T0321936

Social Media for Knowledge Management Applications in Modern Organizations

Francesca Di Virgilio
University of Molise, Italy

A volume in the Advances in
Knowledge Acquisition, Transfer,
and Management (AKATM) Book
Series

Published in the United States of America by
    IGI Global
    Business Science Reference (an imprint of IGI Global)
    701 E. Chocolate Avenue
    Hershey PA, USA 17033
    Tel: 717-533-8845
    Fax: 717-533-8661
    E-mail: cust@igi-global.com
    Web site: http://www.igi-global.com

Library of Congress Cataloging-in-Publication Data

Names: Di Virgilio, Francesca, 1973- editor.
Title: Social media for knowledge management applications in modern
  organizations / Francesca Di Virgilio, editor.
Description: Hershey, PA : Business Science Reference, [2017] | Includes
  bibliographical references.
Identifiers: LCCN 2017013152| ISBN 9781522528975 (h/c) | ISBN 9781522528982
  (eISBN)
Subjects: LCSH: Knowledge management. | Social media.
Classification: LCC HD30.2 .S6359 2017 | DDC 658.4/038--dc23 LC record available at https://
lccn.loc.gov/2017013152

This book is published in the IGI Global book series Advances in Knowledge Acquisition, Transfer, and Management (AKATM) (ISSN: 2326-7607; eISSN: 2326-7615)

British Cataloguing in Publication Data
A Cataloguing in Publication record for this book is available from the British Library.

All work contributed to this book is new, previously-unpublished material.
The views expressed in this book are those of the authors, but not necessarily of the publisher.

For electronic access to this publication, please contact: eresources@igi-global.com.

Advances in Knowledge Acquisition, Transfer, and Management (AKATM) Book Series

ISSN:2326-7607
EISSN:2326-7615

Editor-in-Chief: Murray E. Jennex, San Diego State University, USA

MISSION

Organizations and businesses continue to utilize knowledge management practices in order to streamline processes and procedures. The emergence of web technologies has provided new methods of information usage and knowledge sharing.

The **Advances in Knowledge Acquisition, Transfer, and Management (AKATM) Book Series** brings together research on emerging technologies and their effect on information systems as well as the knowledge society.**AKATM** will provide researchers, students, practitioners, and industry leaders with research highlights surrounding the knowledge management discipline, including technology support issues and knowledge representation.

COVERAGE

- Cognitive Theories
- Cultural Impacts
- Information and Communication Systems
- Knowledge acquisition and transfer processes
- Knowledge management strategy
- Knowledge Sharing
- Organizational Learning
- Organizational Memory
- Small and Medium Enterprises
- Virtual Communities

IGI Global is currently accepting manuscripts for publication within this series. To submit a proposal for a volume in this series, please contact our Acquisition Editors at Acquisitions@igi-global.com or visit: http://www.igi-global.com/publish/.

Titles in this Series

For a list of additional titles in this series, please visit:
http://www.igi-global.com/book-series/advances-knowledge-acquisition-transfer-manage-ment/37159

Bio-Inspired Computing for Information Retrieval Applications
D.P. Acharjya (School of Computing Science and Engineering, VIT University, India) and Anirban Mitra (Vignan Institute of Technology and Management,India)
Information Science Reference • ©2017 • 388pp • H/C (ISBN: 9781522523758) • US $205.00

Managing Knowledge Resources and Records in Modern Organizations
Priti Jain (University of Botswana, Botswana) and Nathan Mnjama (University of Botswana, Botswana)
Business Science Reference • ©2017 • 280pp • H/C (ISBN: 9781522519652) • US $185.00

Analyzing the Role of Citizen Science in Modern Research
Luigi Ceccaroni (1000001 Labs, Spain) and Jaume Piera (ICM-CSIC, Spain)
Information Science Reference • ©2017 • 355pp • H/C (ISBN: 9781522509622) • US $185.00

Scholarly Communication and the Publish or Perish Pressures of Academia
Achala Munigal (Osmania University, India)
Information Science Reference • ©2017 • 375pp • H/C (ISBN: 9781522516972) • US $190.00

Open Source Solutions for Knowledge Management and Technological Ecosystems
Francisco J. Garcia-Peñalvo (University of Salamanca, Spain) and Alicia García-Holgado (University of Salamanca, Spain)
Business Science Reference • ©2017 • 297pp • H/C (ISBN: 9781522509059) • US $195.00

Handbook of Research on Social, Cultural, and Educational Considerations of Indigenous...
Patrick Ngulube (University of South Africa, South Africa)
Information Science Reference • ©2017 • 462pp • H/C (ISBN: 9781522508380) • US $265.00

For an enitre list of titles in this series, please visit:
http://www.igi-global.com/book-series/advances-knowledge-acquisition-transfer-manage-ment/37159

701 East Chocolate Avenue, Hershey, PA 17033, USA
Tel: 717-533-8845 x100 • Fax: 717-533-8661
E-Mail: cust@igi-global.com • www.igi-global.com

Editorial Advisory Board

Table of Contents

Section 1
Social Media

Section 2
Knowledge Management

Section 3
Information Technology

Detailed Table of Contents

Section 1
Social Media

Chapter 1

    Francesca Di Virgilio, University of Molise, Italy

Knowledge sharing is one of the greatest challenges for a business organization. Organizations not only need to focus on innovation of new products and services, but also to pay specific attention to effective knowledge sharing which is of vital importance to their success. In this context, social media have become increasingly popular. They have a profound impact on personal relationships, enable individuals to contribute to a number of issues and generate new possibilities and challenges in order to facilitate knowledge sharing. However, scarce attention has been devoted so far to the theme of social media security and its effects on behavioral intention in relation to knowledge sharing. As a response to this challenge, this chapter illustrates a research roadmap of knowledge sharing which includes important collective variables. This study aims at highlighting a new direction for the evaluation of social media as a tool for knowledge sharing in business organizations. Finally, it concludes with the discussion of several open issues and cutting-edge challenges.

Chapter 2

The advancement of the economy based on knowledge makes knowledge management critical for organizations. The traditional knowledge management systems have presented some shortcomings on their implementation and management. Social media have demonstrated that are not just a buzzword and have been used increasingly by the organizations as a knowledge management component. This chapter was developed aiming at exploring and critically reviewing the literature of social media use in organizational context as a knowledge management component. The review suggests that, while traditional knowledge management systems are static and often act just as knowledge repositories, social media have the potential for supporting different knowledge management processes that will impact on the organizational culture by encouraging on participation, collaboration and knowledge sharing. Despite their recognized impact on knowledge management processes, some uncertainty remains amongst researchers and practitioners and is associated to the difficulty in understanding and measuring their real impact.

Chapter 3

Social media platforms have become a major forum for consumers to interact with firms and other individuals. Drawing on both the customer-dominant logic and the theory of planned behavior, the present chapter aims to advance understanding and encourage research on the variables that drive consumers' online purchase intention. Al though there is a general agreement in recognizing the importance of social media platforms as a source of information about consumer behavior, a complete theorization of the variables that affect the relation between behavioral intention and online purchase intention is still lacking. The proposed theoretical model is an extension of the theory of planned behavior and incorporates trust and electronic word-of-mouth communication as part of the customers' online purchase intention. Finally, the theoretical and managerial implications are further discussed.

Chapter 4

Qiang (Steven) Lu, The University of Sydney, Australia
Zhen Yi Seah, The University of Sydney, Australia

With the popularity of social media, social media influencers have been playing an increasing role in modern marketing. However, there is little research on the impact of social media influencers on consumer brand engagement. To fill this gap, this chapter develops a conceptual framework to examine the impact of the endorsement by social media influencers on online brand engagement. The authors use social distance theories to construct several propositions to provide a deep understanding. They suggest that traditional celebrities and social media influencers have different social distance, therefore generate different types and degrees of consumer online engagement. And the product characteristics moderate the effectiveness of the different types of celebrity endorsement.

Chapter 5

Rocco Agrifoglio, University of Naples "Parthenope", Italy
Concetta Metallo, University of Naples "Parthenope", Italy

The chapter aims to provide an overview of the role of social media for knowledge management in tourism industry. Respect than traditional tools, the social media penetration within such industry is growing thanks to opportunity for travelers and travel professionals to access critical tourism knowledge everywhere and every time. Prior research has mainly focused on how social media are changing the tourism industry, while it is lacking enough the contribution of these technologies to managing touristic knowledge. This chapter seeks to shed light on how social media support knowledge management, with particular attention to knowledge creation, sharing, and preservation processes, in tourism industry. In particular, while knowledge creation and sharing process have attracted the attention of scholars, knowledge preservation via social media seems be still in its infancy stage.

Chapter 6

Stephen Asunka, Ghana Technology University College, Ghana

Against the backdrop that universities are required to generate and disseminate relevant and applicable knowledge for the general good, and with the understanding that social media can be an effective vehicle for such knowledge sharing practices, this study explored the use of social media for knowledge sharing by academics at a university college in Ghana. The study thus examined how instructors use social media for sharing academic knowledge, the factors that promote such knowledge sharing practices, and the barriers to effective knowledge sharing in the academic environment. 47 instructors participated by completing an online questionnaire, whilst 7 participated in focus group discussions. Findings reveal a regular, though not daily, use of social media platforms for academic knowledge sharing. Personal, technological and institutional factors were determined to be contributing in fostering as well as hindering such activities. Implications of these findings as well as suggestions for future research are accordingly discussed.

Chapter 7

Ahmed Elazab, Cairo University, Egypt
Mahmood A. Mahmood, Cairo University, Egypt
Hesham Ahmed Hefny, Cairo University, Egypt

Social media is a powerful communication tool that facilitates the interaction and provide an efficient interconnection among different roles in many fields such as business and media. The power of social media forced its responsibility for the vast dissemination of different information during real time events. Many social networks have emerged since the 90s; however, many of these networks have been abandon while the success of others in providing intelligent and active communication made them the most famous recently. Some examples of these successful social networks are Facebook, and Twitter. In this research, we provide the readers with the main concepts of social media and social networks, and their relation with other fields. We also discuss the current situation with providing the emerging trends and challenges of both fields.

Section 2
Knowledge Management

Chapter 8

Ayşe Aslı Sezgin, Osmaniye Korkut Ata University, Turkey
Esengül İplik, Osmaniye Korkut Ata University, Turkey

The aim of this study is to identify the applications to be used for personal knowledge management, determine their area of use, and specify and analyze the examples obtained for their use at administrative levels in corporations. Within this framework, this study includes the assessment of the work flow of a top manager with the required experience and professionalism in the field of knowledge management. Besides the literature review conducted in line with the content of the subject area in this study, applications that enable personal knowledge management in particular and the similarities between these applications and the features of their social media networks were detected, and their specific purpose of use was clarified. Evernote, chosen as a sample application to be used at corporations, following personal knowledge management, has been assessed within the framework of managers' experiences with the use of depth interview technique.

Chapter 9

This chapter reveals the overview of knowledge transfer; knowledge transfer, labor mobility, and labor diversity; knowledge transfer and subsidiary perspectives; barriers to knowledge transfer; knowledge transfer and absorptive capacity; knowledge transfer and knowledge acquisition; knowledge transfer and virtual teams; and the advanced issues of knowledge transfer in modern organizations. The process of transferring knowledge is an ongoing progression of learning, adjusting, and improving. At the organizational level, knowledge transfer manifests itself through changes in the knowledge of a unit. Most successful knowledge transfer efforts actively involve both the source of the knowledge and its receiver. Establishing performance expectations for those who will use the knowledge further quantifies the value of the transfer. Companies considering or using knowledge transfer processes, should continuously evaluate their social media readiness. The benefits of knowledge transfer for workplaces include the increases in productivity, speed, agility, profits, and growth.

The idea of the chapter is to make a cross-cultural analysis of the various knowledge management processes, with the aim of identifying advantages and disadvantages, perspectives and obstacles for knowledge management (KM) within the boundaries between university and industry. KM strategies revealed the importance of institutionalization and legitimation processes of practitioners' knowledge. In the contemporary networking world with blurring boundaries between professional and non-professional knowledge the position of expert is changing. It immediately influences knowledge flows between university and industry. The chapter will provide a comparative analysis of two KM cases in the field of university-industry relations – Germany and Russia with emphasis on difficulties and advantages of KM implementation for enhancing decision-making process on both sides; evolving stakeholders to participate in activities, building efficient societal capabilities and developing knowledge-based communities.

Chapter 11

Muhammad Khaleel, Universiti Sains Malaysia, Malaysia
Shankar Chelliah, Universiti Sains Malaysia, Malaysia

This chapter discusses the significance of employee wellbeing at the workplace and self-perceived English language proficiency as a predictor variable. The importance of employee wellbeing has been recognized all around the world. To generalize the findings of previous literature this study has examined the proposed model in the context of telecom MNCs in Pakistan. This chapter starts with what is wellbeing at the workplace? And moves towards it significance in the context of developed and underdeveloped countries. Further, this chapter explains the empirical findings of the proposed model. The results revealed a strong correlation between self-perceived English language proficiency and dimensions of employee wellbeing at the workplace. This is a very important chapter for both researchers and managers.

Section 3
Information Technology

Chapter 12

Murat Yaslioglu, Istanbul University, Turkey
Duygu Toplu Yaslioglu, Istanbul University, Turkey

New challenge in all industries is to catch up with the digital revolution. There are some pioneers and some followers in all industries but it is inevitable that digits catch every company by its claws. Our research aims to put forward the dynamics of the digital era or in other words new economy. Companies with a good level of digital maturity and thus high digital quotient become the leaders of their industries. Of course it is in some sectors digitization has become more obvious compared to others, but it is a rising trend in every industry, one can appoint. Banking sector is casts a great example how digital quotient and its factors come into play. Our research tries to define the new concept of digital quotient and illustrate a good practice by evaluating the strategies of a leading bank in Turkey.

Chapter 13

Simone Scalabrino, University of Molise, Italy
Salvatore Geremia, University of Molise, Italy
Remo Pareschi, University of Molise, Italy
Marcello Bogetti, University of Turin, Italy
Rocco Oliveto, University of Molise, Italy

In the last years social media are increasing their importance in the context of digital freelancing by letting companies offer projects to external professionals through the Web. However, the available platforms for digital freelancing are still far from supporting the ecosystem of companies and professionals during the implementation of complex projects through an accurate definition of the required skills, roles, interdependencies and responsibilities. This chapter presents a roundup of the available systems of support to freelancers. The goal is to identify the essential features and structure of a comprehensive social media able to effectively manage and support the potential of an "economy 4.0" characterized by a free and flexible circulation of highly skilled professionals, that can be aggregated to support the needs of organizations.

Foreword

This timely book, edited by Francesca Di Virgilio, Associate Professor of Organization Theory and Human Resources Management at University of Molise (Italy), very cogently addresses the subject of social media and its relationship with knowledge management applications; furthermore, underlining the issue of how this topic can be used to leverage business success.

How can this indeed be effected? Recently, social media technologies have received a lot of attention in scholarly as well as in practitioner-oriented literature and in professional services companies as well as in business organizations from many sectors. Due to the large demand for concepts and theories to support a systematic intervention in the way an organization handles knowledge through social media, the field has attracted researchers from different disciplines and has absorbed a wide array of research questions and approaches.

In the book edited by Francesca Di Virgilio, there is a considerable number of theories, approaches, methods and tools. In addition, the case studies interspersed in several of its chapters, represent an excellent addition to help the reader understand the subject matter discussed in the book, and relate it to real world scenarios.

Together with Francesca Di Virgilio's original work on the stages of growth of social media for knowledge management applications in modern organizations, this will become an indispensable tool, for initiates and practitioners too. In the first section, the book intends to provide concrete hints, models and metaphors on how to go about designing, implementing and deploying social media applications. While maintaining that social media is only a facilitator in helping organizations manage knowledge, this book - in particular with respect to the discussion in the second section - describes how an organization can develop its strategy to align with its knowledge management strategy in different contexts. In the third and last section, we have a set of perspectives on information technology services and infrastructures, as enabler and facilitator, that encourage and support knowledge sharing. This section is related to the knowledge management technology used in the sharing activity, and it makes knowledge sharing easier and more effective in different organizations.

She has sought contributions from around the world to make this happen and was pleased that this volume has acquired an international flavor which offers a wide variety of viewpoints along a set of common themes. Although this area of study continues to receive a lot of attention in the literature, it could be invigorated by additional perspectives not commonly shared or that are in the early stages of development.

The timeliness of this book edited by Francesca Di Virgilio lies in the fact that it does not only conceptually link up these three, relatively separate (at least until now) areas of study — social media, knowledge management and information technology — into a holistic picture, but also theoretically points the way through different chapters to how these disparate areas can actually be aligned in a meaningful way.

I wholeheartedly recommend this book to student and practitioner alike, for each will find a wealth of knowledge within its pages to suit their needs and interests.

The timeliness of this book edited by Francesca Di Virgilio lies in the fact that it not only conceptually links up these three, relatively separate (at least until now) areas of study — social media, knowledge management and information technology — into a holistic picture, but also theoretically points the way through different chapters to how these disparate areas can actually be aligned in a meaningful way.

I wholeheartedly recommend this book to student and practitioner alike, for each will find a wealth of knowledge within its pages to suit their needs and interests.

Gianluigi Mangia
University of Naples "Federico II", Italy

Preface

Social media have modified personal relationships, allowed individuals to contribute to many issues and generated new possibilities and challenges which facilitate collaboration. Consequently, the potential advantages of embracing and implementing social media are enormous. Though the interest in social media is increasing, organizations on the one hand have an urgent need to focus on innovation of new products and services, but must also pay specific attention to effective knowledge sharing, of vital importance for their success. Knowledge workers and managers are hesitating before getting involved in this collaborative world because they may not feel motivated or may not be aware of the advantages of using these tools for work purposes. On the other hand, organizations tend not to allow their employees to use social media technologies because they may be concerned about the risks and consequences of potential misuse or abuse.

The approach implementation for knowledge management is particularly important for organizations where a high quantity of information is necessary for the progress of their many activities but also where access to information is problematic or simply when the organization wishes to structure available knowledge and distribute it to all employees. The fast and complex development of organizations in the public and private sector clearly shows that technological, social or economic changes are tightly interweaved with the quality of the information available and even more so with our ability in managing that information. Particularly in the last couple of years, this has led to an increase in interest for social media tools and knowledge management techniques for the creation and transfer of good practices, given that these have become equally important to both the private and public sectors.

Thus, how to induce and motivate employees to use social media technologies for knowledge management applications was for me an important goal in writing this book. It was written with the help of enterprises and institutions operating in the world of profit and non-profit sectors. Within this field, the book amalgamates a considerable number of theories, approaches, methods and tools. The results are presented in the light of strategic issues, such as organizational design – roles, collectives, tasks and processes, the contents of knowledge management, technologies and systems – as well as the application of social media for knowledge management applications in modern organizations. In addition, this book provides insights into links between social media and knowledge management that students will find vital to their professional success. The book also helps managers and professionals gain competitive advantage from the use of social media for knowledge management applications. Finally, it provides self-help for practitioners.

Because the social media dimension is important for business and management students, this book can be used at both the undergraduate and graduate levels. At the graduate level, more emphasis can be placed on empirical studies and research methodology. The book could be suitable for courses in IT, business information systems, knowledge management, and management studies. It can be considered an introductory text for management undergraduates and for postgraduates who have a multi-disciplinary background.

This book attempts to be strong in concepts coverage. It has many examples drawn from a wide range of international sources. Reviewers of earlier versions have stressed that this is a much needed text in a very important and growing area. It synthesizes strategy, technology and knowledge management. It is based on the premise that it is difficult, if not impossible, to manage a modern business or public organization without at least some understanding of the planning, use, control and benefits of social media to support knowledge creation, transfer and sharing among workers.

The scholarly value of the book and its contribution to the literature in the knowledge management and information technology disciplines is to be found in three main areas: social media, knowledge management and information technology.

I start out by introducing the reader to the contents of each section: social media, knowledge management and information technology with their accompanying chapters

SOCIAL MEDIA (SECTION 1)

The seven chapters within this theme focus on the multi-faceted field of social media, its history, interdisciplinary roots, its tactical goals and strategic ambition; the chapters do not ignore the critics of the field.

The overall perspective considers aspects of social media which impact on the knowledge management applications.

In the first chapter, Di Virgilio discusses the determinants of knowledge sharing and the role of social media in business organizations. Knowledge sharing is one of the greatest challenges for a business organization. Because it not only needs to focus on innovation of new products and services, but also needs to pay specific attention to effective knowledge sharing, which is of vital importance to their success. In this context, social media have become increasingly popular: they have a profound impact on personal relationships, enable individuals to contribute to a number of issues and generate new possibilities and challenges in order to facilitate knowledge sharing. Scarce attention, however, has been devoted so far to the theme of social media security and its effects on behavioral intention in relation to knowledge sharing. As a response to this challenge, the author illustrates a research roadmap of knowledge sharing which includes important collective variables. This study aims at highlighting a new direction for the evaluation of social media as a tool for knowledge sharing in business organizations.

In the second chapter, Chedid and Teixeira discuss by means of a literature review the critical role of social media tools in knowledge management within the organizational context. The authors explore and contribute to understanding the possible impacts and consequences in the use of these tools in knowledge management within the organizational context, and highlight the factors that can be determinants in the potential success of knowledge management based on social media.

In the third chapter, Di Virgilio and Antonelli discuss consumer behavior, trust, and electronic word-of-mouth communication to develop an online purchase intention model. Social media platforms have become a major forum for consumers to interact with firms and other individuals. Drawing on both the customer-dominant logic and the theory of planned behavior, the authors aim to advance understanding and encourage research on the variables that drive consumers' online purchase intentions. Although there is general agreement in recognizing the importance of social media platforms as a source of information about consumer behavior, a complete theorization of the variables that affect the relation between behavioral intention and online purchase intention is still lacking. The proposed theoretical model is an extension of the theory of planned behavior and incorporates trust and electronic word-of-mouth communication too as part of customers' online purchase intention.

In the fourth chapter, Lu and Seah analyze social media influencers and consumer online engagement management. With the popularity of social media, social media influencers have been playing an increasing role in modern marketing. To fill this gap, the authors develop a conceptual framework to examine the impact of the endorsement by social media influencers on online brand engagement. The authors use social distance theories to construct several propositions to provide a deep understanding. They suggest that traditional celebrities and social media influencers have different social distance, therefore generate different types and degrees of consumer online engagement. And the product characteristics moderate the effectiveness of the different types of celebrity endorsement.

In the fifth chapter, Agrifoglio and Metallo investigate the creation, sharing and preservation processes of knowledge trough social media in tourism industry, with the aim of understanding how organizational knowledge can and should be managed effectively. The information system literature pays more attention to the tools – traditional or IT-assisted – for creating, sharing and preserving such knowledge. Respect than traditional tools, social media in particular, are increasingly providing novel ways of supporting processes of knowledge creation, sharing and preservation within and between organizations. Social media are playing an increasingly important role as information sources for organizations and individuals in various industries, such as tourism. The authors investigate the role of social media in tourism industry for knowledge management by identifying the main dynamics and mechanisms supporting the creation, sharing and preservation of the explicit and tacit forms of individual and collective knowledge.

In the sixth chapter, Asunka analyze the use of social media for knowledge sharing by instructors in a higher education institution. Consequently she discusses the study in detail, touching on some theoretical underpinnings and elaborating on the research strategies adopted to help unravel some instructor behaviors and perceptions. She concludes by sharing lessons learnt with the view to contributing to the evolution of best-practice frameworks and models for facilitating the use of social media for knowledge sharing among instructors in institutions of higher learning.

The seventh and final chapter of this section, Abdelrahman, Mahmood and Hefny discuss social media and social networking in the present and in the future directions. The authors provide an understanding of the basic concepts of social media for different aspects related to social media, with presenting different directions for social media analysis.

KNOWLEDGE MANAGEMENT (SECTION 2)

The four chapters of this section examine how organizations can utilize knowledge flows to gain or maintain competitive advantage, and they provide important applications for organizations to consider. In particular, the chapters in this section take a slightly different view of knowledge management: they look at people, processes, and technologies as they manage issues such as the uneven sharing of knowledge across the organization and the differences in appropriateness of explicit and tacit knowledge resources.

In the eighth chapter, Sezgin and İplik identify the applications to be used for personal knowledge management, and specify and analyze the examples obtained for their use at administrative levels in corporations. Within this framework, they include the assessment of the work flow of a top manager with the required experience and professionalism in the field of knowledge management. Besides the literature review conducted in line with the content of the subject area in this study, applications that enable personal knowledge management in particular and the similarities between these applications and the features of their social media networks were detected, and their specific purpose of use was clarified.

In the ninth chapter, Kasemsap analyze the role of knowledge transfer in modern organizations. The author bridge the gap in the literature on the thorough literature consolidation of knowledge transfer. The extensive literature of knowledge transfer provides a contribution to practitioners and researchers by revealing the trends and issues of knowledge transfer in order to maximize the impact of knowledge transfer in modern organizations. In the era of knowledge-based economy, knowledge has become the most important core competence. Knowledge transfer is an important issue for organizational knowledge management programs and is the systematic process of sharing knowledge and learning from the experience of others. Knowledge management system can potentially enhance knowledge transfer by providing the ready access to knowledge across personal, departmental, and organizational boundaries. New knowledge is gained through knowledge acquisition and knowledge transfer processes that can be interpreted as the inbound knowledge flows from the viewpoint of a given organization. Knowledge transfer is enhanced by the ready access to a network of assets by the intended knowledge users.

In the tenth chapter, Hinkelbein and Karnaukhova discuss some critical remarks on the matter of the role and functioning of expert knowledge in the university-industry cooperation. The first one concerns the idea of so-called expert knowledge, or expert systems – as well as it affects the expert term itself. The critical point of this kind of definitions is that the expert is considered very narrow and grouped around special technical skills. With the result that knowledge itself is conceptualized very technocratic. Taking into account practical activity opens the opportunity to investigate knowledge management in a more complex way. This is an absolutely necessary aspect when such different cultures as universities and industries are compared. The second remark concerns digitalization and networking as core mottos and practices in knowledge management today. Finally, the authors provide a comparative analysis of two knowledge management cases in the field of university-industry relations Germany and Russia with emphasis on difficulties and advantages of knowledge management implementation for enhancing decision-making process on both sides; evolving stakeholders to participate in activities, building efficient societal capabilities and developing knowledge-based communities.

The eleventh and final chapter of this section, Khaleel and Chelliah discuss the significance of employee wellbeing at the workplace and self-perceived English language proficiency as an element of knowledge sharing and social interaction. To generalize the findings of previous literature the authors examine the proposed model in the context of telecom MNCs in Pakistan. The empirical findings reveal a strong correlation between self-perceived English language proficiency and dimensions of employee wellbeing at the workplace.

INFORMATION TECHNOLOGY (SECTION 3)

The two chapters of this final section explore information technology (IT) services and infrastructures, a facilitator encouraging and supporting knowledge sharing and analyze how the former are related to the knowledge management technology used in the sharing activity. Moreover, they make knowledge sharing easier and more effective in different organizations.

The twelfth chapter, Yaslioglu and Yaslioglu discuss the Concept of "Digital Quotient". The authors aim to put forward the dynamics of the digital era or in other words new economy. Companies with a good level of digital maturity and thus high digital quotient become the leaders of their industries. Of course it is in some sectors digitization has become more obvious compared to others, but it is a rising trend in every industry, one can appoint. Banking sector is casts a great example how digital quotient and its factors come into play. The authors define the new concept of digital quotient and illustrate a good practice by evaluating the strategies of a leading bank in Turkey.

In the thirteenth and final chapter of this section, Bogetti, Oliveto, Geremia, Pareschi, and Scalabrino do a roundup of the available systems of support to professionals through the digital cloud, both commercially, as exemplified in the above initiatives, and in the broader frame of recommending systems applicable in this area. This analysis is then evaluated with respect to an array of requirements that must be met to finalize effectively the potential of an "economy 4.0" characterized by a free and flexible circulation of highly skilled professionals, that can be aggregated to support the needs of organizations. From here, the authors identify the essential features and structure of a software architecture for systems effectively fulfilling the full gamut of requirements arising from this new ecosystem.

SUMMARY

This book brings together in one volume a truly international perspective in social media for knowledge management applications. The expertise provided herein comes from all over the world, and although there are common themes among the chapters, each provides a unique viewpoint that springs from cultural and geographic differences. I believe that such diversity of thought is a necessary component in the advancement of the body of knowledge, regardless of the discipline involved.

I have considered uniqueness of research methodologies while selecting articles for this book to include ethnographic studies, case studies, research articles, empirical papers, conceptual papers, and review papers. Overall, I feel that these chapters are a good blend of extant and new research. The common link of knowledge among the various disciplines provides an opportunity to enhance understanding of the role played by social media for knowledge management applications in the creation and sustenance of competitive advantage for organizations. I hope this enhanced understanding will stimulate additional research in these areas.

I am confident, indeed quiet certain, that the readers will find the volume interesting and that the complex questions presented will be stimulating.

Francesca Di Virgilio
University of Molise, Italy

Acknowledgment

I have contracted too many debts of gratitude during the many months of work required to put together this book for individual acknowledgements to be possible.

I shall therefore express my collective thanks to the editorial staff at IGI Global for providing the opportunity to create this volume. It was very much a learning experience for parties, and they made the process a smooth and supportive one. We are glad they appreciate the importance of addressing the intersection of Social Media for Knowledge Management Applications.

The quality of this book also owes a lot to my contributors and to the reviewers of the chapters; this volume provided us with the opportunity to compile a resource that we think will benefit both researchers and practitioners. For this, I thank them very much.

I would also like to acknowledge the invaluable suggestions and unfailing support that I have received from the members of the Editorial board. I would like to especially thank Gilda Antonelli (University of Sannio, Italy) member of the editorial board, colleague and friend who motivated me in difficult times and sometimes just smiled at my frantic sessions in front of the computer.

Most importantly, I would like to acknowledge the support and encouragement that my family has provided me: my daughters Alessia and Sara, beacons of my life, who with their love provide me unwitting encouragement; my husband, Massimo, has always stood by me demonstrating a great deal of patience whilst my parents have always provided their continued loving logistical support. And last but not least, I would like to thank my closest friends for being there.

Without each and every one of them, this book would not have been possible.

Many thanks to you all!

Francesca Di Virgilio
University of Molise, Italy

Section 1
Social Media

Chapter 1
Exploring Determinants of Knowledge Sharing and the Role of Social Media in Business Organizations:
Overview and New Direction

Francesca Di Virgilio
University of Molise, Italy

ABSTRACT

Knowledge sharing is one of the greatest challenges for a business organization. Organizations not only need to focus on innovation of new products and services, but also to pay specific attention to effective knowledge sharing which is of vital importance to their success. In this context, social media have become increasingly popular. They have a profound impact on personal relationships, enable individuals to contribute to a number of issues and generate new possibilities and challenges in order to facilitate knowledge sharing. However, scarce attention has been devoted so far to the theme of social media security and its effects on behavioral intention in relation to knowledge sharing. As a response to this challenge, this chapter illustrates a research roadmap of knowledge sharing which includes important collective variables. This study aims at highlighting a new direction for the evaluation of social media as a tool for knowledge sharing in business organizations. Finally, it concludes with the discussion of several open issues and cutting-edge challenges.

DOI: 10.4018/978-1-5225-2897-5.ch001

INTRODUCTION

The rising popularity and the recent development of knowledge management are considered to be the result of the organization's needs to obtain a competitive edge and strategic differentiation, in the face of globalization and of the explosion of media and information phenomena. Industrially developed countries claim that the third era of development has not been recently induced by agriculture or industry, but by information and knowledge (Gaál et al. 2015; Usman, & Oyefolahan, 2014; Yassin, et al. 2013).

This is an era of rapid change and uncertainty, characterized by both the increasing importance of knowledge and knowledge management as well as a wide use of new information technologies which can, potentially, change radically the way organizations work. As it has already been stated, the Internet has been the single most significant technological development in the last 20 years. It allows individuals to connect, collaborate and share knowledge, information, documents, photos, videos, etc. continuously with anyone in any place around the world. As several authors (Gaál et al. 2015; Usman, & Oyefolahan, 2014; Yassin, et al. 2013) have noticed, second generation web-based technologies are increasingly becoming popular in the managerial context.

This phenomenon is emphasized by the dramatic development of social media that constitute a meaningful example of users' involvement in knowledge dissemination and in collaborative content creation. In particular, new web technologies enable people to engage and to share information all over the world and across different platforms through the use of multiple modalities for interaction and contribution (Eijkman, 2011). While relying on the same knowledge framework (Dawson, 2007; Vuori & Okkonen, 2012), these technologies support and encourage collaborative writing (e.g., Wikis), content sharing (e.g., text, video, and images), social networking (e.g., Google+, LinkedIn, Facebook, Twitter), training (e.g. webinar) social bookmarking (e.g. ratings, tagging), and syndication (e.g., web feeds: RSS, Atom) (Dawson, 2008).

More recently, as organizations have recognized the power and purpose of these tools, they have begun incorporating social media into their business processes (Gaál et al., 2014). However, with increased collaboration and communication, there are cyber security risks that a company may monitor and/or face with new technologies, especially with social media (Zhang & Gupta, 2016). Given the numerous cases of data interception, information fraudulence, privacy spying, and copyright infringement from disorganized social organizational forms and non-friendly participation bodies that have been reported and discussed over the last few years, it is now even more crucial that organizations address this fundamental issue.

The first part of this chapter aims to present an overview of previous studies conducted on knowledge and knowledge sharing. In analyzing the literature it becomes evident that there is a research gap between the importance of social media tools as a source of knowledge sharing and the role of security as a level of analysis in knowledge sharing mechanisms. The second part of this chapter develops a research roadmap of knowledge sharing which includes important collective variables of organizational factors: individuals, groups, organizational culture, and technological factors as security, to determine whether they influence users in organizations or institutions to share knowledge via social media. Finally, this study discusses the role of social media tools in knowledge sharing in relation to our roadmap.

Specifically, the present study aims to introduce a new framework which may serve both as a tool for enhancing the understanding of knowledge sharing mechanisms in business organizations and also more generally as a useful guide for future research on knowledge and social media. This study could also be further elaborated, as it would be interesting to make a comparison between knowledge sharing practices and usage of social media across different countries. The content discussed herein attempts to establish the building block toward the development of a theory of knowledge sharing and usage of social media tools. Conclusive comments and managerial implications, as well as new directions for future research, are presented in the final part of this chapter.

BACKGROUND

Knowledge Background

The term "knowledge" is one which has caused confusion in knowledge management research. Within this field, it has acquired a variety of meanings that describe a particular piece or process in the scope of knowledge (Alavi & Leidner, 2001; Grant, 1996; Lehner & Maier, 2000; Stankosky & Baldanza, 2001; Weick, 1995). Drawing from prior studies, we distinguish knowledge from data and information and see it as a "fluid mix of framed experience, values, contextual information and expert insight that provide[s] a framework for evaluation and incorporating new experiences and information" (Davenport & Prusak, 1998, p. 5).

The knowledge process acts on information in order to create new information that allows for greater possibilities to fulfill old or possibly new organizational needs (Gaál et al. 2015; Usman, & Oyefolahan, 2014; Yassin, et al. 2013). Moreover, according to Grover and Davenport (2001), many cycles of generation, codification, and transfer are concurrently occurring in businesses.

To be successful, firms must not only exploit their existing knowledge but must also invest heavily in the exploration of new knowledge in order to determine future strategies and obtain competitive advantages (Sambamurthy et al., 2003).

As I have noted above, knowledge is becoming a strategically important resource and a powerful driver of organizational performance (Yesil & Dereli, 2013). Either located in the minds of the individuals (tacit knowledge) (Polányi, 1966), or embedded in organizational routines and norms, or even codified in technological devices (explicit knowledge) (Nonaka & Takeuchi, 1995), knowledge enables the development of new competencies (Choo, 1998). Successful companies are those that consistently create new knowledge, disseminate this knowledge throughout the organization, and embody it in technologies, products and services (Gottschalk, 2007; Gaál et al., 2008)..

A major concern for researchers and practitioners is to understand how knowledge flow can be facilitated to gain positive results on the organizational level in terms of performance, innovativeness and competitive advantage. For the last few years, the knowledge governance approach has been emerging to address these issues. But a further question needs to be posed: can knowledge be conceived as existing at multiple (individual, group, intra-organizational and inter-organizational relationships) levels?

Significantly, after having recognized the strategic importance of organizational knowledge at multiple levels, a wide range of firms has implemented various knowledge management initiatives. In most studies, the main attention has focused on the knowledge management system architecture, on the building process and on the mechanism for agent-based knowledge sharing. For example, Liu and colleagues (2010) presented a knowledge sharing community model and adopted an agent-based solution to perform the functions of knowledge sharing in virtual enterprises. However, overall, empirical research on knowledge management systems is still limited.

Therefore, there is growing interest of among both researchers and practitioners to understand processes, antecedents, and results of employees' knowledge sharing within organizations. In the following section, I argue for a frame to describe the content of knowledge sharing in the literature review.

MAIN FOCUS OF THE CHAPTER

Knowledge Sharing

Sharing occurs commonly among people, but knowledge sharing within an organization is a complex and complicated issue. Knowledge sharing is the process by which individuals' knowledge is converted into a form that can be understood and used by other individuals (Ipe, 2003). Knowledge sharing refers to the task of helping others through knowledge, and to collaborate with others to solve problems, develop new ideas, or implement processes (Cummings, 2004). The definition implies that knowledge sharing is seen as the willingness act whereby knowledge is capable of being used again or repeatedly in the course of its transfer from one party to another (Lee & Al-Hawamdeh, 2002). Similarly, knowledge sharing is a routine activity that entails guiding individuals or audience to adopt a specific way of thinking and reasoning. It also requires understanding and consideration of the individuals' problem situation (McDermott, 1999; Wang & Noe, 2010).

Knowledge sharing is a key asset to almost all organizations (Chen, et al., 2009; Yu, et al., 2009). It is also a multilevel phenomenon (Foss, 2007), and in order to find out how managerial practices facilitate sharing to get organizational level results, it is essential to identify what kind of knowledge sharing behaviors influence positively organizational performance, also what motivates individuals to share knowledge in a particular way, and finally, how organizations can facilitate that motivation and enable individual sharing behavior (Foss, et al., 2010). Furthermore, in several studies, the differences between various types of knowledge sharing were found (i.e. Teng & Song 2011; van den Hooff & de Ridder, 2004).

Knowledge sharing is understood nowadays as a dynamic social process (Von Krogh, 2011) through which knowledge possessed by one person is translated into a form that can be understood, absorbed and used by another (Ipe 2003). This definition shows that in the process of knowledge sharing there are two types of behavior, namely donating and receiving. Consequently, the success of knowledge sharing is achieved when the knowledge receiver internalizes a piece of knowledge (has a better understanding of the problem or the situation) and is able to use it in the future. This indicates that knowledge sharing is not just passing on some information from one person to another, but it is rather giving the information with some context or explanation. Knowledge sharing is a highly diversified process of interaction (direct and indirect) between the knowledge donator and knowledge receiver – that influences the success of the sharing process. As an example, Haas and Hansen (2007) proved that the behavior of the knowledge donator can hinder the performance of the knowledge recipient. Moreover, Foss and colleagues (2009) found that a reward system influences negatively donating knowledge and positively collecting knowledge. Durmusoglu and colleagues (2013) also identified the different influence of culture and rewards on the behavior of a person that is sharing knowledge, and of a person that is receiving knowledge.

Teng and Song (2011) distinguished two types of knowledge sharing looking from the perspective of a knowledge donator and identified diverse reasons of for sharing, for instance whether sharing is solicited by the receiver (on request) or if it is instead the voluntary decision of the donator. They found that different work unit related factors influence each type of sharing.

Cummings and Teng (2006) differentiated four characteristics of knowledge sharing that influence knowledge internalization and usage of knowledge: source, recipient, relational and environmental. While relational and environmental contexts create opportunities for knowledge sharing; the source, recipient and knowledge context are the key elements of the sharing process and they form what the process looks like.

Several previous studies have shown that both knowledge-sharing types have different antecedents, for example rewards (Hau et al. 2013; Cabrera, et al. 2006; Reychav & Weisberg 2009), and different outcomes (Haas & Hansen 2007) deriving from different theoretical perspectives (i.e. theory of planned behavior/theory of reasoned action; motivation-opportunity-ability framework; social exchange theory, economic exchange theory; social interdependence theory, agency theory), of which the results in many areas are inconsistent. The reward system could be an example, as there is no consensus whether rewards facilitate or hinder sharing (Rudawska, 2015; Witherspoon, 2013).

Bartol and Srivastava (2002) focused on the manner of sharing knowledge proposing four knowledge sharing mechanisms: contribution to databases, informal interactions, formal interactions and communities of practice. Their approach was operationalized by Yi (2009) who proposed a knowledge sharing behavior measure. In this chapter, we draw from the literature which has found several factors that influence knowledge sharing activities (Lin, 2007). Besides personal and organizational factors, researchers have identified the role of the technological factors as the influencing factor in knowledge sharing (e.g., Lin, 2007; Paroutis & Al Saleh, 2009; Wahlroos, 2010; Rehman, et al., 2011; Gaál et al. 2015; Usman, & Oyefolahan, 2014; Yassin, et al. 2013)..

Consequently, individual, group, organizational culture and technological factors are the starting point when investigating knowledge sharing using web technologies (Lin, 2007; Paroutis & Al Saleh, 2009; Wahlroos, 2010; Cabrera & Cabrera, 2002). By giving an account of individual and group characteristics, the theories outlined in this chapter serve as the foundation for developing a new research model. Figure 1 illustrates the research roadmap.

ORGANIZATIONAL FACTORS DETERMINING KNOWLEDGE SHARING

Individuals

Literature indicates that knowledge sharing depends on individual factors (Cummings & Teng 2006; Teng & Song, 2011; Berends et al., 2011; Berends et al., 2006), such as beliefs, experience, values, motivation (Lin, 2007), as well as expectations, perceptions, attitudes and mindset towards knowledge sharing (Volady, 2013). As Van den Hooff, Elving, Meeuwsen, and Dumoulin (2003) show, knowledge sharing

Figure 1. Knowledge Sharing Roadmap

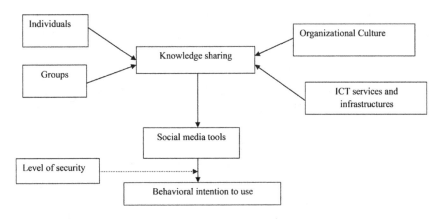

also relies on communication skills comprising both verbal and written practices (Riege, 2005). Moreover, Volady (2013) and Wangpipatwong (2009) claim that an individual's ability to share or willingness to share positively influence the knowledge sharing process. In other words, persons who have enough confidence in their efficacy to share valuable knowledge have greater chances to achieve their goals as well as to experience a higher level of engagement in knowledge sharing (Wang & Noe, 2010). A study by Wahlroos (2010) provides relevant research findings on the role of individual factors (costs and benefits) in the use of social media as a form of organizational knowledge sharing. It was found that the knowledge sharing process is dominated by the intrinsic factors of the employees, rather than by the extrinsic factors. Although the impact of costs is not discussed in her study, the outcome of the research shows that an effective and beneficial use of social media has a significant influence on individual factors. Other studies explain that knowledge sharing takes place in different contexts. For example, Ipe (2003) differentiates purposive and relational learning channels in relation to the conceptual framework of individual knowledge sharing. The former provide an individual with a structured environment for knowledge sharing by giving relevant tools, while the knowledge is explicit in nature. The latter are based on personal contact and relationship between the sharing actors (Ipe 2003). Sometimes the personalized, direct sharing is needed in order to gain knowledge on where and how to retrieve information and knowledge from a non-human knowledge repository.

Groups

The second dimension concerns groups or units as actors engaged in knowledge sharing (Yi, 2009). The most common definition of a group is "a collection of two or more interacting individuals with a stable pattern of relationships between them who share common goals and who perceive themselves as being a group" (Davenport, 1999, p. 71-78). This definition can be applied also to group knowledge conceived as two or more persons in social interaction who share common goals and information. The literature on small groups has shown that the knowledge possessed by group members varies according to the dimensions of the type of knowledge/ability (Jones, 1974; Kennedy, 1971), as well as according to the level of knowledge/ability (Tziner & Eden, 1985), and to the distribution of knowledge (Liang, 1994). Consistent with this argument, Stasser and colleagues (1989) found that broadly distributed or shared information is more likely to be retrieved by the group than unshared information. They further found that as a piece of information was is distributed among more individuals within the group, the retrieval of this information becomes more probable and thus facilitates group decision-making; when instead information is held by multiple members, not only more people within the group possess the information, but group members who possess this information may also provide retrieval cues to one another in order to aid the introduction of the knowledge and the decision making (Okhuysen & Eisenhardt, 2002; Moreland et al., 1997; Liang et al., 1995; Larson et al. 1994; Wegner, 1986).Shared conceptualization of other group members allows to pool information more effectively and to make better group decisions(Gruenfled et al., 1996; Stasser et al., 1995). Conversely, when group members have non-overlapping information, group members have difficulty discussing or sharing that knowledge; and, as a result, the group does not reach the optimal decision (Stasser & Titus, 1987; Stasser & Stewart, 1992). This sharing is based on the direct interaction and communication between the knowledge donor and receiver (personalized sharing), but this interaction is not totally easy-going (rather formal) because it is contrived by a leader, supervisor or manager, who creates the opportunity for that interaction – time, place, subject, and participants.

When information is held by multiple members, not only more people within the group possess the information, but group members who possess the information may also provide retrieval cues to one another in order to aid the introduction of the knowledge and decision making (Bagozzi, 2000; West, Garrod & Carletta, 1997). In this scenario groups bring assets, adding knowledge and creativity, which increases the understanding and the acceptance of ideas (Tosi, et al., 2000). Numerous studies have demonstrated the benefits for groups that engage in information sharing and communication within the group (Keller & Staelin, 1987; Gruenfeld, et al.1996; Rulke & Galaskiewicz, 2000). Emphasis on workgroup to share knowledge has been brought forward in contexts where individuals come together in a particular platform and on a regular basis to share their experience and expertise in order to achieve a common goal (Schermerhorn, et al., 1994).

Though successful groups take advantage of the perspectives, talents, and ideas of different members, a well-designed group can also create a common understanding of the web 2.0 context through shared knowledge. In the next section, this study discusses the organizational culture and technology factors in business organizations that can help to explain the role of social media tools in knowledge sharing.

ORGANIZATIONAL CULTURE AND MANAGERIAL IMPLICATIONS

As observed by previous researchers, organizational factors play a significant role in knowledge sharing (Riege, 2005; Yassin, et al., 2013). According to Wahlroos (2010), in the context of knowledge sharing, knowledge culture is one of the organizational factors that have attracted the attention of some researchers due to the changes in the nature of knowledge generation, production, and distribution in business organizations.

Culture is usually defined as a social or normative "glue" that holds an organization together (Siehl & Martin, 1981; Tichy, 1982). It expresses the values or social ideals and beliefs that organization members come to share (Louis, 1980; Siehl & Martin, 1981). Culture, conceived as shared key values and beliefs, fulfills several important functions. First, it conveys a sense of identity for organization members (Deal & Kennedy, 1982; Peters and Waterman, 1982). Second, it facilitates the generation of commitment to something larger than the self (Schall, 1981; Siehl & Martin, 1981; Peters & Waterman, 1982). Third, culture enhances social system stability (Louis, 1980; Kreps, 1981). Fourth, culture serves as a sense-making device that can guide and shape behavior (Louis, 1980; Meyer, 1981; Pfeffer, 1981; Siehl & Martin, 1981). This is only a sampling of the research on the various dimensions of organizational culture. As the number of studies increases, however, there is some convergence among them the findings tend to converge.

Schein (1985, p. 9) describes organizational culture as the pattern of basic assumptions that a given group has invented, discovered, or developed in learning to cope with its problems of external adaptation and internal integration, and that have worked well enough to be considered valid, and, therefore, to be taught to new members as the correct way to perceive, think, and feel in relation to these problems. It is a perspective for understanding what is occurring in an organization and "refers to a collection of theories that attempt to explain and predict how organizations and the people in them act in different circumstances" (Ott, 1989, p. 32). This theory was developed in response to researchers feeling that the more conventional structural and systematic perspectives of organizations did not include a human factor that acknowledged life within organizations.

To implement a culture of knowledge sharing within an organization, leadership or management play an important role because the responsibility lies not only on workers, but above all on the senior managers who need to create an environment that encourages the sharing of knowledge. Organizational culture involves feedback and valuable contributions and participation from colleagues and the level of collaboration in and across business units; while managerial implications cover the responsibility of providing sufficient training, valuing contributions, giving positive feedback, allowing participation and supplying organizational guidelines for using social media tools (Wahlroos, 2010).

In this study, Information communication technologies (ICT) services and infrastructures serve as facilitators that encourage and support knowledge sharing (Riege, 2005) because they are related to the knowledge management technology used in the sharing activity (Volady, 2013; Lin, 2007).

SOCIAL MEDIA TECHNOLOGIES AND KNOWLEDGE SHARING

The term "Web 2.0" was coined by O'Reilly (2005), and it refers to technologies that allow individuals to interact and share information, allowing to build networks based on mutual personal or professional interest. Web 2.0 facilitates social networking, and therefore is also referred to as the social media.

Social media have a variety of broad definitions, such as "collaborative online applications and technologies which enable and encourage participation, conversation, openness, creation and socialization amongst a community of users" (Bowley, 2009, p.15), web-based tools and practices enabling participation and collaboration based on individuals' activities (Storey et al., 2010). Surowiecki (2005) argued that social media is to make use of the "wisdom of the crowd". Groups of people are better at problem-solving and at fostering decision-making than the individuals alone. New ways of inspiring and exploiting knowledge sharing are forcing organizations to expand their knowledge sharing technologies and practices (Mentzas et al., 2007).

These technologies – blogs (like Blogger), video sharing (like YouTube), presentation sharing (like SlideShare), social networking service (like Facebook, LinkedIn), instant messaging service (like Skype) and groupware (like Google Docs) – foster a more socially connected platform (Anderson, 2007).

Several studies (Vuori, 2011; Jalonen, 2014; Bonson &Flores, 2011) explore how and to what extent social media support communication (social media provide new tools to share, store and publish contents, discuss and express opinions and influences); enhance collaboration (social media enable collective content creation and editing without location and time constraints), aid connection (social media offer new ways of networking with other people, socializing within the community), enable completion (social media tools are used to complete content by describing, adding or filtering information, tagging contents, and showing a connection between contents or mixing and matching contents deriving from separate online environments) and provide a combination of pre-existing web services that allow a certain user within a platform to use another application, in a specific window, without the need to leave the initial website. Tab.1 includes the different purposes of social media tools.

Several research studies have been conducted to investigate the use of social media and Web 2.0 for sharing knowledge in the workplace. Paroutis and Saleh (2009) identified the key determinants of knowledge sharing and collaboration using Web 2.0 technologies within a large multinational enterprise by exploring the reasons for and barriers to employees' active participation across the various platforms. Using insights from both Web 2.0 users and non-users, the following four key determinants were identified: history, outcome expectations, perceived organizational support and trust. Dumbrell and Steele (2014) presented an informal knowledge management framework based on the system capabilities of social media technologies as well as the requirements of older adult users. The system capabilities distinct from social media technologies are the following: public peer-to-peer sharing, content evaluation amongst peers, and the "push" nature of these systems. Behringer and Sassenberg (2015) studied the relation between the importance of knowledge exchange, deficits in knowledge exchange, perceived usefulness of social media for knowledge exchange, as well as social media experience on the one hand and the intention to use knowledge exchange technology on the other. The results showed

Table 1. Five C. (Jalonen, 2014)

Five C	Technologies	Tools
Communication	Blogs	Blogger
	microblogs	Twitter
	Video sharing	YouTube
	Presentation sharing	Slide Share
	Instant messaging service	Skype
Collaboration	Wikis	Wikipedia
	Groupware/shared workspaces	Google Docs
Connecting	Social networking services	Facebook LinkedIn
Completing	Visual bookmarking tool	Pinterest
	News aggregator	Digg
Combining	Mash-ups	Google Maps

that the interplay between these criteria jointly affected the intention to apply social media for knowledge exchange after their implementation.

Another study (Sigalaa & Chalkiti, 2015) investigated the relation between social media use and employee creativity by adopting a knowledge management approach in order to consider the influence of social networks and interactions on individuals' creativity. Their findings highlighted the need to shift focus from identifying and managing creative individuals (micro level) and/or organizational contexts (macro level) to creating and managing creative social networks (meso level). The use of social media for externalizing, disseminating and discussing information with others within various social networks as well as for combining and generating shared (new) knowledge can further trigger, enrich and expand the employees' individual cognitive abilities and provide them with stimuli for generating and (co)-creating more and newer ideas/knowledge.

Social Media Security and User Behavior in Business Organizations

As a form of presentation and typical application of Web 2.0 technology, (mobile) social media have been constituted by the relations between different kinds of agents (individuals, groups, organizations, institutions) with the aids of modern (mobile) Internet technology and platforms. As the Internet has evolved into a more social and communicative venue more undesirable security and privacy risk issues have emerged. In particular, the concerns related to ethical issues such as participant knowledge and consent, data privacy, security, confidentiality, integrity of data and availability of Internet platforms are persisting in social media ecosystems. Further, considering the emergence of trust and cyber risk issues coupled with the proliferation of social media users, as well as their various identifications, roles, groups and corresponding behaviors, the investigation of social media security and vulnerability has become more sophisticated and challenging than ever before. With the ever-increasing craze of mobile tools and apps over the past few years, it has become important for business organizations to have clear social media policy best practices in order to both safely maintain a credible and lasting social profile (Zhang, 2015) and mitigate cyber risks.

Summarily speaking, the available studies on social media technology mainly use traditional security techniques such as cryptography and image processing methods to address problems related to partial security, privacy protection, and copyright protection. Most studies are grounded in social media analysis, searching, exploration, assessment, and sentiment analysis on the basis of machine learning and deep learning.

In this section, an overview of the most prominent cyber attack types directly affecting the intention to engage in knowledge sharing behaviors will be briefly presented (Zhang, & Gupta, 2016; Joshi & Kuo, 2011; Cutillo et al. 2010).

Identity Theft

Identity thefts via social media takes numerous forms. Some of the more common schemes include creating a fictitious social media account. Here, the criminal defendant is able to use a victim's social media site to learn enough personal information with the intent to commit fraudulent activities or cause a reputational damage.

Spam Attack

Email spam, also known as junk email, is unsolicited bulk messages sent through email. Recipients of spam often have had their email addresses obtained by spambots, which are automated programs that crawl the internet looking for email addresses. Spammers use spambots to create email distribution lists. A spammer typically sends an email to millions of email addresses, with the expectation that only a small number will respond or interact with the message. The spam emails sent in bulk cause network congestion and the cost of sending emails falls mostly upon the service providers and sometimes on the user.

Malware Attacks

They are becoming very common among social networking sites. The attackers send malware injected scripts to the legitimate user. On clicking the malicious URL a malware might be installed on the devices or can lead to a fake website which attempts to steal personal information from the target user.

Sybil Attacks

It is an attack wherein a reputation system is subverted by forging identities in peer-to-peer networks. It can be used for the distribution of junk information or even malware over the network.

Social Phishing

Social phishing is the attempt to obtain sensitive information such as usernames, passwords, and credit card details (and, indirectly, money), often for malicious reasons, by disguising as a trustworthy entity in an electronic communication.

Impersonation

Here, the aim of the attacker is to create a fake profile in order to successfully impersonate a real-world person. This attack highly depends on the authentication techniques used for registering new accounts.

Domain Name Hijacking

Domain name hijacking is when someone changes registration data of a domain name without the original holder's permission. Usually this happens by someone pretending to be the domain name holder and convincing the registrar to modify the registration information. Once this information is altered, the hijacker can then transfer the domain to another registrar and take control of websites and emails. Weak passwords are the primary cause for most hijacked accounts. So more complex passwords and mandated password changes are a long-standing security practice.

Fake Requests

The attacker sends a fake request with his/her own profile, so as to enlarge his/her network and steal sensitive information from a victim's profile. The actual dissemination of fake requests cannot be prevented, thus, the individual should make a more responsible use of social media.

Image Retrieval and Analysis

Here, the attacker uses various face and image recognition softwares to find more information about the target and his/her linked profiles. It not only affects the target but also his/her circle. This type of cyber attack aims to steal images, videos and other sensitive information from the target.

   In earlier studies, Barbara and colleagues (2011) pointed out that an enhanced access control system for social networks is the first step to address online security and privacy risks. With regard to the personal information disclosure and privacy protection of social media users, Fogues and colleagues (2015) argued that given the massive number of social media users in the last few years, the current beneficial services of Social Networking Service (SNS), such as Facebook and Twitter, while providing social users with convenient and rich experiences, are being overshadowed due to the existence of privacy hazards. Therefore, they listed all the types of privacy hazards that may potentially affect SNSs privacy settings and provided insight on the privacy mechanism enabling the restraint of threats and the protection of data in physical, virtualized and cloud-based environments. They further described and analyzed the current solutions that can be put into place to fulfill the whole range of needs and specifications. Viejo and colleagues (2016) indicated that the big data available on social media platforms contains sensitive personal information that can be collected and used for various types of profit fraud and security lapses. Moreover, current practical solutions mainly adopt strict access control systems only to protect, but not support, users in identifying what information is sensitive or confidential. However, this may not be practically feasible since the set of software programs and/or services that companies employ to prevent cyber attacks require a direct involvement of social media operators which should intervene to optimize the control mechanism.

RECOMMENDATIONS FOR BUSINESS ORGANIZATIONS: MAJOR CONCERNS AND CHALLENGES

The never-ending security breaches over social media have entitled the organizations to safeguard the information that is shared over the network. Any violation of security hinders directly with economic growth of the organization. Social media can be analyzed by studying online behavior, whether the user is an individual or a group. Internet users need to be well informed of the threats posed by the circulation of their personal and financial information. Moreover, they should have the capability to employ appropriate and reliable security measures at their disposal. However, it must be observed that online users' behavior is influenced by subjective factors and personal experience. For example, the experience of being a cyber victim will make a difference in the way that social media consumption behavior is experienced (Scott, & Weems, 2010). Business organizations are also making more efforts in protecting their consumers' private information because the consumers' trust in the service might be greatly diminished or lost. The existing social media research is still on its way towards obtaining a sufficient security analysis from both a qualitative and quantitative point of view.

With regard to the fundamental and common features of the newly developed social media applications, this chapter suggests a novel research direction for the security of the main social media platforms by defining the attacks as evidence-driven research on knowledge sharing. The aim is to encourage or to direct more attention towards the construction of "a behavioral intention, to use security-preserving social media for optimizing knowledge sharing" (Zhang & Gupta, 2016).

As of today, researchers and practitioners in the field of social media networks are still tackling various attacks from (or against) social network and social platforms (NaliniPriya & Asswini, 2015) and endeavor to cope with those challenging security (Guerar et al., 2016, Dhouioui, et al., 2016), privacy and measurement (Sarkar &

Banerjee, 2016; Alduaij, et al., 2016) issues. Social media on the one hand allow us to share our information with people across the globe, but on the other it gives organizations that handle our information access control to our private information. These issues need to be addressed as user trust can only be gained by increasing perceived user control and lowering such risks.

Consequently, the current study addresses the following important scientific questions regarding the role of social media and their integration in the knowledge sharing process: are social media able to develop organizational memory classified in internal (group's skills and organizational culture) and external (formal policies, procedures, manual and computer files)? Is security-preserving social media able to optimize knowledge sharing? Is social media security able to influence the behavioral intention of the group/individual to continue to use social media tools? Is organizational culture positively influenced by knowledge sharing via web 2.0 technologies?

In considering social media, I argue that it is not if and how social media and security can play a role in our knowledge sharing system, but rather what we want social media to be capable of doing. Thus, with the rapid advancement of IT (Information Technologies), the question is not actually what social media can do for researchers and practitioners, but instead what we want social media to do for all people in business organizations.

FUTURE RESEARCH DIRECTIONS

Although the study contributes to fill a research gap due to the lack of theoretical and empirical literature on the role of social media in knowledge sharing, there are some limitations that should be taken into account. Contrasting findings on the use of IT tools were however shown in previous studies (Olivera, 2000). For example, Goodman and Darr (1998) found that, in the absence of external rewards, employees were not willing to update shared databases, while Constant et al. (1996) found that employees usually liked to answer posted questions to help each other despite the absence of external rewards. Research also found that the decision of not updating the systems was partially explained by the lack of motivation to be held accountable for posted contributions (Orlikowski, 1996).

The lack of attention on individuals' interactions was also addressed as one of the main limits of the knowledge sharing debate (Hansen, 1999). As Brown and Duguid wrote "[a] great deal of hope (and money) is thus being placed on the value of Intranets. Intranets are indeed valuable, but social knowledge suggests that there is more to consider both with regards to search and retrieval" (1998, p. 98), because as also pointed out by Gherardi and colleagues (1998) knowledge is out there somewhere, stored in places (books, databases, minds) waiting to be transferred to and acquired by another mind for future use.

Currently, another obvious drawback is that the study of knowledge sharing security across social media in business settings is still in its infancy and is very limited in scope. Nowadays it is very difficult to evaluate the role of security in this field because no one is able to learn and evaluate the dynamics of security and to understand how to support knowledge sharing. Anyway, considering that social media is a global phenomenon, cross-cultural research on the knowledge sharing effect would be a promising area for further investigation.

This chapter highlights the existing opportunities for an active involvement of social media tools in business organizations. Numerous social-based strategies can be adopted to increase the operational performance or reduce corporate costs, but the following may serve as practical examples and procedures: communication between employees can be encouraged to support problem-solving (if organization needs an expert for a specific task, a post can be placed on a blog and likely receive a response from another employee or search on LinkedIn to find the person who can help); the conversion of personal knowledge into shared knowledge (if the senior employees record videos about their work and share them with the new employees, the organization can use these videos instead of expensive training programs to explain the details); the discussion of work-related problems (with a group of people who are active practitioners in a particular area; professional communities can be useful because they are neutral and can provide a way to share best practices, to ask questions and to provide support for each other outside the organization). Reduction of time and costs through integrated tools (the digital calendar, for example, which allows to organize and share events, meetings, and expedite matters, as compared to phone calls or e-mails). Several managerial processes can also be implemented. For example, it is recommended that the introduction of new social media technologies be supported for establishing the terms and conditions of usage, communicating the benefits or providing the necessary training. Moreover, organizations should develop a reward system to encourage employees' willingness to use social media tools for knowledge sharing.

CONCLUSION

From a research perspective, this chapter sets a broad agenda for future research. Due to the fact that only limited research has examined knowledge sharing and the role of social media in business organizations, it is believed that this study can inspire subsequent scientific inquiries in this recently emerging, but promising area of research. Possible future research directions may provide some responses to my initial questions about the role of security and the way social media can be successfully applied in order to interpret the impact of determinants on knowledge sharing. Moreover, my study can be tested by a team of experts (e.g. Delphi methodology).

It also aims to contribute to the management and organizational fields in two separate but related ways. First, future studies may compare firms that use social media tools with those that do not and determine their impact on knowledge sharing. At a larger scale, a comparison could be made between a firm that uses this approach and one that does not in terms of the impact on job satisfaction, employee loyalty, and development of a new idea. The issue of how to effectively design and deploy security policies is the second recommended research direction. It has become clear that security offers many opportunities for firms to interact with their groups along the entire knowledge-sharing process. Future research could also analyze and develop a training system for employees and companies to gather security data with respect to the variables governing relations and dynamics between individuals and groups. In general, firms have only a few opportunities to gather knowledge.

Using the determinants interpretation and the knowledge sharing theory, and guided by the theoretical approaches from related research in business and management, this chapter provides an analytical approach to explore the knowledge sharing by investigating the influence of social media tools and security on knowledge sharing systems. Here some important potential applications of knowledge sharing representation in the study of social media have been discussed. In particular, an outline of the major theoretical approaches to these applications has been provided. Gaining and utilizing consistent knowledge sharing by an organizational group is not a simple or straightforward task. It is a highly involved and multidimensional process, which is seldom complete or errorless. Furthermore, companies have to clearly identify what information and knowledge are to be kept confidential and what instead can be shared and made available to others. Such practices such as crowdsourcing and open innovation practices have demonstrated the value of sharing information and knowledge that has previously been considered to be confidential. In this study, social media emerge as a new perspective. Enormous information and knowledge can be shared using powerful tools in a world in which social factors play an essential role. In our new, accelerated world, numerous technologies have been developed to support social capital connections (social networking services like Facebook, LinkedIn) and to communicate in a more effective way (instant messaging services like Skype, Viber). For organizations that ensure value to knowledge sharing, integrating social media tools into their daily business life is essential to enable employees an easy access and to offer training to inexperienced users. For example, it would be a gross mistake to underestimate the power of social media that everyone uses daily while developing documents or knowledge management systems.

As previously stated, social media can be analyzed by studying online behavior, whether the user is an individual or a group. The Internet users need to be well informed about the threats posed by the circulation of their personal and financial information. Moreover, they should have the capability to employ appropriate and reliable security measures to aid them. Building and strengthening trustworthiness will provide awareness and safeguard all users.

Practitioners can use this study not only to evaluate knowledge sharing and the role of social media in targeting better future security interventions in business settings, but also to gain a better understanding of the determinants of knowledge sharing that a company needs to be aware of and responsive to human resources' needs and expectations.

REFERENCES

Alavi, M., & Leidner, D. E. (2001). Review: Knowledge Management and Knowledge Management Systems: Conceptual Foundations and Research Issues. *Management Information Systems Quarterly*, *25*(1), 107–136. doi:10.2307/3250961

Alduaij, S., Chen, Z., & Gangopadhyay, A. (2016). Using crowd sourcing to analyze consumers response to privacy policies of online social network and financial institutions at micro level. *International Journal of Information Security and Privacy*, *10*(2), 41–63. doi:10.4018/IJISP.2016040104

Anderson, P. (2007). *What is Web 2.0? Ideas, technologies and implications for education*. JISC reports. Available: http://www.jisc.ac.uk/media/documents/techwatch/tsw0701b.p

Bagozzi, R. P. (2000). On the concept of intentional social action in consumer research. *The Journal of Consumer Research*, *27*(3), 388–396. doi:10.1086/317593

Barbara, C., Elena, F., & Raymond, H. (2011). Semantic web-based social network access control. *Computers & Security*, *30*(2), 108–115.

Bartol, K. M., & Srivastava, A. (2002). Encouraging Knowledge Sharing: The Role of Organizational Reward Systems. *Journal of Leadership & Organizational Studies*, *9*(1), 64–76. doi:10.1177/107179190200900105

Behringer, N., & Sassenberg, K. (2015). Introducing social media for knowledge management: Determinants of employees intentions to adopt new tools. *Computers in Human Behavior*, *48*, 290–296. doi:10.1016/j.chb.2015.01.069

Bonson, E., & Flores, F. (2011). Social media and corporate dialogue: The response of the global financial institutions. *Online Information Review*, *35*(1), 34–49. doi:10.1108/14684521111113579

Bowley, R. C. (2009). A comparative case study: Examining the organizational use of social networking sites (Thesis). Hamilton: The University of Waikato. Available http://researchcommons.waikato.ac.nz/bitstream/handle/10289/3590/thesis.pdf?sequence=1&isAllowed=y

Brown, J. S., & Duguid, P. (1998). Organizing knowledge. *California Management Review*, *40*(3), 90–111. doi:10.2307/41165945

Cabrera, A., & Cabrera, E. F. (2002). Knowledge-Sharing Dilemmas. *Organization Studies*, *23*(5), 687–710. doi:10.1177/0170840602235001

Cabrera, Á., Collins, W. C., & Salgado, J. F. (2006). Determinants of individual engagement in knowledge sharing. *International Journal of Human Resource Management*, *17*(2), 245–264. doi:10.1080/09585190500404614

Chen, I.Y., & Chen, N.S., & Kinshuk. (2009). Examining the Factors Influencing Participants' Knowledge Sharing Behavior in Virtual Learning Communities. *Journal of Educational Technology & Society*, *12*(1), 134–148.

Choo, C. (1998). *The Knowing Organization: How Organizations Use Information for Construct Meaning, Create Knowledge and Make Decisions*. New York: Oxford Press.

Constant, D., Sproull, L. S., & Kiesler, S. B. (1996). The kindness of strangers: The usefulness of electronic weak ties for technical advice. *Organization Science*, *7*(2), 119–135. doi:10.1287/orsc.7.2.119

Cross, R., & Sproull, L. (2004). More than an answer: Information relationships for actionable knowledge. *Organization Science*, *15*(4), 446–462. doi:10.1287/orsc.1040.0075

Cummings, J. L., & Teng, B. S. (2006). The keys to successful knowledge sharing. *Journal of General Management*, *31*(4), 1–18. doi:10.1177/030630700603100401

Cummings, J. N. (2004). Work groups, structural diversity, and knowledge sharing in a global organization. *Management Science*, *50*(3), 352–364. doi:10.1287/mnsc.1030.0134

Cutillo, L. A., Manulis, M., & Strufe, T. (2010). Security and privacy in online social networks. In *Handbook of Social Network, Technologies and Applications*. Springer. doi:10.1007/978-1-4419-7142-5_23

Davenport, T. H. (1999). Groups and teams. In *Organisational behaviour*. London: Financial Times Pitman Publishing.

Davenport, T. H., & Prusak, L. (1998). *Working Knowledge: How Organizations Manage What They Know*. Boston: Harvard Business School Press.

Dawson, R. (2007). *Future of Media Report 2007*. Available at: www.rossdawsonblog. com/Future_of_Media_Report2007.pdf

Dawson, S. (2008). A study of the relationship between student social networks and sense of community. *Journal of Educational Technology & Society, 11*(3), 224–238.

Deal, T. E., & Kennedy, A. A. (1982). *Corporate Cultures*. Reading, MA: Addison-Wesley.

Dhouioui, Z., Ali, A. A., & Akaichi, J. (2016). Social networks security policies. *Proceedings of 9th KES International Conference on Intelligent Interactive Multimedia Systems and Services*, 395–403.

Di Pietro, L., Di Virgilio, F. & Pantano, E (2013). Negative eWOM in user-generated contents: recommendations for firms and organizations. *International Journal of Digital Content Technology and its Applications, 7*(5), 1-8.

Dumbrell, D., & Steele, R. (2014). Social Media Technologies for Achieving Knowledge Management Amongst Older Adult Communities. *Procedia: Social and Behavioral Sciences, 147*, 229–236. doi:10.1016/j.sbspro.2014.07.165

Eijkman, H. (2011). Dancing with Post Modernity: Web 2.0+ as a New Epistemic Learning Space. IGI Global.

Fogues, R., Such, J. M., Espinosa, A., & Garcia-Fornes, A. (2015). Open challenges in relationship-based privacy mechanisms for social network services. *International Journal of Human-Computer Interaction, 31*(5), 350–370. doi:10.1080/10447318 .2014.1001300

Foss, N. J., Husted, K., & Michailova, S. (2010). Governing Knowledge Sharing in Organizations: Levels of Analysis, Governance Mechanisms, and Research Directions. *Journal of Management Studies, 47*(3), 455–482. doi:10.1111/j.1467-6486.2009.00870.x

Foss, N. J., Minbaeva, D. B., Pedersen, T., & Reinholt, M. M. (2009). Encouraging knowledge sharing among employees: How job design matters. *Human Resource Management, 48*(6), 871–893. doi:10.1002/hrm.20320

Gaál, Z., Szabó, L., Kovács, Z., Obermayer-Kovács, N., & Csepregi, A. (2008). Knowledge Management Profile Maturity Model. *ECKM 2008 - Conference Proceedings, 9th European Conference on Knowledge Management*, 209-216.

Gaál, Z., Szabó, L., & Obermayer-Kovács, N. (2014). Personal knowledge sharing: Web 2.0 role through the lens of Generations. *ECKM 2014 – Conference Proceedings, 15th European Conference on Knowledge Management*, 362-370.

Gaál, Z., Szabó, L., Obermayer-Kovács, N., & Csepregi, A. (2015). Exploring the role of social media in knowledge sharing. *Electronic Journal of Knowledge Management*, *13*(3), 185–197.

Gherardi, S., Nicolini, D., & Odella, F. (1998). Toward a social understanding of how people learn in organizations: The notion of situated curriculum. *Management Learning*, *29*(3), 273–297. doi:10.1177/1350507698293002

Goodman, P. S., & Darr, E. D. (1998). Computer-aided systems and communities: Mechanisms for organizational learning in distributed environment. *Management Information Systems Quarterly*, *22*(4), 417–440. doi:10.2307/249550

Gottschalk, P. (2007). *CIO and corporate strategic management: changing role of CIO to CEO.* Hershey, PA: Idea Group Publication. doi:10.4018/978-1-59904-423 1

Grant, R. M. (1996). Prospering in dynamically-competitive environments: Organizational capability as knowledge integration. *Organization Science*, *7*(4), 375–387. doi:10.1287/orsc.7.4.375

Grant, R. M. (1996). Toward a Knowledge-Based Theory of the Firm. *Strategic Management Journal*, *17*(2), 109–122. doi:10.1002/smj.4250171110

Grover, V., & Davenport, T. (2001). General Perspectives on Knowledge Management: Fostering a Research Agenda. *Journal of Management Information Systems*, *18*(1), 5–22.

Gruenfeld, D. H., Mannix, E. A., Williams, K. Y., & Neale, M. A. (1996). Group composition and decision making: How member familiarity and information distribution affects process and performance. *Organizational Behavior and Human Decision Processes*, *67*(1), 1–15. doi:10.1006/obhd.1996.0061

Guerar, M., Migliardi, M., & Merlo, A. (2016). Using screen brightness to improve security in mobile social network access, IEEE Trans. *Dependable Secure Computer*, *99*, 1545–5971.

Haas, M. R., & Hansen, M. T. (2007). Different knowledge, different benefits: Toward a productivity perspective on knowledge sharing in organizations. *Strategic Management Journal, 28*(11), 1133–1153. doi:10.1002/smj.631

Hansen, M. T., Nohria, N. & Tierney, T. (1999, March). What is your strategy for managing knowledge. *Harvard Business Review,* 106-116.

Hau, Y. S., Kim, B., Lee, H., & Kim, Y. G. (2013). The effects of individual motivations and social capital on employees tacit and explicit knowledge sharing intentions. *International Journal of Information Management, 33*(2), 356–366. doi:10.1016/j.ijinfomgt.2012.10.009

Ipe, M. (2003). Knowledge sharing in organizations: A conceptual framework. *Human Resource Development Review, 2*(4), 337–359. doi:10.1177/1534484303257985

Jalonen, H. (2014). Social media and emotions in organisational knowledge creation. *Conference Proceedings, Federated Conference on Computer Science and Information Systems,* 1371–1379. doi:10.15439/2014F39

Jones, M. B. (1974). Regressing group on individual effectiveness. *Organizational Behavior and Human Performance, 11*(3), 426–451. doi:10.1016/0030-5073(74)90030-0

Joshi, P., & Kuo, C. C. (2011). Security and privacy in online social networks: A survey. *Proceedings of IEEE International Conference on Multimedia and Expo.* doi:10.1109/ICME.2011.6012166

Keller, K. L., & Staelin, R. (1987). Effects of Quality and Quantity of Information and Decision Effectiveness. *The Journal of Consumer Research, 14*(2), 200–213. doi:10.1086/209106

Kennedy, J. L. (1971). The system approach: A preliminary exploratory study of the relation between team composition and financial performance in business games. *The Journal of Applied Psychology, 55*(1), 46–49. doi:10.1037/h0030599

Kreps, G. (1981). *Organizational folklore: The packaging of company history at RCA.* Paper presented at the ICA/SCA Conference on interpretive approaches to organizational communication, Alta, UT.

Larson, J., Christensen, C., Foster-Fishman, P. G., & Keys, C. B. (1994). Discussion of shared and unshared information in decision-making groups. *Journal of Personality and Social Psychology, 67*(3), 446–461. doi:10.1037/0022-3514.67.3.446

Lee, C. K., & Al-Hawamdeh, S. (2002). Factors impacting knowledge sharing. *Journal of Information & Knowledge Management*, 49-56.

Lehner, F., & Maier, R. K. (2000). How can organizational memory theories contribute to organizational memory systems? *Information Systems Frontiers*, 2(3/4), 277–298. doi:10.1023/A:1026516627735

Liang, D. W., Moreland, R., & Argote, L. (1995). Group versus individual training and group performance: The mediating role of transactive memory. *Personality and Social Psychology Bulletin*, 21(4), 384–393. doi:10.1177/0146167295214009

Lin, H. F. (2007). Knowledge sharing and firm innovation capability: An empirical study. *International Journal of Manpower*, 28(3/4), 315–332. doi:10.1108/01437720710755272

Liu, K. L., Chang, C. C., & Hu, I. L. (2010). Exploring the Effects of Task Characteristics on Knowledge Sharing in Libraries. *Library Review*, 59(6), 455–468. doi:10.1108/00242531011053968

Louis, M. R. (1980). *A cultural perspective on organizations: The need for and consequences of viewing organizations as culture-bearing milieux*. Paper presented at the National Academy of Management Meetings, Detroit, MI.

McDermott, R. (1999). Why information technology inspired but cannot deliver knowledge management. *California Management Review*, 41(4), 103–117. doi:10.2307/41166012

Mentzas, G., Kafentzis, K., & Georgolios, P. (2007). Knowledge services on the Semantic Web. *Communications of the ACM*, 50(10), 53–58. doi:10.1145/1290958.1290962

Meyer, A. (1981). How ideologies supplant formal structures and shape responses to environments. *Journal of Management Studies*, 19(1), 45–61. doi:10.1111/j.1467-6486.1982.tb00059.x

Moreland, R. L., Argote, L., & Krishnan, R. (1997). Training people to work in groups. In Applications of Theory and Research on Groups to Social Issues. Plenum.

NaliniPriya, G., & Asswini, M. (2015). A survey on vulnerable attacks in online social networks. *Proceedings of 2015 International Conference on Innovation Information in Computing Technologies*, 1–6.

Nonaka, I., & Takeuchi, H. (1995). *The Knowledge-creating Company*. New York: Oxford University Press.

O'Reilly, T. (2005). *What is Web 2.0? Design patterns and business models for the next generation of software*. Available: http://www.oreilly.com/pub/a/web2/archive/what-is-web-20.html

Okhuysen, G. A., & Eisenhardt, K. M. (2002). Integrating Knowledge in Groups: How Formal Interventions Enable Flexibility. *Organization Science, 13*(4), 370–386. doi:10.1287/orsc.13.4.370.2947

Olivera, F. (2000). Memory systems in organizations: An empirical investigation of mechanisms for knowledge collection, storage and access. *Journal of Management Studies, 37*(6), 811–832. doi:10.1111/1467-6486.00205

Orlikowski, W. J. (1996). Improving organizational transformation over time: A situated change perspective. *Information Systems Research, 7*(1), 63–92. doi:10.1287/isre.7.1.63

Ott, J. S. (1989). *The organizational culture perspective*. Pacific Grove, CA: Brooks/Cole Publishing Company.

Paroutis, A., & Al Saleh, A. (2009). Determinants of knowledge sharing using Web 2.0 technologies. *Journal of Knowledge Management, 13*(4), 52–63. doi:10.1108/13673270910971824

Peters, T. J., & Waterman, R. H. Jr. (1982). *In Search of Excellence: Lessons from America's Best-Run Companies*. New York: Harper & Row.

Pfeffer, J. (1981). Management as symbolic action: The creation and maintenance of organizational paradigms. In L. L. Cummings & B. M. Staw (Eds.), Research in Organizational Behavior (vol. 3, pp. 1-52). Greenwich, CT: JAI Press.

Polányi, M. (1966). *The Tacit Dimension*. London: Routledge & Kegan Paul.

Rehman, M., Mahmood, K. B., Salleh, R., & Amin, A. (2011). Review of Factors Affecting Knowledge Sharing Behavior. *2010 International Conference on E-business, Management and Economics*, 3, 223-227.

Reychav, I., & Weisberg, J. (2009). Good for Workers, good for Companies: How Knowledge Sharing benefits Individual Employees. *Knowledge and Process Management, 16*(4), 186–197. doi:10.1002/kpm.335

Riege, A. (2005). Three dozen knowledge sharing barriers managers must consider. *Journal of Knowledge Management, 9*(3), 18–35. doi:10.1108/13673270510602746

Rudawska, A. (2015). System nagród jako mechanizm wspierający wewnątrzorganizacyjne dzielenie się wiedzą. *Studia i Prace Wydziału Nauk Ekonomicznych i Zarządzania, 34*(4), 289–301.

Rulke, D. L., & Galaskiewicz, J. (2000). Distribution of Knowledge, Group Network Structure, and Group Performance. *Management Science, 46*(5), 612–625. doi:10.1287/mnsc.46.5.612.12052

Sambamurthy, V., Bharadwaj, A., & Grover, V. (2003). Shaping Agility through Digital Options: Reconceptualizing the Role of Information Technology in Contemporary Firms. *Management Information Systems Quarterly, 27*(2).

Sarkar, M., & Banerjee, S. (2016). Exploring social network privacy measurement using fuzzy vector commitment. *Intelligent Decision Technologies, 10*(3), 285–297. doi:10.3233/IDT-160256

Schall, M. S. (1981). *An exploration into a successful corporation's saga-vision and its rhetorical community*. Paper presented at the ICAl SCA Conference on Interpretive Approaches to Organizational Communication, Alta, UT.

Schein, E. H. (1985). *Organizational Culture and Leadership*. San Francisco, CA: Jossey-Bass.

Schermerhorn, J. R., Hunt, J. G., & Osborn, R. N. (1994). *Managing organizational behavior*. New York: Wiley.

Scott, B. G., & Weems, C. F. (2010). Patterns of actual and perceived control: Are control profiles differentially related to internalizing and externalizing problems in youth? *Anxiety, Stress, and Coping, 23*(5), 515–528. doi:10.1080/10615801003611479 PMID:20155530

Serdar, D., Jacobs, M., Nayir, D. Z., Khilji, S., & Wang, X. (2013). The quasi-moderating role of organizational culture in the relationship between rewards and knowledge shared and gained. *Journal of Knowledge Management, 18*(1), 19–37.

Siehl, C., & Martin, J. (1981). *Learning organizational culture*. Working paper, Graduate School of Business. Stanford University.

Sigalaa, M., & Chalkiti, K. (2015). Knowledge management, social media and employee creativity. *International Journal of Hospitality Management, 45*, 44–58. doi:10.1016/j.ijhm.2014.11.003

Stankosky, M., & Baldanza, C. (2001). *A systems approach to engineering a KM system*. Unpublished Manuscript.

Stasser, G., & Stewart, D. (1992). Discovery of hidden profiles by decision-making groups: Solving a problem versus making a judgment. *Journal of Personality and Social Psychology, 63*(3), 426–434. doi:10.1037/0022-3514.63.3.426

Stasser, G., & Titus, W. (1987). Effects of information load and percentage of shared information on the dissemination of unshared information during group discussion. *Journal of Personality and Social Psychology, 53*(1), 81–93. doi:10.1037/0022-3514.53.1.81

Stasser, G., Titus, W., & Wittenbaum, G. M. (1995). Expert roles and information exchange during discussion: The importance of knowing who knows what. *Journal of Experimental Social Psychology, 31*(3), 244–265. doi:10.1006/jesp.1995.1012

Storey, M. A., Treude, C., Deursen, A., & Cheng, L. T. (2010). The Impact of Social Media on Software Engineering Practices and Tools. *FoSER '10 Proceedings of the FSE/SDP workshop on Future of software engineering research*, 359-364. doi:10.1145/1882362.1882435

Surowiecki, J. (Ed.). (2005). *The Wisdom of the Crowds*. New York: Anchor Books.

Teng, J. T. C., & Song, S. (2011). An exploratory examination of knowledge sharing behaviors: Solicited and voluntary. *Journal of Knowledge Management, 15*(1), 104–117. doi:10.1108/13673271111108729

Tichy, N. M. (1982). Managing change strategically: The technical, political, and cultural keys. *Organizational Dynamics, 11*(Autumn), 59–80. doi:10.1016/0090-2616(82)90005-5 PMID:10298937

Tosi, H. L., Mero, N. P., & Rizzo, J. R. (2000). *Managing organizational behaviour* (4th ed.). Oxford, UK: Blackwell Blackwell Business.

Tziner, A., & Eden, D. (1985). Effects of crew composition on crew performance: Does the whole equal the sum of its parts? *The Journal of Applied Psychology, 70*(1), 85–93. doi:10.1037/0021-9010.70.1.85

Usman, S., H. & Oyefolahan, O. (2014). Determinants of Knowledge Sharing Using Web Technologies among Students in Higher Education. *Journal of Knowledge Management, Economics and Information Technology, 4*(2).

Van den Hooff, B., & de Ridder, J. A. (2004). Knowledge sharing in context: The influence of organizational commitment, communication climate and CMC use on knowledge sharing. *Journal of Knowledge Management, 8*(6), 117–130. doi:10.1108/13673270410567675

Van den Hooff, B., Elving, W. J. L., Meeuwsen, J. M., & Dumoulin, C. M. (2003). *Knowledge Sharing* in Knowledge Communities. In M. H. Huysman, V. Wulf, & E. Wenger (Eds.), *Communities and Technologies*. Deventer: Kluwer Academic Publishers. doi:10.1007/978-94-017-0115-0_7

Viejo, A., & Sánchez, D. (2015). Enforcing transparent access to private content in social networks by means of automatic sanitization. *Expert Systems with Applications*, *42*(23), 9366–9378. doi:10.1016/j.eswa.2015.08.014

Volady, L. (2013). *An Investigation of Factors Influencing Knowledge Sharing Among Undergraduate Teacher Education Students*. Retrieved September 9, 2013, from http://volady0002.wordpress.com/knowledge-sharingamong-undegraduate-students/

Von Krogh, G. (2011). Knowledge Sharing in Organizations: The role of communities. In E.-S. Mark & L. Marjorie (Eds.), *Handbook of Organizational Learning and Knowledge Management* (pp. 403–432). Wiley & Sons.

Vuori, V. (2011). *Social Media Changing the Competitive Intelligence Process: Elicitation of Employees' Competitive Knowledge*. Academic Dissertation. Available: http://dspace.cc.tut.fi/dpub/bitstream/handle/123456789/20724/vuori.pdf

Vuori, V., & Okkonen, J. (2012). Refining information and knowledge by social media applications: Adding value by insight. *VINE Information and Knowledge Management*, *42*(1), 117–128.

Wahlroos, J. K. (2010). *Social Media as a Form of Organizational Knowledge Sharing. A Case Study on Employee Participation*. Unpublished thesis of the University of Helsinki. Retrieved from https://helda.helsinki.fi/bitstream/handle/10138/24624/Thesis.Johanna.Wahlroos.pdf?sequence=1

Wang, S., & Noe, R. A. (2010). Knowledge sharing: A review and directions for future research. *Human Resource Management Review*, *20*(2), 115–131. doi:10.1016/j.hrmr.2009.10.001

Wang, S., & Noe, R. A. (2010). Knowledge sharing: A review and directions for future research. *Human Resource Management Review*, *20*(2), 115–131. doi:10.1016/j.hrmr.2009.10.001

Wangpipatwong, S. (2009). Factors Influencing Knowledge Sharing Among University Students. *Proceedings of the 17th International Conference on Computers in Education*, 800-807.

Wegner, D. M. (1986). Transactive memory: A contemporary analysis of the group mind. In G. Mullen & G. Goethals (Eds.), *Theories of Group Behavior*. New York: Springer-Verlag.

Weick, K. E. (1995). *Sensemaking in Organizations*. Thousand Oaks, CA: Sage.

West, M. A., Garrod, S., & Carletta, J. (1997). Group decision-making and effectiveness: unexplored boundaries. In C. L. Cooper & S. E. Jackson (Eds.), *Creating tomorrow's organizations a handbook for future research in organizational behaviour*. New York: John Wiley & Sons.

Witherspoon, C. L., Bergner, J., Cockrell, C., & Stone, D. N. (2013). Antecedents of organizational knowledge sharing: A meta-analysis and critique. *Journal of Knowledge Management, 17*(2), 250–277. doi:10.1108/13673271311315204

Yassin, F., Salim, J., & Sahari, N. (2013). The Influence of Organizational Factors on Knowledge Sharing Using ICT among Teachers. *Procedia Technology, 11*, 272–280. doi:10.1016/j.protcy.2013.12.191

Yesil, S., & Dereli, S. F. (2013). An empirical investigation of organisational justice, knowledge sharing and innovation capability. *SciVerse Science Direct, 75*, 199–208.

Yi, J. (2009). A Measure of Knowledge Sharing Behavior: Scale Development and Validation. *Knowledge Management Research & Practice, 7*(1), 65–81. doi:10.1057/kmrp.2008.36

Yu, T., Lu, L., & Liu, T. (2009). Exploring factors that influence knowledge sharing behavior via weblogs. *Computers in Human Behavior*. doi:10.1016/j.chb.2009.08.002

Zhang, Z., & Gupta, B. B. (2016). Social media security and trustworthiness: Overview and new direction. *Future Generation Computer Systems*. doi:10.1016/j.future.2016.10.007

Zhang, Z. Y. (2015). Security, trust and risk in multimedia social networks. *The Computer Journal, 58*(4), 515–517. doi:10.1093/comjnl/bxu151

KEY TERMS AND DEFINITIONS

Content Sharing: Is the textual, visual, or aural content that is encountered as part of the user experience on websites. It may include—among other things—text, images, sounds, videos, and animations.

Groupware: Is an application software designed to help people involved in a common task to achieve their goals. One of the earliest definitions of collaborative software is intentional group processes plus software to support them.

Mash-Ups: Is a song or composition created by blending two or more pre-recorded songs, usually by overlaying the vocal track of one song seamlessly over the instrumental track of another.

Messaging Service: Is a service that is process oriented and exchanges messages/data calls.

Social Bookmarking: Is a centralized online service which allows users to add, annotate, edit, and share bookmarks of web documents.

Social Networking: (Also social networking site, SNS or social media) Is an online platform that is used by people to build social networks or social relations with other people who share similar personal or career interests, activities, backgrounds or real-life connections.

Web Tools: Are tools used for testing the user facing interface of a website or web application.

Chapter 2
The Role of Social Media Tools in the Knowledge Management in Organizational Context:
Evidences Based on Literature Review

Marcello Chedid
University of Aveiro, Portugal

Leonor Teixeira
University of Aveiro, Portugal

ABSTRACT

The advancement of the economy based on knowledge makes knowledge management critical for organizations. The traditional knowledge management systems have presented some shortcomings on their implementation and management. Social media have demonstrated that are not just a buzzword and have been used increasingly by the organizations as a knowledge management component. This chapter was developed aiming at exploring and critically reviewing the literature of social media use in organizational context as a knowledge management component. The review suggests that, while traditional knowledge management systems are static and often act just as knowledge repositories, social media have the potential for supporting different knowledge management processes that will impact on the organizational culture by encouraging on participation, collaboration and knowledge sharing. Despite their recognized impact on knowledge management processes, some uncertainty remains amongst researchers and practitioners and is associated to the difficulty in understanding and measuring their real impact.

DOI: 10.4018/978-1-5225-2897-5.ch002

INTRODUCTION

In the last twenty years knowledge management emerges as a distinct area of study, consolidating as a significant source of competitive advantage and as one of the most important resources in the capacity of progress of modern organizations (Mårtensson, 2000; Pekka-Economou & Hadjidema, 2011). The ability to define, implement and manage business opportunities depends largely on the availability and quality of knowledge.

To meet the challenge of capturing, organizing and disseminating knowledge, the organizations have undertaken heavy investments in technology, however, with "significant failure rates" (Malhotra, 2005, p. 8). In general, the system was not appropriated or the organization was not prepared for the required cultural change.

Despite the wide agreement that knowledge management occurs within a social context, some authors have the opinion that organizations have been focused primarily on the technology and little on people and process (Kakabadse, Kakabadse, & Kouzmin, 2003), and most of the solutions were centralized within the organization with lack of interactivity (Panahi, Watson, & Partridge, 2012).

Social media became a global phenomenon (Schlagwein & Hu, 2016) and have been used increasingly by the organizations. There are several examples of social media use in line with different organization objectives across countries and different types of industries. According to Von Krogh (2012, p. 154), "the increased use of social software by firms is often the result of a strategic imperative for more openness toward the outside", including, for example, universities, suppliers, customers, and users.

Social media, also called social software, has become in a driving force by exploiting the collective intelligence (Chatti, Klamma, Jarke, & Naeve, 2007). Social media are a set of features, grouped into software applications, which enables to recreate online various types of social interactions that are possible to find in physical environments.

The strategically chosen social media can be internal or external to organization and its use can have as objective to achieve internal or external goals. Schlagwein and Hu (2016, p. 3) add that "technologically different social media tools might achieve the same organizational purpose, or technologically similar social media tools might achieve very different organizational purposes". These purposes can be such as to improve productivity, increase the interaction between departments and team workers, create a channel with consumers or enhance the management of knowledge.

Truly, almost none of the social media acts alone. The combination of different tools in an appropriate measure can produce excellent results for organizations.

However, often identifying the perfect match of tools can be somewhat difficult due to the dynamism and versatility of social media tools (Schlagwein & Hu, 2016).

Social media are very close in its principle and attributes to knowledge management (Levy, 2009), providing inexpensive alternatives and solutions that can overcome many failures of traditional knowledge management models (von Krogh, 2012). These tools have also shown to be an efficient mechanism in supporting knowledge sharing, particularly tacit knowledge, helping organizations to capture knowledge based on the knowledge from different stakeholders (Al Saifi, Dillon, & McQeen, 2016; Clark et al., 2015; Costa et al., 2009; Panahi et al., 2012; Paroutis & Al Saleh, 2009; Tee & Karney, 2010). Based on the crowd-wisdom, the social media enable to keep knowledge relevant and up-to-date (Chatti et al., 2007).

According to Kane et al. (2014, p. 276) "the impact of social media on and for organizations, represents an important area for information systems research".

Given that knowledge management is critical for organizations and social media tools have the potential to be enablers for knowledge management processes, through a literature review, the chapter's authors aim to explore and contribute to understanding the possible impacts and consequences in the use of these tools in knowledge management in organizational context, and highlight the factors that can be determining to the eventual success of a knowledge management based on social media. The chapter also aims to address some further research directions.

This chapter is to be understood as being exploratory in its nature and is organized as follows. In the next section, the authors through the theoretical background introduce social media and knowledge management. The following section, based on the literature reviewed, provides a critical discussion of the role of social media in the knowledge management processes. Following this section, the authors discuss about the main benefits and threats of social media in the knowledge management context. Conclusion and directions for future research are in the final part of this chapter.

BACKGROUND

Initially, it is important to make a brief theoretical background of the study. In this section, the authors provide an overview of social media tools and traditional knowledge management.

Social Media Tools

Social media have demonstrated that is not just a buzzword. After influencing how organizations and society operate (Ford & Mason, 2013b), social media in the organization have been boosting collaboration and participation among knowledge workers, helping to create a social network in which people are more connected and knowledge can flow more efficiently between participants (Gaál, Szabó, Obermayer-Kovács, & Csepregi, 2015; Levy, 2009).

Kaplan and Haenlein (2010, p. 59) argue that in the literature "there seems to be very limited understanding of what the term "social media" exactly means", and what exactly should be included under this term (Kaplan & Haenlein, 2010). Practitioners and researchers have used the term social media interchangeably and as synonym for Web 2.0 (Kaplan & Haenlein, 2010; O'Reilly, 2007). This situation causes some confusion, so it is necessary to clarify the terms. The term Web 2.0 is credited to O'Reilly (Paroutis & Al Saleh, 2009) and it refers to a set of technology of online tools that supports social interaction among users. Social media are the platforms created using the Web 2.0 technologies being, according to Kaplan and Haenlein (2010, p. 61), defined as "a group of Internet-based applications that build on the ideological and technological foundations of Web 2.0, and that allow the creation and exchange of User Generated Content". Also De Wever et al. (2007, p. 512) define social media as "software that enables communication through digital technologies during which people connect, converse, collaborate, manage content and form online networks in a social and bottom-up fashion".

Harrysson et al. (2016) state that, based on their survey "The evolution of social technologies" carried out among 2750 global executives over each year from 2005 to 2015, since the beginning of the social-technology era, organizations have recognized potential of social media in strengthen lines of company communication and collaboration, and to boost knowledge sharing. In their article, Kane et al. (2014) support that the adoption of social media by organizations has just begun. Interestingly though, a more recent survey of McKinsey&Company (Bughin, 2015) points out that organizational use of social media grew rapidly, but currently growth is flattening.

The availability of popular, and free, open source software, that are simpler, smarter and more flexible has fostered the increased use of social media (Avram, 2006; Leonardi, Huysman, & Steinfield, 2013).

Social media are based on integration between people and comprise a set of technological tools that support organizational purpose enabling people to connect, communicate, and collaborate by self-organizing social networks and engaging in conversational interactions and social feedback (Hemsley & Mason, 2011; Schlagwein & Hu, 2016; Sigala & Chalkiti, 2015).

According to Levy (2009), the decision to use social media tools by the organizations is taken based on two dimensions: technology adoption (software infrastructure or software application), and user orientation (use by and for organizational members, or use by organization facing stakeholders - customers, partners and suppliers).

These tools typically consist in: blogs and micro-blogs, discussion forums, social networks or relationship maps, document or media sharing, and wikis (Ford & Mason, 2013b; Hemsley & Mason, 2011).

At the strategic level, according to the Harrysson et al.'s survey (2016), around 30% of the organizations use social tools for strategy development, and 25% of organizations make decisions and setting strategic priorities from bottom up. The survey results also point to the fact that, according to the 47% of surveyed executives, the strategy of priorities from the bottom up would intensify over the next three to five years, with organizations using mainly social networks that have their use expanded and become better integrated.

However, organizations do not work the same way the Internet community does, and a model that is working out there could fail in the organizational context. Consequently, social media use in organizations faces two main barriers. The first on the part of organizations that are concerned about the risks and consequences of a potential misuse, and the second on the part of workers and managers that are not motivated or are not aware of the benefits of using these tools for work purposes (Gaál et al., 2015).

The same social media tool can be used for very different organizational purposes (Schlagwein & Hu, 2016). However, this versatile characteristic brings a challenge. According to McAfee (2006) the challenge lies in ability of each organization to exploit these tools, and he adds that the significant difference in organizations' abilities that will make all the difference.

Due to the combination of their main characteristics, such as user-generated content, peer to peer communication, networking, multimedia oriented, and user friendly (Panahi et al., 2012), these tools represent a successful mechanism that enables knowledge sharing and knowledge creation, keeps people connected, can supply endless reusable knowledge, or even facilitates to access expert's knowledge (Bharati, Zhang, & Chaudhury, 2015).

Traditional Knowledge Management

After the information management, a neutral and normative system in the organizations (Gloet & Terziovski, 2004), knowledge management emerges as a distinct area of study, establishing as a significant source of competitive advantage and as one of the most important resources in the capacity of progress of organizations in today's hypercompetitive and globalized marketplace (Ford & Mason, 2013b; Mårtensson, 2000; Pekka-Economou & Hadjidema, 2011).

The advancement of an economy based on knowledge has increased the visibility and importance of organizations that create and disseminate knowledge. Through knowledge, organizations can disrupt limitations, enhancing development and create new opportunities (Pekka-Economou & Hadjidema, 2011). Several authors consider that new knowledge and innovation are heavily dependent on knowledge management practices (Gaál et al., 2015; Gloet, 2006; Inkinen, 2016), thus constituting knowledge management practices as a key driver of innovation performance.

According to the classical division introduced by Polanyi (1966), and widely spread by Nonaka et al. (1996) knowledge can be explicit or tacit.

Explicit knowledge is a type of knowledge that can be easily codified, articulated, documented and archived, and usually, it is stored and expressed in the form of text, data, scientific formulae, maps, manuals and books, websites, etc. (Alavi & Leidner, 2001; Iacono, Nito, Esposito, Martinez, & Moschera, 2014; Nonaka & Konno, 1998; Polanyi, 1966; Santoro & Bierly, 2006; Seidler-de Alwis & Hartmann, 2008).

Tacit knowledge is the basis of knowledge creation, it is complex and not codified, and presents some difficulty in its reproduction in document or database. Smith (2001) reported that ninety percent of the knowledge in any organization is tacit knowledge and it is embedded and synthesized in peoples' heads.

Among several authors knowledge management is a multidimensional concept (e.g., Gaál et al., 2015). In the present chapter the authors adopt the Davenport and Prusak's (1998) definition, that is one of the most cited in the literature: "knowledge management is concerned with the exploitation and development of the knowledge assets of an organization with a view to furthering the organization's objectives."

Knowledge management is based on three main pillars (technology, people and process), and occurs within a social context (Kalkan, 2008; Prieto, Revilla, & Rodríguez-Prado, 2009) (Figure 1).

With substantial investments in highly structured technological solutions, organizations have been carried to focus primarily on the technology and little on people and process (Kakabadse et al., 2003), not enabling the interactivity and opportunity of the people in influencing (McAfee, 2006; Panahi et al., 2012). According to Sultan (2013, p. 162) "working people are more likely to seek work-related advice from fellows workers than from a knowledge-based system".

Technologies are not creator of knowledge, but are considered as one of the key enablers in the knowledge management process (Malhotra, 2005).

Knowledge management describes the processes of sharing and transfer, capture, and application of organizational knowledge to improve organizations' competitiveness.

Kang et al.'s (2010) state that knowledge by itself is not a useful resource that creates value and competitive advantage until it can be shared and transferred. Knowledge emerges from sharing knowledge in a social context (Jakubik, 2008) resulting of interactions between people. However, several authors (e.g., Ford & Mason, 2013b; Sigala & Chalkiti, 2015; von Krogh, 2012) identify the knowledge sharing process, a weak point of traditional models of knowledge management.

Figure 1. Knowledge Management Pillars

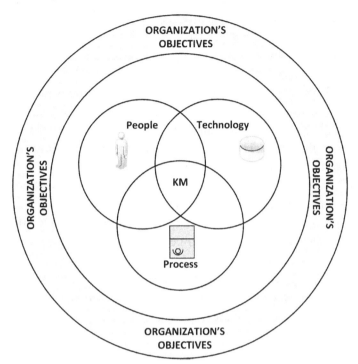

The successful sharing and transfer of knowledge is an important factor in knowledge management performance (Gaál et al., 2015; Wang & Noe, 2010), and according to Gaál et al. (Gaál et al., 2015, p. 185) "actually, the organizations are faced with the challenge how to get people to share their knowledge". Faced with this challenge, organizations have been forced to improve their knowledge sharing practices and to adopt new technologies.

Knowledge needs to be captured, stored and then disseminated (Huzita et al., 2012). The knowledge capture is a key process of preserving and formalizing knowledge (Becerra-Fernandez & Sabherwal, 2010) and the result is the inclusion of the knowledge into the stock of knowledge. The process of capture has various methods and the selected method depends on the type of knowledge. The process of capture must be disposed of properly, responding to the challenge of capturing only the relevant and valuable knowledge (Nielsen, 2006). Once captured, knowledge should be continuously evaluated to ensure their quality and relevance.

Knowledge application is the process management that justifies the existence all of others processes. It makes no sense to create knowledge, capture it, share it and download it, if not be disseminated and applied. Starbuck (1992) argued that merely storing knowledge does not preserve it.

New knowledge is disseminated through several channels available among the members of a social system (Graham et al., 2006) promoting their application (Becerra-Fernandez & Sabherwal, 2010). Social system is considered a set of interactions between people who have connection between themselves and that belong to the same context (Figure 2).

Traditional knowledge management are complex environments which have as organizational purposes to capture knowledge through documents repositories, share that knowledge with groupware tools, and make it accessible via corporate portals (von Krogh, 2012). These solutions often require an effort of investment and presents some difficulty in its application (Sultan, 2013).

In general, traditional knowledge management system consist in a collection of knowledge management technologies (Figure 3), which support the knowledge management processes, and a set of communication media widely diffused in the organizations, such as e-mail, person-to-person instant messaging, and telephone (McAfee, 2006; von Krogh, 2012). The usage of communication media use, according to McAfee (2006, p. 22), enable that digital knowledge "can be created and distributed by anyone, but the degree of commonality of this knowledge is low", i.e., it's only viewable by the few people who are part of the subject.

Figure 2. Social System

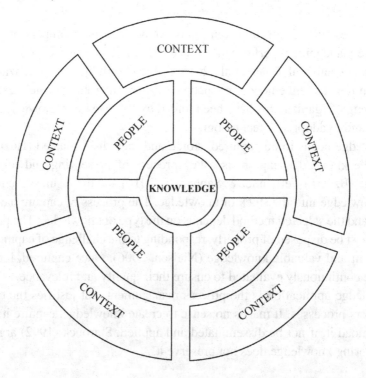

Figure 3. Knowledge Management Technologies

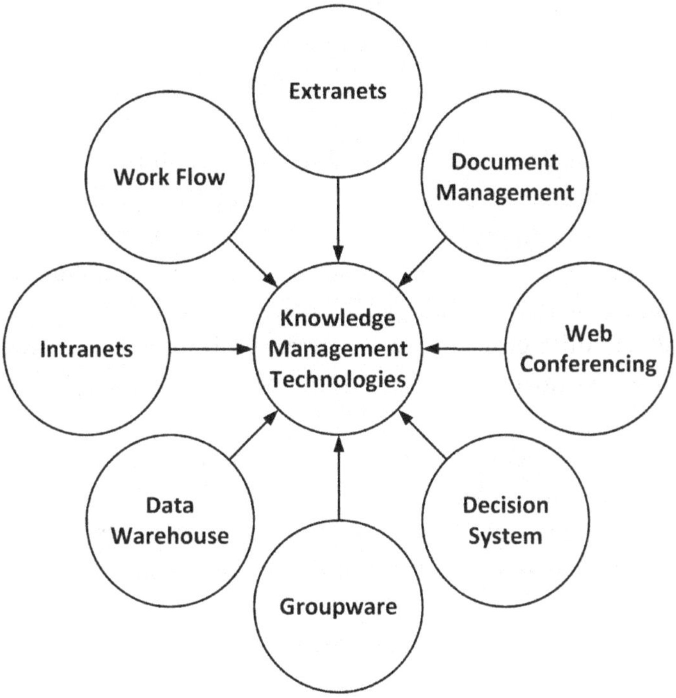

THE ROLE OF SOCIAL MEDIA TOOLS IN THE KNOWLEDGE MANAGEMENT IN ORGANIZATIONAL CONTEXT

Knowledge Management 2.0

The expression "knowledge management 2.0" refers to the knowledge management system that enables self-organization of people, by utilization of appropriate social media tools (Becerra-Fernandez & Sabherwal, 2010; Levy, 2009). In contrast to the traditional knowledge management models, knowledge management 2.0 is characterized by the content that is generated in decentralized and distributed way and in a bottom-up condition, from workers (internal social media use) and stakeholders (external social media use) (Avram, 2006; Schlagwein & Hu, 2016; von Krogh, 2012). Ford and Mason (2013a, p. 8) highlight that "the two types may have different risks, costs, and benefits for organizations".

As well as with the knowledge management, the use of social media by organizations has become a global phenomenon (Schlagwein & Hu, 2016). Bharati et al. (2015) cite in their study that, based on the 2011 McKinsey's survey, around 70% of the organizations use social media tools to increase speed to access knowledge.

The social media tools, that organizations can buy or develop, are close to some principles of knowledge management (Ford & Mason, 2013b; Levy, 2009; McAfee, 2006; von Krogh, 2012), since both involve people using technology to capture or acquire knowledge, create knowledge, and share this knowledge (Bradley & McDonald, 2011).

According to von Krogh (2012) social media have three aspects of relevance to knowledge management: (i) it is founded on socially oriented principles; (ii) it consists of a series of intuitive and easy to use applications (e.g., blogs and wikis); (iii) it is based on infrastructures (e.g. open platforms and enabling services) that make possible to reach considerable economies of scale.

The significant difference consists in the centralization and controlled attitude of knowledge management, in contrast to the uncontrolled and decentralized one of social tools (Levy, 2009).

The traditional knowledge management systems are technology-centric with a rigid and hierarchic knowledge structure. However, Malhotra (2000) in his work "Knowledge management and new organization forms: a framework for business model innovation" points to the fact that knowledge management technologies, in itself, do not assure knowledge creation and knowledge evolution. In this era characterized by discontinuous change, there is an increasing importance of the "human function of ensuring the reality check - by means of repetitive questioning, interpretation and revision of the assumptions underlying the knowledge system" (Malhotra, 2000, p. 11).

Social media technologies are people-centric with priority to the relationship and collaborative knowledge management processes (Sigala & Chalkiti, 2015). This second generation of knowledge management solutions puts technology in the background and focuses on people, promoting the participation of knowledge workers, who will be more willing to share and innovate by using tools they already know and like (Levy, 2009).

Figure 4 illustrates the difference between these two approaches.

McAfee (2006) alerts to the fact that social technologies are not incompatible with traditional knowledge management systems. Existing channels and platforms can be enhanced, improving and reducing gaps in processes and technologies, by adoption of social tools that provide the essential ingredients needed to succeed in the organizations. These ingredients are summarized in an acronym formulated by McAfee (2006) (see Figure 5).

Knowledge management 2.0, with structures more open and informal with short communication lines, arises to answer the request for effective ways to support knowledge sharing, and collaborative work. Organizations have been looking for secure, flexible environments where workers can add, organize, share and socialize knowledge through close interpersonal relationships with higher degree of trust.

Figure 4. Technology-Centric and People-Centric Approaches

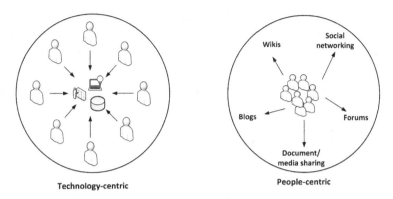

Figure 5. SLATES Infrastructure – Based on McAfee (2006)

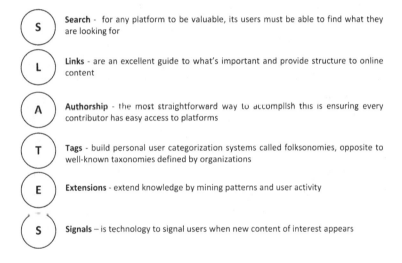

Social media tools seem to be suited to increase knowledge sharing, and improve organizational competences.

Social Media as a Knowledge Management Component

The usage of social media as a component of the knowledge management system has a great potential to leverage the existing knowledge management initiatives in organizations (Ford & Mason, 2013a; Richter, Stocker, Müller, & Avram, 2011), and to foster and to support the human participation in the processes. It is important that organizations embrace them and consciously utilize them to support their knowledge management initiatives (Levy, 2009; von Krogh, 2012).

The social media use as a knowledge management component can facilitate communication and collaboration between users within and outside an organization (Bharati et al., 2015), enabling users to easily share what they have learned, created and experienced, creating opportunities and conditions that promote the flow of tacit knowledge (Panahi et al., 2012), as well as allowing the storage of knowledge directly on social media or the use of social media to post links to knowledge management system (Schlagwein & Hu, 2016).

The Figure 6 represents a conceptual model of tacit knowledge sharing in social media according Panahi et al. (2012).

Citing Bebensee et al. (2011), von Krogh (2012) argues that social media have three layers of relevance to knowledge management, namely, they are based on socially oriented principles, the tools are intuitive to understand and easy to use, and they are infrastructures as open platforms that achieve considerable economics scale. Dave and Koskela (2009) add two other relevant aspects. They mention search capabilities, that make easy to retrieve knowledge, and anytime/anywhere and widespread availability.

The knowledge management evolution is characterized by the adoption of appropriate social media tools including, among others, wikis, blogs and social networks. The use of one or a combination of these tools as a knowledge management component has been providing to the organizations a new knowledge environment (Hemsley & Mason, 2011) with enhancement of organizational knowledge management and collaborative sharing of knowledge (Bharati et al., 2015; O'Reilly, 2007; von Krogh, 2012).

The paradigm shift taking place in the new forms of interaction and knowledge sharing requires that organizations will adopt more flexibility in roles and control, with greater individual responsibilities (Ford & Mason, 2013a). Social media tools

Figure 6. Tacit Knowledge Sharing in Social Media From Panahi et al. (2012)

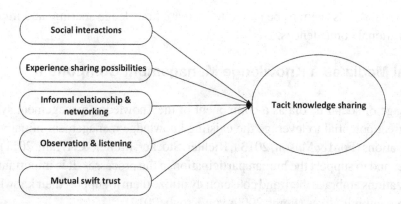

can facilitate this shift, supporting and providing fundamental changes in traditional knowledge management processes (Bharati et al., 2015; Richter et al., 2011).

Social media embodied with a business mindset can move organizational knowledge management, with impacts within and outside the organizations (Dave & Koskela, 2009), towards to a more flexible structure, thereby leading to fundamental change in such a way that enables interactions among individuals with rich and diverse types and contents knowledge (Richter et al., 2011; Sigala & Chalkiti, 2015). This change enable self-organization of workers, promote social interactions, networking and different ways of knowledge sharing (Bharati et al., 2015; Dave & Koskela, 2009; Sigala & Chalkiti, 2015), in particular regarding the tacit knowledge (Dave & Koskela, 2009).

Sigala and Chalkiti (2015) suggest that according the existing literature, social media can support all the four circles of the SECI model (Nonaka et al., 1996) by empowering people to create and renew knowledge in a dynamic, conversational and flexible way (Figure 7). The SECI model is based on the assumption that the creation and expansion of organizational knowledge occur by the continuing interaction between tacit and explicit knowledge resulting from the interactions between groups or individuals.

Although their significant impact, some organizations remain uncertain of their usage (Ford & Mason, 2013a). This uncertainty, according to several authors (Kane et al., 2014; Richter et al., 2011; Schlagwein & Hu, 2016), is associated to the difficulty amongst researchers and practitioners in understanding the real impact of the social media adoption in the organizations. In recent study Schlagwein and Hu (2016) discuss about this issue and identify three social media characteristics that can hinder this understanding. Social media are continuously in development, encompass a wide range of different tools and content, and the same social media tool at the same time can be used for very different organizational purposes or different social media tools might achieve the same organizational purpose (Schlagwein & Hu, 2016).

Based on the literature reviewed, the Table 1 presents several empirical studies about the usage of social media in the knowledge management context.

Benefits of Using Social Media as Knowledge Management Component

Considering that organizations do not have the mass of people as the Web does (Levy, 2009), the collaborative use of social media by organizations assumes an important role in the development of a collective intelligence knowledge environment which can represent a competitive advantage (Charband & Navimipour, 2016; Hemsley & Mason, 2011).

Figure 7. Knowledge Conversion Circles Enabled by Social Media – Based on Nonaka et al. (2000) and Adapted From Sigala and Chalkiti (2015)

SOCIALIZATION	EXTERNALIZATION
Tacit ———— Tacit	Tacit ———— Explicit
. Participation in online discussions/ forums and social networks	. Users placing tags to their bookmarks, to their documents
. Update of profile and sharing of knowledge in social networks	. Users posting comments to online discussions
. Space creation of social interaction	
EMPATHIZING	ARTICULATING
INTERNALIZATION	COMBINATION
Tacit ———— Explicit	Explicit ———— Explicit
. Sense-making and learning processes	. Users creation a collective knowledge
. Passive learning by reading others' comments and online discussions	. Users sharing knowledge on a social network or a wiki
Keeping notes and writing reflections of reading/discussions	
EMBODYING	CONNECTING

Knowledge management 2.0 with structures more open and informal with short communication lines, can provide workers close interpersonal relationships with higher degree of trust. This context is extremely favorable to knowledge sharing activities (Al Saifi et al., 2016).

Social media enable that knowledge becomes more articulated and explicit through discussions within workers and different stakeholders with creation of particular knowledge outputs as well as products and services (Schlagwein & Hu, 2016), overcoming many of failings of traditional knowledge management solutions (Chatti et al., 2007).

Leonardi et al. (2013) highlight that social media are distinguished with respect to other communication technologies since maintain the visibility and persistence of communicative actions, expanding the environment whom workers can learn. Social media also promotes the knowledge reuse, or as Schlagwein and Hu (2016, p. 19) say "may prevent that organization from forgetting what it already knows", with workers taking advantage of past experiences and learning from what others already know within and outside organization. As well as, compared to traditional knowledge management systems, social media enable easily that knowledge be

Table 1. Social Media in Knowledge Management Context

Author	Study	Method
Al Saifi et al. (2016)	This paper explores the relationship between face-to-face social networks and knowledge sharing. The results reveal that face to face social networks facilitate knowledge sharing in diverse ways.	Semi- structured interview
Schlagwein & Hu (2016)	This study examines the relation between social media use and the absorptive capacity of organizations.	Semi- structured interview
Bharati et al. (2015)	This study highlights both the potential and limitations of social media in promoting organizational knowledge management.	Case study
Gaál et al. (2015)	This research investigates how internal or external social media technologies are being used for knowledge sharing during work or for professional development.	Survey
Sigala & Chalkiti (2015)	The study investigates the relation between social media use and employee creativity by adopting a knowledge management approach in order to consider the influence of social networks and interactions on individuals' creativity.	Case study
Soto-Acosta et al. (2014)	This paper extends previous studies on the use of internet technologies and knowledge management by analyzing factors affecting knowledge sharing through Web 2.0 technologies within small and medium-sized enterprises.	Survey
Giuffrida & Dittrich (2013)	This paper reviews and map empirical studies on the usage of social software in Software Engineering projects and in distributed teams. Social software is reported as being chiefly used as a support for collaborative work, fostering awareness, knowledge management and coordination among team members.	Systematic mapping study
Bebensee et al. (2011)	This article aims at identifying Web 2.0 applications for bolstering up organizations' knowledge management practices.	Case study
García et al. (2011)	The aim of this work is to provide a set of guidelines to develop knowledge-based Process Asset Libraries to store software engineering best practices, implemented as a Wiki.	Fieldwork case study
Richter et al. (2011)	This study analyzed social software adoption in 23 companies and derived six main goals of corporate social software adoption. These goals were compared with the goals of knowledge management projects and initiatives, as identified in a series of well-known knowledge management studies.	Case study
Costa et al. (2009)	This case study describes the effects of using a Web Based Social Network approach to Knowledge Management in a Brazilian software development organization.	Case study
Dave & Koskela (2009)	This paper discusses a range of solutions and presents a case study where a collaborative knowledge management solution is implemented across a multi-functional construction company.	Case study
Paroutis & Al Saleh (2009)	The purpose of this paper is to investigate the key determinants of knowledge sharing and collaboration using Web 2.0 technologies by exploring the reasons for and barriers to employees' active participation in its various platforms.	Case study design

edited, updated and searched, what encourages workers to participate in creation and use of relevant knowledge, fostering and enriching the individual and collective processes of cognitive interactions. (Harrysson et al., 2016; Schlagwein & Hu, 2016; Sultan, 2013).

McAfee (2006, p. 26) address another important issue related to the integration capability of social media in large organizations, that makes organizations "in some ways more searchable, analyzable and navigable than smaller ones". The workers are able to find knowledge more readily and to identify experts on various topics.

Due to their characteristics, social media also emerge as an opportunity for the small and medium enterprises. These organizations work in a scenery of shortage of resources, and in the knowledge era they will be competitive if they take advantage of their peculiarities and peculiarities of their environment (Starbuck, 1992). Social media can meet the knowledge management needs of these type of organizations (Sultan, 2013).

Richter et al. (2011) in their study "Knowledge management goals revisited - A cross-sectional analysis of social software adoption in corporate environments" identify the main benefits that organizations expect to reach with the adoption of social media (Table 2).

Social media have also shown to be an important and efficient mechanism in supporting tacit knowledge sharing, helping organizations to capture knowledge based on the knowledge from different stakeholders (Al Saifi et al., 2016; Clark et al., 2015; Costa et al., 2009; Tee & Karney, 2010). With the creation of social interactive and collaborative spaces - so-called *Ba* by Nonaka et al. (2000), provided by these technologies, the individual and collective cognitive processes are facilitated (Sigala & Chalkiti, 2015), occurring great opportunity for effective flow of tacit knowledge between workers or communities of experts (Chatti et al., 2007; Panahi et al., 2012).

Threats of Using Social Media as Knowledge Management Component

The flexibility seems to be the watchword of social media. The new forms of communication and knowledge sharing, arising from the adoption of social media as a knowledge management component, require greater flexibility by organizations with impact on organizational culture of control and management.

However, Richter et al. (2011, p. 8) highlight that "flexibility in use does not come without threats".

Based on the literature reviewed, the chapter's authors identify some threats related with knowledge protection, knowledge quality, and management approach.

Table 2. Main Goals for the Adoption of Social Media - Adapted From Richter et al. (2011)

Main Goal	Characteristics of the Goal
Efficient, goal-oriented employee communication and avoidance of information overload	Implementation of open communication channels, support of employees' goal orientation by enhancing communication, improvement of employee- to-employee communication, prevention and control of information overload, decrease of e-mail usage
Efficient knowledge transfer	Preservation and restoration of internal knowledge, break up of knowledge silos, facilitation of intra-organizational knowledge transfer, better access to best practices
The establishment of networks of experts	Improvement of networking among employees and identification of experts, connecting people with similar contexts, development of expert communities (e.g. yellow pages), support for wisdom of crowds
Participation of employees and creation of open corporate culture	Sustainable involvement of employees i.e. each employee should be able to contribute actively, prevent employee anonymity within the organization, improve exchange and discussion among the employees to get better insights to support the corporate culture, development of a creative climate, openness of corporate culture allowing employees to participate more
Increased awareness and transparency	Provide better visibility to common tasks and competences, more transparency within decisions and processes, employees and management are aware of each other, cross-cutting issues can be revealed
Support for the innovation potential and secure the future viability of the enterprise	Innovation can be communicated faster and will be better understood, innovation can be started from inside and outside, new systems guarantee future-orientation and flexibility, sustainability is demonstrated by including the younger generations

Knowledge Protection

The advent of social media as a knowledge management component may represent large efficiency gains, and knowledge sharing within and across organization boundaries (von Krogh, 2012) stands out as one of the most significant benefit. However, knowledge sharing achieved with the use of social media can turn into a relevant threat for the organizations.

Due to the ease with that knowledge can be disseminated and shared, result of social media characteristics, such as speed of knowledge distribution, blurry audience, and easily collectible (Ford & Mason, 2013b; Richter et al., 2011), and the way that organization perceive knowledge in this new environment, social media could represent as a knowledge protection threat (Ford & Mason, 2013b).

This threat may mean potential loss in the organization's value resulting from disclosure of critical knowledge assets (Ford & Mason, 2013b; von Krogh, 2012), misuse of knowledge (Ford & Mason, 2013b), or risk of exposure of existing gaps in organizational knowledge (von Krogh, 2012).

The philosophy of traditional knowledge management concerning the notion of knowledge protection seems to be conflicting with knowledge management 2.0's philosophy. Restrictive rules, and monitoring at the individual level may be impractical and counterproductive (von Krogh, 2012), and can seriously inhibit or even stop spontaneous workers' interactions and collaborations.

Knowledge Quality

The quality of knowledge created in this new environment derived of the adoption of social media is often questioned in the literature (von Krogh, 2012). Whereas knowledge quality is essential to manage business opportunities, this issue may be also viewed as a possible threat.

The environment that enables quality of knowledge should be rich and diverse in sources of knowledge in order to benefit knowledge creation, thus avoiding the influence of existing biases within and among of small groups of workers (Kane, 2015). McAfee (2006) also alerts for the fact of that, due to the versatility of social media, despite the correct use of them by the workers, the knowledge reached by the organization may not being the intended.

Another issue which arises when talking about quality of knowledge is the overload of knowledge that results from the diversity in the knowledge sharing process fostered by the social media use in knowledge management. It will therefore be fundamental for the organizations to ensure the increased efficiency and effectivity at knowledge sharing (Charband & Navimipour, 2016; Richter et al., 2011).

The overload knowledge effect may cause some difficulty to workers in processing a vast quantity of knowledge (Kane et al., 2014) or in differentiating the relevant knowledge (Kane et al., 2014; Leonardi et al., 2013). Which, according to Leonardi et al. (2013, p. 12), "could force workers to become even more insulated and in-group focused than they were before of social media use".

The business emphasis of knowledge management plays a central role in bridging the threat of knowledge quality in the social media use (Bharati et al., 2015; Dave & Koskela, 2009).

Management Approach

Ford and Mason (2013b) highlight that the adoption of social media causes emergence of some tensions between these technologies and knowledge management initiatives arise. The tensions arise from the necessity to redefine previously accepted organizational mechanisms (e.g., roles, control) that become difficult to maintain in what is emerging as a dynamic, complex knowledge environment (Ford & Mason, 2013a, 2013b). The formality will not disappear entirely, however management style will play an important role in this process, and their involvement in the adoption and utilization of social media as a component of knowledge management practices will be crucial (Bharati et al., 2015). The management should clearly support the adoption of new technologies, explicit expectations about the outcomes (Paroutis & Al Saleh, 2009), and embrace social media as a part of organization's knowledge strategic component (von Krogh, 2012).

In the literature several authors point out some issues that the management faces when organizations adopt social media. For example, McAfee (2006) has the opinion that knowledge workers, in general, are busy, do not help to development social media platforms, and just use them as user. Ford and Mason (2013a) comment that when organization supports empowerment and engagement, these initiatives may fail if they are seen as attempts to control the knowledge and to make workers expendable. According to Sultan (2013, p. 164) "a large proportion of the content created on social media platforms is the contribution of a small proportion of the people who use those tools", making it necessary to encourage as many of workers as possible to engage and contribute to knowledge creation process in a collaborative manner (Al Saifi et al., 2016; Richards, 2007).

FUTURE RESEARCH DIRECTIONS

The adoption of social media by organizations has increased quickly and the implementation approaches vary from organization to organization (Bharati et al., 2015; Richter et al., 2011; von Krogh, 2012). The research opportunities are vast on the usage impact of these tools for knowledge management into organizations. It is possible to find in the existing literature studies which are devoted to the opportunities or needs of research on this subject (e.g., Kane et al., 2014; Leonardi et al., 2013; von Krogh, 2012).

The chapter's authors highlight some questions which should be addressed in future research:

- First of all, does exist difference among the types of organization that social media is more suitable than traditional knowledge management?
- How does organization balance the social media and traditional knowledge management uses to enable knowledge processes?
- How does organization protect their knowledge exploiting the benefits and mitigating the threats?

- It seems to be consensus among authors that capture and sharing of knowledge may become easier with social media use. What are the best practices to boost them?
- Finally, due to the phenomenon of globalization of organizations, would be interesting further researches on the identification of the impact of cultural differences in social media adoption.

CONCLUSION

This chapter was developed aiming at exploring and critically reviewing the literature of social media use in organizational context as a knowledge management component, and highlight which roles that these tools have played enabling and improving the development of knowledge management in the organizations.

In the extensive literature the term "easy" is the most commonly used by different authors in relation to social media (e.g., Avram, 2006; Leonardi et al., 2013; Levy, 2009; von Krogh, 2012). However, the abilities to exploit these tools will make significant difference among organizations.

Despite some authors claim that social media oriented to knowledge management will require much less of the "management" component, the chapter's authors have the opinion that the adoption of these tools often requires management actions more intense than in the traditional knowledge management, since the workers are used to use social media in a very spontaneous way and in accordance with their interests. According to Gaál et al. (2015, p. 196), "it is recommended for management to support introducing social media tools, establish the terms and conditions of usage, communicate the benefits and provide the necessary trainings".

The review suggests that, while traditional knowledge management systems are static and often act just as knowledge repositories, social media have the potential for supporting different knowledge management processes that will impact on the organizational culture by encouraging on participation, collaboration and knowledge sharing. This impact provides capabilities, which are difficult in traditional model that can make knowledge management processes, mainly knowledge creation and sharing, more effectively and efficiently.

Social media, probably due to its continuous change and variety of platforms, have not yet been fully exploited, but it seems be clear their potential as a significant component of knowledge management system.

REFERENCES

Al Saifi, S. A., Dillon, S., & McQeen, R. (2016). The relationship between face to face social networks and knowledge sharing: An exploratory study of manufacturing firms. *Journal of Knowledge Management, 20*(2), 308–326. doi:10.1108/JKM-07-2015-0251

Alavi, M., & Leidner, D. E. (2001). Review: Knowledge management and knowledge management systems: Conceptual foundations and research issues. *Management Information Systems Quarterly, 25*(1), 107–136. doi:10.2307/3250961

Avram, G. (2006). At the crossroads of knowledge management and social software. *Electronic Journal of Knowledge Management, 4*(1), 1–10.

Bebensee, T., Helms, R., & Spruit, M. (2011). Exploring Web 2.0 applications as a means of bolstering up knowledge management. *Electronic Journal of Knowledge Management, 9*(1), 1–9.

Becerra-Fernandez, I., & Sabherwal, R. (2010). *Knowledge management: systems and processes*. Armonk, NY: M.E. Sharpe, Inc.

Bharati, P., Zhang, W., & Chaudhury, A. (2015). Better knowledge with social media? Exploring the roles of social capital and organizational knowledge management. *Journal of Knowledge Management, 19*(3), 456–475. doi:10.1108/JKM-11-2014-0467

Bradley, A. J., & McDonald, M. P. (2011). Social media versus knowledge management. *Harvard Business Review*, 1–4. Retrieved from https://hbr.org/2011/10/social-media-versus-knowledge

Bughin, J. (2015). Taking the measure of the networked enterprise. *McKinsey Quarterly Survey*. Retrieved from http://www.mckinsey.com/business-functions/business-technology/our-insights/taking-the-measure-of-the-networked

Charband, Y., & Navimipour, N. J. (2016). Online knowledge sharing mechanisms: A systematic review of the state of the art literature and recommendations for future research. *Information Systems Frontiers*, 1–21.

Chatti, M. A., Klamma, R., Jarke, M., & Naeve, A. (2007). The Web 2.0 driven SECI model based learning process. In *Seventh IEEE International Conference on Advanced Learning Technologies (ICALT 2007)* (Vol. 5, pp. 780–782). IEEE. doi:10.1109/ICALT.2007.256

Clark, S. S., Berardy, A., Hannah, M. A., Seager, T. P., Selinger, E., & Makanda, J. V. (2015). Group tacit knowledge and globally distributed virtual teams: Lessons learned from using games and social media in the classroom. *Connexions - International Professional Communication Journal, 3*(1), 113–151.

Costa, R. A., Silva, E. M., Neto, M. G., Delgado, D. B., Ribeiro, R. A., & Meira, S. R. L. (2009). Social knowledge management in practice: A case study. In L. Carriço, N. Baloian, & B. Fonseca (Eds.), *Groupware: Design, Implementation, and Use* (Vol. 5784, pp. 94–109). Springer Berlin Heidelberg. doi:10.1007/978-3-642-04216-4_8

Dave, B., & Koskela, L. (2009). Collaborative knowledge management - A construction case study. *Automation in Construction, 18*(7), 894–902. doi:10.1016/j. autcon.2009.03.015

Davenport, T. H., & Prusak, L. (1998). *Working knowledge: How organizations manage what they know*. Boston, MA: Harvard Business School Press.

De Wever, B., Mechant, P., Veevaete, P., & Hauttekeete, L. (2007). E-learning 2.0: Social software for educational use. *Ninth IEEE International Symposium on Multimedia Workshops (ISMW 2007)*, 511–516. doi:10.1109/ISM.Workshops.2007.91

Ford, D. P., & Mason, R. M. (2013a). A multilevel perspective of tensions between knowledge management and social media. *Journal of Organizational Computing and Electronic Commerce, 23*(1–2), 7–33. doi:10.1080/10919392.2013.748604

Ford, D. P., & Mason, R. M. (2013b). Knowledge management and social media: The challenges and benefits. *Journal of Organizational Computing and Electronic Commerce, 23*(1–2), 1–6. doi:10.1080/10919392.2013.748603

Gaál, Z., Szabó, L., Obermayer-Kovács, N., & Csepregi, A. (2015). Exploring the role of social media in knowledge sharing. *Electronic Journal of Knowledge Management, 13*(3), 185–197.

García, J., Amescua, A., Sánchez, M. I., & Bermón, L. (2011). Design guidelines for software processes knowledge repository development. *Information and Software Technology, 53*(8), 834–850. doi:10.1016/j.infsof.2011.03.002

Giuffrida, R., & Dittrich, Y. (2013). Empirical studies on the use of social software in global software development - A systematic mapping study. *Information and Software Technology, 55*(7), 1143–1164. doi:10.1016/j.infsof.2013.01.004

Gloet, M. (2006). Knowledge management and the links to HRM. *Management Research News, 29*(7), 402–413. doi:10.1108/01409170610690862

Gloet, M., & Terziovski, M. (2004). Exploring the relationship between knowledge management practices and innovation performance. *Journal of Manufacturing Technology Management, 15*(5), 402–409. doi:10.1108/17410380410540390

Graham, I. D., Logan, J., Harrison, M. B., Straus, S. E., Tetroe, J., Caswell, W., & Robinson, N. (2006). Lost in knowledge translation: Time for a map? *The Journal of Continuing Education in the Health Professions, 26*(1), 13–24. doi:10.1002/chp.47 PMID:16557505

Harrysson, M., Schoder, D., & Tavakoli, A. (2016). *The evolution of social technologies.* McKinsey Quarterly Survey. Retrieved from http://www.mckinsey.com/industries/high-tech/our-insights/the-evolution-of-social-technologies

Hemsley, J., & Mason, R. M. (2011). The nature of knowledge in the social media age: Implications for knowledge management models. *Proceedings of the Annual Hawaii International Conference on System Sciences,* 3928–3937.

Huzita, E. H. M., Leal, G. C. L., Balancieri, R., Tait, T. F. C., Cardoza, E., Penteado, R. R. D. M., & Vivian, R. L. (2012). Knowledge and contextual information management in global software development: challenges and perspectives. In *2012 IEEE Seventh International Conference on Global Software Engineering Workshops* (pp. 43–48). IEEE. doi:10.1109/ICGSEW.2012.12

Iacono, M. P., De Nito, E., Esposito, V., Martinez, M., & Moschera, L. (2014). Investigating the relationship between coordination mechanisms and knowledge in a wine firm. *Knowledge and Process Management, 21*(4), 280–291. doi:10.1002/kpm.1436

Inkinen, H. (2016). Review of empirical research on knowledge management practices and firm performance. *Journal of Knowledge Management, 20*(2), 230–257. doi:10.1108/JKM-09-2015-0336

Jakubik, M. (2008). Experiencing collaborative knowledge creation processes. *The Learning Organization, 15*(1), 5–25. doi:10.1108/09696470810842475

Kakabadse, N. K., Kakabadse, A., & Kouzmin, A. (2003). Reviewing the knowledge management literature: Towards a taxonomy. *Journal of Knowledge Management, 7*(4), 75–91. doi:10.1108/13673270310492967

Kalkan, V. D. (2008). An overall view of knowledge management challenges for global business. *Business Process Management Journal, 14*(3), 390–400. doi:10.1108/14637150810876689

Kane, G. C. (2015). Enterprise social media: Current capabilities and future possibilities. *MIS Quarterly Executive, 14*(1), 1–16.

Kane, G. C., Labianca, G., & Borgatti, S. P. (2014). What's different about social media networks? A framework and research agenda. *Management Information Systems Quarterly, X*(X), 1–30.

Kang, J., Rhee, M., & Kang, K. H. (2010). Revisiting knowledge transfer: Effects of knowledge characteristics on organizational effort for knowledge transfer. *Expert Systems with Applications, 37*(12), 8155–8160. doi:10.1016/j.eswa.2010.05.072

Kaplan, A. M., & Haenlein, M. (2010). Users of the world, unite! The challenges and opportunities of social media. *Business Horizons, 53*(1), 59–68. doi:10.1016/j.bushor.2009.09.003

Leonardi, P. M., Huysman, M., & Steinfield, C. (2013). Enterprise social media: Definition, history, and prospects for the study of social technologies in organizations. *Journal of Computer-Mediated Communication, 19*(1), 1–19. doi:10.1111/jcc4.12029

Levy, M. (2009). WEB 2.0 implications on knowledge management. *Journal of Knowledge Management, 13*(1), 120–134. doi:10.1108/13673270910931215

Malhotra, Y. (2000). Knowledge management and new organization forms: A framework for business model innovation. *Information Resources Management Journal, 13*(1), 5–14. doi:10.4018/irmj.2000010101

Malhotra, Y. (2005). Integrating knowledge management technologies in organizational business processes: Getting real time enterprises to deliver real business performance. *Journal of Knowledge Management, 9*(1), 7–28. doi:10.1108/13673270510582938

Mårtensson, M. (2000). A critical review of knowledge management as a management tool. *Journal of Knowledge Management, 4*(3), 204–216. doi:10.1108/13673270010350002

McAfee, A. P. (2006). Enterprise 2.0: The dawn of emergent collaboration. *IEEE Engineering Management Review, 34*(3), 38–47. doi:10.1109/EMR.2006.261380

Nielsen, A. P. (2006). Understanding dynamic capabilities through knowledge management. *Journal of Knowledge Management, 10*(4), 59–71. doi:10.1108/13673270610679363

Nonaka, I., & Konno, N. (1998). The concept of ba: Building a foundation for knowledge creation. *California Management Review*, *40*(3), 40–54. doi:10.2307/41165942

Nonaka, I., Takeuchi, H., & Umemoto, K. (1996). A theory of organizational knowledge creation. *International Journal of Technology Management*, *11*(7–8), 833–845.

Nonaka, I., Toyama, R., & Konno, N. (2000). SECI, Ba and leadership: A unified model of dynamic knowledge creation. *Long Range Planning*, *33*(1), 5–34. doi:10.1016/S0024-6301(99)00115-6

Nonaka, I., Toyama, R., & Nagata, A. (2000). A firm as a knowledge-creating entity: A new perspective on the theory of the firm. *Industrial and Corporate Change*, *9*(1), 1–20. doi:10.1093/icc/9.1.1

O'Reilly, T. (2007). What is Web 2.0: Design patterns and business models for the next generation of software. *Communications & Stratégies*, *1*(65), 17–37.

Panahi, S., Watson, J., & Partridge, H. (2012). Social media and tacit knowledge sharing : Developing a conceptual model. *World Academy of Science. Engineering and Technology*, *64*, 1095–1102.

Paroutis, S., & Al Saleh, A. (2009). Determinants of knowledge sharing using Web 2.0 technologies. *Journal of Knowledge Management*, *13*(4), 52–63. doi:10.1108/13673270910971824

Pekka-Economou, V., & Hadjidema, S. (2011). Innovative organizational forms that add value to both organizations and community: The case of knowledge management. *European Research Studies*, *14*(2), 81–95.

Polanyi, M. (1966). The logic of tacit inference. *Philosophy (London, England)*, *41*(155), 1–18. doi:10.1017/S0031819100066110

Prieto, I. M., Revilla, E., & Rodríguez-Prado, B. (2009). Managing the knowledge paradox in product development. *Journal of Knowledge Management*, *13*(3), 157–170. doi:10.1108/13673270910962941

Richards, D. (2007). Collaborative knowledge engineering: Socialising expert systems. In *11th International Conference on Computer Supported Cooperative Work in Design* (pp. 635–640).

Richter, A., Stocker, A., Müller, S., & Avram, G. (2011). Knowledge management goals revisited - A cross-sectional analysis of social software adoption in corporate environments. In *22nd Australasian Conference on Information Systems* (pp. 1–10).

Santoro, M. D., & Bierly, P. E. (2006). Facilitators of knowledge transfer in university-industry collaborations: A knowledge-based perspective. *IEEE Transactions on Engineering Management, 53*(4), 495–507. doi:10.1109/TEM.2006.883707

Schlagwein, D., & Hu, M. (2016). How and why organisations use social media: Five use types and their relation to absorptive capacity. *Journal of Information Technology*, (May): 1–28.

Seidler-de Alwis, R., & Hartmann, E. (2008). The use of tacit knowledge within innovative companies: Knowledge management in innovative enterprises. *Journal of Knowledge Management, 12*(1), 133–147. doi:10.1108/13673270810852449

Sigala, M., & Chalkiti, K. (2015). Knowledge management, social media and employee creativity. *International Journal of Hospitality Management, 45*(February), 44–58. doi:10.1016/j.ijhm.2014.11.003

Smith, E. A. (2001). The role of tacit and explicit knowledge in the workplace. *Journal of Knowledge Management, 5*(4), 311–321. doi:10.1108/13673270110411733

Soto-Acosta, P., Perez-Gonzalez, D., & Popa, S. (2014). Determinants of Web 2.0 technologies for knowledge sharing in SMEs. *Service Business, 8*(3), 425–438. doi:10.1007/s11628-014-0247-9

Starbuck, W. H. (1992). Learning by knowledge-intensive firms. *Journal of Management Studies, 29*(6), 713–740. doi:10.1111/j.1467-6486.1992.tb00686.x

Sultan, N. (2013). Knowledge management in the age of cloud computing and Web 2.0: Experiencing the power of disruptive innovations. *International Journal of Information Management, 33*(1), 160–165. doi:10.1016/j.ijinfomgt.2012.08.006

Tee, M. Y., & Karney, D. (2010). Sharing and cultivating tacit knowledge in an online learning environment. *International Journal of Computer-Supported Collaborative Learning, 5*(4), 385–413. doi:10.1007/s11412-010-9095-3

von Krogh, G. (2012). How does social software change knowledge management? Toward a strategic research agenda. *The Journal of Strategic Information Systems, 21*(2), 154–164. doi:10.1016/j.jsis.2012.04.003

Wang, S., & Noe, R. A. (2010). Knowledge sharing: A review and directions for future research. *Human Resource Management Review, 20*(2), 115–131. doi:10.1016/j.hrmr.2009.10.001

KEY TERMS AND DEFINITIONS

Knowledge Capture: A fundamental process of preservation and formalization of knowledge.

Knowledge Management: The exploitation and development of the knowledge assets of an organization with a view to furthering the organization's objectives.

Knowledge Management 2.0: Knowledge management system that enables self-organization of people, by utilization of appropriate social media tools, such as wikis, blogs and social networks.

Knowledge Sharing: Sharing and transfer interchangeable, and commonly appear with the same sense in the literature. Knowledge sharing promotes the creation of new theories and ideas, and establishment of new research principles. It is a key driver of innovation process.

Social Media: A set of features, grouped into software applications and websites, which enables people and organizations to recreate online various types of social interactions that enable to create and share content.

Social Networks: Web sites that enable users to articulate a network of connections of people with whom they wish to share access to profile information, news, or other forms of content.

Tacit Knowledge: Knowledge that is complex, not codified, and presents some difficulty in its reproduction in a document or in a database. It can be get from experience, perceptions and individual values, and depends on the context in which is inserted.

Web 2.0: The second generation of the World Wide Web, that emphasizes the concept of exchange of information and collaboration through the Internet sites and virtual services. The idea is that the online environment becomes more dynamic and, in this way, users to collaborate to organize content.

Chapter 3
Consumer Behavior, Trust, and Electronic Word-of-Mouth Communication:
Developing an Online Purchase Intention Model

Francesca Di Virgilio
University of Molise, Italy

Gilda Antonelli
University of Sannio, Italy

ABSTRACT

Social media platforms have become a major forum for consumers to interact with firms and other individuals. Drawing on both the customer-dominant logic and the theory of planned behavior, the present chapter aims to advance understanding and encourage research on the variables that drive consumers' online purchase intention. Al though there is a general agreement in recognizing the importance of social media platforms as a source of information about consumer behavior, a complete theorization of the variables that affect the relation between behavioral intention and online purchase intention is still lacking. The proposed theoretical model is an extension of the theory of planned behavior and incorporates trust and electronic word-of-mouth communication as part of the customers' online purchase intention. Finally, the theoretical and managerial implications are further discussed.

DOI: 10.4018/978-1-5225-2897-5.ch003

INTRODUCTION

Social media are dramatically changing the relationship among individuals, firms, and societies (Leung, 2013; Oakley & Salam, 2014). Web 2.0 technologies, as the basis of social media platforms and social networking sites (e.g. Alibaba, eBay), enable the acquisition of products through supporting users' interactions and contributions (Liang & Turban, 2011).

A growing number of companies recognizes the significant role that social media play as a means of communication and as a driving force in creating new business opportunities (Kim & Ko, 2012; Sashi, 2012). They enable consumers and firms to interact and exchange different categories of information, including comments, evaluations, images, photos and videos.

Hence, consumer's behavior information allows firms to strategically position themselves ahead of their competitors. The capability of managing information becomes a core competence of the firm in creating competitive long term strategies. Since social media websites are powerful tools used to expand one's network and help in connecting with acquaintances and strangers (Chang et al., 2015), as the proliferation and the use of social media apps improve, firms have a great opportunity to determine consumers' requirements and needs by involving consumers in panel questionnaires and interviews. A broad variety of social media tools enable firms to connect with a wide range of potential and existing customers (Briones, et al., 2011; Chang, Yu, & Lu, 2015; Wu, 2016; Bianchi & Andrews, 2015; Curran & Lennon, 2011), to post contents, share ideas, learn and fulfill social needs (Ferreira, et al, 2014). In particular, a growing number of companies recognize that social media provide a means to communicate and change the business model while creating new opportunities (Kim & Ko, 2012; Sashi, 2012, Wu, 2016; Chang et al , 2015; Culnan et al., 2010). Specifically, through social media information, it becomes possible to describe the customer's buying behavior (Culnan, et al., 2010; Zaglia, 2013).

In the context of high rather than low customer involvement in social media, consumers that are more involved and believe that social media are important and interesting will be more dependent on them in searching for suggestions and sharing information on products and services.

From a customer-dominant logic perspective, understanding how social media obtains maximum benefits is still a research gap. The literature attributes this research gap to a combination of factors such as cost, time and lack of top management knowledge, unproven success metrics, and the company's perceived loss of control

(Whelan, et al., 2011). Because of a number of technology-related challenges, firms are slow in adopting social media as a strategy to leverage business opportunities (Kaplan & Haenlein, 2010).

To address these research gaps, we have designed a theoretical model based on the theory of planned behavior (TPB) (Ajzen, 1991; Fishbein & Ajzen, 1975) in order to identify the underlying factors and conditions that drive consumers to engage in social media so that they purchase online.

In particular, our chapter aims to fill the research gap in consumer behavior on purchase intention on social media platforms and adopts a customer-dominant logic perspective with its integration of the following important approach: TPB (Ajzen, 1991; Fishbein & Ajzen, 1975).

Our theoretical model of consumer behavior intention analyzes the direct effects of two important factors on consumers' purchase intentions: trust and Electronic word-of-mouth communication (eWOM). Trust – a belief in the reliability, truth, and ability of the exchange party – is recognized as one of the main variables that refrain customers from electronic purchases (Gefen, 2000; Liang & Turban, 2011; Kim & Pak, 2013; Hajli, et al., 2016). However, given the context of social media, users acquire knowledge of a specific product from social media and may engage in a purchase. Thus, in the context of the social media and embedded content provided by peers, trust may increase the users' purchase intentions from an e-vendor (Kim & Park; 2013).

Electronic word-of-mouth eWOM is the exchange of product or service evaluations among people who meet, talk, and text each other within a variety of online environments (King et al., 2014; Yoon, 2012; Barreto, 2014).

In this scenario, we organized the chapter in different parts. In the first part we make a contribution to the body of literature by examining first the role of social media platforms for the improvement of decision making as compared to more traditional methods; second, the customer-dominant logic as an innovative way of interpreting the relationship between consumers and firms; and last, the theory of planned behavior. In the second part, we analyze trust in social platforms and e-word-of-mouth communication as important variables which may mediate the effect of consumers' behavior intentions for online purchasing; and then we identify four directions which are the results of the literature review and the observation of real consumers' behaviors. Finally, we construct a theoretical model based on digital consumer purchase intention. We close the chapter by discussing future research directions for this work.

BACKGROUND

Social Media

The literature defines social media as a group of Internet-based applications that build on the ideological and technological foundations of Web 2.0 technology, and that allow the creation and exchange of user-generated content (Bianchi & Andrews, 2015; Chang et al., 2015; Kaplan & Haenlein, 2010). Kaplan and Haenlein (2011) and Sashi (2012) define social media marketing as electronic-word-of-mouth (Di Pietro et al. 2013) and as a sort of marketing message of a firm, brand, or product. Despite buyers' strong enthusiasm, many firms remain skeptical about embracing social media to assist the marketing function (Ferreira et al., 2014; Sashi, 2012; Bruhn et al., 2012).

Social media have changed the classic business dynamics. Through more efficient communication means, such as weblogs, social networks, social bookmarking sites, wikis, and virtual worlds (Curran & Lennon, 2011), social media facilitate promotion among dispersed individuals with seemingly, marginal concerns (Rodriguez, Peterson, & Krishnan, 2012), they foster mutual enrichment through conversation, exchange, and participation (Whelan et al., 2011) and they reduce transaction and coordination costs. In addition, social media platforms allow salespeople to coordinate internal value-creating functions and deliver superior value in customer relationships (Bharadwaj, 2000; Kaplan & Haenlien, 2009). In doing so, they represent an important marketing strategy in which organizations build relationships with customers (Agnihotri et al., 2012; Culnan et al., 2010). Social media also capture the attention of managers. A recent global survey of managers has found that almost half of the buyers pay attention to social media's role when involved in the buying process (Agnihotri, et al., 2012).

This expanded role of social media platforms can better contribute to improving decision making than traditional methods (Bruhn, et al., 2012) on purchase intention. Consequently, firms can adopt a customer-dominant logic and become involved in consumers' lives and businesses (Cheung & To, 2015; Heinonen & Strandvik, 2015; Heinonen et al., 2010).

The Customer-Dominant Logic

Customer-dominant logic is an innovative way of interpreting the relationship between consumers and firms (Heinonen & Strandvik, 2015; Heinonen et al., 2010; Cheung & To, 2016). This kind of management perspective is dominated by consumer-related aspects rather than by a focus on services, products, systems, profits, and costs.

Customer-dominant logic is grounded in an understanding of consumers' lives and their use of services or products (Heinonen & Strandvik, 2015; Cheung & To, 2016).

Following the neo-institutionalism theory, institutional logics define the content and meaning of institutions (which are believed to exert some kind of 'pressure' at firm level in order to gain endorsement from important referent audiences) providing means both of understanding the social world and of acting confidently within it (Greenwood et al., 2011; Tolbert et al., 2011). As useful constructs for the organizational studies, the institutional logic concept was introduced by Jackall (1988), Friedland and Alford (1991) who defined it as a set of material practices and symbolic construction that surely influence individual or collective actors but that, in turn, may be also modified by them. For Jackall (1988) an institutional logic is the way a particular social world works; for Friedland and Alford (1991) it provides social actors with vocabularies of motive and sense of self. The main institutions, namely, the capitalist market, the bureaucratic state, families, democracy, and religion, which have a central logic, while constraining both the means and ends of individual behavior and being constitutive of individuals, organizations, and society, also provide sources of agency and change. Moreover, institutional complexity becomes an opportunity for transforming individual identities, organizations and society.

By putting together the structural and normative approach of Jackall (1988) and the structural and symbolic approach of Friedland and Alford (1991), Thornton and Ocasio defined the institutional logics as "the socially constructed, historical patterns of material practices, assumptions, values, beliefs, and rules by which individuals produce and reproduce their material subsistence, organize time and space, and provide meaning to their social reality" (1999, p. 804).

As a result, the interests, identities, values, and assumptions are embedded within prevailing institutional logics. Moreover, to locate behavior in a context requires theorizing an inter-institutional system of societal actors in which each sector represents a different set of expectations and human and organizational behavior, allowing sources of heterogeneity and agency coming from the contradictions between the logics of different institutional orders. Each of the institutional orders in society has both material and cultural characteristics so that institutions develop and change as a result of the interplay between both of these forces. In addition, institutional logics may develop at a variety of different levels (i.e. organizations, markets, industries, inter-organizational networks, geographic communities, and organizational fields), and in order to apply the institutional logics approach it is critical that the level of analysis at which institutionalization occurs be clearly specified.

Actors may transform social relations within and among institutions, in order to create new practices and models of actions, obviously if they loosen their embeddedness into the social context. This in other words, as taken-for-granted assumptions and practices, institutional logics are strongly embedded in individual and organizational actors' cognition and give appropriateness and meaningfulness to what should be preferred, also, influencing the perceptive, attentive, evaluative and responsive processes to environmental stimuli of actors (Almandoz, 2014).

While Friedland and Alford (1991) pointed to such societal logics as 'capitalism', 'democracy', 'family', and 'religion'; currently, the major types of rationalized institutional logics are 'family', 'religion', 'state', 'market', 'profession', 'corporation', and 'community' (Thornton et al., 2012; Thornton & Ocasio, 2008).

Institutional logics become, over time, both a theory and a method of analysis which enable researchers and scholars to understand the role that societal-level culture has on individual and organizational actors' cognition and behavior (DiMaggio, 1997).

According to this, organizational forms, managerial practices, and individual behaviors are the result of existing institutional logics so that they may become a way to interpret tensions and change dynamics observed in contemporary organizations and organization fields due to the competition and struggle among various categories of actors committed to constraining institutional logics (Scott, 2014; Thornton, 2004).

Components of Theory of Planned Behavior

The theory of planned behavior (TPB) (Ajzen, 1991; Fishbein & Ajzen, 1975) posits that an individual's intention to engage in a behavior is shaped by his or her attitudes toward the behavior, the subjective norms and the perceived behavioral control; whereas his or her intentions and perceived behavioral control have an impact on actual behavior. The TPB has been used to explore the acceptance of computer and ICT technologies since the 1980s (Davis et al., 1989; Jiang et al., 2016; Kim, et al., 2016; Mou & Lin, 2015; Taylor & Todd, 1995). Cho et al. (2015) suggested that the TPB is useful for exploring the influence of social and psychological variables on consumers' behavioral intention.

When consumers perceive social media to have a high rather than a low level of usefulness in terms of obtaining updated information and suggestions on products and services, they may tend to spend more time and effort in learning about the products and the services and rely more directly on social media websites. Increased participation in online purchasing provides a viable means for consumers to develop a favorable attitude toward service firms testified by a more active involvement in the improvement of the features and perceived benefits of products and services (Cheung & To, 2016). A growing body of literature published over the last three decades underlines the importance of consumer behavior as an avenue of research worthy of attention from the research community. The same literature, however, suggests that it is extremely complex to analyze consumer's behavior, and that traditional research measures may catch only a portion of its richness (Myers, et al., 1979; Pfeffer, 1993; Summers, 2001; McInnis, 2004; Levy, 2006). Consumer's behavior is a complex topic that includes different perspectives and uses several disciplinary approaches such as consumer culture theory research, transformative consumer research, social cognition research stream, motivation research area, behavioral decision theory.

Nevertheless, the evolution of consumer's behavior shows that a "theory of consumer" (Teas & Palan, 1997; Summers, 2001) is still not available and many scholars are trying to build a more comprehensive theory.

Several articles published in top-tier management journals have focused primarily on intra-individual behaviors and, in particular, on measuring cognitive processes by studying individuals' performance when purchasing consumptions goods (Bagozzi, 2000; Briley & Wyer, 2002; Thomas-Hunt, et al., 2003; Cummings, 2004). The general premise of the TPB is that an individual is more likely to adopt a behavior when he or she holds a favorable attitude towards it; he or she perceives what other individuals think about his or her behavior, with the result of taking more control over the expected barriers (Ajzen, 1991). According to the TPB (Ajzen, 1991; Fishbein & Ajzen, 1975), an individual's attitude toward a particular behavior is one of the most significant predictors of an individual's intention to engage in that behavior and as well as of his/her actual behavior. The attitude toward the behavior is defined as the degree to which the individual has a positive evaluation of the behavior in question.

Fishbein and Ajzen (1975) identified two other important factors that affect behavioral intention: subjective norms that can be seen as the perceived social pressure on the individual to engage in a specific behavior; perceived behavioral control, which refers to the individual's perception of the ease of engaging in a behavior. In addition, an individual's behavioral intention and perceived behavioral control directly influence his or her actual behavior. Bai, Tang, Yang and Gong (2014) highlighted that subjective norms or perceived pressure from significant others have a great impact on an individual's intention to make choices more freely.

As stated above, attitude is a strong predictor of behavioral intention (Ajzen,1991; Mou & Lin, 2015). When consumers develop a favorable attitude toward social media, they may be interested in initiating a strong intention of fulfilling their beliefs.

Studies of the acceptance of computer or information and communication technologies (ICT) suggest that attitudes toward the use of a computer/ICT technology are determined by its perceived usefulness and ease of use (Davis, Bagozzi, & Warshaw, 1989; Porter & Donthu, 2006; Taylor & Todd, 1995; Di Virgilio et al. 2017). Perceived usefulness is defined as the degree to which an individual believes that the use of a particular system may increase his or her performance (Davis et al., 1989). Perceived usefulness has a much stronger effect on consumers' attitudes toward the use of a new technology than perceived ease of use (Davis et al., 1989; Porter & Donthu, 2006; Taylor & Todd, 1995; Di Pietro et al. 2013). When consumers trust that using social media will broaden their understanding of the products and services, they have a more favorable attitude toward their engagement in social media platforms. In addition, consumers may recognize social media as an effective channel for sharing their opinions on products and services with friends and relatives as well as a helpful resource to aid the decision-making process for the purchasing of products and services they are interested in. Thus, a high level of perceived usefulness will lead consumers to develop a favorable attitude toward engaging in social media. Indeed, perceived usefulness represents a key determinant of consumer attitudes and behavioral intention toward online shopping (Childers, et al., 2002; O'Cass & Fenech, 2003).

In the present study, we focus on consumer attitudes toward engaging in social media purchasing. Since social media are pervasive in people's daily lives (Midyette, et al., 2014; Yan, et al., 2014), we drop the variable of perceived ease of use and retain perceived usefulness as an antecedent of the attitude construct.

MAIN FOCUS OF THE CHAPTER

Purchase Intention: The Effects of Trust and Ewom

Trust

In the theoretical model we present here, we consider trust in social media platforms and eWOM as important variables which may mediate the effect of individuals' behavior in online purchasing intentions. Purchase intentions in social media contexts refer to the customers' intentions to engage in online purchases from e-vendors in social media platforms. Intentions are the determinants of behavior and are defined as "the strength of one's intentions to perform a specific behavior" (Fishbein & Ajzen, 1975, p.288).

Ba & Pavlou (2002) posit that trust is an individual's belief that an exchange will happen in a manner consistent with one's confident expectations. Trust is a unidimensional or a multidimensional concept (Gefen, 2002). However, a better understating of trust comes from the recognition of its dimensions. Cognitive and affective trust are the main types of trust (Aiken & Boush, 2006): cognitive trust is the customer's belief in and willingness of dependency on an exchange partner's ability and consistency. Affective trust is a customer's belief about a firm's level of care and concerns based on emotions (Kim & Park, 2013). Both cognitive and affective trust contain dimensions of credibility (one's belief that the exchange party is reliable) and benevolence (beliefs that the exchange partner is motivated by seeking joint gain) (Aiken & Boush, 2006).

For the purpose of the present study, trust is used as the sense of trusting beliefs, referring to the beliefs that "one can rely upon a promise made by another and that the other, in unforeseen circumstances, will act toward oneself with goodwill and in a benign fashion" (Suh & Han, 2003, p. 137). In online contexts, trust is based on beliefs in the trustworthiness of an exchange party and the characteristics of competence, integrity, and benevolence (McKnight, et al., 2002). Given the context of social media platforms, uncertainty is usually higher due to the high level of user-generated contents and the lack of face-to-face interactions (Featherman & Hajli, 2015). Despite this, the enhancement of experience with exchange parties could reduce the uncertainty and increase tendencies for online commerce adoption through the increase in trust (Gefen & Straub, 2004).

The lack of face-to-face interactions could result in customers' suspicion of truthfulness in online exchanges and the paucity of knowledge about the e-vendors could further heighten the adverse influence of risk in online shopping (Kaiser & Müller-Seitz, 2008). Kim & Park (2013) investigate the antecedents of trust and its direct effects on purchase intentions and word-of-mouth intentions on social commerce platforms. Seven social commerce characteristics are identified as the key antecedents of trust: reputation, size, information quality, transaction safety, communication, economic feasibility, and word-of-mouth referrals. It is noteworthy that customer reviews and experiences posted in forums and communities can improve trust in a specific website.

Previous literature found that the purchase from an e-vendor depends on customer trust in the e-vendor (Gefen, et al., 2003). We propose that trust in a social media platform could increase customers' purchase intentions. Social media platforms bring customers into contact with e-vendors and provide the facilities for the value exchange between the parties. Within social media platforms, customers see advertisements, pictures/videos/news, recommendations and Likes related to the e-vendors. However, according to Hajli et al. (2016), trust in the social media platforms could determine the customer's reliance on the credibility of the contents and of the e-vendors' activities. Credibility encompasses integrity and ability of the platform in providing the expected outcomes, which in turn, increases intentions to buy on the platform (Kaiser & Müller-Seitz, 2008).

As suggested by McKnight and Chervany (2001), there could be four variables that affect consumers' trust in social media platforms: 1) competence or power of the social media platforms to fulfill a successful exchange or the provision of recovery if the failure occurs from the e-vendor side; 2) benevolence, indicating the concern of the social media platforms to favor users regardless of the profit utilitarian aim; 3) integrity, related to ethical behavior of the social media platforms and their fulfillment of promises; 4) predictability, as the consistency of the action of the social media platforms, enabling users to forecast future exchanges. These variables enhance customer's reliance on the user-generated contents, reducing the uncertainty of exchanging outcomes and extending the duration of the relationship between SMP and consumers (Suh & Han, 2003). Kim and Park (2013) indicated that users who trust social commerce sites are more likely to spread positive word-of-mouth and purchase on these platforms.

Electronic Word-of-Mouth Communication

Electronic word-of-mouth (eWOM) is defined as the exchange of product or service evaluations among people who meet, talk and text each other in the virtual world (King et al., 2014; Yoon, 2012; Barreto, 2014). EWOM is emerging as a more influential knowledge sharing tool than traditional word-of-mouth (WOM) (Katz & Lazarsfeld, 1955). Social media have become among the most prevalent eWOM channels because of their ubiquity, mobility, and interactivity (French & Read, 2013; Zmuda, 2013). These characteristics enable social media users to communicate and connect with each other more frequently and more closely (Laroche et al., 2013; Kleina et al., 2015).

Despite the benefits of using social media to improve eWOM effectiveness, the effects of network closeness and network strength on the diffusion of eWOM remain unclear (Wang et al., 2016).

Relevant studies have investigated the key drivers (Cheung & Lee, 2012; Chu & Kim, 2011) of eWOM and their impact on sales (Chevalier & Mayzlin, 2006), on the consumer decision-making process (De Bruyn & Lilien, 2008), and on the attitude toward both brands and websites (Lee et al., 2009). In particular, through the social digital media, *ad hoc* virtual communities and blogs, eWOM provides additional and highly-customized information related to the research on social media platform. Then, it measures the popularity and the inclinations for a specific brand, when a product or service are concerned (Casaló et al., 2010; Chan & Li, 2010; Park & Kim, 2008). As a consequence, in the process of choosing what to buy, consumers are compelled to use social media to search for information on possible product or service, to visualize images, and access other's opinions in order to gain a larger amount of info to make a more effective choice. According to Bickart and Schindler (2001), eWOM has the potential to reduce the risk, uncertainty, and ambiguity associated with a product or service.

Potential consumers thus depend on referrals from their friends, family members, and social networks. In this sense, eWOM becomes a powerful tool for catching consumers' attention and influencing their behaviors (Litvin et al., 2008; Chan & Li, 2010).

THE THEORETICAL MODEL

Considering the research literature and the above description of individuals' actual behavior in online purchases, we have constructed a theoretical model of the online customer purchase intention. The TPB states that there is a direct effect of the customers behavioral intention on their purchase intention. When we come to purchasing on social media platforms, this occurrence becomes even more apparent since the use of the web is pervading everyday life and online transactions are increasing at an exponential rate. Beside the specific application of the relation to the specific channel, we add some value to the model considering the mediation effect which is played on the purchase intention by trust in the specific platform and the availability of eWOM communication. The latter propositions come from the following statements which are the results of the literature review and the observation of the concrete consumer's behaviors:

- *Trust in the social media platform affects the perceived usefulness of the channel as supporting tool for purchase intentions.*
- *Trust has a direct influence on the attitude towards the online purchase intention that can reinforce the customer behavioral intention.*
- *E-word-of-mouth communication has a direct influence on the perceived usefulness of the social media platform in online purchasing, therefore, amplifying the online purchased intention.*
- *E-word-of-mouth communication affects the perceived trust in the social media platform and therefore influences online purchase intention.*

Figure 1 describes our theoretical model to enlighten the mediation effect of the variables on online purchasing intention

CONCLUSION AND FUTURE RESEARCH

The theoretical model that we propose will accomplish an important goal with respect to consumer's behavior. Using the theory of planned behavior interpretation and customer-dominant logic and guided by the theoretical approaches from related research in consumer behavior, this chapter provides an analytical framework to explore the consumer's online purchase intention. It introduces the mediation effect of trust in social media platform and eWOM communication on the direct effect performed by the customers' behavioral intentions on the purchase intention and it expands the area of effect to the social media platform. This study is one of the first that examine the antecedents and boundary condition of the TPB in the context of

Figure 1. The Theoretical Model of Online Purchase Intention

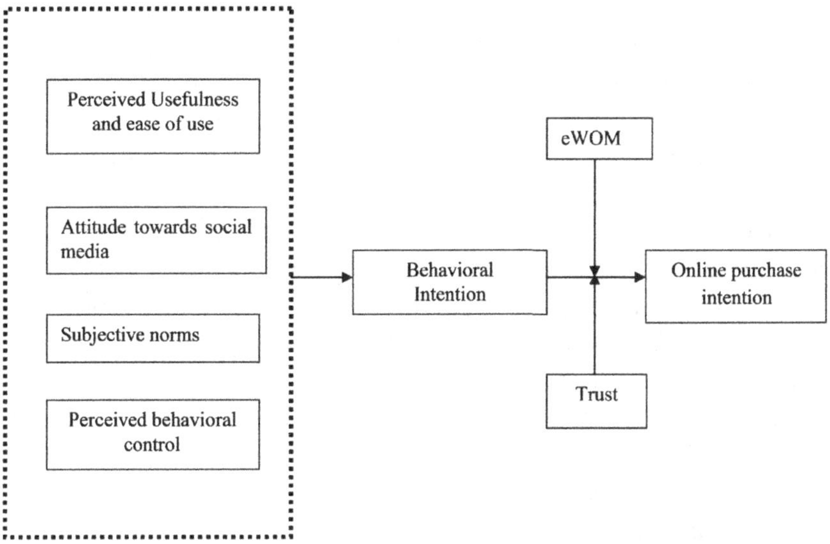

social media platforms. We found that perceived usefulness was a key determinant of attitudes toward engaging in social media and that consumer behavior was a moderator of the link between perceived usefulness and attitudes toward engaging in social media. Moreover, using TPB theory and dominant logic literature, we speculate that the trust in social media platform and eWOM communication has a mediating effect on online purchase intention.

Practitioners can use our theoretical model to increase purchase intention of consumers and better target future marketing strategies to increase the online amount of transactions. In fact, the outcome of this study is of benefit to both, the consumers and the firms. From a better understanding of the variables that influence the consumer's purchase intention a company will have a greater understanding of consumers' expectations and will be able to implement social media platforms and to improve the support of the purchasing decision-making process.

In addition, the consumer's attitudes toward purchasing on social media platforms could be implemented by improving trust and eWOM communication, which in turn, can lead to a higher level of engagement in online purchasing. Trust is a critical issue in a social commerce contexts and specifically, it plays an important role in increasing purchase intentions. The more customers trust the platform, the more they engage in the purchasing process. Social media platform designers are able to increase customers' trust by enhancing the characteristic of the platforms, including reputation, size, information quality, transaction safety, communication, economic feasibility, and word-of-mouth referrals (Kim & Park, 2013). However, trust is not the only factor and other elements are also important in increasing purchase intentions.

These studies open a new path of research on how consumer behavior can take place through the combined effect of trust and eWOM on behavioral intentions.

This study contributes to the development of research on consumer's online behavior. Since only a few analysis on customer-dominant logic have been carried out in the field of consumer's research, this study can act as a catalyst for future scientific inquiries in this important area.

Today the development and use of eWOM for supporting and influencing consumers on their online purchasing intentions play a key role for both managers and researchers. EWOM could be quite effective in helping a customer to make decisions about purchasing. It should be interesting to introduce digital content and technologies that understand consumers behavior, to facilitate the decision making process through a user-friendly interface, by giving information related to products, promotions, new arrivals. In order to achieve an efficient, flexible and meaningful feeling of human-computer interaction, the main features to develop are the interactivity and the multimodality. The quality of interactions affects the knowledge creation, which is capable of influencing the decision-making process (Yoo et al., 2010).

The issue of how to effectively design and deploy social media platforms in this approach is most certainly an additional future research direction. It is clear that the social media platforms offer companies many opportunities to interact with consumers along with the entire decision-making process.

A future research direction can assess the model empirically by targeting a panel of online buyers in order to observe them in their purchasing process. It should increase the number of different control variables to explore the effect of the decision-making unit on other information acquisition variables, such as the content and sequence of the information acquired. Findings from the alternative models indicate that those who use social media information to a greater extent (information seekers) tend to more likely engaged in online relationships with e-vendors independently of their trust in that specific social media platform. Future studies may also examine our model in different cultural contexts and generations, in which consumers will have different orientations (Bilgihan, 2016); it is possible that some consumers may place higher values on some preferred networks because they better fit their needs. Such differences in individual network value may affect the intensity of consumers' intentions to purchase. Finally, future studies could test whether and to what extent the degree of customer engagement moderates the link between perceived usefulness and attitude toward co-creation in social media (Chathoth, et al., 2016; Zhang, et al., 2015)

REFERENCES

Agnihotri, R., Kothandaraman, P., Kashyap, R., & Singh, R. (2012). Bringing social into sales: The impact of salespeoples social media use on service behaviors and value creation. *Journal of Personal Selling & Sales Management, 22*(3), 333–348. doi:10.2753/PSS0885-3134320304

Aiken, K. D., & Boush, D. M. (2006). Trustmarks, objective-source ratings, and implied investments in advertising: Investigating online trust and the context-specific nature of internet signals. *Journal of the Academy of Marketing Science, 34*(3), 308–323. doi:10.1177/0092070304271004

Ajzen, I. (1991). The theory of planned behavior. *Organizational Behavior and Human Decision Processes, 50*(2), 179–211. doi:10.1016/0749-5978(91)90020-T

Almandoz, J. (2014). Founding teams as carriers of competing logics: When institutional forces predict banks risk exposure. *Administrative Science Quarterly, 59*(3), 442–473. doi:10.1177/0001839214537810

Ba, S., & Pavlou, P. A. (2002). Evidence of the effect of trust building technology in electronic markets: Price premiums and buyer behavior. *Management Information Systems Quarterly, 26*(3), 243–268. doi:10.2307/4132332

Bagozzi, R. P., & Dholakia, U. (1999). Goal Setting and Goal Striving in Consumer Behavior. *Journal of Marketing, 63*, 19–32. doi:10.2307/1252098

Bai, L., Tang, J., Yang, Y., & Gong, S. (2014). Hygienic food handling intention: An application of the theory of planned behavior in the Chinese cultural context. *Food Control, 42*, 172–180. doi:10.1016/j.foodcont.2014.02.008

Barreto, A. M. (2014). The word-of-mouth phenomenon in the social media era. *International Journal of Market Research, 56*(5), 631–654.

Benbasat, I., & Weber, R. (1996). Research Commentary: Rethinking Diversity in Information System Research. *Information Systems Research, 7*(4), 389–399. doi:10.1287/isre.7.4.389

Bharadwaj, A. S. (2000). A resource-based perspective on information technology capability and firm performance: An empirical investigation. *Management Information Systems Quarterly, 24*(1), 169–196. doi:10.2307/3250983

Bianchi, C., & Andrews, L. (2015). Investigating marketing managers perspectives on social media in Chile. *Journal of Business Research, 68*(12), 2552–2559. doi:10.1016/j.jbusres.2015.06.026

Bickart, B., & Schindler, R. M. (2001). Internet forums as influential sources of consumer information. *Journal of Interactive Marketing, 15*(3), 31–40. doi:10.1002/dir.1014

Bickart, B., & Schindler, R. M. (2001). Internet forums as influential sources of consumer information. *Journal of Interactive Marketing, 15*(3), 31–40. doi:10.1002/dir.1014

Bilgihan, A. (2016). Gen Y customer loyalty in online shopping: An integrated model of trust, user experience, and branding. *Computers in Human Behavior, 61*, 103–113. doi:10.1016/j.chb.2016.03.014

Briones, R. L., Kuch, B., Liu, B. F., & Jin, Y. (2011). Keeping up with the digital age: How the American Red Cross uses social media to build relationships. *Public Relations Review, 37*(1), 37–43. doi:10.1016/j.pubrev.2010.12.006

Bruhn, M., Schoenmueller, V., & Schafer, D. B. (2012). Are social media replacing traditional media in terms of brand equity creation? *Management Research Review, 35*(9), 770–790. doi:10.1108/01409171211255948

Casaló, L. V., Flaviàn, C., & Guinlalìu, M. (2010). Determinants of the intention to participate in firm-hosted online travel communities and effects on consumer behavioural intentions. *Tourism Management, 31*(6), 898–911. doi:10.1016/j.tourman.2010.04.007

Chan, K. W., & Li, S. Y. (2010). Understanding consumer-to-consumer interactions in virtual communities: The salience of reciprocity. *The Journal of Business, 63*, 1033–1040.

Chan, K. W., & Li, S. Y. (2010). Understanding consumer-to-consumer interactions in virtual communities: The salience of reciprocity. *The Journal of Business, 63*, 1033–1040.

Chang, Y., Yu, H., & Lu, H. (2015). Persuasive messages, popularity cohesion, and message diffusion in social media marketing. *Journal of Business Research, 68*(4), 777–782. doi:10.1016/j.jbusres.2014.11.027

Chathoth, P. K., Ungson, G. R., Harrington, R. J., & Chan, E. S. (2016). Co-creation and higher order customer engagement in hospitality and tourism services: A critical review. *International Journal of Contemporary Hospitality Management, 28*(2), 222–245. doi:10.1108/IJCHM-10-2014-0526

Cheung, C. M. K., & Lee, M. K. O. (2012). What drives consumers to spread electronic word of mouth in online consumer-opinion platforms. *Decision Support Systems, 53*(1), 218–225. doi:10.1016/j.dss.2012.01.015

Cheung, M. F. Y., & To, W. M. (2015). Do task- and relation-oriented customers co-create a better quality of service? An empirical study of customer-dominant logic. *Management Decision, 53*(1), 179–197. doi:10.1108/MD-05-2014-0252

Chevalier, J. A., & Mayzlin, D. (2006). The effect of word of mouth on sales: Online book reviews. *JMR, Journal of Marketing Research, 43*(3), 345–354. doi:10.1509/jmkr.43.3.345

Childers, T. L., Carr, C. L., Peck, J., & Carson, S. (2002). Hedonic and utilitarian motivations for online retail shopping behavior. *Journal of Retailing, 77*(4), 511–535. doi:10.1016/S0022-4359(01)00056-2

Cho, S. H., Chang, K. L., Yeo, J. H., Head, L. W., Zastrow, M., & Zdorovtsov, C. (2015). Comparison of fruit and vegetable consumption among Native and non-Native American population in rural communities. *International Journal of Consumer Studies, 39*(1), 67–73. doi:10.1111/ijcs.12153

Choi, B., & Lee, I. (2016). *Trust in open versus closed social media: The relative influence of user- and marketer generated content in social network services on customer trust.* Telematic Information. doi:10.1016/j.tele.2016.11.005

Chu, S. C., & Kim, Y. (2011). Determinants of consumer engagement in electronic word-of-mouth (eWOM) in social networking sites. *International Journal of Advertising, 30*(1), 47–75. doi:10.2501/IJA-30-1-047-075

Culnan, M., McHugh, P., & Zubillaga, J. (2010). How large U.S. companies can use twitter and other social media to gain business value. *MIS Quarterly Executive, 9*(4), 243–259.

Curran, J., & Lennon, R. (2011). Participating in the conversation: Exploring usage of social media. *Academy of Marketing Studies Journal, 15*(1), 21–38.

Davis, F. D., Bagozzi, R. P., & Warshaw, P. R. (1989). User acceptance of computer technology: A comparison of two theoretical models. *Management Science, 35*(8), 982–1003. doi:10.1287/mnsc.35.8.982

De Bruyn, A., & Lilien, G. L. (2008). A multi-stage model of word-of-mouth influence through viral marketing. *International Journal of Research in Marketing, 25*(3), 151–163. doi:10.1016/j.ijresmar.2008.03.004

Di Maggio, P. J. (1997). Culture and cognition. *Annual Review of Sociology, 23*(1), 263–287. doi:10.1146/annurev.soc.23.1.263

Di Pietro L., Di Virgilio F. & Pantano E. (2013). Negative eWOM in user-generated contents: recommendations for firms and organizations. *International Journal of Digital Content Technology and its Applications, 7*(5), 1-8.

Di Virgilio, F., Camillo, A. A., & Camillo, I. (2017). The Impact of Social Network on Italian Users Behavioural Intention for the Choice of a Medical Tourist Destination. *International Journal of Tourism and Hospitality Management in the Digital Age, 1*(1), 36–49. doi:10.4018/IJTHMDA.2017010103

Featherman, M. S., & Hajli, N. (2015). Self-service technologies and e-services risks in social commerce era. *Journal of Business Ethics*, 1–19.

Ferreira, J. B., da Rocha, A., & Ferreira da Silva, J. (2014). Impacts of technology readiness on emotions and cognition in Brazil. *Journal of Business Research, 67*(5), 865–873. doi:10.1016/j.jbusres.2013.07.005

Fishbein, M., & Ajzen, I. (1975). *Belief, attitude, intention and Behavior: An introduction to theory and research*. Reading, MA: Addison-Wesley.

French, A. M., & Read, A. (2013). My moms on Facebook: An evaluation of information sharing depth in social networking. *Behaviour & Information Technology, 32*(10), 1049–1059. doi:10.1080/0144929X.2013.816775

Friedland, R., & Alford, R. R. (1991). Bringing society back in: Symbols, practices, and institutional contradictions. In W. Powell & P. J. DiMaggio (Eds.), *The New Institutionalism in Organizational Analysis* (pp. 232–263). Chicago: University of Chicago Press.

Gefen, D. (2002). Reflections on the dimensions of trust and trustworthiness among online consumers. *The Data Base for Advances in Information Systems, 33*(3), 38–53. doi:10.1145/569905.569910

Gefen, D., Karahanna, E., & Straub, D. W. (2003). Trust and TAM in online shopping: An integrated model. *Management Information Systems Quarterly, 27*(1), 51–90.

Gefen, D., & Straub, D. (2000). The relative importance of perceived ease of use in IS adoption: A study of E-commerce adoption. *Journal of the Association for Information Systems, 1*, 1–30.

Gefen, D., & Straub, D. W. (2004). Consumer trust in B2C e-commerce and the importance of social presence: Experiments in e-products and e-services. *Omega, 32*(6), 407–424. doi:10.1016/j.omega.2004.01.006

Greenwood, R., Raynard, M., Kodeih, F., Micelotta, E. R., & Lounsbury, M. (2011). Institutional Complexity and Organizational Responses. *The Academy of Management Annals*, 5(1), 317–371. doi:10.1080/19416520.2011.590299

Hajli, N. et al.. (2016). A social commerce investigation of the role of trust in a social networking site on purchase intentions. *Journal of Business Research*. doi:10.1016/j.jbusres.2016.10.004

Heinonen, K., & Strandvik, T. (2015). Customer-dominant logic: Foundations and implications. *Journal of Services Marketing*, 29(6/7), 472–484. doi:10.1108/JSM-02-2015-0096

Heinonen, K., Strandvik, T., Mickelsson, K. J., Edvardsson, B., Sundström, E., & Andersson, P. (2010). A customer-dominant logic of service. *Journal of Service Management*, 21(4), 531–548. doi:10.1108/09564231011066088

Jackall, R. (1988). *Moral Mazes: The World of Corporate Managers*. New York: Oxford University Press.

Jiang, C., Zhao, W., Sun, X., Zhang, K., Zheng, R., & Qu, W. (2016). The effects of the self and social identity on the intention to microblog: An extension of the theory of planned behavior. *Computers in Human Behavior*, 64, 754–759. doi:10.1016/j.chb.2016.07.046

Kaiser, S., & Müller-Seitz, G. (2008). Leveraging lead user knowledge in software development: The case of weblog technology. *Industry and Innovation*, 15(2), 199–221. doi:10.1080/13662710801954542

Kaplan, A. M., & Haenlein, M. (2009). Consumers, companies, and virtual social worlds: A qualitative analysis of Second Life. *Advances in Consumer Research. Association for Consumer Research (U. S.)*, 36(1), 873–874.

Kaplan, A. M., & Haenlein, M. (2010). Users of the world, unite! The challenges and opportunities of social media. *Business Horizons*, 53(1), 59–68. doi:10.1016/j.bushor.2009.09.003

Katz, E., & Lazarsfeld, P. F. (1955). *Personal Influence: The Part of Played by People in The Flow of Mass Communications*. Free Press.

Kim, A. J., & Ko, E. (2012). Do social media marketing activities enhance customer equity? An empirical study of luxury fashion brand. *Journal of Business Research*, 65(10), 1480–1486. doi:10.1016/j.jbusres.2011.10.014

Kim, E., Lee, J. A., Sung, Y., & Choi, S. M. (2016). Predicting selfie-posting behavior on social networking sites: An extension of theory of planned behavior. *Computers in Human Behavior, 62*, 116–123. doi:10.1016/j.chb.2016.03.078

Kim, S., & Park, H. (2013). Effects of various characteristics of social commerce (s-commerce) on consumers trust and trust performance. *International Journal of Information Management, 33*(2), 318–332. doi:10.1016/j.ijinfomgt.2012.11.006

King, R. A., Racherla, P., & Bush, V. D. (2014). What we know and dont know about online word-of-mouth: A review and synthesis of the literature. *Journal of Interactive Marketing, 28*(3), 167–183. doi:10.1016/j.intmar.2014.02.001

Kleina, A., Ahlfb, H., & Sharmac, V. (2015). Social activity and structural centrality in online social networks. *Telematics and Informatics, 32*(2), 321–332. doi:10.1016/j.tele.2014.09.008

Laroche, M., Habibi, M. R., & Richard, M. O. (2013). To be or not to be in social media: How brand loyalty is affected by social media? *International Journal of Information Management, 33*(1), 76–82. doi:10.1016/j.ijinfomgt.2012.07.003

Lee, M., Rodgers, S., & Kim, M. (2009). Effects of valence and extremity of eWOM on attitude toward the brand and website. *Journal of Current Issues and Research in Advertising, 31*(2), 1–11. doi:10.1080/10641734.2009.10505262

Leung, L. (2013). Generational differences in content generation in social media: The roles of the gratifications sought and of narcissism. *Computers in Human Behavior, 29*(3), 997–1006. doi:10.1016/j.chb.2012.12.028

Levy, S. J. (2006). How New, How Dominant? In R. F. Lusch & S. L. Vargo (Eds.), *The Service-Dominant Logic of Marketing. Dialog, Debate, and Directions*. Armonk, NY: M.E. Sharpe.

Liang, T. P., & Lai, H. J. (2002). Effect of store design on consumer purchase: An empirical study of online bookstores. *Information & Management, 39*(6), 431–444. doi:10.1016/S0378-7206(01)00129-X

Liang, T. P., & Turban, E. (2011). Introduction to the special issue, social commerce: A research framework for social commerce. *International Journal of Electronic Commerce, 16*(2), 5–14. doi:10.2753/JEC1086-4415160201

Litvin, S. W., Goldsmith, R. E., & Pan, B. (2008). Electronic word-of-mouth in hospitality and tourism management. *Tourism Management, 29*(3), 458–468. doi:10.1016/j.tourman.2007.05.011

McInnis, D.J. (2004). Where Have All the Papers Gone? Reflections on the Decline of Conceptual Articles. *ACR News*, 1-3.

McKnight, D. H., & Chervany, N. L. (2001). What trust means in e-commerce customer relationships: An interdisciplinary conceptual typology. *International Journal of Electronic Commerce*, *6*(2), 35–59.

McKnight, D. H., Choudhury, V., & Kacmar, C. (2002). Developing and validating trust measures for e-commerce: An integrative typology. *Information Systems Research*, *13*(3), 334–359. doi:10.1287/isre.13.3.334.81

Midyette, J. D., Youngkin, A., & Snow-Croft, S. (2014). Social media and communications: Developing a policy to guide the flow of information. *Medical Reference Services Quarterly*, *33*(1), 39–50. doi:10.1080/02763869.2014.866482 PMID:24528263

Millissa, F. Y. (2016). Service co-creation in social media: An extension of the theory of planned behavior. *Computers in Human Behavior*, *65*, 260–266. doi:10.1016/j.chb.2016.08.031

Mou, Y., & Lin, C. A. (2015). Exploring podcast adoption intention via perceived social norms, interpersonal communication, and theory of planned behavior. *Journal of Broadcasting & Electronic Media, 59*(3), 475-493.

Myers, J. G., Greyser, S. A., & Massy, W. F. (1979). The Effectiveness of Marketings R&D for Marketing Management: An Assessment. *Journal of Marketing*, *43*(1), 17–29. doi:10.2307/1250754

Oakley, R. L., & Salam, A. F. (2014). Examining the impact of computer-mediated social networks on individual consumerism environmental behaviors. *Computers in Human Behavior*, *35*, 516–526. doi:10.1016/j.chb.2014.02.033

OCass, A., & Fenech, T. (2003). Web retailing adoption: Exploring the nature of internet users web retailing behavior. *Journal of Retailing and Consumer Services*, *10*(2), 81–94. doi:10.1016/S0969-6989(02)00004-8

Park, D. H., & Kim, S. (2008). The effects of consumer knowledge on message processing of electronic word-of-mouth via online consumer reviews. *Electronic Commerce Research and Applications*, *7*(4), 399–410. doi:10.1016/j.elerap.2007.12.001

Pfeffer, J. (1993). Barriers to the Advance of Organizational Science: Paradigm Development as a Dependent Variable. *Academy of Management Review*, *18*(4), 599–620.

Porter, C. E., & Donthu, N. (2006). Using the technology acceptance model to explain how attitudes determine Internet usage: The role of perceived access barriers and demographics. *Journal of Business Research, 59*(9), 999–1007. doi:10.1016/j.jbusres.2006.06.003

Rodriguez, M., Peterson, R. M., & Krishnan, V. (2012). Social medias influence on business-to-business sales performance. *Journal of Personal Selling & Sales Management, 32*(2), 365–378. doi:10.2753/PSS0885-3134320306

Sashi, C. M. (2012). Customer engagement, buyer–seller relationships, and social media. *Management Decision, 50*(2), 253–272. doi:10.1108/00251741211203551

Sashi, C. M. (2012). Customer engagement, buyer–seller relationships, and social media. *Management Decision, 50*(2), 253–272. doi:10.1108/00251741211203551

Scott, W. R. (2014). *Institutions and Organizations: Ideas, Interests, and Identities.* Los Angeles, CA: Sage.

Suh, B., & Han, I. (2003). The impact of customer trust and perception of security control on the acceptance of electronic commerce. *International Journal of Electronic Commerce, 7*(3), 135–161.

Summers, J. O. (2001). Guidelines for Conducting Research and Publishing in Marketing: From Conceptualization Though the Review Process. *Journal of the Academy of Marketing Science, 29*(4), 405–415. doi:10.1177/03079450094243

Taylor, S., & Todd, P. A. (1995). Understanding information technology usage: A test of competing models. *Information Systems Research, 6*(2), 144–176. doi:10.1287/isre.6.2.144

Teas, K. R., & Palan, K. M. (1997). The Realms of Scientific Meaning Framework for Constructing Theoretically Meaningful Nominal Definitions of Marketing Concepts. *Journal of Marketing, 61*(4), 52–67. doi:10.2307/1251830

Thornton, P. H. (2004). *Markets From Culture: Institutional Logics and Organizational Decisions in Higher Education Publishing.* Stanford, CA: Stanford University Press.

Thornton, P. H., & Ocasio, W. (1999). Institutional logics and the historical contingency of power in organizations: Executive succession in the higher education publishing industry, 19581990. *American Journal of Sociology, 105*(3), 801–843. doi:10.1086/210361

Thornton, P. H., & Ocasio, W. (2008). Institutional logics. In R. Greenwood, C. Oliver, K. Sahlin, & R. Suddaby (Eds.), *The Sage Handbook of Organizational Institutionalism* (pp. 99–129). Los Angeles, CA: Sage. doi:10.4135/9781849200387. n4

Thornton, P. H., Ocasio, W., & Lounsbury, M. (2012). *The Institutional Logics Perspective: A New Approach to Culture, Structure, and Process*. Oxford, UK: Oxford University Press. doi:10.1093/acprof:oso/9780199601936.001.0001

Tolbert, P. S., David, R. J., & Sine, W. D. (2011). Studying choice and change: The intersection of institutional theory and entrepreneurship research. *Organization Science*, *22*(5), 1332–1344. doi:10.1287/orsc.1100.0601

Wang, T., Keng-Jung Yeh, R., Chen, C., & Tsydypov, Z. (2016). What drives electronic word-of-mouth on social networking sites? Perspectives of social capital and self-determination. *Telematics and Informatics*, *33*(4), 1034–1047. doi:10.1016/j. tele.2016.03.005

Whelan, E., Parise, S., De Valk, J., & Aalbers, R. (2011). Creating employee networks that deliver open innovation. *MIT Sloan Management Review*, *53*(1), 37–44.

Wu, C.-W. (2016). The performance impact of social media in the chain store industry. *Journal of Business Research*, *69*(11), 5310–5316. doi:10.1016/j.jbusres.2016.04.130

Yan, G., He, W., Shen, J., & Tang, C. (2014). A bilingual approach for conducting Chinese and English social media sentiment analysis. *Computer Networks*, *75*, 491–503. doi:10.1016/j.comnet.2014.08.021

Yoon, S. J. (2012). A social network approach to the influences of shopping experiences on E-WOM. *Journal of Electronic Commerce Research*, *13*(3), 213–223.

Zaglia, M. E. (2013). Brand communities embedded in social networks. *Journal of Business Research*, *66*(2), 216–223. doi:10.1016/j.jbusres.2012.07.015 PMID:23564989

Zhang, T. T., Kandampully, J., & Bilgihan, A. (2015). Motivations for customer engagement in online co-innovation communities (OCCs): A conceptual framework. *Journal of Hospitality and Tourism Technology*, *6*(3), 311–328. doi:10.1108/JHTT-10-2014-0062

Zmuda, N. (2013). *Pepsi Beverage Guru Unveils His Plan to Win the World Over*. Retrieved from <http://adage.com/article/news/pepsi-beverage-guruunveils- plan-win-world/228641>

KEY TERMS AND DEFINITIONS

Co-Creation: Is a management initiative, or form of economic strategy, that brings different parties together (for instance, a company and a group of customers), in order to jointly produce a mutually valued outcome.

Customer-Dominant Logic: Is grounded in an understanding of consumers' lives and the use they make of services or products.

Embeddedness: Refers to the degree to which economic activity is constrained by non-economic institutions.

E-Vendor: Is an individual or company that sells goods or services to someone else in the economic production chain through the Internet as well as networking systems.

EWOM: Is defined as the exchange of product or service evaluations among people who meet, talk and text each other in the virtual world.

Intention: Purpose or attitude toward the effect of one's actions or conduct.

Social Media Platform: (Also social networking site or social media) is an online platform that is used by people to build social networks or social relations with other people who share similar personal or career interests, activities, backgrounds or real-life connections, and where can purchase online.

Chapter 4
Social Media Influencers and Consumer Online Engagement Management

Qiang (Steven) Lu
The University of Sydney, Australia

Zhen Yi Seah
The University of Sydney, Australia

ABSTRACT

With the popularity of social media, social media influencers have been playing an increasing role in modern marketing. However, there is little research on the impact of social media influencers on consumer brand engagement. To fill this gap, this chapter develops a conceptual framework to examine the impact of the endorsement by social media influencers on online brand engagement. The authors use social distance theories to construct several propositions to provide a deep understanding. They suggest that traditional celebrities and social media influencers have different social distance, therefore generate different types and degrees of consumer online engagement. And the product characteristics moderate the effectiveness of the different types of celebrity endorsement.

INTRODUCTION

Late 1983, Pepsi's popularity skyrocketed, overtaking their main competitor Coca cola, when Michael Jackson was hired as the endorser (University of Michigan, 1987). The effect of this campaign has become a good example in celebrity advertising.

DOI: 10.4018/978-1-5225-2897-5.ch004

It is believed that celebrity endorsers are able to create a profound impact on brands, particularly in the social media domain (Kramer, 2011). It is certainly "a ubiquitous feature of modern marketing" (McCracken, 1989). Marketers use celebrity endorsements as an effective promotional tool and there are approximately one-sixth of ads worldwide featuring celebrities (Shimp & Andrews, 2013). Given the importance of celebrities on the effectiveness of advertising, consumer engagement, company's investment in promotional dollars, the selection of celebrity endorsers is crucially important (Choi & Rifon, 2012).

Despite the importance of social media influencers in modern marketing, there are not many prior studies explored on the impact of social media influencers. To fill the gap in the literature, this study investigates the effects of different types of celebrity endorsers in social media on the emergence of different amount as well as types of consumer brand engagements. The two types of celebrity endorsers are the traditional celebrities, who are movie stars, sport stars and singers, and the 'new' celebrities, who are the social media influencers (Saul, 2016). In this study, we use the terms 'new' celebrities" and "social media influencers" interchangeably. The brand engagement is investigated in quantity and the form of abstract engagement versus concrete engagement. The study further explains the underlying mechanism: the perceived social distance. As such, the study presumes that traditional and new types of celebrities generate different perceptions of social distance among consumers which then makes them engage in brands differently (i.e., in an abstract vs concrete manner) and in different amount in the social media. The study also investigates the impact of different celebrities on brand engagement when they endorse different goods (hedonic versus utilitarian). Lastly, this research contributes to literature of celebrity endorsement, social media and construal level theory.

BACKGROUND

Celebrity Endorsement

The use of celebrities as endorsers has been a common but expensive practice in the advertising industry since the nineteenth centuries (Choi, Lee, & Kim, 2005). It is suggested that attributes acquired by celebrities, such as trustworthiness, likeability, expertness, dynamism, and objectivity are essential for drawing attention, enhance source credibility, and increase the likelihood of message recall (Ohanian, 1990). Source credibility model (Sternthal, Dholakia, & Leavitt, 1978) and source attractiveness model (McGuire, 1969) are widely used by researchers in celebrity endorsement literature to assess the effectiveness of messages conveyed through celebrity endorsement (McCracken, 1989). Additionally, "match-up hypothesis" is another stream of research on this topic to examine the congruence between a celebrity and the endorsed product (Kahle & Homer, 1985; Solomon, Ashmore, & Longo, 1992). Nevertheless, there are still several disadvantages or pitfalls in utilising celebrity endorsements. For instance, celebrities are costly to be hired as endorsers and sometimes they might overshadow the endorsed products (Erdogan, 1999). Also, results from (Mehta, 1994) study show that there were no statistically significant differences in consumers' attitudes towards brand and purchase intentions stimulated by celebrity endorsers and other type of endorsers.

Social Media Influencers

The emergence of *social media influencers* has become more apparent recently (Freberg, Graham, McGaughey, & Freberg, 2011). Social media influencers are a new group of independent third party endorser, who own at least thousands of followers by sharing their daily life, tips and tricks in social media (Morgan, 2016). They have the power to influence and shape consumers attitudes towards a brand (Freberg, et al., 2011). Also, they are redefining celebrities and emerged as the *new celebrities* (Saul, 2016). However, not many researchers have introduce social media influencer into the academic literature. There is a study focused on the identification of social media influencers in a social identity context to help companies market their products more effectively to this group of people (Langner, Hennigs, & Wiedmann, 2013) and a book written to guide marketers on how to utilize social media influencers as a promotional tool (Gillin & Moore, 2009).

MAIN FOCUS OF THE CHAPTER

Consumer Brand Engagement

CBE refers to the way consumers engage with marketer-generated content on brands (Yang, Lin, Carlson, & Ross Jr, 2016). Positive word-of-mouth and consumers' motivation to interact with the brands are one of the examples of CBE (Leckie, Nyadzayo, & Johnson, 2016). Also, it involves cognitive processing, affection and interactions (Hollebeek, Glynn, & Brodie, 2014). Research reveals that CBE can enhance consumer brand loyalty and strengthen the emotional bond between the brand and the consumer (Brodie, Ilic, Juric, & Hollebeek, 2013). Thus, the concept of CBE has recently gained much attention from both researchers and marketers (Hollebeek, et al., 2014). The literature claims that the ads of products featuring celebrities are perceived to be credible (Sternthal, et al., 1978). It is believed that celebrity credibility has an impact on brand engagement (Dwivedi, McDonald, & Johnson, 2014). Thus, we have:

P1: *Celebrity endorsement has positive impact on customer brand engagement.*

Social Distance

Construal level theory (Liberman & Trope, 1998) is a theory that describes how psychological distance affects the extent to which people's thinking is abstract or concrete. There are multiple dimensions of psychological distance such as temporal, social, hypothetically, and spatial (Trope & Liberman, 2011). Research reveals that interpersonal similarity is one form of social distance, which a person feel socially closer to similar others than dissimilar others (Liviatan, Trope, & Liberman, 2008). This concept has been widely recognized in social psychological literature, and supported by many researchers (Liviatan, et al., 2008). (Heider, 2013) claimed that interpersonal similarity could be referring to similarity in personality traits, family background, or beliefs; while other scholars also argued that gender and age also could be the similarity indicator (Tesser & Paulhus, 1983).

According to the social distance theory mentioned above, interpersonal similarity is one of the indicators to measure social distance (Liviatan, et al., 2008). The greater the interpersonal similarity between the individual and the target, the lower the social distance (Liviatan, et al., 2008). Consumers feel there is shorter social distance when they compare themselves to the social media influencers than traditional celebrities due to the fact that traditional celebrities have higher popularity and they do not share their private life with their fans, meanwhile social media influencers' life are all documented in social media channels (Morgan, 2016). Hence, consumers are able to relate themselves better when there is a shorter social distance, which leads to an increase in consumers' motivation to engage with the brand endorsement ads.

P2: *Social distance mediates the impact of types of celebrity endorsement on brand engagement: There is greater perceived social distance between traditional celebrities and consumers than between 'new' celebrities and consumers; the lower the social distance between the celebrity and the consumer, the more the brand engagement.*

Hedonic and Utilitarian Product

Hedonic goods are goods that satisfy human desire for sensual pleasure, fantasy, and fun (designer clothes, luxury cars, etc.) while utilitarian goods are goods that are functional and satisfy human basic needs (electronic appliances, laptop, etc.) (Dhar

& Wertenbroch, 2000). There is no doubt that every product contains different level of hedonic and utilitarian attributes; some products can be perceived as more hedonic in nature and vice versa (Okada, 2005). In line with the findings of (Bazerman, Tenbrunsel, & Wade-Benzoni, 1998) that the want/should distinction can be easily identified judging by a person's preferences, whether it is affective-driven ("wants") or cognitive-driven ("shoulds"). There are considerable amount of prior studies on hedonism and utilitarianism. For instance, scholars assess how consumer make a choice between hedonic and utilitarian products, as influenced by the nature of the decision task (Dhar & Wertenbroch, 2000), the emotional experiences evoked by hedonic and utilitarian benefits (Chitturi, Raghunathan, & Mahajan, 2008).

According to the construal level theory, 'high-level construal corresponds with desirability while low-level construal corresponds with feasibility' (Dhar & Kim, 2007). Thus, humans are more likely to have positive attitudes towards hedonic products when they are in high-level construal, as both hedonic goods and high-level construal are related to human's desirability meanwhile they will have positive attitudes towards utilitarian products when they are in low-level construal condition as both of these are related to feasibility. Therefore, a product type may gain lesser consumer brand engagement when there is a mismatch between the congruency of the endorser and the product type (Solomon, et al., 1992). If there is greater social distance between a consumer and a traditional celebrity than a *new celebrity*, consumer therefore is more likely to be in high-level construal condition. Hence, he/she will be more motivated to engage with the brand if the brand's product endorsed by celebrity is perceived as more hedonic. In this case, a traditional celebrity endorsement, as opposed to a new celebrity endorsement, will receive more brand engagement and more effective in increasing the amount of brand engagement. We have:

P3: *Product type moderates the effect of social distance on consumer brand engagement.*

Based on the construal level theory, people are more likely to form a perception on an object in terms of abstract characteristics in a high construal level condition, meanwhile construe an object in terms of concrete characteristics in low construal level condition (Trope, Liberman, & Wakslak, 2007). Individuals are more likely to process information about others' action in terms of their primary features, and superordinate in high construal level condition; which is when there is a lower level of similarity between them and the target (Liviatan, et al., 2008). If there are differences in social distance between an individual and a celebrity, it may then affect that individual's brand engagement. His/her comment may contain either more abstract or concrete characteristics on a brand's social media post featuring that celebrity. Comments in concrete manner are focused on the product detail such as price and the design of it, whereas comments in abstract manner are comments that described the overall picture, for instance, consumers' express their love towards the celebrities. We have:

P4: *Traditional celebrity endorsement stimulates more abstract engagement than 'new' celebrity endorsement.*

FUTURE RESEARCH DIRECTIONS

The rise of social media has given consumers the power to control programmed advertisements, hence, consumers prefer to use social media such as Facebook and Instagram for the purpose of gaining knowledge and making purchase decision (Xiang & Gretzel, 2010). Therefore, marketing practitioners started to leverage the benefit of these platforms to better communicate and stay at the top-of-mind with target audiences by creating online communities (Weinberg & Pehlivan, 2011.). Additionally, scholars have gradually introduced the concept of social media into academic literature, as social media has given them the opportunity to utilize the free data from social media platforms to understand its critical effects on consumer behavior and engagement through content analysis (Ertimur & Gilly, 2012). For instance, Park, Rodgers, and Stemmle (2011) collected 1760 wall comments from organisations' Facebook page to investigate how organisations use this medium to manage their image, and (Parsons, 2013) used 70 Facebook pages of international brands to justify what approaches these brands employed to develop relationships with customers. There is also another stream of research observed on the impact of online communities on brand loyalty (Laroche, Habibi, & Richard, 2013), particularly brand engagement on these communities (Trusov, Bucklin, & Pauwels, 2009). The launch of Instagram, a popular online mobile photo capturing and sharing application introduced in October 2010 (Hu, Manikonda, & Kambhampati, 2014) has hit approximately 500 million active users today (Statista, 2016). It is a remarkable achievement and it is reported that Instagram has generated the most brand engagement amongst other social media channels (Clifford, 2015), however, to the authors' knowledge, currently there are very few studies that focus on Instagram, or introduce this particular social media into the academic literature to analyze how brand managers stimulate consumer brand engagement in this platform. Hence, it can be very important future research direction.

CONCLUSION

With the world's Internet accessibility growing exponentially, as of 2015, Internet users have grown to a peak of 3 billion, which accounts for approximately half the global population (World Internet Usage and Population Statistics, 2015). Online social media channels have since became the emerging platform for consumers and marketers to exchange and disseminate information. The increase in social media channels usage has resulted in a rising phenomenon within this medium, where a group of people emerged as "social media influencers". These individuals have possessed the power to significantly influence a brand's online engagement, awareness and perception. Our study provides a conceptual framework to help academics and practitioners to have a better understanding of consumers' behavior online. It provides insights on how social media influences can have different impact from traditional celebrities and how the impact is moderated by product characteristics.

REFERENCES

Bazerman, M. H., Tenbrunsel, A. E., & Wade-Benzoni, K. (1998). Negotiating with Yourself and Losing: Making Decisions with Competing Internal Preferences. *Academy of Management Review*, *23*(2), 225–241. doi:10.2307/259372

Brodie, R. J., Ilic, A., Juric, B., & Hollebeek, L. (2013). Consumer engagement in a virtual brand community: An exploratory analysis. *Journal of Business Research*, *66*(1), 105–114. doi:10.1016/j.jbusres.2011.07.029

Chitturi, R., Raghunathan, R., & Mahajan, V. (2008). Delight by design: The role of hedonic versus utilitarian benefits. *Journal of Marketing*, *72*(3), 48–63. doi:10.1509/jmkg.72.3.48

Choi, S. M., Lee, W. N., & Kim, H.-J. (2005). Lessons from the Rich and Famous: A Cross-Cultural Comparison of Celebrity Endorsement in Advertising. *Journal of Advertising*, *34*(2), 85–98. doi:10.1080/00913367.2005.10639190

Choi, S. M., & Rifon, N. J. (2012). It is a match: The impact of congruence between celebrity image and consumer ideal self on endorsement effectiveness. *Psychology and Marketing*, *29*(9), 639–650. doi:10.1002/mar.20550

Clifford, C. (2015). Instagram Is Crushing Twitter and Facebook Brand Engagement. *Entrepreneur*. Retrieved from https://www.entrepreneur.com/article/253838

Dhar, R., & Kim, E. Y. (2007). Seeing the forest or the trees: Implications of construal level theory for consumer choice. *Journal of Consumer Psychology, 17*(2), 96–100. doi:10.1016/S1057-7408(07)70014-1

Dhar, R., & Wertenbroch, K. (2000). Consumer choice between hedonic and utilitarian goods. *JMR, Journal of Marketing Research, 37*(1), 60–71. doi:10.1509/jmkr.37.1.60.18718

Dwivedi, A., McDonald, R. E., & Johnson, L. W. (2014). The impact of a celebrity endorsers credibility on consumer self-brand connection and brand evaluation. *The Journal of Brand Management, 21*(7-8), 559–578. doi:10.1057/bm.2014.37

Erdogan, B. Z. (1999). Celebrity endorsement: A literature review. *Journal of Marketing Management, 15*(4), 291-314.

Ertimur, B., & Gilly, M. C. (2012). So whaddya think? Consumers create ads and other consumers critique them. *Journal of Interactive Marketing, 26*(3), 115–130. doi:10.1016/j.intmar.2011.10.002

Freberg, K., Graham, K., McGaughey, K., & Freberg, L. A. (2011). Who are the social media influencers? A study of public perceptions of personality. *Public Relations Review, 37*(1), 90–92. doi:10.1016/j.pubrev.2010.11.001

Gillin, P., & Moore, G. A. (2009). *The new influencers: A marketer's guide to the new social media*. Linden Publishing.

Heider, F. (2013). *The psychology of interpersonal relations*. Psychology Press.

Hollebeek, L. D., Glynn, M. S., & Brodie, R. J. (2014). Consumer brand engagement in social media: Conceptualization, scale development and validation. *Journal of Interactive Marketing, 28*(2), 149–165. doi:10.1016/j.intmar.2013.12.002

Hu, Y., Manikonda, L., & Kambhampati, S. (2014). What we instagram: A first analysis of instagram photo content and user types. In *Proceedings of the 8th International Conference on Weblogs and Social Media, ICWSM 2014* (pp. 595-598). The AAAI Press.

Kahle, L. R., & Homer, P. M. (1985). Physical Attractiveness of the Celebrity Endorser: A Social Adaptation Perspective. *The Journal of Consumer Research, 11*(4), 954–961. doi:10.1086/209029

Kramer, L. (2011). The Power of Celebrity Endorsement Enhanced By Social Media. *Business Insider Australia*. Retrieved from http://www.businessinsider.com.au/the-power-of-celebrity-endorsements-enhanced-by-social-media-2011-3?r=US&IR=T

Langner, S., Hennigs, N., & Wiedmann, K.-P. (2013). Social persuasion: Targeting social identities through social influencers. *Journal of Consumer Marketing*, *30*(1), 31–49. doi:10.1108/07363761311290821

Laroche, M., Habibi, M. R., & Richard, M. O. (2013). To be or not to be in social media: How brand loyalty is affected by social media? *International Journal of Information Management*, *33*(1), 76–82. doi:10.1016/j.ijinfomgt.2012.07.003

Leckie, C., Nyadzayo, M. W., & Johnson, L. W. (2016). Antecedents of consumer brand engagement and brand loyalty. *Journal of Marketing Management*, *32*(5-6), 558–578. doi:10.1080/0267257X.2015.1131735

Liberman, N., & Trope, Y. (1998). The role of feasibility and desirability considerations in near and distant future decisions: A test of temporal construal theory. *Journal of Personality and Social Psychology*, *75*(1), 5–18. doi:10.1037/0022-3514.75.1.5 PMID:11195890

Liviatan, I., Trope, Y., & Liberman, N. (2008). Interpersonal similarity as a social distance dimension: Implications for perception of others actions. *Journal of Experimental Social Psychology*, *44*(5), 1256–1269. doi:10.1016/j.jesp.2008.04.007 PMID:19352440

McCracken, G. (1989). Who is the Celebrity Endorser? Cultural Foundations of the Endorsement Process. *The Journal of Consumer Research*, *16*(3), 310–321. doi:10.1086/209217

McGuire, W. J. (1969). The nature of attitudes and attitude change. The Handbook of Social Psychology, 3(2), 136-314.

Mehta, A. (1994). How advertising response modeling (ARM) can increase ad effectiveness. *Journal of Advertising Research*, *34*, 62–62.

Morgan, E. (2016). Influencers cash in on social media's power. *ABC News*. Retrieved from http://www.abc.net.au/news/2016-03-24/influencers-cash-in-on-social-media-power/7274678

Ohanian, R. (1990). Construction and Validation of a Scale to Measure Celebrity Endorsers Perceived Expertise, Trustworthiness, and Attractiveness. *Journal of Advertising*, *19*(3), 39–52. doi:10.1080/00913367.1990.10673191

Okada, E. M. (2005). Justification Effects on Consumer Choice of Hedonic and Utilitarian Goods. *JMR, Journal of Marketing Research*, *42*(1), 43–53. doi:10.1509/jmkr.42.1.43.56889

Park, H., Rodgers, S. & Stemmle, J. (2011). Health organizations' use of Facebook for health advertising and promotion. *Journal of Interactive Advertising, 12*(1), 62-77.

Parsons, A. (2013). Using social media to reach consumers: A content analysis of official Facebook pages. *Academy of Marketing Studies Journal, 17*(2), 27.

Saul, H. (2016,). Instafamous: Meet the social media influencers redefining celebrity. *Independent.* Retrieved from http://www.independent.co.uk/news/people/instagram-model-natasha-oakley-iskra-lawrence-kayla-itsines-kendall-jenner-jordyn-woods-a6907551.html

Shimp, T., & Andrews, J. C. (2013). *Advertising promotion and other aspects of integrated marketing communications.* Cengage Learning.

Solomon, M. R., Ashmore, R. D., & Longo, L. C. (1992). The Beauty Match-up Hypothesis: Congruence between Types of Beauty and Product Images in Advertising. *Journal of Advertising, 21*(4), 23–34. doi:10.1080/00913367.1992.10673383

Statista. (2016). *Leading social networks worldwide as of April 2016, ranked by number of active users (in millions).* Retrieved from http://www.statista.com/statistics/272014/global-social-networks-ranked-by-number-of-users/

Sternthal, B., Dholakia, R., & Leavitt, C. (1978). The Persuasive Effect of Source Credibility: Tests of Cognitive Response. *The Journal of Consumer Research, 4*(4), 252–260. doi:10.1086/208704

Tesser, A., & Paulhus, D. (1983). The definition of self: Private and public self-evaluation management strategies. *Journal of Personality and Social Psychology, 44*(4), 672–682. doi:10.1037/0022-3514.44.4.672

Trope, Y., & Liberman, N. (2011). Construal level theory. In P. Van Lange, A. W. Kruglanski, & E. T. Higgins (Eds.), *Handbook of Theories of Social Psychology.* London: Sage Publications.

Trope, Y., Liberman, N., & Wakslak, C. (2007). Construal levels and psychological distance: Effects on representation, prediction, evaluation, and behavior. *Journal of Consumer Psychology: The Official Journal of the Society for Consumer Psychology, 17*(2), 83.

Trusov, M., Bucklin, R. E., & Pauwels, K. (2009). Effects of Word-of-Mouth versus Traditional Marketing: Findings from an Internet Social Networking Site. *Journal of Marketing, 73*(5), 90–102. doi:10.1509/jmkg.73.5.90

Weinberg, B. D., & Pehlivan, E. (2011). Social spending: Managing the social media mix. *Business Horizons, 54*(2), 275–282. doi:10.1016/j.bushor.2011.01.008

Xiang, Z., & Gretzel, U. (2010). Role of social media in online travel information search. *Tourism Management*, *31*(2), 179–188. doi:10.1016/j.tourman.2009.02.016

Yang, S., Lin, S., Carlson, J. R., & Ross, W. T. Jr. (2016). Brand engagement on social media: Will firms social media efforts influence search engine advertising effectiveness? *Journal of Marketing Management*, *32*(5-6), 526–557. doi:10.1080 /0267257X.2016.1143863

KEY TERMS AND DEFINITIONS

Consumer Brand Engagement: The two-way interaction between brand and consumers, whereby consumers engage with marketer-generated content on brands that involves cognitive processing and affection.

Economic Brand: A brand that offers great value or quality products, which produce in great quantity and it is reasonably priced.

Hedonic Product: Goods that are consumed for luxury purposes and satisfy human desire for sensual pleasure and enjoyment.

Instagram: An application on smartphone that allows its user to share visual content, i.e., photo and video publicly or privately online and connect with other like-minded people around the world.

Luxury Brand: A brand that provides symbolic and experiential value at a premium price, and gives it users a unique identity to differentiate themselves from the others.

New Celebrities: New celebrities are generally known as social media influencers. This group of celebrities emerged since the introduction of social media and it can be anyone who possesses the power to influence others within their social sphere.

Social Distance: The degree of similarity between oneself to another in terms of gender, age, personality, ethnicity, social class or beliefs.

Traditional Celebrities: Celebrities who receive their fame from entertainment or sport and they are the iconic figures who enjoy public attention around the world.

Utilitarian Product: Goods that are practical, functional, and generally are basic human necessities.

Chapter 5
Knowledge Management and Social Media in Tourism Industry

Rocco Agrifoglio
University of Naples "Parthenope", Italy

Concetta Metallo
University of Naples "Parthenope", Italy

ABSTRACT

The chapter aims to provide an overview of the role of social media for knowledge management in tourism industry. Respect than traditional tools, the social media penetration within such industry is growing thanks to opportunity for travelers and travel professionals to access critical tourism knowledge everywhere and every time. Prior research has mainly focused on how social media are changing the tourism industry, while it is lacking enough the contribution of these technologies to managing touristic knowledge. This chapter seeks to shed light on how social media support knowledge management, with particular attention to knowledge creation, sharing, and preservation processes, in tourism industry. In particular, while knowledge creation and sharing process have attracted the attention of scholars, knowledge preservation via social media seems be still in its infancy stage.

DOI: 10.4018/978-1-5225-2897-5.ch005

INTRODUCTION

The chapter aims to provide an overview of the role of social media for knowledge management in tourism industry.

According to Davenport and Prusak (1998, p. 5) knowledge is defined as "a fluid mix of framed experience, values, contextual information, and expert insights that provides a framework for evaluating and incorporating new experiences and information. It originates in and is applied in the minds of knowers". This perspective focuses on the dynamic character of knowledge, that is conceived both as an outcome and a process for "incorporating new experiences and information" (e.g., Tsoukas & Vladimirou, 2001; Nonaka & Takeuchi, 1995). The managerial literature agrees that one of the major problems of knowledge is its exploitation. Often individuals and organizations possess an enormous amount of information, but they are not able to exploit it for getting sustainable competitive advantage. When organizations operating in non-traditional markets and/or information-intensive industry, the management and processing of knowledge are considered even more critical factors for sustainability and organizational survival.

Knowledge management is a process that enables organizations to identify, capture and effectively leverage collective knowledge in an organization (Von Krough, 1999). It consists of various sets of socially enacted "knowledge processes," such as knowledge creation (known as contraction or development), knowledge sharing (known as transfer, distribution or dissemination), and knowledge preservation (known as storage and retrieval). Knowledge management, and the managing of explicit or tacit and individual or collective forms of knowledge, has been investigated by various authors from many countries and disciplines. However, while managerial literature mainly focuses on the process of knowledge management, with the aim of understanding how organizational knowledge can and should be managed effectively, the Information Systems (IS) literature pays more attention to the tools – traditional or Information Technology-assisted (IT-assisted) – for creating, sharing and preserving such knowledge. The IS literature recognized the IT-assisted tools as enablers of knowledge creation, sharing and preservation (e.g., Alavi & Leidner, 2001; Sher & Lee, 2004; Pezzillo Iacono, Martinez, Mangia, & Galdiero, 2012, Agrifoglio, 2015). Respect than traditional tools, IT-assisted tools, and social media in particular, are increasingly providing novel ways of supporting processes of knowledge creation, sharing and preservation within and between organizations.

Social media have been defined as "a group of Internet-based applications that build on the ideological and technological foundations of Web 2.0, and that allow the creation and exchange of user-generated content" (Kaplan & Haenlein, 2010).

The literature agrees that social media are a set of the Internet-based applications based on the peer-to-peer communication, which enables the creation, collaboration and exchange of information between organizations, communities and individuals (e.g., Kaplan & Haenlein, 2010). Social media are playing an increasingly important role as information sources for organizations and individuals in various industries, such as tourism. Tourism is an information-intensive industry whereby social media usage was recognized as critical in many aspects and for different levels. In particular, social media enable to exchange information between travellers and industry suppliers (e.g., hotels, transportation sectors, attractions), intermediaries (e.g., travel agents), controllers (e.g., governments and administrative bodies) (Werthner &Klein, 1999). Thanks to social media, the enormous amount of information is now exploitable for improving many aspects of tourism, especially in information search and decision-making behaviours, tourism promotion and in focusing on best practices for interacting with consumers (Zeng & Gerritsen, 2014). More in general, the considerable adoption of social media has extended organizational boundaries of companies operating in tourism industry, changing the way their communicate, collaborate and managing knowledge. For these reasons, growing role of social media in tourism has been increasingly an emerging research topic (e.g., Leung, Law, Van Hoof, & Buhalis, 2013; Zeng & Gerritsen, 2014).

This chapter focuses on the role of social media for knowledge management in tourism industry. In particular, it seeks to shed light on how organizations, destinations and, more in general, tourism sector create, share and preserve tourism knowledge. The structure of the chapter is as follows. Firstly, we introduce the theoretical background on knowledge management (Section 2) and on knowledge management issues in tourism industry (Section 3). Furthermore, we provide an overview of the role of social media in tourism industry (Section 4) and of the main dynamics of knowledge management through social media in tourism industry (Section 5). Finally, we show the summary of the chapter (Section 6).

From Knowledge to Knowledge Management in Organizations

Defining organizational knowledge is not an easy task. Knowledge represents a complex topic because of being abstract, it is difficult to define and quantify. Agreement with Davenport et al. (1998), knowledge tends to be fuzzy in nature and it is usually deeply and closely attached to the individuals who hold it, thus this issue is challenging to define, measure and manage in any organizational settings (Ipe, 2003).

Since the classical Greek era, the history of philosophy has taught us that the pursuit of the meaning of knowledge is a never-ending search (Nonaka, 1994). The research on rationalism advanced by Descartes and other philosophers in the 17th century, as well as subsequent research on empiricism (Locke and others in the 18th century) and interactionism (Kant and others in the 19th century) are some examples. More in general, the Greek philosophers have focused on absolute, static and nonhuman nature of knowledge, which can typically be expressed in propositional structures in formal logic. Overcoming the debates related to the Greek philosophy, more recent research looks at knowledge as a "dynamic human process of justifying personal beliefs as part of an aspiration for the truth" (Nonaka 1994, p. 15). Specifically, according to Nonaka (1994) and Huber (1991), knowledge has been conceived as the specific and justified belief of an individual that is able to increase his/her capacity to take effective action. In this context several factors are necessary in order to take the action, such as physical skills and competencies (e.g., playing football, or handicraft), cognitive/intellectual activity (e.g., problem solving), or both (e.g., in the surgery both manual skills and cognitive elements, that is knowledge of human anatomy and medicine, are required).

Without going into too much detail, it clear that the concept of knowledge has taken on different meanings over time that change depending on the various research fields and the analytical perspectives.

In particular, scholars from the IS field tend to define knowledge mainly making a distinction between knowledge, information, and data. At first, the IS literature does not clearly distinguish the terms knowledge and information, in fact they were sometimes used interchangeably. Consistent with this point of view, information was defined as "that commodity capable of yielding knowledge, and what information a signal carries is what we can learn from it" (Dretske, 1981, p. 44). It is a flow of messages or meanings which might be able to enrich, restructure or change knowledge (Machlup, 1983). Then, Vance (1997) provides a clear distinction between knowledge and information. In his opinion, information is a flow of messages, while knowledge is the result of a process of creation and management by the flow of information, related to the commitment and beliefs of its holder. Also, as suggested by Maglitta (1996), data is raw numbers and facts, instead information is processed data, and knowledge is "information made actionable". In this perspective, the emphasis is on the human action for knowledge and each term is conceptualized considering the differences among them clarifying when information becomes knowledge[1].

Unlike prior research, another interesting perspective looks at the dynamic character of knowledge. It could be defined as "a fluid mix of framed experience, values, contextual information, and expert insights that provides a framework for evaluating and incorporating new experiences and information. It originates in and is applied in the minds of knowers. In organizations, it often becomes embedded not only in documents or repositories but also in organizational routines, processes, practices, and norms" (Davenport & Prusak, 1998, p. 5). In agreement with this point of view, other research, such as Nonaka (1991) and Nonaka and Takeuchi

(1995), looks at dynamic dimension of knowledge, focusing on the interplay between knowledge and action in an organizational settings. Indeed, as Nonaka (1991) pointed out an organization is not merely an information-processing machine, but an entity that creates knowledge through such action and interaction. In this regard, organizational knowledge is could be defined as a 'stock' of knowledge emerging from interaction and stored in rules, procedures, routines, and shared norms of an organization (Walsh & Ungson 1991; Lam 2000). This perspective has been also stressed by other managerial scholars who mainly emphasized the interplays between what people know (knowledge) and what people do (knowing) in organizational settings (e.g., Weick, 1991; Cook & Brown, 1999; Agrifoglio, 2015).

Since defining 'what organizational knowledge is a very complex task, it should be easier to understand 'what constitutes it'. The taxonomy of organizational knowledge was investigated along two dimensions, such as epistemological (explicit and tacit forms of knowledge) and ontological (individual and collective forms of knowledge). With reference to the epistemological dimension, we can distinguish explicit and tacit forms based on the modes of expression of knowledge. Explicit is a kind of knowledge that can be formalized and codified, since it is easy to identify, store, and retrieve (Brown & Duguid, 1998). As Nonaka (1994) stated, it is that form of knowledge codified and communicated by symbolic and natural language, and appears valuable. From a managerial perspective, explicit knowledge can be easily and effectively handled within organizations. Unlike explicit, tacit knowledge refers to knowledge that is largely experience based. Polanyi (1966) defines tacit knowledge as something everyone knows but cannot describe. It referred to know-how, that is, that part of the knowledge that is intuitive, hard to define and to communicate, as well as deeply rooted in action, commitment, and involvement (Nonaka, 1994). Since tacit knowledge cannot be formalized and codified and is often context dependent and personal in nature, it can be developed through access to the sources of knowledge, rather than to the information itself. From a managerial perspective, managing tacit knowledge is a very complicated task, since it is often embodied in people rather than organizations. With reference to the ontological dimension, we can distinguish individual and collective forms based on the locus of knowledge that resides at individual and collective level. Leaving aside the older ontological debate on the subject, and the anthropomorphic view of knowledge in particular, the managerial literature looks at individual form of knowledge as that knowledge created by and inherent in the individual, while collective form of knowledge (well-known as social knowledge) as that knowledge created by and inherent in the collective actions of a group (e.g., Alavi & Leidner 2001).

Knowledge management is largely regarded as a process that enables organizations to identify, capture and effectively leverage collective knowledge (Von Krough 1999; Alavi & Leidner, 2001). As remarked by Agrifoglio (2015, p. 10), knowledge management consists of "various sets of socially enacted 'knowledge processes', such as knowledge creation (known as contraction or development), knowledge sharing (known as transfer, distribution or dissemination), and knowledge preservation (known as storage and retrieval)". In particular, knowledge creation is "the process of making available and amplifying knowledge created by individuals as well as crystallizing and connecting it with an organization's knowledge system" (Nonaka, von Krogh, & Voepel, 2006, p. 1179). It concerns the process of knowledge transformation from an individual to a collective state through dynamic interactions among individuals, organization and environment (Nonaka & Takeuchi, 1995; Nonaka & Toyama, 2002). On the contrary, knowledge sharing is that process whereby organizational knowledge is made available to others. According to Ipe (2003, p. 341), it is a voluntary act through which "knowledge held by an individual is converted into a form that can be understood, absorbed, and used by other individuals". Knowledge preservation, instead, is the process of selection, storage and effective actualization of organizational knowledge (Agrifoglio, 2015). After knowledge has been developed or acquired, it must be carefully preserved in order to avoid memory loss. Preserving knowledge is recognized as one of the most relevant processes of organizational knowledge management. It concerns a process constituted of three phases, such as selection, storage, and actualization. The selection is related to the identification of that organizational knowledge that must be saved because it is usable for a third party in the future. The storage is the second stage of knowledge preservation process. After selecting the organizational knowledge that is worth protecting, storage enables individuals to save it in an effective way and in a suitable form (Romhardt, 1997; Agrifoglio, 2015). Finally, the last stage of preservation process is the actualization of organizational knowledge previously stored. The actualization stage of knowledge preservation consists of making the previously stored organizational knowledge available in acceptable quality for decision-making.

KNOWLEDGE MANAGEMENT IN TOURISM

The creation and use of knowledge to feed innovation and product development was recognized as critical for both organizations and industries. In many economic sectors, such as primary industries, the knowledge, and knowledge creation and sharing processes in particular, has emerged as a topic of growing interest among academics and practitioners because of it was acknowledged as basis for competitive advantage in firms. Unlike other industries, although academic tourism research did not pay sufficient attention to knowledge management approach in the past, the sector is not as competitive as it could be (e.g., Ruhanen & Cooper, 2004; Cooper, 2015). This is true for two reasons. First, the tourism sector is mainly composed of micro and small companies, including family businesses, where often missing that managerial skills that are usually more oriented to knowledge management. Second, tourism organizations are traditionally research averse (Ruhanen & Cooper, 2004). Indeed, although the growth of academic research on knowledge management in tourism sector in the last years, entrepreneurs and practitioners are often not able to look at managing knowledge for tourism enterprises, destinations and governments (Cooper, 2006, 2015). This result once again confirms that the academic research seldom influences working practice.

More in general, although the managerial research in tourism has unquestionably grown in recent years, the presence of the barriers to the implementation of knowledge management in such sector makes this sector as less competitive than other ones (e.g., Grizelj, 2003; Ruhanen & Cooper, 2004; Cooper, 2006, 2015). The remaining part of the paragraph provides a review of the main contributes on knowledge management in tourism. Such contributes agree to recognize the need for tourism organizations, destinations and, more in general, industry to adopt a knowledge management approach to transform tourism research and intellectual property into capabilities for the sector.

Cooper's (2006) research provided one of the first and most important contributes to apply a knowledge management approach for tourism. He proposed a model for tourism aimed at explaining how tourism organizations and destinations managing knowledge, by focusing on the creation, transmission and use processes of tourism knowledge. Cooper's (2006) research has also pointed out the critical role of tacit form of knowledge in tourism due to the difficult of absorptive capacity of micro and small sized enterprises that often are not able to take advantage of business relationships and cooperation. Similarly, other research (e.g., Grizelj, 2003; Ruhanen & Cooper, 2004; Cooper, 2015) also suggested the need of contractual and cooperative forms, such as networks and communities of practice, that ensure the continuity of knowledge transfer and adoption in tourism. There is no doubt that networks are a traditionally suited contexts for generating and sharing knowledge among organizations that belong to them. Destinations as inter-organizational networks are composed of enterprises, governments and other organizations where how learning takes place and knowledge is transferred. In particular, as Cooper (2015, p. 114) suggested, destinations enable to articulate "tacit knowledge at the individual organization level into explicit knowledge, which is transmitted through the wider network of organizations through the usual processes of KM". The tourism academic literature was widely recognized the critical role of social relationships in destinations, as well as the important contribution that these knowledge networks make to knowledge transfer (e.g., Grizelj, 2003; Xiao & Smith, 2010; Cooper, 2015).

Like the destinations, community of practice also contributes to knowledge transfer in tourism, even if with a different degree of effectiveness than other sectors (e.g., Shaw & Williams, 2009; Cooper, 2015). Indeed, people are "members of different communities and also act as 'boundary spanners' across such divides and help knowledge more between these communities" (Shaw & Williams, 2009, p. 329). Also, as Cooper (2015, p. 116) suggested, "a COP differs from a destination is in the fact that a COP depends upon a high degree of trust [..] this notion of trust – or lack of it – that is central to the issues surrounding effective KM in tourism". However, such research has also remarked some criticisms on communities of practice's contribution to knowledge transfer in tourism. Community of practice tends often to be constrained by the shared word view of the members and thus it aids more the knowledge movement rather than new creation.

Furthermore, other research has also investigated the role of other mechanisms, such as the interlocking directorships and the human mobility, in aiding the tacit knowledge transfer in tourism industry (e.g., Shaw & Williams, 2009; Beritelli, Strobl, & Peters, 2013). While the contribution of human mobility was recognized, interlocking directorship leads to obtain divergent results. Indeed, although interlocking directorates are considered as 'boundary spanners' that link across organizations, the use of mechanisms of interlocking directorships with local board members could obtain greater benefits in terms of knowledge acquisition and transfer and, more in general, the development of social capital, than interlocking directorships with non-local board members (Beritelli, Strobl, & Peters, 2013).

SOCIAL MEDIA IN TOURISM INDUSTRY

Tourism is a an information-intensive industry (Sheldon, 1997; Werthner & Klein, 1999), in which the web-based technologies are changing the way in which tourism-related information is created and distributed (Xiang & Gretzel, 2010) as well as the way for planning and consuming travel (Buhalis & Law, 2008). Research on the role of information and communication technologies (ICTs) in the tourism industry is a widely studied topic in literature (Poon, 1993; Buhalis, 1998; Buhalis & Schertler, 1999; Fesenmaier, Klein, & Buhalis, 2000; Buhalis & Licata, 2001). In fact, ICTs have always been an important support for management practices' tourism organizations, especially for allowing information sharing (for example, such as prices and availability) regarding to reservation management (Poon, 1993). Therefore, tourism industry is interesting field for the investigation of the potential offered by new technologies (Lee, 2000). The tourist product consists of information on price, availability, qualitative characteristics and convenience of the single services of the holiday; it cannot be evaluated prior to consumption, as it is intangible. As a consequence, the ability to arouse interest and attract potential consumers is mostly determined by amount of information available, communicated and exchanged for describe and presentation the tourist product. Not surprising that the web-based technologies have found in the tourist industry the first and most popular applications, accompanied by a change that, in parallel, covered the behaviours and attitudes of consumers (Buhalis, 1998; O'Connor, 1999; Smith & Jenner, 1998; Werthner & Klein, 1999; O'Connor & Frew, 2002; Buhalis & Licata, 2001).

In the past few years, there has been considerable growth of the use of Web 2.0 applications in the tourism industry, commonly known as Travel 2.0 (Leung, Law, van Hoof, & Buhalis, 2013). Recently, Travel Weekly has published a study on social media usage in tourism, showing the rise in travelers with social media accounts from 2013 to 2016. Figure 1 shows the travellers with social media accounts from 2013 to 2016.

Results show the growth of social media usage, such as Facebook (+8%), YouTube (+23%), Pinterest (+23%), Twitter (+25%), and Instagram (+26%), in tourism in the last 3 years.

More in general, social media have become an important and popular tool for increasing information potentially available to travellers. Virtual context such as, for example, travelblog.org, travelpod.com, blog.realtravel.com, yourtraveljournal. com, worldnomads.com, travelpost.com, represent the specialized blogs that receive information by travellers (Pan, MacLaurin, & Crotts, 2007; Schmallegger & Carson, 2008). Moreover, travel agencies (statravelblogs.com, tui.com) or travel guides (lonelyplanet.com, community.roughguides.com, frommers.com), as well as several

Figure 1. Rise in Travellers with Social Media Accounts (Tobin, 2016)
Source: Tobin, 2016.

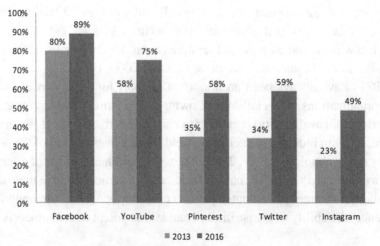

countries (on their official destination websites) provide a web space for tourists to share their experiences (Schmallegger & Carson, 2008).

Social Media Usage in Tourism Industry

The Travel Weekly has published the results of a survey based on responses from 1,193 travel agents about the current social media trends for consumers (c) and travel professionals (t). The survey's results have shown that more than 90% of travellers and travel agents have a Facebook account (c=94%; t=94%), while other platforms, such as Twitter (c=76%; t=37%), LinkedIn (c=75%; t=41%) and Instagram (c=74%; t=33%), are less used above all for business reasons. Also, the results shown that the most popular medium used for travel agents is the e-mail (78%), following by social media (67%), agency website (57%), newsletter (28%), and others media (less than 28%). Respect than e-mail, the usage of social media (+3%), agency website (+2%) and newsletter (+1%) is respectively increased from 2015 to 2016. *Source:* http://www.travelweekly.com/IndustrySurvey2016/Social-media

Through social media, people can share travel-related comments, opinions, stories and personal experiences about holidays, as well as can obtain information to support the trip-planning process and to assist in decision-making about destinations, accommodation, restaurants, tours, and attractions (Buhalis & Law, 2008; Xiang & Gretzel, 2010; Hays, Page, & Buhalis, 2013). Moreover, social media users can enrich the shared contents uploading images, audios, and videos, helping to create an objective and reliable information source in travel planning (Kang & Shuett, 2013).

For example, these contributions can elicit review sites, such as Tripadvisor. com, providing reviews and ratings, or online travel communities, such as that of Lonely Planet, to engage consumers in conversations. The recommendations shared on social media applications seem be the main tool for supporting the choice of services of the holiday; travellers rely on other travellers' advice (Hays et al., 2013). In fact, findings of the BrightLocal's Annual Local Consumer Review Survey 2015 has shown that the 92% of consumers read online reviews and about the 40% of consumers form an opinion by reading just 1-3 reviews. For Search Engine Land (2014) the 85% of consumers read up to 10 reviews before they feel that they can trust a business. Research by Deloitte (2015) found that 42% of holidaymakers use review websites and these sites are the most important sources that influenced the booking decisions (59%).

The role and use of social media in tourism and hospitality industry has become an interesting area of inquiry (see for a review Leung, Law, Hoof, & Buhalis, 2013 and Zeng & Gerritsen, 2014), for analysing the effect of social media on travellers' decision-making as well as in tourism operations and management. For example, some scholars investigated the effect of users' shared travel experiences on holiday planning processing (e.g., Di Pietro, Di Virgilio, & Pantano, 2011; Fotis, Buhalis, & Rossides, 2012; Jacobsen & Munar, 2012; Litvin, Goldsmith, & Pan, 2008) showing that people prefer independent travel-related information provided by the individuals who have travelled previously. Other studies deepened the use of social media tools as destination marketing tools (Mariani, Di Felice, & Mura, 2016; Hays et al., 2013; Stankov, Lazic, & Dragicevic, 2010; Xiang & Gretzel, 2010). Overall, for tourism organizations, social media are a challenge to increase their service quality because the use of feedback or negative postings also by travellers should represent an input to improve the efficiency and effectiveness of their processes (Kang & Shuett, 2013). Thus, tourism organizations, considering the consumer perspective in every business decision, would be able to identify new ways for reengineer business models and operations, such as customer service, marketing, networking and knowledge management (Zeng & Gerritsen, 2014).

USING SOCIAL MEDIA FOR KNOWLEDGE MANAGEMENT IN TOURISM INDUSTRY

As information-intensive industry, the management practices' tourism organizations are highly focused on the information exchanges and knowledge transfer because the tourism product is a combination of many different services offered by several actors, resulting in complex and intense interdependence conditions amongst tourism firms (Cooper, 2006). The information and knowledge sharing is fundamental for any coordination and interaction to occur among parties. Particularly, one way in which inter-organizational relationships materialize is through the exchange of information (Czepiel, 1975; Levine & White, 1961), and this is a prerequisite to cooperative inter-organizational activity (Schermerhorn, 1977; Van de Ven & Koening, 1975). Therefore, information sharing, as a set of information flows exchanged between more actors in a collective action, is a prerequisite of cooperation between different organizations.

Many scholars have recognized the knowledge management as an important topic for tourism research (e.g., Yang & Wan, 2004; Cooper, 2006; Hallin & Marnburg, 2008; Sigala & Chalkiti, 2014), deepening knowledge management applications across destination networks (Baggio & Cooper 2010; Scott, Cooper, & Baggio, 2008; Hays et al., 2013) or in the hospitality industry (Hallin & Marnburg 2008; Kyriakidou & Gore, 2005; Yang & Wan, 2004). For example, hotel chains are collections of hotel services organizations, differentiated in physical space, that are linked together into a larger organization. The distance in geographical space among the components of a chain suggests that each hotel affiliated belongs at least to two kinds of networks, the local destination network and the chain network. The linkage with a chain affects its components by giving resources, reputation and market power; moreover, the collection in a chain of organizations of different destinations fosters a transfer of knowledge within the local network (Buonocore & Metallo, 2004). In fact, Baum and Ingram (1997) shown that the value of the experience of a chain to a component depends on the similarity between the environment of the component and the environment of the chain. To the extent the chain has experience in the component's local environment it should result in a significant and valuable transfer of knowledge to component organizations.

ICTs have been regarded as one of the main enablers of knowledge creation and sharing activities (e.g., Sigala & Chalkiti 2014; Skok & Kalmanovitch, 2005; Sher & Lee, 2004). Traditionally, ICT in support of knowledge creation and sharing process in organizations are viewed as applications for (Alavi & Leidner, 2001): the coding and sharing of best practices; the creation of corporate knowledge directories; the creation of knowledge networks.

The ICTs have a crucial role for information exchange between all actors of tourism industry (Werthner & Klein, 1999; Xiang & Gretzel 2010): consumer, suppliers (e.g., hotels, transportation sectors, attractions), intermediaries (e.g., travel agents, tour operators), controllers (e.g., governments and administrative bodies), non-profit organizations (e.g., destination marketing organizations). For example, Ingram and Roberts (2000) described that relationships among managers of Sydney hotels supported by web tools allowed knowledge sharing and the consolidation of many best practices, improving the hotels' performance. In fact, in the hotel industry, the implementation of knowledge management (KM) systems is a very common practice for benefits resulting from hotel chains requirements of an overall quality standard of their geographically dispersed hotels (see for a review Hallin & Marnburg, 2008). Bouncken (2002) described Accor Hotel Group's KM systems, with 3500 hotels worldwide, that has implemented a KM system based on three components: IT-based knowledge accumulation; access to the IT-based knowledge system; and motivation for knowledge use and creation. In tourism destination management, ICTs are tools able to support the integrated offer of facilities and attractions for tourists, facilitating knowledge management in the geographical area.

The Case of the Visittrentino.it

Nowadays, Web 2.0 tools allow people to take an active role in knowledge co-creating and sharing, by contributing and debating content with others through a collaborative approach (e.g., Sigala & Chalkiti, 2012, 2014; Yu, Lu, & Liu, 2010; Wagner & Bolloju, 2005). For example, knowledge sharing in online travel communities occurs when people share travel-related comments, opinions, experiences, and prospective travellers can consult this information, posting questions and interacting with members

(Lee, Reid, & Kim, 2014; Arsal, Woosnam, Baldwin, & Backman, 2010; Ip, Lee, & Law, 2010). Moreover, in these communities, the accumulation of knowledge shared by traveller is a particularly important factor for the success of the online travel communities (Hsu et al., 2007; Shen et al., 2010; Qu & Lee, 2011). Munar and Jacobsen (2014) have shown that in social media, tourists share not only knowledge, aspects about holiday attributes (e.g., prices or weather conditions), but typically also tourism experiences defined as an individual's subjective evaluation of events related to his/her tourist activities (Tung & Ritchie, 2011). Travel experiences can be shared through storytelling, artefacts (such as photographs and videos) or both; Noor and colleagues (2005) observed that experience sharing is one form of tacit knowledge sharing. Therefore, social media provide the opportunity for users to share also tacit knowledge that relies on experience and practices (Nezakati et al., 2015).

The Case of the Castagna di Montella IGP

Montella is an small mountain village of less than 10,000 inhabitants located in Campania, a southern region of Italy. The village has always had a vocation for producing chestnuts, cheese and other typical local products thanks to its specific territorial location, climate and the fertility soil. The chestnuts were always considered as extremely important because of they provided food and work to whole generations of rural people in the Montella village and more in general in the Avellino Province. The Montella Chestnut is so highly valued to obtain a certificate of the recognition of the IGP label (Protected Geographical Indication). After harvesting of chestnut that begins in September and October, the inhabitants of Montella organizes the annual festivity (well-known as 'Sagra della Castagna di Montella IGP') of the Montella Chestnut (now in its 34th edition) which has become a famous tourist attraction not only for locals, but also for tourists from the region of Campania. It is a way for promoting the typical local products and for preserving the traditional handcrafted methods that have been handed down from generation to generation. The annual festivity, the chestnut's museum, etc. are some examples of touristic initiatives aimed at promoting and preserving the cultivation techniques and processing of chestnuts. Such touristic destination is also known thanks to Internet web sites and social media, such as Facebook fan page (34a Sagra della Castagna di Montella IGP), which are increasingly used for sharing touristic knowledge. The Facebook fan page (https://www.facebook.com/SagraCastagnaDiMontella/) of the '34a Sagra della Castagna di Montella IGP' has more than 2.800 likes and 1.400 fans are talking about this. It contains information, photos and videos posted by local organizers and tourists on various initiatives organized during the festivity, so representing an important medium for promoting and for preserving the typical local product and for enhancing sustainable tourism. Source: http://www.castagnamontella.it/; https://www.facebook.com/SagraCastagnaDiMontella/.

Buhalis and Licata Hays (2002) suggested that technology applications can encourage the diffusion of the knowledge about typical customs and traditions of a destination, promoting visibility of cultural resources, and supporting relationships between cultural and tourism operators (Jamhawi & Hajahjah, 2016). Therefore, it seems that social media tools could favour the destination sustainability and, thus, to reduce the negative impacts of the tourism growth through the promotion of local events such as markets or festivals that characterize the community culture and the local identity. Local traditions are an important way of preserving the community knowledge and its sustainability. However, many destinations, mainly rural areas, risk the loss of local traditions as well as the abandonment of some professions and as Silberman (2005, p. 12) observed digital technology allows a "quicker and more efficient methods of recording endangered data ... to deal with cultural heritage emergencies". Trough social media it is possible the digital storytelling of the tourism experiences or the description of the customs, form of art, social practices, values, lifestyles, or typical products that distinguish local identity of the destination. Preserving cultural heritage appears to be a key factor for supporting tourism development as well as tourism product differentiation (Cuccia & Cellini, 2007).

CONCLUSION AND FUTURE RESEARCH DIRECTIONS

This chapter focused on the role of social media for knowledge management in tourism industry.

Although prior academic literature has mainly deepened the effects of social media on organizations, destinations and, more in general, tourism industry, there is limited research addressing how social media support knowledge management and, in particular the processes of knowledge creation (known as contraction or development), knowledge sharing (known as transfer, distribution or dissemination), and knowledge preservation (known as storage and retrieval). Further research should be addressed to investigate how social media usage influences the processes of creation, sharing and preservation of touristic knowledge.

Furthermore, while the tourism academic literature has paid particular attention to knowledge creation and sharing processes, knowledge preservation issue is still in its infancy stage. Indeed, with reference to knowledge creation and sharing processes, social media tools have been regarded as an important enabler of knowledge creation and sharing activities in destination management and/or hospitality industry, so allowing people to take an active role in knowledge co-creating and sharing trough a collaborative approach (e.g., Baggio & Cooper 2010; Yu, Lu, & Liu, 2010). On the contrary, with reference to knowledge preservation process, there are only few studies that highlight as social media can favour community knowledge and cultural heritage for development tourism product (e.g., Munar & Ooi, 2012; Silberman, 2005). Managerial literature underlined that after knowledge has been developed or acquired, it must be carefully preserved in order to avoid memory loss, emphasizing the process of selection, storage and effective actualization of knowledge. According to these arguments, we think that future research should work along these lines by investigating the use of social media for knowledge preservation in terms of customs, traditions and cultural resources. In this way, organizations and tourism destinations could use social media for preserving history and heritage, which affect the brand marketing and characterizes the place, playing a significant role for destination sustainability and competitiveness.

REFERENCES

Agrifoglio, R. (2015). *Knowledge Preservation Through Community of Practice. Theoretical Issues and Empirical Evidence. Information Systems Series*. Springer. doi:10.1007/978-3-319-22234-9

Alavi, M., & Leidner, D. E. (2001). Review: Knowledge management and knowledge management systems: Conceptual foundations and research issues. *Management Information Systems Quarterly*, *25*(1), 107–136. doi:10.2307/3250961

Arsal, I., Woosnam, K. M., Baldwin, E. D., & Backman, S. J. (2010). Residents as Travel Destination Information Providers: An Online Community Perspective. *Journal of Travel Research*, *49*(4), 400–413. doi:10.1177/0047287509346856

Baggio, R., & Cooper, C. (2010). Knowledge transfer in a tourism destination: The effects of a network structure. *Service Industries Journal*, *30*(10), 1757–1771. doi:10.1080/02642060903580649

Baum, J. A. C., & Ingram, P. (1997). Chain affiliation and the failure of Manhattan hotels, 1898-1980. *Administrative Science Quarterly*, *42*(1).

Beritelli, P., Strobl, A., & Peters, M. (2013). Interlocking directorships against community closure: A trade-off for development in tourist destinations. *Tourism Review*, *68*(1), 21–34. doi:10.1108/16605371311310057

Bouncken, R. B. (2002). Knowledge management for quality improvements in hotels. *Journal of Quality Assurance in Hospitality & Tourism*, *3*(3-4), 25–59. doi:10.1300/J162v03n03_03

BrightLocal. (2015). *Local Consumer Review Survey*. Retrieved from https://www.brightlocal.com/learn/local-consumer-review-survey/

Brown, J. S., & Duguid, P. (2000). Mysteries of the region: knowledge dynamics in Silicon Valley. *The Silicon Valley Edge*, 16-45.

Buhalis, D. (1998). Strategic use of information technologies in the tourism industry. *Tourism Management*, *19*(5), 409–421. doi:10.1016/S0261-5177(98)00038-7

Buhalis, D., & Law, R. (2008). Progress in information technology and tourism management: 20 years on and 10 years after the Internet—The state of eTourism research. *Tourism Management*, *29*(4), 609–623. doi:10.1016/j.tourman.2008.01.005

Buhalis, D., & Licata, M. C. (2002). The future eTourism intermediaries. *Tourism Management*, *23*(3), 207–220. doi:10.1016/S0261-5177(01)00085-1

Buhalis, D., & Schertler, W. (1999). Information and Communication Technologies in tourism. *ENTER 99 Conference Proceedings*.

Buonocore, F., & Metallo, C. (2004). Tourist Destination Networks, Relational Competencies and "Relationship Builders"–the Central Role of Information Systems and Human Resource Management. In *Networking and partnerships in destination development and management: Proceedings of the ATLAS annual conference* (pp. 377-398).

Cook, S. D. N., & Brown, J. S. (1999). Bridging Epistemologies: The Generative Dance Between Organizational Knowledge and Organizational Knowing. *Organization Science*, *10*(4), 381–400. doi:10.1287/orsc.10.4.381

Cooper, C. (2006). Knowledge management and tourism. *Annals of Tourism Research*, *33*(1), 47–64. doi:10.1016/j.annals.2005.04.005

Cooper, C. (2015). Managing tourism knowledge. *Tourism Recreation Research*, *40*(1), 107–119. doi:10.1080/02508281.2015.1006418

Cuccia, T., & Cellini, R. (2007). Is cultural heritage really important for tourists? A contingent rating study. *Applied Economics*, *39*(2), 261–271. doi:10.1080/00036840500427981

Czepiel, J. A. (1975). Patterns of interorganizational communications and the diffusion of a major technological innovation in a competitive industrial community. *Academy of Management Journal*, *18*(1), 6–24. doi:10.2307/255621

Davenport, T. H., & Prusak, L. (1998). *Working Knowledge*. Boston: Harvard Business School Press.

Davidavičienė, V., & Raudeliūnienė, J. (2010). ICT in Tacit Knowledge Preservation. In *The 6th International Scientific Conference "Business and Management 2010"* (pp. 822-828).

Deloitte, L. L. P. (2015). *Travel Consumer 2015. Engaging the empowered holidaymaker*. Retrieved from http://www2.deloitte.com/content/dam/Deloitte/uk/Documents/consumer-business/deloitte-uk-travel-consumer-2015.pdf

Di Pietro, L., Di Virgilio, F., & Pantano, E. (2012). Social network for the choice of tourist destination: Attitude and behavioural intention. *Journal of Hospitality and Tourism Technology*, *3*(1), 60–76. doi:10.1108/17579881211206543

Dretske, F. (1981). *Knowledge and the Flow of information*. MIT Press.

Fesenmaier, D., Klein, S., & Buhalis, D. (2000). *Information and Communication Technologies in Tourism*. Vienna: Springer.

Fotis, J., Buhalis, D., & Rossides, N. (2012). *Social media use and impact during the holiday travel planning process*. Springer-Verlag. doi:10.1007/978-3-7091-1142-0_2

Grizelj, F. (2003). Collaborative knowledge management in virtual service companies-approach for tourism destinations. *Tourism*, *51*(4), 371–385.

Hallin, C. A., & Marnburg, E. (2008). Knowledge management in the hospitality industry: A review of empirical research. *Tourism Management*, *29*(2), 366–381. doi:10.1016/j.tourman.2007.02.019

Hays, S., Page, S. J., & Buhalis, D. (2013). Social media as a destination marketing tool: Its use by national tourism organisations. *Current Issues in Tourism*, *16*(3), 211–239. doi:10.1080/13683500.2012.662215

Hsu, M., Ju, T. L., Yen, C., & Chang, C. (2007). Knowledge sharing behavior in virtual communities: The relationship between trust, self-efficacy, and outcome expecta- tions. *International Journal of Human-Computer Studies*, *65*(2), 153–169. doi:10.1016/j.ijhcs.2006.09.003

Huber, G. (1991). Organizational Learning: The Contributing Processes and the Literatures. *Organization Science*, *2*(1), 88–115. doi:10.1287/orsc.2.1.88

Ingram, P., & Roberts, P. W. (2000). Friendships among competitors in the Sydney Hotel Industry1. *American Journal of Sociology*, *106*(2), 387–423. doi:10.1086/316965

Ip, C., Lee, H., & Law, R. (2010). Profiling the users of travel websites for planning and online experience sharing. *Journal of Hospitality & Tourism Research (Washington, D.C.)*, *36*(3), 418–426. doi:10.1177/1096348010388663

Ipe, M. (2003). Knowledge sharing in organizations: A conceptual framework. *Human Resource Development Review, 2*(4), 337–359. doi:10.1177/1534484303257985

Jacobsen, J. K. S., & Munar, A. M. (2012). Tourist information search and destination choice in a digital age. *Tourism Management Perspectives, 1*, 39–47. doi:10.1016/j. tmp.2011.12.005

Jamhawi, M. M., & Hajahjah, Z. A. (2016). It-Innovation and Technologies Transfer to Heritage Sites: The Case of Madaba, Jordan. *Mediterranean Archaeology and Archaeometry, 16*(2), 41–46.

Kang, M., & Schuett, M. A. (2013). Determinants of sharing travel experiences in social media. *Journal of Travel & Tourism Marketing, 30*(1-2), 93–107. doi:10.10 80/10548408.2013.751237

Kaplan, A. M., & Haenlein, M. (2010). Users of the world, unite! The challenges and opportunities of Social Media. *Business Horizons, 53*(1), 59–68. doi:10.1016/j. bushor.2009.09.003

Kyriakidou, O., & Gore, J. (2005). Learning by example: Benchmarking organizational culture in hospitality, tourism and leisure SMEs. *Benchmarking: An International Journal, 12*(3), 192–206. doi:10.1108/14635770510600320

Lam, A. (2000). Tacit Knowledge, Organizational Learning and Societal Institutions: An Integrated Framework. *Organization Studies, 21*(3), 487–513. doi:10.1177/0170840600213001

Lee, A. (2000). *Computer reservation systems: an industry of its own. Centre for Asian Business Cases, School of business*. The University of Hong Kong.

Lee, H., Reid, E., & Kim, W. G. (2014). Understanding knowledge sharing in online travel communities: Antecedents and the moderating effects of interaction modes. *Journal of Hospitality & Tourism Research (Washington, D.C.), 38*(2), 222–242. doi:10.1177/1096348012451454

Leung, D., Law, R., Van Hoof, H., & Buhalis, D. (2013). Social media in tourism and hospitality: A literature review. *Journal of Travel & Tourism Marketing, 30*(1-2), 3–22. doi:10.1080/10548408.2013.750919

Levine, S., & White, P. E. (1961). Exchange as a conceptual framework for the study of interorganizational relationships. *Administrative Science Quarterly, 5*(4), 583–601. doi:10.2307/2390622

Litvin, S. W., Goldsmith, R. E., & Pan, B. (2008). Electronic word-of-mouth in hospitality and tourism management. *Tourism Management*, *29*(3), 458–468. doi:10.1016/j.tourman.2007.05.011

Machlup, F. (1983). *The study of information: Interdisciplinary messages.* Retrieved from http://philpapers.org/rec/MACTSO-9

Maglitta, J. (1996). Smarten up! *Computerworld*, *29*(23), 84–86.

Mariani, M. M., Di Felice, M., & Mura, M. (2016). Facebook as a destination marketing tool: Evidence from Italian regional Destination Management Organizations. *Tourism Management*, *54*, 321–343. doi:10.1016/j.tourman.2015.12.008

Munar, A., & Ooi, C. (2012). *What Social Media Tell Us About The Heritage Experience.* Retrieved from https://www.researchgate.net/profile/can_seng_ooi/publication/265060043_what_social_media_tell_us_about_the_heritage_experience_what_social_media_tell_us_about_the_heritage_experience/links/55faa40c08aeba1d9f369106.pdf

Munar, A. M., & Jacobsen, J. K. S. (2014). Motivations for sharing tourism experiences through social media. *Tourism Management*, *43*, 46–54. doi:10.1016/j.tourman.2014.01.012

Nelson, R. R., & Winter, S. G. (1982). *An Evolutionary Theory of Economic Change.* Cambridge, MA: Belknap Press.

Nezakati, H., Amidi, A., Jusoh, Y. Y., Moghadas, S., Aziz, Y. A., & Sohrabinezhadtalemi, R. (2015). Review of social media potential on knowledge sharing and collaboration in tourism industry. *Procedia: Social and Behavioral Sciences*, *172*, 120–125. doi:10.1016/j.sbspro.2015.01.344

Nonaka, I. (1991). The knowledge-creating company. *Harvard Business Review*, *69*, 96–104.

Nonaka, I. (1994). A Dynamic Theory of Organizational Knowledge Creation. *Organization Science*, *5*(1), 14–37. doi:10.1287/orsc.5.1.14

Nonaka, I., & Konno, N. (1998). The concept of Ba: Building a foundation for knowledge creation. *California Management Review*, *40*(3), 40–55. doi:10.2307/41165942

Nonaka, I., & Takeuchi, H. (1995). *The Knowledge-Creating Company: How Japanese Companies Create the Dynamics of Innovation.* New York: Oxford University Press.

Nonaka, I., & Toyama, R. (2002). A firm as a dialectical being: Towards a dynamic theory of a firm. *Industrial and Corporate Change, 11*(5), 995–1009. doi:10.1093/icc/11.5.995

Nonaka, I., & Toyama, R. (2003). The knowledge-creating theory revisited: knowledge creation as a synthesizing process. *Knowledge Management Research & Practice, 1*(1), 2-10.

Nonaka, I., von Krogh, G., & Voepel, S. (2006). Organizational knowledge creation theory: Evolutionary paths and future advances. *Organization Studies, 27*(8), 1179–1208. doi:10.1177/0170840606066312

Noor, N. L. M., Hashim, M., Haron, H., & Aiffin, S. (2005). Community acceptance of knowledge sharing system in the travel and tourism websites: an application of an extension of TAM. *ECIS 2005 Proceedings,* 71.

O'Connor, P. (1999). *Electronic information distribution in tourism and hospitality.* CAB international.

O'Connor, P., & Frew, A. J. (2002). The future of hotel electronic distribution: Expert and industry perspectives. *The Cornell Hotel and Restaurant Administration Quarterly, 43*(3), 33–45. doi:10.1016/S0010-8804(02)80016-7

Pan, B., MacLaurin, T., & Crotts, J. C. (2007). Travel blogs and their implications for destination marketing. *Journal of Travel Research, 46*(1), 35–45. doi:10.1177/0047287507302378

Pezzillo Iacono, M., Martinez, M., Mangia, G., & Galdiero, C. (2012). Knowledge creation and inter-organizational relationships: The development of innovation in the railway industry. *Journal of Knowledge Management, 16*(4), 604–616. doi:10.1108/13673271211246176

Polanyi, M. (1966). *The Tacit Dimension.* New York: Doubleday.

Poon, A. (1993). *Tourism, Technology and Competive Strategies.* Wallingford, UK: CAB International.

Qu, H., & Lee, H. (2011). Travelers social identification and membership behaviors in online travel community. *Tourism Management, 32*(6), 1262–1270. doi:10.1016/j.tourman.2010.12.002

Romhardt, K. (1997). Processes of knowledge preservation: Away from a technology dominated approach. In Proceedings der 21, "Deutschen Jahrestagung für Künstliche Intelligenz", 9.

Ruhanen, L., & Cooper, C. (2004). Applying a knowledge management framework to tourism research. *Tourism Recreation Research, 29*(1), 83–87. doi:10.1080/02508281.2004.11081434

Schermerhorn, J. R. Jr. (1977). Information sharing as an interorganizational activity. *Academy of Management Journal, 20*(1), 148–153. doi:10.2307/255469 PMID:10305920

Schmallegger, D., & Carson, D. (2008). Blogs in tourism: Changing approaches to information exchange. *Journal of Vacation Marketing, 14*(2), 99-110.

Scott, N., Cooper, C., & Baggio, R. (2008). Destination networks: Four Australian cases. *Annals of Tourism Research, 35*(1), 169–188. doi:10.1016/j.annals.2007.07.004

Search Engine Land. (2014). *About Local Consumer Review Survey 2014*. Retrieved from http://searchengineland.com/88-consumers-trust-online-reviews-much-personal-recommendations-195803

Shaw, G., & Williams, A. (2009). Knowledge transfer and management in tourism organisations: An emerging research agenda. *Tourism Management, 30*(3), 325–335. doi:10.1016/j.tourman.2008.02.023

Sheldon, P. (1997). *Tourism Information Technologies*. Oxford, UK: CAB.

Shen, K. N., Yu, A. Y., & Khalifa, M. (2010). Knowledge contribution in virtual communities: Accounting for multiple dimensions of social presence through social identity. *Behaviour & Information Technology, 29*(4), 337–348. doi:10.1080/01449290903156622

Sher, P. J., & Lee, V. C. (2004). Information technology as a facilitator for enhancing dynamic capabilities through knowledge management. *Information & Management, 41*(8), 933–945. doi:10.1016/j.im.2003.06.004

Sigala, M., & Chalkiti, K. (2012). Knowledge management and Web 2.0: preliminary findings from the Greek tourism industry. *Social Media in Travel, Tourism and Hospitality: Theory, Practice and Cases*, 261.

Sigala, M., & Chalkiti, K. (2014). Investigating the exploitation of web 2.0 for knowledge management in the Greek tourism industry: An utilisation–importance analysis. *Computers in Human Behavior, 30*, 800–812. doi:10.1016/j.chb.2013.05.032

Silberman, N. A. (2005). Beyond theme parks and digitized data: what can cultural heritage technologies contribute to the public understanding of the past? *Interdisciplinarity or The Best of Both Worlds: The Grand Challenge for Cultural Heritage Informatics in the 21st Century.* Available at: http://works.bepress.com/neil_silberman/39/

Skok, W., & Kalmanovitch, C. (2005). Evaluating the role and effectiveness of an intranet in facilitating knowledge management: A case study at Surrey County Council. *Information & Management, 42*(5), 731–744. doi:10.1016/j.im.2004.04.008

Smith, C., & Jenner, P. (1998). Tourism and the Internet. *Travel & Tourism Analyst,* (1), 62-81.

Stankov, U., Lazic, L., & Dragicevic, V. (2010). The extent of use of basic Facebook user-generated content by the national tourism organizations in Europe. *European Journal of Tourism Research, 3*(2), 105.

Tobin, R. (2016). Social media: Platform use keeps rising. *Travel Weekly.* Retrieved from http://www.travelweekly.com/ConsumerSurvey2016/Social-media-platform-use-keeps-rising

Tsoukas, H., & Vladimirou, E. (2001). What is organizational knowledge? *Journal of Management Studies, 38*(7), 973 993. doi:10.1111/1467-6486.00268

Tung, V. W. S., & Ritchie, J. B. (2011). Exploring the essence of memorable tourism experiences. *Annals of Tourism Research, 38*(4), 1367–1386. doi:10.1016/j.annals.2011.03.009

Van de Ven, A. H., & Koenig, R. Jr (1975). *Pair-Wise Inter-Agency Relationships: theory and preliminary findings.* Working Paper, Department of Administrative Sciences, Kent State University.

Vance, D. M. (1997). Information, knowledge and wisdom: the epistemic hierarchy and computer-based information system. In B. Perkins & I. Vessey (Eds.), *Proceedings of the Third Americas Conference on Information Systems.* Academic Press.

Von Krogh, G. (1999). *Developing a knowledge-based theory of the firm.* St. Gallen: University of St. Gallen.

Wagner, C., & Bolloju, N. (2005). Supporting knowledge management in organizations with conversational technologies: Discussion forums, weblogs, and wikis. *Journal of Database Management, 16*(2), 1–8.

Walsh, J. P., & Ungson, G. R. (1991). Organizational Memory. *Academy of Management Review, 16*(1), 57–91. doi:10.5465/AMR.1991.4278992

Weick, K. E. (1991). The nontraditional quality of organizational learning. *Organization Science*, *2*(1), 116–123. doi:10.1287/orsc.2.1.116

Werthner H., & Klein S. (1999). *Information technology and tourism. A challenging relationship*. Springer Computer Science.

Werthner, H., & Klein, S. (1999). ICT and the changing landscape of global tourism distribution. *Electronic Markets*, *9*(4), 256–262. doi:10.1080/101967899358941

Xiang, Z., & Gretzel, U. (2010). Role of social media in online travel information search. *Tourism Management*, *31*(2), 179–188. doi:10.1016/j.tourman.2009.02.016

Xiao, H., & Smith, S. L. J. (2010). Professional communication in an applied tourism research community. *Tourism Management*, *31*(3), 402–411. doi:10.1016/j.tourman.2009.04.008

Yang, J. T., & Wan, C. S. (2004). Advancing organizational effectiveness and knowledge management implementation. *Tourism Management*, *25*(5), 593–601. doi:10.1016/j.tourman.2003.08.002

Yoo, K. H., & Lee, W. (2015). Use of Facebook in the US heritage accommodations sector: An exploratory study. *Journal of Heritage Tourism*, *10*(2), 191–201. doi:10.1080/1743873X.2014.985228

Yu, T. K., Lu, L. C., & Liu, T. F. (2010). Exploring factors that influence knowledge sharing behavior via weblogs. *Computers in Human Behavior*, *26*(1), 32–41. doi:10.1016/j.chb.2009.08.002

Zeng, B., & Gerritsen, R. (2014). What do we know about social media in tourism? A review. *Tourism Management Perspectives*, *10*, 27–36. doi:10.1016/j.tmp.2014.01.001

KEY TERMS AND DEFINITIONS

e-Tourism: The use of Web 2.0 applications in the tourism industry (commonly known also as Travel 2.0).

Knowledge Creation: Is a process that enables organizations to transform knowledge created by individuals from an individual to a collective state.

Knowledge Management: Is a set of socially enacted processes that enable to identify, capture and effectively leverage collective knowledge within an organizational context.

Knowledge Preservation: The process of selection, storage and effective actualization of organizational knowledge.

Knowledge Sharing: Is a process that enables to make available knowledge to others within an organizational context.

Social Media: A set of Web 2.0 applications for creating, organizing, combining, sharing, commenting, and rating user-generated content.

Tourism Destination: Local agglomerations of actors of different nature (tourist firms, local governments, public agencies, cultural organizations, etc.) that cooperate for the development of local tourism product.

Tourism Industry: An information-intensive industry comprised by several activities which need to be combined and assembled, gathering together actors geographically and/or organizationally dispersed such as industry suppliers (e.g., hotels, transportation sectors, attractions), intermediaries (e.g., travel agents), and controllers (e.g., governments and administrative bodies).

ENDNOTE

[1] Contrary to the hierarchical structure of knowledge discussed above, other scholars proposed an inverse perspective in defining knowledge from knowledge to data. From this point of view, knowledge exists before formulating information and measuring data, because of it is a results from a cognitive processing triggered by the inflow of new stimuli (Alavi & Leidner, 2001; Nonaka, von Krogh, & Voelpel, 2009). In this regard, information could be converted to knowledge because processed by people's minds, while knowledge becomes information once it is structured and formally represented through text, graphics, words, or other symbolic forms.

Chapter 6
Use of Social Media for Knowledge Sharing by Instructors in a Higher Education Institution:
An Exploratory Case Study

Stephen Asunka
Ghana Technology University College, Ghana

ABSTRACT

Against the backdrop that universities are required to generate and disseminate relevant and applicable knowledge for the general good, and with the understanding that social media can be an effective vehicle for such knowledge sharing practices, this study explored the use of social media for knowledge sharing by academics at a university college in Ghana. The study thus examined how instructors use social media for sharing academic knowledge, the factors that promote such knowledge sharing practices, and the barriers to effective knowledge sharing in the academic environment. 47 instructors participated by completing an online questionnaire, whilst 7 participated in focus group discussions. Findings reveal a regular, though not daily, use of social media platforms for academic knowledge sharing. Personal, technological and institutional factors were determined to be contributing in fostering as well as hindering such activities. Implications of these findings as well as suggestions for future research are accordingly discussed.

DOI: 10.4018/978-1-5225-2897-5.ch006

INTRODUCTION

The Oxford English Dictionary defines knowledge as "facts, information, and skills acquired through experience or education; the theoretical or practical understanding of a subject" (Oxforddictionaries.com, 2016). For an individual or organisation, knowledge represents the sum of all this theoretical and practical understanding of several subject areas, and residing in the intelligence and competence of the said individual, or in the case of an organisation, all individuals within the organisation. Knowledge also provides a framework for evaluating and incorporating new experiences and information (Davenport & Prusak, 2000). In the current information age, knowledge, better known as intellectual capital, is increasingly being recognized as a greater contributor to organizational wealth (Hislop, 2013), and applying knowledge-based resources is at the heart of competitive advantage for enterprises (Jasimuddin & Zhang, 2014).

Being such a very critical resource, individuals and organisations need to appropriately manage knowledge so that the right knowledge will always be available to the right people at the right time and place etc. The processes of knowledge acquisition, creation, refinement, storage, transfer, sharing, and utilization that are used to get the most out of an individual's or organization's knowledge are collectively referred to as Knowledge Management, a discipline which has, in recent times, been a primary focus of attention for enterprises interested in the innovative development and maintenance of competitive advantages (Hakami, et al., 2014; King, 2009).

One crucial component of knowledge management is knowledge sharing - a process where knowledge is reciprocally shared between individuals within a group, negotiated and refined until it becomes common knowledge to the group (Yang, 2004). This sharing process often consists of collecting, organizing and conversing knowledge from one to another (Van-den-Hooff & De-Ridder, 2004). Indeed, knowledge management practitioners assert that, to get the most value from one's intellectual assets, knowledge must be shared and serve as the foundation for collaboration. This is so because, when managed properly, knowledge sharing can greatly improve work-quality and decision- making skills, problem-solving efficiency as well as competency that will benefit individuals and the organization at large (Syed-Ihksan & Rowland, 2004; Yang, 2007). Knowledge sharing is therefore emerging as a key topic of interest in many fields including innovation management, technology transfer, strategic management etc. (Cummings, 2003).

It must however be emphasized that knowledge can be classified broadly as either explicit or tacit (Miller, 1998). Explicit knowledge consists of facts, rules, relationships and policies that can be codified on paper or electronic form. This form of knowledge can thus be easily shared among individuals. Tacit knowledge on the other hand is knowledge that is held by individuals based on their observations, insights, emotions, experiences, intuition etc., and cannot be easily codified, written down or verbalized (Usoro, 2013). It is acquired largely through association with other people, and is therefore integral to the entirety of a person's consciousness (BusinessDictionary.com, 2016). Tacit knowledge is not easily transferable, and most often gets transferred from one individual to another through joint or shared activities. Incidentally, tacit knowledge constitutes the bulk of what one knows, and forms the underlying framework that makes explicit knowledge possible. For effective knowledge sharing therefore, facilitating systems and processes should not stop at only transmitting explicit knowledge, but must also provide the appropriate communication and collaborative tools that will facilitate sharing of tacit knowledge.

In academia, and higher education in particular (which are regarded as knowledge based organisations), students are expected to be responsible of their education proactively by "learning with both individual responsibility and communal sharing" (Brown, 1988). Instructors on the other hand, become learning facilitators who design and implement learning environments that provide appropriate settings for the collaborative exchange of ideas and knowledge sharing among students, and between students and instructors. In addition, and as part of their duties in academia, instructors are obliged to conduct research in their respective fields of study, and publish their findings as book chapters, journal articles etc. Since achieving these feats requires effective knowledge co-creation and sharing practices among instructors, the general expectation is that higher education institutions will be places where knowledge is shared freely among academics (Ramayah, et al., 2013). Indeed, several higher education institutions in the developed world have been receiving grants to implement knowledge sharing practices among their respective academic staff (Sohail & Daud, 2009). Christensen (2007) also indicates that sharing knowledge helps academics improve upon their teaching abilities, develop quality research and avoid repeating past mistakes.

Knowledge sharing among academics within and between institutions has therefore been the norm in academia, and includes processes such as lectures, workshops, debates, group discussions, group problem solving, presentations, scholarly publications etc. Prior to the advent of microcomputers and the Internet, these knowledge sharing practices were largely through personal contact and face-to-face interactions. However, the rapid development in information and communication technologies (ICTs) over the last decade or two, and the resultant increasing use of these technologies for teaching and learning in higher education (Hyman, 2012), is offering platforms for virtual interaction and more effective knowledge sharing. Moreover, higher education institutions the world over are steadily moving teaching and learning practices onto the virtual environment by implementing blended and online learning initiatives (Norberg, Dziuban, & Moskal, 2011), and instructors as well as students are expected to involve these computing and communication technologies in most, or all, instructional and learning activities, including knowledge sharing.

One of such enabling technologies is social media, a term collectively applied to Internet-based archiving and communication applications that enable people to interact with each other by creating and sharing information. Social media thus includes popular networking websites, like Facebook and Twitter; social bookmarking sites like Digg or Reddit, photo and video sharing sites like Instagram and YouTube, blogs, wikis, online discussion forums, instant messaging (e.g. WhatsApp), and any aspect of an interactive presence which allows individuals' ability to engage in conversations with one another (Obar & Wildman, 2015).

Social media use worldwide is estimated to cover over 31% of world population, and with adoption increasing at a rate of over 10% each year (Smartinsights. com, 2016). As these technologies are known to encourage, support and facilitate effective knowledge and information sharing between individuals and groups (Panahi, Watson, & Partridge, 2012), their increased use over the past decade has impacted on almost every aspect of humanity including work, play, politics, news consumption, communications patterns, community engagement, teaching and learning etc. (Perrin, 2015).

Given that all these social media applications are operable on mobile devices including the smartphone, and with cellular mobile voice and data services now covering about 97% of the adult population globally (GSM Association, 2015), chances are that most, if not all, higher education instructors, particularly those in the developing world, will be highly connected via social media. Indeed, a casual observation of instructors on any university campus will reveal almost all of them handling one particular Internet-enabled device or the other, and there is no doubt that they have high levels of digital skills and are comfortable using these devices to retrieve and share information and knowledge (Lichy & Kachour, 2016).

However, with http://wearesocial.com (2016) reporting that only 11% of Africa's population actively use social media, a question that comes to mind is whether Africa's higher education instructors are engaging in effective knowledge sharing behaviours on social media platforms. And if they do (not), what personal, contextual and environmental factors influence such knowledge sharing behaviours. Understanding such factors, particularly within peculiar cultural settings, will not only help institutions appropriately define the role of social media in knowledge sharing, but also contribute towards evolving workable strategies that will help motivate knowledge sharing among learning communities on social media platforms. Within the Ghanaian higher education context however, no studies pertaining to instructor use of social media for knowledge sharing practices, have thus far been reported in the literature.

It is against this backdrop that this preliminary exploratory study was conducted among lecturers at a private university college in Ghana with the objective of answering the following questions:

1. What specific social media technologies are commonly used by these instructors?
2. Do instructors consider knowledge sharing among colleagues to be vital for individual and institutional growth?
3. What specifically do these instructors consider as knowledge that they are sharing on social media platforms?
4. How frequently do these instructors use social media for sharing scholarly knowledge?
5. What personal and environmental factors do these instructors consider to be influencing their ability and willingness to share knowledge on social media?

The study adopted a qualitative approach as it considered the experiences and perceptions of those being studied as very crucial. As Marshall and Rossman (2006) point out, qualitative research is an inquiry process aimed at building a holistic understanding of complex social issues, and is characterized by data collection - typically within natural settings - in which the researcher acts as a key instrument. Data for the study were gathered using survey questionnaire and focus group discussions, and analysed using descriptive statistics and Grounded Theory methods.

The rest of the chapter discusses the study in detail, touching on some theoretical underpinnings and elaborating on the research strategies adopted to help unravel some instructor behaviours and perceptions. It concludes by sharing lessons learnt with the view to contributing to the evolution of best-practice frameworks and models for facilitating the use of social media for knowledge sharing among instructors in institutions of higher learning.

LITERATURE REVIEW

Social Media for Knowledge Sharing in Academia

Social media has been defined and categorized severally based on the various dimensions of value and affordances they bring to users. However, the categorization by Erkolla (2008, cited in Vuori, 2011), offers a comprehensive summary of the features, functionalities and characteristics that make social media such a valuable resource (Table 1)

As Table 1 shows, the features and functionalities of social media are quite numerous and varied, but critical among these is that, in addition to supporting user-

Table 1. Categorization of Social Media (Source: Erkolla 2008)

Category	Features
Differs from traditional media	User-originated, interactive, two-way, many-to-many communication, not a mass medium, personal, open, social, human-related, opinion and perspective related, democratic
Different perspective of knowledge	Uncontrollable, fragmented, global, local, fast, real-time, groupable, linkable, knowledge-intensive
Technology related	Instrumental, uses the Internet, technology-based
Collective	Supports shared meanings and their building, based on collective intelligence, supports collective intelligence, supports peer-production, supports communities, content centered, challenges traditional operating models
Interwoven	Diverse, modular, editable, multimedial, structured, intricate

content generation, communication and collaboration, social media also supports collective intelligence and (democratic) knowledge building through authorship and sharing. It is therefore not surprising that several social media platforms are available as user-friendly mobile applications, online portals and websites, most of which are free to use. Table 2 lists examples of these tools together with their respective purposes and uses.

It is however worth noting that the categories outlined in Table 2 are not mutually exclusive, but only represent the dominant purposes to which each of the respective tools can be put. Thus a resource like Facebook which is categorized as a predominantly social networking tool, and thus basically keeps people connected, can also be used for communication, collaboration etc.

The foregoing demonstrates that any Internet or web-based application that qualifies to be classified as social media, should be able to provide the requisite

Table 2. Social Media Technologies (Adapted from Vuori, 2011)

	Tools/Technologies	Purpose	Examples
1	Blogs, Discussion Forums, Instant Messaging, Podcasting	Communication: publish, discuss, express oneself, show opinion, share, influence, store	Blogger, YouTube, Skype, SlideShare, WordPress, Flickr, WhatsApp
2	Wikis, shared workspaces	Collaboration: collective content creation	Wikis, Wikipedia, Google Drive
3	Social networks, communities, virtual worlds	Connecting: network, socialize, connect, play, entertain	Facebook, LinkedIn, SecondLife, Instagram, Twitter
4	Tagging, social bookmarking, RSS, add-ons	Completing: describing, adding, tagging content, news aggregation	Delicious, Pinterest, Digg, Reddit
5	Mash-ups, platforms	Combining:	Google maps

platform or environment for facilitating and enhancing knowledge sharing among its users. Also, in the education sector, social media applications should be capable of facilitating the co-construction of knowledge, as the environments provide learners and instructors the opportunity to reflect on newly shared knowledge, reevaluate their thoughts with them, and externalize them by transforming the internal processes into public processes (Choi, Land, & Turgeon, 2005). It is therefore only natural that research works aimed at establishing knowledge sharing practices among instructors in higher education settings will gain significant traction, particularly in the present Web 2.0 era.

Accordingly, several recent studies have invested considerable attention into finding, first, if appreciable knowledge sharing via social media applications exists among academics in higher education institutions, and if they do, what the determinants of these knowledge sharing behaviors are. Adopting theoretical frameworks such as Theory of Reasoned Action (TRA), Theory of Planned Behaviour (TPB), Technology Acceptance Model (TAM), Social Power Theory (SPT) etc., these studies have reported findings which can be placed under three broad categories namely: (i) Individual attitudes and behaviors, (ii) Technology and (iii) Organizational culture and practices (Cheng, Ho, & Lau, 2009; Hakami et al., 2014; Hassandoust & Perumal, 2011; Ramayah et al., 2013). These are discussed in the subsequent sections.

Individual Attitudes and Behaviors

With the general understanding that knowledge sharing is strongly influenced by individuals' willingness to engage in the process, majority of the studies reported in the literature on the use of social media for knowledge sharing by academic staff in universities largely focus on the individuals staff members' behavioral intentions to engage in the practice, their actual knowledge sharing practices, and the main factors enhancing or hindering such practices. Salient findings are summarized as follows:

- Academicians, at least within the developing world context, tend to be individualistic, independent and autonomous, and therefore place a higher priority on individual scholarly achievement than on sharing their knowledge for the common good (Ramayah et al., 2013). Consequently, knowledge sharing among individual academics within and between institutions has been determined to be quite scanty (Ridzuan, et al., 2008).
- Individual academics tend to engage more in knowledge sharing processes in the online environment when motivated with financial incentives, recognition and reputation (Hassandoust & Perumal, 2011).
- Trust - defined as the degree to which members believe that there is honesty and reliability in a community (Mayer, et al., 1995) - has been determined to

be one of the critical antecedents of effective knowledge sharing behaviours among academics. Indeed, Powell, Piccoli and Ives (2004), argue that virtual communities with high level of trust have better social collaboration, willingness toward knowledge sharing and significant and timely feedback about other member's performance.

- The degree to which academics believe that they can improve mutual relationships through knowledge sharing - known as anticipated reciprocal relationships - has been determined to have a positive effect on knowledge sharing by academics (Bock, et al. 2005). Thus higher education instructors will be more willing to share knowledge through social media if they anticipate an equal and rewarding response from colleagues. Indeed, Lin and Hung (2009), contend that these exchanges tend to cease when the expected reactions are not forthcoming.

- There is a strong positive relationship between attitude towards knowledge sharing and intention to share knowledge. Attitude towards knowledge sharing refers to the degree of one's positive feelings about sharing one's knowledge (Ramayah et al., 2013), and several research works have consistently found that each individual academic's intention to share knowledge is driven by their attitude towards knowledge sharing (Cheng et al., 2009; Hassandoust & Perumal, 2011; Ramayah et al., 2013; Seonghee & Boryung, 2008).

- Subjective norm - defined as "the perceived social pressure to perform or not to perform the behaviour" (Ajzen, 1991, p. 188) - has been determined to have an influence on knowledge sharing. Thus, a high subjective norm leads to a high intention towards knowledge sharing (Goh & Sandhu, 2013).

Technology

As highlighted in Table 1, social media is technology based, i.e. requires Internet enabled devices and mostly a live Internet connection. Effective use of the various social media applications also requires some level of user understanding of the features and functionalities of the respective platforms and interfaces. In addition, the networking functionalities (e.g. friending and unfriending, tagging, following, liking etc.), and in some cases, the multimedia content requirements (audio, video, animations etc.) signifies that users have to be fairly adept in manipulating these affordances in order to effectively use social media for knowledge sharing.

Depending on each particular situation or context therefore, technology can either be a facilitator, or a barrier to effective knowledge sharing as evidenced by research works which have established the following:

- Individual perceptions of the usefulness of social media technologies for knowledge sharing, and their experiences in social media use jointly affect their intention to apply social media for knowledge sharing (Behringer & Sassenberg, 2015).

- The intensity and effectiveness of knowledge sharing through social media largely depends on the usability and user-friendliness of the various technical features of these platforms (DiGangi & Wasko, 2016). Social media applications are fairly easy to use, respond appropriately to specific user needs, are mostly available for free, work seamlessly on all types of mobile devices, and have been designed to be visually appealing to users. They therefore tend to be more rapidly adopted by potential users.

- User perceptions of possible imperfections of social media, especially when it comes to data privacy, have also been demonstrated to have an influence on knowledge sharing on social media (Hakami et al., 2014). Academics generally tend to place a higher priority on individual scholarly achievement (Kim & Ju, 2008), and so fears that one's intellectual property might be appropriated or stolen when put out on social media, is one technology reason that discourages copious knowledge sharing (Cheng et al., 2009).

Organizational Culture and Practices

According to McLaughlin (2016);

Organizational culture is a system of shared assumptions, values, and beliefs, which governs how people behave in organizations. These shared values have a strong influence on the people in the organization and dictate how they dress, act, and perform their jobs. Every organization develops and maintains a unique culture, which provides guidelines and boundaries for the behavior of the members of the organization (para. 5).

As discussed previously, higher education institutions, by virtue of their core mandates of producing and disseminating knowledge, are expected to provide the right climate and cultural contexts for the free sharing of knowledge, particularly among the academics (Ramayah, et. al., 2013). Additionally, universities are now operating in a competitive environment, and are therefore striving to increase their performance and visibility both locally and globally. With knowledge production and sharing being one way of achieving these objectives, it is only natural that they will be creating the right the cultural climate to foster knowledge sharing. In this regard, some empirical research works have established the following:

- The more academicians feel they are within a culture that pressures them to share knowledge, the higher there is the tendency for them to do so (Ramayah, et. al., 2013). Indeed, the adage "publish or perish" emanates from this culture of pressurizing academics to generate and disseminate knowledge effectively to users of the knowledge, the absence of which their positions will be untenable.

- A strong feeling of affiliation (i.e. togetherness or closeness), encourages members within an organisation to help each other by sharing knowledge (Goh & Sandhu, 2013). Organisations can foster a climate of affiliation by encouraging employees to develop a sense of care and empathy for each other, particularly during times of need. Such a climate encourages employees to go beyond their responsibility to help each other in the organization (Bock & Kim, 2002), and in the case of academia, share knowledge with the view to helping improve individual and organisational performance.

- Knowledge sharing among academics flourishes when institutions actively promote and support these activities (Hakami et al., 2014). Such institutions occasionally train staff on the importance and usefulness of social media as a tool for knowledge sharing, and even reward staff members who are seen to be actively engaging in it.

- Institutions that exhibit a culture of collective cognitive responsibility, i.e. create environments where efforts are being made by all members to secure group rather than individual success, tend to experience improved knowledge sharing behaviours. In such contexts, individuals not only take responsibility for knowing what needs to be known, but also ensure that others know what needs to be known through effective knowledge sharing (Scardamalia, 2002)

Summary

A review of the literature pertaining to the use of social media for knowledge sharing by academicians in higher education institutions reveals a plethora of individual and institutional factors that can potentially impact this phenomenon either positively or negatively. The findings, though numerous, are however not easily generalizable, due to the peculiarity of most of the cases studied, and particularly as all these studies pertain to situations in the developed world, or in some cases, the more endowed developing countries, notably Malaysia. It is therefore imperative that such studies be extended to the least developed parts of the world where access to Internet services can be quite a challenge.

THEORETICAL PERSPECTIVE

According to Schutt (2006), social exploratory research seeks to find out how people get along in particular settings, what meanings they give to their actions, what issues concern them, and so forth: "The goal is to learn 'what is going on here?' and to investigate social phenomena without explicit expectations" (p. 12). Exploratory research thus fits with Grounded Theory, the basic tenet of which is that a theory must emerge from (or be grounded in) the data (Glaser & Strauss, 1967). Grounded theory is mostly an inductive approach, which means the researcher does not begin with a hypothesis about the phenomenon to be studied, but instead remains open to whatever theory emerges from the data (Glaser & Strauss, 1967; Strauss & Corbin, 1990).

Grounded theory thus emphasizes the use of "real world" data and a systematic set of procedures to develop a theory about a phenomenon, rather than deductively generating theories in abstraction. The intent of this approach is to develop an account of a phenomenon that identifies the major constructs, or categories, their relationships, and the context and process, thus providing a theory of the phenomenon that is much more than a descriptive account (Becker, 1993). Table 3 summarises some of the common Grounded Theory methods.

Given that the phenomenon of knowledge sharing via social media by academics within higher education institutions remain largely unexplored, particularly within the Sub-Saharan African context, this study adopted a grounded theory approach to gathering and analysing data. Thus, working within a context of no preconceived hypotheses or conceptual frameworks, this study hoped to acquire new insights into the phenomenon in order to formulate a more precise problem or to develop some hypotheses

Table 3. Grounded Theory Methods (Adapted from Silerman, 2006)

Step	Processes
1	Try to generate theories through data rather than through prior hypotheses
2	Code data line by line to show action and process
3	Raise significant codes into analytic categories for purposes of comparison through three methods: open coding (the preliminary process of breaking down, examining, comparing, conceptualizing and categorizing data), axial coding (putting data back together in new ways after open coding by making connections between categories); and selective coding (selecting the core category, systematically relating it to other categories, and filling in categories that need further refinement and development.
4	Check and fill out categories through theoretical sampling and integrate categories into a theoretical framework
5	Develop these categories into more general analytic frameworks with relevance outside the setting (formal theories)

METHODOLOGY

Study Context and Participants

The institution involved in this study is a Ghanaian University College that offers programs leading to the award of undergraduate and postgraduate degrees in mostly the sciences and business fields. Established in August 2006, the college grew rapidly over the last 10 years, and presently has a student population of over six thousand (6,000), and an instructor population of about one hundred and twenty (120). The college's vision is to be a center of academic excellence providing training in technology oriented education to meet the needs of Ghana and the sub-region whilst its mission includes promoting relevant cutting-edge technologies to enhance education delivery. The school thus prides itself as being in the forefront of harnessing the affordances of Information & Communications Technologies (ICTs) for effective education delivery and research, and has been living up to this mantra since its inception.

As a technology oriented higher education institution therefore, it will not be farfetched to presume that its academic staff members will probably be more technology oriented. It is with this understanding that this study focused on the instructors who thus constituted the population of the study

Data Collection

Two research methods were used in the study; (i) survey, based on the general understanding that it is the most popular research method for obtaining data on behaviours, interests and opinions shared by people (Engel & Schutt, 2005), and (ii) focus group discussions, since this is a fast and efficient way of gaining further information and deeper insights into attitudes, opinions and behaviours of research participants (Krueger, 1988). The university's internal review board reviewed and approved the data collection methods prior to their use in the study.

Survey

As an exploratory study that sought to answer some specific questions, the survey questionnaire was designed along the lines of the research questions and some of the findings enumerated in the literature review. It was thus not based on any theoretical framework or standard practice etc. The questionnaire was divided into two parts - Section A comprising questions eliciting demographic characteristics of respondents, and Section B comprising questions designed to obtain data on instructor use of social media, their views on the significance of knowledge sharing, how frequently they use social media for knowledge sharing activities, and what they consider to be the critical factors facilitating or hindering their knowledge sharing activities. A five point Likert scale was mostly used in this section, and respondents were required to state the extent to which they agreed or disagreed with the statements in the questionnaire.

The questionnaire was reviewed by a university faculty member with expertise in survey data analysis and then tested among 10 instructors who were randomly approached on the school's campus and asked to help in the test. A few modifications were made resulting in a final questionnaire which was administered online using the QuestionPro online survey tool (http://www.questionpro.com). Using the university's mailing list of instructors, an email was first sent to all one hundred and twenty six (126) full-time instructors a week prior, informing them of the impending survey and its purpose. Subsequently, a link to the online survey was sent to all instructors, again by email, informing them of the availability of the survey, and also imploring them to complete it as objectively and sincerely as they could. The survey was active for two weeks, and so a reminder was sent a week later, and again a day to the deadline which was June 30, 2016. Forty seven (47) responses were received by the deadline - a return rate of 37%. Responses were anonymous.

Focus Group Discussion

Following the survey, the researcher again sent an email to all instructors appealing to them to volunteer and participate in a one hour group discussion on the research topic. The research questions were attached to the email. On the given date and time, seven (7) instructors turned up and all participated in the hour-long discussion. The researcher moderated the discussions which centred mainly on the research questions. At the end of the discussion, one person orally presented the groups' consensus on the issues. The researcher recorded the presentation which lasted for about 10 minutes.

Data Analysis

The research methods adopted yielded numerical and textual data. The QuestionPro software produced descriptive results of the responses to the survey questions. At a confidence interval of 95%, the system reported means and standard deviations of all responses to each question. Some of these data were inputted into Microsoft Excel, sorted and displayed graphically for easy visualization of the comparisons. The textual responses to the open-ended questions in the survey, as well as those in the transcript from the focus group discussion were analysed using traditional grounded theory coding techniques as outlined by Strauss and Corbin (1990). Coding involved examining the textual data line by line to identify key issues (codes). Codes were then grouped inductively to construct categories, which were given unique names.

Findings of numerical and textual data were integrated using a contiguous staged narrative approach (Fetters, Curry, & Creswell, 2013). In this approach, numerical findings are first presented, followed by textual responses, with categories and themes interwoven in the discussion. This is to give a holistic and comprehensive understanding of the issue being explored.

DISCUSSION OF RESULTS

Participant Demographics

Table 1 above displays the demographic information of respondents to the survey questionnaire. The male to female ration of respondents is about 7:1, which is fairly representative of the university's instructor population which stands at an 8:1 male: female ratio. Likewise, majority of respondents are in the 30 - 49 year age group, and most hold the position of a lecturer, a reflection of the young nature of the university which is just 10 years. Another instructor attribute that was relevant to the study was what instructors considered to be their level of proficiency with regard to the use of technology. Majority chose the intermediate level, which meant they

Table 4. Participant Demographics (N=47)

Respondent Profile	Classification	Frequency
Gender	Male	41
	Female	6
Age Group (years)	Below 30	2
	30 - 39	23
	40 - 49	18
	50 - 59	4
	60 and above	0
Proficiency in Technology	Beginner	0
	Intermediate	29
	Expert	18
Position	Lecturer	45
	Senior Lecturer	2
	Associate Professor	0

were capable of using most hardware and software, accessing and using Internet based applications, creating, storing and sharing digital content etc. Those in the expert category were the computer scientists and information technologists. As no instructor chose the beginner category, the study proceeded on the understanding that all research participants had the ability to use social media for knowledge sharing purposes.

Instructor Use of Social Media

The first research question sought to determine the social media tools that instructors typically use in their academic and other social activities. The questionnaire thus provided a list of twenty (20) of the most popular social media applications (excluding the popular Chinese sites) as ranked by http://wearesocial.com (2016). Respondents were required to indicate whether or not they use these tools on a regular basis, i.e. at least once a day. Figure 1 below summarises the responses

As Figure. 1 shows, all respondents indicated that they regularly use Facebook and WhatsApp. Other popular social media among respondents were Twitter, Facebook Messenger, Skype, LinkedIn and Instagram, with over 50% of respondents indicating that they regularly use these. These findings are not surprising given that majority of the instructors are fairly young, and are also working in a technology oriented university. During the focus group discussion, participants were asked whether the finding that Facebook and WhatsApp enjoyed 100% usage among instructors was valid, to which the response was in the affirmative. It was also emphasized during

Figure 1. Use of the Various Social Media Applications by Respondents

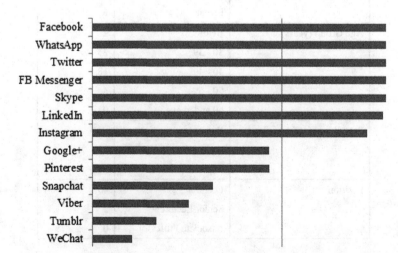

the focus group discussion that email was another main vehicle that instructors use extensively, though it was not categorized as social media.

Instructor Views of What Constitutes Knowledge

A second objective of the study was to clearly establish what higher education instructors consider to be knowledge, particularly with regard to their sharing or collaborative activities on social media. An open ended question asked respondents to list what in their opinion constitutes knowledge that can be shared with others through social media. Responses to the questionnaire as well as information gleaned from the focus group discussion were quite varied. Reading through and categorising the responses revealed the following as constituting knowledge:

1. Lecture notes.
2. PowerPoint slides.
3. Teaching and research strategies.
4. Research findings.
5. Computer code/program.
6. Institutional policies, regulations, structure, processes etc.
7. Information on latest happenings in one's field.
8. Administrative experience.
9. Other skills such as negotiation, people management, teamwork etc.

Participants in the focus group discussion were however quick to point out the fact that it is only the kind of knowledge that can be rendered as digital artifacts (text, audio, graphics and video) that can be effectively shared through social media, and that most of the knowledge required by instructors to survive and succeed in academia cannot be easily transferred through social media. As discussed previously, this finding only affirms the general understanding that whilst explicit knowledge can easily be transferred, tacit knowledge can only be transferred through shared experiences.

Instructor Perceptions of Knowledge Sharing

A third objective of the study was to assess the degree to which instructors considered knowledge sharing to be critical for their individual and collective development. A five point Likert scale requiring respondents to state the extent to which they agreed or disagreed with some statements was used. As Table 5 shows, no respondent disagreed with the statements stated in the questionnaire.

Table 5. Instructor perceptions of knowledge sharing (N=47)

Statement	SD	D	N	A	SA
Knowledge sharing is critical for my individual success	-	-	-	12 (26%)	35 (74%)
Knowledge sharing among instructors is critical for the growth and reputation of the university	-	-	-	5 (11%)	42 (89%)

All respondents were therefore of the view that knowledge sharing among instructors is an important contributor to their success as well as that of the institution. A curious finding however was that more respondents (89%) strongly agreed that knowledge sharing was critical for the growth and reputation of the university, as against 74% who strongly agreed that knowledge sharing was critical for their individual success. The focus group discussion however brought up a suggestion that some instructors might be of the opinion that sharing will mean they are sacrificing their individual intellectual property which can be used for their personal development, for institutional progress, particularly as most are still young and developing their careers.

Instructor Use of Social Media for Knowledge Sharing

The fourth research question sought to ascertain the frequency of use of social media for knowledge sharing by instructors. Respondents to the questionnaire were required to make a single choice of whether they shared knowledge on social media daily, about twice a week, occasionally, rarely or never. The results are shown in Figure 2.

Figure 2. Frequency of instructor use of social media for knowledge sharing

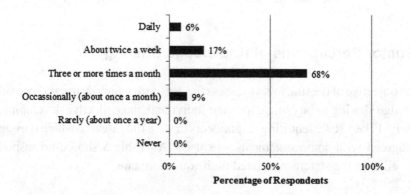

The findings displayed in Figure. 2 can be interpreted to mean that most instructors tend to share knowledge on social media platforms on a regular, though not daily, basis. Another finding that is worthy of note is that none of the respondents indicated that they either rarely, or never use social media for knowledge sharing purposes. The focus group discussion corroborated the findings when the presenter stated the following:

Most of us tend to share knowledge on a regular basis because we collaborate to work on research projects, publications and conference presentations. Social media therefore comes in handy as we cannot meet on regular basis, but can use a platform like Google Drive to co-create documents. For others such as Facebook and WhatsApp, we all use them on a daily basis, but mostly for social networking purposes rather than for academic purposes. Occasionally one might come across something on these platforms that they think will be relevant to colleagues, and so they pass it on.

One thing we also discussed and agreed on is that most knowledge sharing among instructors is on a one-to-one basis, and mostly involves using email to request and receive content. Though social media is an effective tool when one is on the move, the fact that email is also enabled on mobile devices, and even alerts users when mail arrives, means that it will be more preferable for such one-to-one interactions.

Factors That Enhance or Hinder Knowledge Sharing via Social Media

The final research question sought to explore what instructors consider to be the main factors enhancing or hindering their ability and willingness to use social media for knowledge sharing. This was thus an open-ended asking respondents to write down their opinions on the issue. The focus group discussion also dwelt extensively on the issue. Twenty four (24) of the forty seven (47) respondents wrote comments in answer to this question. These responses together with the transcribed text from the focus group presentation were subjected to relational content analysis in line with grounded theory techniques. This involved first reading line by line to decipher and categorize any emerging patterns which were then grouped into broader categories and represented by a word or phrase. The findings are summarised below.

Enhancing Factors

1. **Ubiquitous Nature of Social Media:** Since instructors move around with mobile devices, it is easy for them to quickly send or receive information anytime and anyplace.

2. **The Open Access Paradigm:** *Open* access to academic literature means "it is freely available and permits any user to read, download, copy, distribute, print, search, or link to the full texts of these articles, crawl them for indexing, pass them as data to software, or use them for any other lawful purpose, without financial, legal, or technical barriers..." (Budapest Open Access Initiative, 2016, para. 3). This free availability of high quality academic literature on the Internet was identified by instructors as a phenomenon that also encourages knowledge sharing. As one instructor noted:

   a. I for one, I browse open access repositories a lot, and any time I find relevant content, I bookmark the link and sometimes share with people I feel will benefit from...

3. **The Need to Help Colleagues Keep up With Current Knowledge:** Instructors who come across trending issues, particularly in their academic fields, are always willing to share with others as quickly as possible, and social media becomes the preferred vehicle. Obviously instructors who share new knowledge also expect to benefit from their colleagues' new knowledge at a future date.

4. **The Need to Get Some Work Done:** Instructors who work in teams on research or study projects tend to readily share new knowledge so as to get the work done.

5. **The Need to Respond to Some Specific Requests:** Instructors occasionally ask colleagues for one form of assistance or the other with regard to the academic pursuits. Recipients of such requests who are able to assist most often use social media to honor such requests.

6. **Peer Review of Academic Work:** Most academics do not hesitate to assist their colleagues enhance their scholarly output and academic careers by reviewing their works and giving feedback. Social media thus becomes the ideal platform for such interactions.

7. **A Feeling of Satisfaction for Helping Address Colleagues' Concerns, Requests etc.:** Instructors who are dedicated to their work are always willing to help others succeed. Thus, by sharing knowledge that will benefit a colleague, they gain some satisfaction. Such academics always have the urge to respond to their colleagues' requests in a timely manner, hence the use of social media.

Hindering Factors

1. **Lack of Institutional Support:** There is no policy or practice framework within the institution that encourages instructors to share either academic or organisational knowledge. Most knowledge sharing thus happens on a voluntary basis.

2. **High Internet Cost:** As social media applications ride on the Internet, accessing and using them requires a live Internet connection and at appreciable speed. Instructors typically subscribe to Internet data services provided by the various telecom operators in the country. Unlike in the developed countries where Internet is cheaply (and sometimes freely) available, most developing countries still have to contend with high Internet costs, sometimes compounded with power outages etc. This situation tends to dampen motivation for using social media extensively for knowledge sharing.

3. **Reluctance on the Part of Most Instructors to Share Knowledge:** Probably by virtue of their training in a school system that encouraged competition and individual work, some instructors tend to hoard knowledge. Thus when they create or acquire knowledge through their individual efforts, they are reluctant to share it for fear of losing the status of being the sole repository of such critical knowledge that might pay some future dividends.

4. **Face-to-Face Meetings:** Academics spend several hours each week attending meetings, workshops, lectures etc., where the opportunity exists for them to interact and share ideas. Consequently, the use of social media for knowledge sharing purposes will be an exception rather than the norm.

IMPLICATION OF FINDINGS

The foregoing discussion has first, established what instructors in a typical Ghanaian university consider to be knowledge in the academic sense, and second, how these instructors use social media to share such knowledge for both individual and institutional benefit. Universities are expected to be places where knowledge is shared freely (Ramayah et al., 2013), and given that social media provide suitable platforms for such knowledge sharing, it is anticipated that academics will be using these resources enthusiastically to share knowledge. This has however been proven not to be entirely the case as the instructors in this study, though extensive users of social media, do not quite use these technologies in similar ways when it comes to sharing their academic knowledge. This is quite understandable given that though there are several factors that motivate the sharing of knowledge, there are equally several factors that tend to dampen instructors' enthusiasm to share knowledge.

Interestingly, whilst instructors identify their personal attributes and capabilities as being the factors that mostly enhance their use of social media for knowledge sharing, they see the lack of institutional support as one significant barrier. This is however not surprising, as these instructors expressed the feeling that the institution stands to benefit more from their knowledge sharing activities than they benefit as individuals. The onus thus lies on institutions of higher learning to implement strategies that will encourage instructors to freely share knowledge. Such strategies might include:

1. Providing instructors with reliable, and possibly, free wireless Internet access on campus.
2. Offering monetary and other non-monetary rewards to instructors who are seen to be actively engaging in academic knowledge sharing.
3. Encouraging and supporting instructors to publish their academic and research works in open institutional repositories where such knowledge can be easily accessed and shared.
4. Ensuring that academicians benefit from their intellectual property by providing the appropriate protective legal frameworks and services. In so doing, academics will have the confidence and trust to share knowledge, knowing that their intellectual capital is protected from appropriation by colleagues or external entities.
5. Sensitizing instructors on the potential benefits of their knowledge to the wider society, given the fact that one of the core mandates of institutions of higher learning is community service.
6. Including knowledge sharing in the job appraisals of instructors.
7. Creating a conducive work place culture that builds trust, welcomes new ideas, encourages constructive criticisms, and fosters mutual social exchange relationships among instructors.

LIMITATIONS AND FUTURE RESEARCH

The study has some limitations which are attributable to the following issues and assumptions:

1. First, the research was limited to a single institution, and this institution happens to ran technology biased programs. It is therefore possible that the instructors in the institution will not be a fair representation of the instructor population of Ghanaian higher education institutions. Consequently, the findings of the

study may be prone to the threat of a single-source bias, and can therefore not be easily generalized to the entire Ghanaian context.

2. The response rate was quite low (37%) as this was an online survey, though the respondents were demographically a fair representation of instructors of the University. Even though the survey findings were triangulated with focus group discussion, the results must be interpreted with caution as it is possible that those who voluntarily and enthusiastically participated in the research are the "technophiles" or social media enthusiasts.

3. As this was an exploratory study, it did not consider the influence on possible moderator variables on instructors' perceptions, beliefs and attitudes towards using social media for knowledge sharing.

4. To increase the generalizability of the findings, future research could involve different institutions. Also study participants should be randomly sampled to ensure that all categories of instructors, i.e. the technophobes and the technophiles are fairly represented.

5. This study only relied on participants' self-reported activities and perceptions, which cannot be objectively verified. Future studies can therefore also consider obtaining more objective data such as transaction logs of user activities on specific social media platforms. This will provide objective data on how users are actually sharing knowledge, and also the types of knowledge that is typically shared by instructors.

CONCLUSION

Institutions of higher learning are the ideal places for, not only creating knowledge, but freely sharing such knowledge for the benefit of the wider society. Studies however suggest that most academics do not spontaneously share knowledge as expected, but will likely do so only if the right facilitating resources and conditions are in place. For its dynamism, interaction, collaboration, participation and trusting environment (Usoro, 2013), social media has been determined to be the singular avenue that can provide the appropriate resources and facilitating conditions for knowledge sharing practices. Exploring this phenomenon in an academic institution of higher learning, this study found uncovered, as with the case of a few other studies, a plethora of factors that can possibly impact on the use of social media for effective knowledge sharing among instructors of the institution.

Such factors are directly related to the individual, the social media technologies and the institutional work culture and environment. Though it is understandable that knowledge sharing is the ultimate responsibility of the each individual, it is the environment within which such individuals operate that contributes greatly in either fostering or hindering their knowledge sharing tendencies and behaviours. As academics mostly operate within the higher education institutional setting, a greater responsibility lies with these institutions to create the enabling environments for effective and efficient knowledge sharing. Further studies on this phenomenon should therefore be looking at contributing towards evolving best practice frameworks for enhancing knowledge sharing for the benefit of the individual academics, the institutions and society at large.

REFERENCES

Ajzen, I. (1991). The theory of planned behavior. *Organizational Behavior and Human Decision Processes*, *50*(2), 179–211. doi:10.1016/0749-5978(91)90020-T

Becker, P. H. (1993). Common pitfalls in published grounded theory research. *Qualitative Health Research*, *3*(2), 254–260. doi:10.1177/104973239300300207

Behringer, N., & Sassenberg, K. (2015). Introducing social media for knowledge management: Determinants of employees intentions to adopt new tools. *Computers in Human Behavior*, *48*, 290–296. doi:10.1016/j.chb.2015.01.069

Bock, G. W., Zmud, R., Kim, Y. G., & Lee, J. N. (2005). Behavioral intention formation in knowledge sharing: Examining the roles of extrinsic motivators, social-psychological forces, and organizational climate. *Management Information Systems Quarterly*, *29*(1), 87–111.

Brown, A. L. (1988). Motivation to learn and understand: On taking charge of ones own learning. *Cognition and Instruction*, *5*(4), 311–321. doi:10.1207/s1532690xci0504_4

Budapest Open Access Initiative. (2016). *Read the Budapest open access initiative.* Retrieved October 10, 2016, from http://www.budapestopenaccessinitiative.org/read

BusinessDictionary.com. (2016). *Tacit knowledge.* Retrieved September 30, 2016, from http://www.businessdictionary.com/definition/tacit-knowledge.html

Cheng, M. Y., Ho, J. S. Y., & Lau, P. M. (2009). Knowledge sharing in academic institutions: A study of Multimedia University Malaysia. *Electronic Journal of Knowledge Management*, *7*(3), 313–324.

Christensen, P. H. (2007). Knowledge sharing: Moving away from the obsession with best practices. *Journal of Knowledge Management*, *11*(1), 36–47. doi:10.1108/13673270710728222

Cummings, J. (2003). *Knowledge sharing: A review of the literature.* Washington, DC: The World Bank.

Davenport, T., & Prusak, L. (2000). *Working knowledge: How organizations manage what they know.* Boston, MA: Havard Business School Press.

DiGangi, P. M., & Wasko, M. (2016). Social media engagement theory: Exploring the influence of user engagement on social media usage. *Journal of Organizational and End User Computing, 28*(2), 53–73. doi:10.4018/JOEUC.2016040104

Engel, R. J., & Schutt, R. K. (2005). *The practice of research in social work.* Thousand Oaks, CA: Sage Publications.

Fetters, M. D., Curry, L. A., & Creswell, J. W. (2013). Achieving integration in mixed methods design principles and practices. *Health Services Research, 48*(6.2), 2134-2156.

Glaser, B. G., & Strauss, A. L. (1967). *The discovery of grounded theory.* Chicago, IL: Aldine Pub. Co.

Goh, S. K., & Sandhu, M. S. (2013). Knowledge sharing among Malaysian academics: Influence of affective commitment and trust. *Electronic Journal of Knowledge Management, 11*(1), 38–48.

GSM Association. (2015). *The mobile economy.* Retrieved October 1, 2016, from http://www.gsmamobileeconomy.com/GSMA_Global_Mobile_Economy_Report_2015.pdf

Hakami, Y., Tam, S., Busalim, A. H., & Husin, A. R. C. (2014). A review of factors affecting the sharing of knowledge in social media. *Science International, 26*(2), 679–688.

Hassandoust, F., & Perumal, V. (2011). Online knowledge sharing in institutes of higher learning: A Malaysian perspective. *Journal of Knowledge Management Practice, 12*(1). Retrieved October 1, 2016, from http://www.tlainc.com/articl247.htm

Hislop, D. (2013). *Knowledge management in organisations: A critical introduction.* Oxford, UK: Oxford University Press.

Hyman, P. (2012). In the year of disruptive education. *Communications of the ACM, 55*(12), 20–22. doi:10.1145/2380656.2380664

Jasimuddin, S. M., & Zhang, Z. (2014). Knowledge management strategy and organizational culture. *The Journal of the Operational Research Society*, *65*(10), 1490–1500. doi:10.1057/jors.2013.101

Kim, S., & Ju, B. (2008). An analysis of faculty perceptions: Attitudes toward knowledge sharing and collaboration in an academic institution. *Library & Information Science Research*, *30*(4), 282–290. doi:10.1016/j.lisr.2008.04.003

King, W. R. (2009). Knowledge management and organizational learning. In W. R. King (Ed.), Knowledge Management and Organizational Learning (pp. 3-13). Annals of Information Systems.

Krueger, R. A. (1988). *Focus groups: A practical guide for applied research.* Newbury Park, CA: Sage Publications Inc.

Lichy, J., & Kachour, M. (2016). Understanding how students interact with technology for knowledge-sharing: The emergence of a new social divide in France. *International Journal of Technology and Human Interaction*, *12*(1), 83–104. doi:10.4018/IJTHI.2016010106

Lin, J., Hung, S., & Chen, C. (2009). Fostering the determinants of knowledge sharing in professional virtual communities. *Computers in Human Behavior*, *25*(4), 929–939. doi:10.1016/j.chb.2009.03.008

Marshall, C., & Rossman, G. B. (2006). *Designing qualitative research* (4th ed.). Thousand Oaks, CA: Sage Publications Inc.

Mayer, R. C., Davis, J. H., & Schoorman, F. D. (1995). An integrative model of organisational trust. *Academy of Management Review*, *20*(3), 709–734.

McLaughlin, J. (2016). What is organizational culture? Definition & characteristics. *Business 107: Organizational Behavior.* Retrieved September 28, 2016, from http://study.com/academy/lesson/what-is-organizational-culture-definition-characteristics.html#transcriptHeader

Miller, P. (1998). *Mobilising the power of what you know.* London: Random House.

Norberg, A., Dziuban, C. D., & Moskal, P. D. (2011). A time-based blended learning model. *On the Horizon*, *19*(3), 207–216. doi:10.1108/10748121111163913

Obar, J. A., & Wildman, S. (2015). Social media definition and the governance challenge: An introduction to the special issue. *Telecommunications Policy*, *39*(9), 745–750. doi:10.1016/j.telpol.2015.07.014

Oxforddictionaries.com. (2016). *Definition of knowledge in English*. Retrieved October 10, 2016, from http://www.oxforddictionaries.com/definition/english/knowledge

Panahi, S., Watson, J., & Partridge, H. (2012). Social media and tacit knowledge sharing: Developing a conceptual model. *World Academy of Science, Engineering and Technology, 64*, 1095-1102.

Perrin, A. (2015). Social media usage: 2005 - 2015. *PewResearchCenter: Internet, Science & Tech*. Retrieved October 10, 2016,from http://www.pewinternet.org/2015/10/08/social-networking-usage-2005-2015/

Powell, A., Piccoli, G., & Ives, B. (2004). Virtual teams: A review of current literature and directions for future research. *ACM SIG MIS Database, 35*(1), 6–36. doi:10.1145/968464.968467

Ramayah, T., Yeap, J. A. L., & Ignatius, J. (2013). An empirical inquiry on knowledge sharing among academicians in higher learning institutions. *Minerva: A Review of Science, Learning and Policy, 51*(2), 131–154.

Ridzuan, A. A., Sam, H. K., & Adanan, M. A. (2008). Knowledge management practices in higher learning institutions in Sarạwak. *Asian Journal of University Education, 4*(1), 69–89.

Scardamalia, M. (2002). Collective cognitive responsibility for the advancement of knowledge. In B. Smith (Ed.), *Liberal education in a knowledge society* (pp. 67–98). Chicago, IL: Open Court.

Schutt, R. K. (2006). *Investigating the social world: The process and practice of research*. Thousand Oaks, CA: Sage.

Seonghee, K., & Boryung, J. (2008). An analysis of faculty pereceptions: Attitudes toward knowledge sharing and collaboration in an academic institution. *Library & Information Science Research, 30*(4), 282–290. doi:10.1016/j.lisr.2008.04.003

Silerman, D. (2006). *Interpreting qualitative data* (3rd ed.). Thousand Oaks, CA: Sage Publications.

Smartinsights.com. (2016). *Global social media research summary*. Retrieved October 11, 2016,from http://www.smartinsights.com/social-media-marketing/social-media-strategy/new-global-social-media-research/

Sohail, M. S., & Daud, S. (2009). Knowledge sharing in higher education institutions: Perspectives from Malaysia. *VINE: The Journal of Information and Knowledge Management Systems, 39*(2), 125-142.

Strauss, A., & Corbin, J. (1990). *Basics of qualitative research: Grounded theory procedures and techniques.* Newbury Park, CA: Sage Publications.

Syed-Ihksan, S. O. S., & Rowland, R. (2004). Knowledge management in a public organization: A study on the relationship between organizational elements and the performance of knowledge transfer. *Journal of Knowledge Management, 8*(2), 95–111. doi:10.1108/13673270410529145

Usoro, A. (2013). Social media for knowledge sharing in African development institutions: A viewpoint paper. *Computing and Information Systems, 17*(1), 28–30.

Van-den-Hooff, B., & De-Ridder, J. A. (2004). Knowledge sharing in context: The influence of organizational commitment, communication climate and CMC use on knowledge sharing. *Journal of Knowledge Management, 8*(6), 117–130. doi:10.1108/13673270410567675

Vuori, V. (2011). *Social media changing the competitive intelligence process: Elicitation of employees' competitive knowledge.* Tampere University of Technology. Retrieved October 10, 2016, from http://dspace.cc.tut.fi/dpub/bitstream/handle/123456789/20724/vuori.pdf

wearesocial.com. (2016). *Digital in 2016.* Retrieved October 10, 2016, from http://wearesocial.com/uk/special-reports/digital-in-2016

Yang, J. (2007). The impact of knowledge sharing on organizational learning and effectiveness. *Journal of Knowledge Management, 11*(2), 83–90. doi:10.1108/13673270710738933

Yang, J.-T. (2004). Job-related knowledge sharing: Comparative case studies. *Journal of Knowledge Management, 8*(3), 118–126. doi:10.1108/13673270410541088

KEY TERMS AND DEFINITIONS

Academia: A community of academics (or academicians), typically teachers, researchers and auxiliary staff who work on producing and disseminating knowledge for the benefit of society.

Exploratory Research: A research approach aimed at gaining insights into a phenomenon, and also identifying issues that merit further research.

Focus Group: A qualitative research approach in which a group of select individuals are asked about the opinions, perceptions etc. towards the issue under study. Typical focus groups are given the opportunity to discuss the issue and come to a common understanding or agreement.

Grounded Theory: An inductive research methodology involving a set of research procedures that are conducted with the aim of generating conceptual categories, and subsequently the emergence of a theory. In short, a theory grounded in research data.

Higher Education: Also known as post-secondary or tertiary education, this represents the final level of formal learning, and often delivered in institutions known as universities, colleges, advanced professional institutes etc.

Higher Education Instructors: Persons who teach in higher education institutions - often referred to as tutors, lecturers and professors.

Knowledge: Information, facts and skills the individuals or organisations acquire by virtue of education, experience and interactions with other individuals or organisations.

Knowledge Sharing: The act of reciprocally transferring knowledge between individuals for the mutual benefit of both.

Social Media: Internet and Web based technologies that allow users to create and share information, build relationships and networks.

Chapter 7

Social Media and Social Networking:
The Present and Future Directions

Ahmed Elazab
Cairo University, Egypt

Mahmood A. Mahmood
Cairo University, Egypt

Hesham Ahmed Hefny
Cairo University, Egypt

ABSTRACT

Social media is a powerful communication tool that facilitates the interaction and provide an efficient interconnection among different roles in many fields such as business and media. The power of social media forced its responsibility for the vast dissemination of different information during real time events. Many social networks have emerged since the 90s; however, many of these networks have been abandon while the success of others in providing intelligent and active communication made them the most famous recently. Some examples of these successful social networks are Facebook, and Twitter. In this research, we provide the readers with the main concepts of social media and social networks, and their relation with other fields. We also discuss the current situation with providing the emerging trends and challenges of both fields.

DOI: 10.4018/978-1-5225-2897-5.ch007

INTRODUCTION

The internet has changed the way of communication forever, the way people buy things, work, and even socialize. Although some are convinced that internet decrease the communication level among people, however, others think totally the opposite in the presence of many electronic communication methods such as social media. Social media plays a vital role in all online aspects now, including personal communication, business, economic, it even affects political aspects seriously. In Canada, a study considered the impact of social media has found a raise of the economic level from 1.9% in 2011 to be 3.8% in 2012 (Industry Canada, 2012). In business field, social media effect is increasing tremendously, many businesses now are getting benefits from people's opinions to raise the level of their products and services, which is considered one of basis in their growth. For example, the Public Health Agency of Canada" has been using social media to provide valuable information considering the public health with demonstrating the threats and suggesting health plans.

The idea of Social Media is top of the plan for some business officials today. Chiefs, and in addition advisors, attempt to recognize routes in which firms can make beneficial utilization of uses, for example, Wikipedia, YouTube, Facebook, Second Life, and Twitter. However in spite of this enthusiasm, there is by all accounts exceptionally restricted comprehension of what the term ''Social Media'' precisely implies; this article plans to give some elucidation. Kaplan and Haenlein (2010), start by depicting the idea of Social Media, and talk about how it varies from related ideas, for example, Web 2.0 and User Created Content. In light of this definition, Kaplan and Haenlein then give a characterization of Social Media which bunches applications as of now subsumed under the summed up term into more particular classes by trademark: collective tasks, online journals, content groups, interpersonal interaction locales, virtual diversion universes, and virtual social universes. At long last, they display 10 recommendations for organizations which choose to use Social Media (Kaplan & Haenlein, 2010)

With the rapid evolution of content and communication styles in social media, this emerging media has become a powerful communication channel, as evidenced by many recent events like "Egyptian Revolution" and the "Tohoku earthquake and tsunami. Text is changing too. Different from traditional textual data, the text in social media is not independent and identically distributed data anymore. A comment or post may reflect the user's interest, and a user is connected and influenced by his friends. Based on internet users' feelings that were measured from their texts, (Hu & Liu, 2012) was able to investigate their political opinion as well as their confidence.

Kuan-Yu Lin applies arrange externalities and inspiration hypothesis to disclose why individuals keep on joining SNS. This review utilized an online survey to lead exact research, and gathered and investigated information of 402 specimens by auxiliary condition displaying (SEM) approach. The discoveries demonstrate that delight is the most compelling component in individuals' proceeded with utilization of SNS, trailed by number of associates, and convenience. The quantity of companions and saw complementarity have more grounded impact than the quantity of individuals on saw benefits (convenience and happiness). This work additionally ran grouping examination by sexual orientation, which discovered striking contrast in both number of associates and number of individuals amongst men and ladies. The quantity of companions is an imperative component influencing the proceeded with goal to use for ladies yet not for men; the quantity of individuals has no noteworthy impact on delight for men. The discoveries recommend that sexual orientation contrast likewise delivers diverse impacts. The ramifications of research and exchanges gives reference to SNS administrators in advertising and operation (Lin & Lu, 2011).

However, sharing this amount of personal information may have its consequences, as a person may be involved in a situation as a result of posting inappropriate post, or he may receive incorrect information about himself which is posted from others. For example, Facebook gives the user the ability to restrict friends or set page viewing, however, the subject of privacy still an issue in social media. Other problems arise in social media, claiming to be another person is one of the main issues, a person may create a Facebook page claiming to be someone else, using his photos and other known personal information which may cause a lot of problems to the original person. To conclude, we can claim that privacy is lost in social media even with the current status.

Social media web sites contain various types of services and thus create different formats of data, including text, image, video etc. For example, the media sharing sites Flickr and YouTube allow to observe what "ordinary" users do when given the ability to more readily incorporate images and video in their everyday activity. People engaged in the creation and sharing of their personal photography. As a result, a large amount of image and video data is archived in the sites. Besides, in blogging sites, the users post frequently and create a huge number of textual / text-based data; in social bookmarking sites, users share with each other tags and URLs.

The chapter presents the basic understanding of these analysis approaches with demonstrating different work performed by researchers on the aspect with the required enhancements for further development. This structure of the chapter is as follows: presents basic definitions for social media and social networking, a comparison between them. Also it provides the relation between the information extraction and social media, and then presents different information extraction approaches with focusing on the approaches applied in social media by presenting different work done in this research area. And the text analytics direction in social media is discussed with presenting the issues arise in this field in section 7, and finally the conclusion is discussed.

The main focus of this chapter is to provide an understanding of the basic concepts of social media. The chapter provides an understanding for different aspects related to social media, with presenting different directions for social media analysis.

BACKGROUND

Social media and social Networking are two paradigms that usually used for one another by users who do not actually understand the scientific concept that differentiate the two terms. In this section, we demonstrate the basic concepts of both social media and social networking.

Social Media

Social media is not a new concept, it has been evolving since the beginning of human interaction where the social media has transformed the interaction and communication of individuals throughout the world. However Hu and Liu (2012) defines social media as applying a set of online tools to support the efficient communication among users for sharing information and experiences (Hu & Liu, 2012). The social media sites play a very important role in current web applications. Social media such as blogs, microblogs, discussion forums and multimedia sharing sites are increasingly used for users to communicate breaking news, participate in events, and connect to each other anytime, from anywhere.

Benefits of Social Media

OSN acts as a powerful way to communicate also facilitate open forms of communication. Social media is best for many situations, the following are some examples:

On the level of employees, Social media enables employees to share project ideas and work in teams effectively, which helps in sharing knowledge and experiences, it also promotes open communication between employees and management. Also, it encourages supporting members, or part of the company's employees, to become members of a well-recognized community (Edosomwan, 2011).

On the level marketing, social media becomes a good place for discussions and a classic goal of marketing and communications, however, also OSN promotes better content, such as webcast and videos, than just simple text. OSN also helps to communicate collaboratively between current and new customers, in receiving feedback, product definition, product development, or any forms of customer service and support.

Social Media Platforms

Nowadays with the evolution of technology, supported by global and speedy communication network, online social media has been growing rapidly in the form of collaboratively created content which is presents new opportunities and challenges to both producers and consumers of information. With the large data presented by various social media services, text analytics provides an effective way to meet users' diverse information needs. There are many types of social media presented based on their category as shown on Table 1 (Treem & Leonardi, 2012).

In the Sensis Social media report (Social, 2015), and Social media update report Duggan and collegues (2015) which are conducted in 2015, a discussion for some of the most popular social networks is presented on Australia and American societies respectively. The first report showed that 93% of Australians access Facebook, 28% of them access LinkedIn, 26% for Instagram, 17% for Pinterest, and 17% for Twitter on the daily basis. While Americans have different statistics as 71% of American access Facebook, 28% of them access LinkedIn, 28% for Instagram, 26% for Pinterest, and 23% for Twitter on the daily basis. This comparison is presented graphically in Figure 1.

Table 1. Social Media Platforms (Treem & Leonardi, 2012)

Category	Representative Sites	URL
Wiki	Wikipedia, Scholarpedia	https://en.wikipedia.org/wiki/Main_Page http://www.scholarpedia.org/article/Main_Page
Blogging	Blogger, LiveJournal, WordPress	https://www.blogger.com http://www.livejournal.com/ https://ar.wordpress.org/
Social News	Digg, Mixx, Slashdot	http://digg.com/ http://www.mixxx.org/ http://slashdot.org/
Micro Blogging	Twitter	www.twitter.com
Opinion & Reviews	EPinions, Yelp	http://www.epinions.com/ http://www.yelp.com/
Question Answering	Yahoo! Answers, BaiduZhidao	https://answers.yahoo.com/ http://www.chinainternetwatch.com/tag/baidu-zhidao/
Media Sharing	Flickr ,Youtube	www.youtube.com https://www.flickr.com/
Social Bookmarking	Delicious, CiteULike	http://www.citeulike.org/ https://delicious.com/
Social Networking	Facebook, LinkedIn, MySpace	www.facebook.com https://www.linkedin.com https://myspace.com/

Figure 1. Comparison Among Social Media Platform

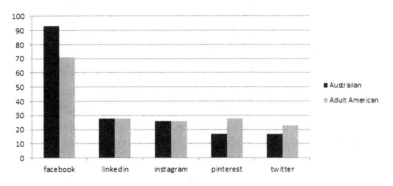

Moreover, in the American adult report (Duggan, et al., 2015), the study revealed that 42% of adult Americans usually use more than one social media sites in 2014, while this percentage increased in 2015 to be 52%.While for Australians, a different comparison is presented in the Sensis social media report (Social, 2015)as it is mentioned, that the percentage of the Australians who check social media daily was 41% in 2014 which increased in 2015 to be 45%. Senisi report (Social, 2015)focused on business field, it applied a study on 1,100 of businesses and 800 consumers, and this study revealed that social network is currently one of the essential methods that businesses depend on. Finally as shown in the Figure 1, it is clear that Facebook still has the lead for popularity in general in both report segments.

Social Networking

In the 1990s, many social networking sites appeared. The first well known OSN site, is called "Six Degrees". Other examples include "BlackPlanet, Asian Avenue, and MoveOn". These are, or have been, online socialsites where people can interact, including sites for public policy support and a social network based on a web of contacts model. In addition, blogging services such as "Blogger and Epinions" were created. "Epinions" is a site where opinions about products are submitted by different customers, these opinions support other consumers to have a near correct decision (Golbeck, 2005). In the 90s, the software applications named "Third Voice and Napster" (Edosomwan, 2011) were created but have been removed from the market. Third Voice was a free plug-in to allowed users which provided them with an access to post comments onWebPages. Napster was a software application that allowed peer-to-peer file sharing in which users were allowed to share music files bypassing normal distribution methods. However, in the end, this situation was determined to been violation of copyright laws (Edosomwan, 2011).

However, many social networks such as Yahoo 360, YouTube, and Facebook are introduced and are currently popularly used. Facebook was initiated only for the Harvard community, however, it became accessible by high school students in the year of 2005, then later in the 2007 the rapidly growth of Facebook was gained over 1 million new users every week (Ellison, 2007) Other method for interaction among people by "Yahoo! 360"which was a website launched by Yahoo! Inc., in which people could create a profile with photo albums and interact with other people with similar interests or get in contact with some of their friends like in any other social network. Another idea is "YouTube" which is provided and has currently a wide usage. The idea started when some of PayPal employees wanted to upload their videos, then they created the YouTube system (Rautio, 2012).

Social Media vs. Social Networking

In order to discriminate between the two terms, in this section, we will provide a short comparison between Social Media and Social Networks according to some determined criteria. As a start, Social Media can be defined as a strategy and an access for broadcasting, while Social Networking is a tool and a utility for connecting with others. The differences between the two terms are not only semantics but also

Table 2. Comparison between Social Media and Social Networking

Item	Social Media	Social Networking
Definition	A media which is mostly used to transfer or share information with a widely audience. (Treem & Leonardi, 2012).	An act of correlation as people with common interests associate together and build relationships through community (Cohen, 2009; Hartshorn, 2010).
Communication style	It is simply a system, a communication channel. It is not a location that you visit (Bedell, 2010).	A two-way communication method where conversations are at the essence, and through which relationships are developed. (Bedell, 2010; Digital Likeness,2008; Hartshorn,2010)
ROI (The return on investment)	Difficult to determine specific numbers for the ROI from social media, this situation is due to the difficulty of the ability to determine the time spent by the company in observing social media and compare this cost with the results gain. (Down, T. Y. T. U., 2010).	The return is clearly determined due to the ability to calculate the traffic rate in the social network which is one of the measure to determine if the social network is successful or not. (Hartshorn, 2010; Hoffman & Fodor, 2010; Wilfong, 2010)
Timely responses	Hard work, as it takes time in which individual conversations can't be automated. Moreover, it does not allow users to manipulate comments, correct errors or other data for personal or business benefit (Bedell, 2010; Cohen, 2009; Hartshorn, 2010; Nations, 2010; Stelzner, 2009).	Communicationis direct between the user and the people that he chooses to connect with people can write blogs or discuss any topic.

in the features and functions which is included in these websites by their creators, these features dictate the way they are designed and used. Moreover, the differences between social media and social networks are summarized as shown in Table 2.

MAIN FOCUS OF THE CHAPTER

Information Extraction From Social Media

In general, information extraction is a field that is concerned with obtaining information from different sources. Focusing on online sources such as online databases and web resources services including websites, according of the dynamic nature of the World Wide Web, it became important to find tools for information extraction from the web as end users and application programs have some difficulties when it comes to finding useful information (Alim, et al., 2011).

Extracting information from social media had applied different learning approaches as HTML is the common language for implementing Web pages and it is widely supported by The World Wide Web Consortium (W3C). HTML pages can be as a form of semi-structured data in which information follows a nested structure (Ferrara, et al., 2014). This section present different research that have been presented to apply different information extraction approaches on social media.

Generally the evolution of technology, supported by global and speedy communication network online Web services, has been growing rapidly which presents new opportunities and challenges to both producers and consumers of information. The volumes of click stream and client information, gathered by web-based associations in their everyday operations, have come to galactic extents. Analysis of such information helps these organizations to focus on the life-time estimation of customers (Mobasher, 2006).

Data mining technique that automatically discovers or extracts the information from web documents in general usually consists of following tasks (Srivastava, et al., 2005); (Bhisikar & Sahu, 2013).

- **Resource Finding:** It involves the task of retrieving intended web documents. It is the process by which we extract the data either online or offline resources available on web.
- **Information Selection and Pre-Processing:** It involves the automatic selection and preprocessing of specific information from retrieved web resources. This process transforms the original retrieved data into information. The data is transformed into useful information by using suitable transformation. The transformation could be renewal of stop words, or it may

be aimed for obtaining the desired representation such as finding particular format of data.

- **Generalization:** It automatically discovers general patterns at individual web sites as well as across multiple sites. Data Mining techniques and machine learning are used in generalization.
- **Analysis:** It involves the validation and interpretation of the mined patterns. It plays an important role in pattern mining. A human plays an important role in information on knowledge discovery process on web.

However, in the extraction process, many issues arise for the target of discovering useful information from online pages. One of these issues considering data representation, as website pages can be found in different formats. HTML is designed for present unstructured information, while XML and XHTML are intended for more organized information which elements help the parsers of web crawlers to communicate with the site pages' substance all the more proficiently (Alim, et al., 2011).

Information Extraction Approaches

Researchers began to use statistical techniques and machine learning algorithms to automatically create information extraction systems for new domains. In the following subsections, overviews of information extraction approaches are presented. In general, approaches of information extraction can be under the category of either supervised, weakly supervised, or unsupervised learning approaches. Supervised learning can be applied for extracting different information including patterns, rules, and sequential information. Moreover, weakly supervised and unsupervised learning methods for information extraction are applied for more global or discourse-oriented approaches to information extraction. The following subsections will demonstrate the work performed by researchers in this field.

Supervised Learning of Extraction Patterns and Rules

Soderland (1999) developed an approach to apply learned rules on text which had been annotated with the information to be extracted. However, the annotated text required for training is often difficult and time consuming to obtain. An alternative approach is to use weakly supervised learning algorithms, these do not require large amounts of annotated training data and rely on a small set of examples instead. These approaches greatly reduced the burden on the application developer by alleviating the knowledge acquisition bottleneck. Weakly supervised algorithms have the benefit of requiring only small amounts of annotated training data (Stevenson & Greenwood, 2006)

Several systems use rule learning algorithms to automatically generate information extraction patterns from explained text corpora. Relational learning methods have also been used to learn rule like structure for information extraction and applied by more researchers such as (Roth, Yih2001; Cali &Mooney 2003; Bunescu & Mooney, 2004; Bunescu & Mooney, 2007).

On the same way Mooney and Cali used relational learning methods to generate information extraction rules, where each rule has a pre-filler and post-filler component each component is a pattern that consists of words, POS tags, and semantic classes (Mooney, 1999).

Another research by (Dahab, et al., 2010) proposed an extraction method for extracting Arabic patterns representing concepts. The research aimed to extract the concept in the agriculture domain with avoiding using the required tools for information extraction such as stemmer and lexicon. However, the proposed method can be further enhanced to extend its output to have a complete hierarchical tree or extract semantic relations.

A recent research by (Hassan, et al., 2014) in which an approach was proposed to propose an answer to user's queries over the web. The approach combined three information extraction approaches to improve the efficiency and accuracy of the extracted answer. These approaches are "Rhetorical Structure Theory (RST), the query processing approach, and the Network Representation approach (NRA). (Hassan, et al., 2014) ". However, the proposed approach raised the problem of the synonyms and anatomies in the text to focus for finding a solution. Moreover, another research by the same authors in 2015 (Hassan, et al., 2015) in which they conducted a classification method for Arabic document for the same answering user query target. Their aim was to classify the document to avoid redundancy in the extracted information for answering the query, however, the research also raised the problem of the lack of resources such as the corpora.

Supervised Learning of Sequential Classifier Models

There are other approaches that view information extraction as a classification problem that can be tackled using sequential learning models. Instead of using explicit patterns or rules to extract information, a machine learning classifier is trained to sequentially scan text from left to right and label each word as an extraction or a non-extraction.

A typical labeling scheme is called "IOB" is presented by (Hobbs & Riloff, 2010) in which each word is classed as an 'I' if it is inside a desired extraction, 'O' if it is outside a desired extraction, or 'B' if it is the beginning of a desired extraction. The proposed scheme has been applied for extracting facts about a bombing incident.

Also Gentile, Lanfranchi, Mazumdar and Ciravegnain (2011) presented an approach to automatically and dynamically provide a model for user expertise from informal communication exchanges. The research depended on generating semantic user profiles from emails (and more generally from any textual user generated content) guaranteeing flexibility, dynamicity and providing ways to connect these data with Linked Open Data (LOD).

Cui (2014) introduced different techniques such as Natural Language Processing to extract traffic information from text based on data hidden in social media. Some examples of the extracted information is which social media available platform in the mobile Internet (weibo.com) which is a Twitter equivalent in China. The research developed a prototype system that published and captured traffic status through an Android based application.

On widely view, Gattani and his colleagues in (2013) described an end-to-end system for industrial that performed element extraction, linking, classification, and tagging for social data. By generate and use contexts and social signals to improve task accuracy, and how the system scale the entire Twitter. Their experiments showed that the system outperforms current proposed approaches such as a Wikipedia-based global "real-time" knowledge base that is well suited for social data). They showed that while not perfect, the system has proved useful in a variety of real-world applications. They presented that it is important to exploit contexts and social signals to maximize the accuracy of such systems.

Hamasaki and collegues (2006) related an integrated method for social network extraction including three kinds of networks, they are: user-registered Know link network, Web-mined Web link network, and face-to-face Touch link network, however, their integration needs improvement of network integration and advanced applications.

Also Arjan and his colleagues in (Alim, et al, 2011) developed an automated web crawler using the ruby programming language. The crawler would visit profile pages based on a randomly generated list of id numbers using the rand function of Microsoft excel. Regular expressions were used to collect the relevant bits of data for classify age differences in online social networking

Weakly Supervised and Unsupervised Approaches

While supervised learning techniques reduced the manual effort required to initiate an information extraction system for a new domain. However, annotating training texts still requires a substantial investment of time, and annotating documents for extraction of information can be fake complex. Also if we have a set of documents as a training set to the system. The documents are either relevant (contain the description of an event relevant to the scenario) or irrelevant. However, the documents are not annotated and the algorithm does not have access to this information (Srivastava, et al., 2005) since 1980 the attempt research to extract data from the Web are two of strategies emerged learning techniques and knowledge engineering techniques also called learning-based and rule-based approaches, respectively. These approaches depends on domain expertise it need programming experience and a good knowledge of the domain in which the data extraction system (Chang, et, al. 2006).

Statistical and Learning Methods

Learning in natural language processing, statistical methods have gained new popularity, and are being applied to new domains. They are usually characterized by using large text corpora and performing some analysis which uses primarily the text characteristics without adding significant linguistic or world knowledge. An example of the current widely used text corpora which have been built is Brown corpus. Annotation of corpora with part of speech tags or parse trees has been a focus of corpus based language analysis. Additional important application areas of statistical techniques to written natural language are thesaurus-building (or lexical clustering) and probabilistic grammar learning. Statistical techniques that have been used for these tasks are n-gram techniques, unsupervised clustering and hidden Markov models (e.g. a special case is grammar induction, which uses context-free grammars in addition to probabilistic information from text (Hobbs & Riloff, 2010)

Rajiv, Pfeil, and Zaphiris (2008) developed an automated web crawler using the Ruby programming language. The crawler depended on the visits of the profile pages based on a randomly generated list of id numbers using the RAND function of Microsoft excel. Regular expressions were used to collect the relevant bits of data.

Challenges of Web Data Extraction Techniques

Different approaches are applied for information extraction from web such as natural language processing, machine learning, and logic. Many factors affect selecting the suitable web extraction method, a major factor is the dependency level of the application domain features, and consequently it then affects the proposing of an effective solution.

Some of the key challenges can be addressed for web data extraction systems. Generally, a need for experts is required for performing the extraction task, therefore, one of the main challenges is applying automatic techniques for extraction, although one of the main targets is to minimize the human interference, however, receiving feedback from users is a very important role. Therefore, balancing between the ability to build automatic based web data extraction systems and human interference is one of the main targets in the field for achieving the most accurate results. Another challenge is the ability of web data extraction methods to analyze large amount of data. This challenge is considered one of the most important targets especially in the business fields (Balke, 2012).

A third challenge is to maintain the user privacy in the network. Moreover, a need for having a large set of training data is one of the main challenges that should be considered, as training data needs to be labeled, this task is usually time consuming. Finally, as web structure usually changes over time, coping with this change and finding a method for extracting information from different structure is not an easy task to be performed.

TEXT ANALYTICS DIRECTIONS IN SOCIAL MEDIA

Social media had its own multi-data sources which include images, video, audio, spatial data, and text. This variety gives us insights into social networks and groups that were not previously possible in both scale and extent. Unfortunately, textual data in social media presents many new challenges due to its distinct characteristics. Text analytics have challenging features of text in social media, including time sensitivity, short length, unstructured phrases, and abundant information (Hu & Liu, 2012)

Text Analytics of Social Media had been growing up rapidly than traditional methods to process textual data in social media. Recently, a number of methods have been proposed to handle the textual data with new features. In this section, we introduce a variety of applying text analytics to social media as:

- Event Detection.
- Collaborative Question Answering.
- Social Tagging.
- Opinion Mining.
- Fraud Detection.

Event Detection

Monitoring a data source and detecting the event that was taken within that source is the target of Event Detection. Monitoring and tracking of news articles, digital books receives much attention for extracting useful information in real time but variety of texts in traditional media, microblogging texts are noisy, short, and embedded with social relations (Hu, et al., 2013).

There are four tasks related to analyzing events from social media data. The four tasks are, new event detection, event tracking, event summarization, and event association. The four tasks enable the organization of methods and systems based on a task-specific view. For example, organizations could help in evaluating the methods for addressing each task and potentially, identify the missing pieces to practically tackle individual tasks when analyzing social media data (Weikum & Theobal, 2010)

Considering the real-time nature of Twitter (Sakaki, et al., 2013) used Twitter users as a sensor to detect an event based on sensory observations. His aim was to monitor the event such as earthquake by semantic analyses where applied to tweets. It classifies the event into a positive and a negative class.. Location estimation methods such as Kalman filtering and particle filtering are used to calculate the locations of events. (Sakaki et, al., 2013) presented an earthquake reporting system, which is a novel approach to notify people of an earthquake event.

COLLABORATIVE QUESTION ANSWERING

Answered to answer questions posted by other people is common define as Collaborative Question Answering such as Yahoo!. Collaborative question answering services started to develop with blooming of OSN. A large volume of questions are asked and answered every day on social Question and Answering (QA) web sites such as Yahoo! Answers. Collaborative question answering portals are a popular destination for users looking for advice with a particular situation, for gathering opinions, for sharing technical knowledge, for entertainment, for community interaction, and for satisfying one's curiosity about a countless number of things (Liu & Eugene, 2011)

(Dou, et al., 2012) proposed a graph based approach to perform question retrieval by segmenting multi-sentence questions. The authors' first attempt to detect question sentences using a classifier built from both lexical and syntactic features, and use similarity and reference chain based methods to measure the closeness score between the question and context sentences. On the other hand, systems provide corresponding quality QA pairs from answer's point of view. Adamic and collegues (2008) evaluated the quality of answers for specific question by analyzing Yahoo! Answer's knowledge sharing activity. First, forum categories are clustered according to the content characteristics and patterns of interaction among users. The interactions in different categories reveal different characteristics. Some categories are more like expertise sharing forums, while others incorporate discussion, everyday advice, and support. Similarly, some users focus narrowly on specific topics, while others participate across categories. Second, the authors utilize this feature to map related categories and characterize the entropy of the users' interests. Both user attributes and answer characteristics are combined to predict, within a given category, whether a particular answer will be chosen as the best answer by the asker (Adamic et al., 2012).

In order to improve QA archives management, there are a number of works done by evaluating the quality of QA pairs. Harper et al. tried to determine which questions and answers have archival value by analyzing the differences between conversational questions and informational questions (Adamic et, al. 2008; Harper et, al., 2009)

Social Tagging

Social tagging is a method for Internet users to organize, store, manage and search for tags / bookmarks (also as known as social bookmarking) of resources online. Where User-generated keywords – tags – have been suggested way of enhancing descriptions of online information resources, and improving their access through broader indexing. "Social Tagging" refers to the practice of publicly labeling or classification resources in a shared, online environment. Unlike file sharing, the resources themselves aren't shared, merely the tags that describes them or bookmarks that reference them. The rise of social tagging services presents a potential great deal of data for mining useful information on the web. The users of tagging services have created a large volume of tagging data which has attracted recent attention from the research community (Trant, 2009).

Opinion Mining

"What other people think" (Lee, et al., 2010), one of the main critical questions in business field. A question that has an answer which may change the whole plan of business and affects tremendously the decision makers' direction. One of the main sources to extract people's opinion is social media, therefore, many work have been performed following this aspect (Agrawal, 2003). A research that focused on the characteristics of social media that can support opinion extraction, it provided a classification method which aim is to classify the person's opinion into negative or positive, however, the work performed can be further enhanced by considering active submitted opinions for more accurate results. Another work by (Sobkowicz, et al. 2012)is a framework for analyzing the contents of social media with providing a mining method for extracting political opinions which needs to be further extended to consider the policy-making in social media sources. Another research by Vijaya (2013), which was a general study of the impact on opinion mining on different fields including business, politics, and others. The study discusses the social media relation with opinion mining and provided different approaches for extracting opinions from different social media platforms.

Fraud Detection

There are many approaches to detecting fake or false user accounts. Some approaches attempt to systematically rank potentially fake accounts by their probability of being fake; others use supervised learning algorithms, while others still use social honey pots. One approach (Benevenuto et al., 2010) to detecting cloned profiles on different OSN involves extracting information from a real account and querying the Internet with information from that account. According results, user information is categorized as common or user specific. Account data were queried to find possible profiles that are real account. According a list of possible clones, which given a similarity score in relation to the real account. f Toward the process end, the user is ranked by similarity score, by human intervention. Also SybilRank (Cao, et al., 2012),was used to detect fake accounts by properties of the social graph to rank users by their probilty of being fake SybilRank use random walk from real account with higher normalized probility than fake account. also other approaches use social honeypots (Egele, et al., 2013). Honeypots are created to trap attackers and begin monitoring and logging attackers' activity. When a honeypot's profile receives an unexpected friend request, the user sending the request is put under observation. The user's activity is tracked for later use as evidence by a classifier to decide if the suspected user is a spammer or not. In this way, the authors identify spammers with a low false positive rate and are able to identify characteristics of spammers' profiles that can be applied to detecting previously unknown spammers.

Elazab and colleagues (2016),present fake accounts detection in Twitter based on minimum weighted Feature. The minimum set of attributes for detecting the fake accounts on Twitter has been determined and tested. Five of the best classification algorithms have been applied and the results have been compared 3. Evaluating both steps is applied and compared with other researchers' results which proved the advancement in the accuracy level of the proposed approach (Elazab, et al, 2016)

The final class of approaches to detecting spammers assigns users a vector of values ("feature" values) (Camasani &Calzolari, 2012; Martinez-Romo & Araujo, 2013; Yang et, al. 2010; Stringhini, et al. 2010) capturing different attributes of their profiles, Tweet history, local social graph, etc. Features are carefully constructed using empirical user data, before they are used as input to a supervised machine learning algorithm along with a set of users that have been pre-classified as being spammers or not. The resulting classifier can then be used on the broader social network. Approaches based on machine learning can be augmented using statistical analysis of the language used in Tweets (Kontaxis et, al., 2011). For example, a suspicious Tweet about a trending topic can be compared to the broader thread of Tweets about the topic using the concept of Kullback–Leibler divergence. Augmenting typical profile-based features with technique Tweet-based features can improve the performance of a spammer-classification system. Detecting subversion on twitter our work uses a machine learning framework with profile and Tweet based features. We synthesize diverse ideas from the literature and describe our proof of-concept system that samples the Twitter social, computes interesting features on the data, and classifies users as being fake or not.

So far, social networking websites lack automated systems to detect fake accounts because it is very difficult to monitor of fake and real online social network Profiles Using hacked accounts to send spam can be viewed as an instance of a Sybil attack on a social network.

There are two types of Sybil attacks: one involves creating many fake accounts, and the other employs hijacked legitimate accounts to perform a desired function., the first attack is common for Twitter,. An attacker may respond to such a defense by hacking into legitimate users' accounts and using them to carry out their attack. The compromised accounts, being legitimate for the most part, are not readily Identifiable, as their behavior is less divergent from that of a real user (Benevenuto, et al., 2010).

Issues of Textual Data Analytics in Social Media

The analysis of the new features of textual data in social media from four different perspectives: Time Sensitivity, Short Length, Unstructured Phrases, and Abundant Information (Hu & Liu, 2012).

Time Sensitivity

Time Sensitivity is important element of numerous OSN administrations is their real-time nature. bloggers examine their sites like clockwork, Which they post news and data a few times day by day. Clients may need to speak in a flash with companions about "What are you doing?" (Twitter) or "What is at the forefront of your thoughts" (Facebook). At the point when presenting a question to Twitter, the returned results are just a few minutes old (Sakaki et al., 2013)

Short Length

Short Length is one of the limitations in OSN sites as they more often than not confine the length of clients' made substance, for example, micro blogging messages, item audits, QA sections and image inscriptions, and so forth. Twitter permits clients to constrained to 140 characters. Likewise, Picasa remarks are constrained to 512 characters, and Windows Live Messenger are confined to 128 characters. Information with a short length is universal on the web at present. As a result, these short messages have assumed expanding vital parts in applications of OSN. Fruitful preparing short messages is essential to content examination routines. (Cai et al., 2008).

Unstructured Phrases

the quality of the content is different between text in osn and traditional media. The variance of quality originates from people's attitudes when posting a microblogging message or answering a question in a forum. Some users are experts for the topic and post information very carefully, while others do not post as high of quality. The main challenge posed by content in social media sites is the fact that the distribution of quality has high variance: from very high-quality items to low-quality, sometimes abusive content, this makes the tasks of filtering and ranking in such systems more complex than in other domains (Ventola, 2014)

Moreover, when composing a message, users may use or coin new abbreviations or acronyms that seldom appear in conventional text documents. For example, messages like "How r u?", "Good 9t" are not really words, but they are intuitive and popular in social media. They provide users convenience in communicating with each other, however it is very difficult to accurately identify the semantic meaning of these messages.

Exploiting the Power of Abundant Information

Online networking when all is said in done show a rich assortment of data sources. In expansion to the substance itself, there is a wide exhibit of non-content information accessible. For instance, Twitter permits clients to use the"#" image, called hashtag, to stamp decisive words or points in a Tweet (tag data); a picture is normally connected with numerous labels which are described by diverse districts in the picture; clients are able to fabricate association with others (interface data) in Facebook and other interpersonal organization locales; Wikipedia gives an effective approach to users to sidetrack to the equivocalness idea page or larger amount idea page(semantic pecking order information). All these outer data presents open doors for traditional tasks. Past content examination sources dependably show up as< user, content>structure, while the content investigation in online networking has the capacity infer data from different perspectives, which incorporate client, substance, connection, label, time stamp and others (Battaglino et al., 2013)

CONCLUSION AND FUTURE RESEARCH DIRECTIONS

With the advent of Online Social media a revolutionary change has occurred in the social interactions of people of this decade. Many popular Social media platforms such as Facebook, Orkut, Twitter, and LinkedIn have become increasingly popular. Nowadays, these Social media allow many easy-to-learn online activities including chatting, online shopping, gaming, tweeting, etc.

In fact social networking is considered to be the second-fastest growing activity, behind only entertainment. Social media and blogging sites are nowadays the fourth most popular activity on the Internet; this means that more than two-thirds of the global online population visit and participate in social networks and blogs. Social media have also pulled ahead of e-mail in the rank of the most popular online activities. Another interesting finding is that social media and blogging accounts for nearly 10% of all time spent on the Internet. Social media have become a fundamental part of the online experience on the WWW throughout the world.

This chapter demonstrated basic aspects in social media and related fields including social networks, text analysis, information extraction, and others. The chapter has tried to present the most interesting work that has been performed in the field of social media, however, more research can be explored with many issues arise in the field when relating to different targets such as fraud detection, opinion summarization business impact, and others. The chapter can be further extended to cover the mentioned aspects in details with even proposing new ideas for the arisen issues.

REFERENCES

Adamic, L., Zhang, J., Bakshy, E., & Ackerman, M. (2008). Knowledge sharing and yahoo answers: everyone knows something. In *Proceeding of the 17th international confrerence on world wide web*, (pp. 665-674). doi:10.1145/1367497.1367587

Adamic, L., Zhang, J., Bakshy, E., & Ackerman, M. (2012). Knowledge sharing and yahoo answers: everyone knows something. *17th international conference on World Wide Web*, (pp. 665–674).

Agrawal, R. (2003). Mining newsgroups using Networks arising from social behavior. *Proceedings of 12th international Conference on WWW.*

Alim, S., Abdulrahman, R., Neagu, D., & Ridley, M. (2011). Online social network profile data extraction for vulnerability analysis. *International Journal of Internet Technology and Secured Transactions, 3*(2), 194–209. doi:10.1504/IJITST.2011.039778

El Azab, Amira, M., Idrees, A. A., Mahmoud, M. A., & Hefny, H. (2016). Fake Accounts Detection in Twitter based on Minimum Weighted Feature. World Academy of Science, Engineering and Technology. *International Journal of Computer, Electrical, Automation, Control and Information Engineering, 10*(1).

Battaglino, C., Bosco, C., Cambria, E., Damiano, R., Patti, V., & Rosso, P. (2013). *Emotion and Sentiment in Social and Expressive Media. Proceedings of the workshop of AIIA 2013 - 25th Year Anniversary.*

Benevenuto, F., Magno, G., & Rodrigues, T., & Almeida. (2014). Detecting spammers on twitter, Collaboration, Electronic messaging. *Anti-Abuse and Spam Conference (CEAS).*

Bhisikar, P., & Sahu, P. (2013). Overview on Web Mining and Different Technique for Web Personalisation. *International Journal of Engineering Research and Applications, 3*, 2.

Cai, K., Spangler, S., Chen, Y., & Zhang, L. (2008). Leveraging sentiment analysis for topic detection. *Proceedings of the 2008 IEEE/WIC/ACM International Conference on Web Intelligence and Intelligent Agent Technology*, 265-271.

Cao, Q., Sirivianos, M., Yang, X., & Pregueiro, T. (2012). Aiding the detection of fake accounts in large scale social online services. In *Proceedings of the 9th USENIX Conference on Networked Systems Design and Implementation.* USENIX Association.

Dahab, M. Y., & Edrees, A., & Rafea, A. (2010). Pattern Based Concept Extraction for Arabic Documents. *International Journal of Intelligent Computing and Information Sciences, 10*(2).

Dou, W., Wang, K., & Ribarsky, W., & Zhou. (2012). Event detection in social media data. In *Proceedings IEEE VisWeek Workshop on Interactive Visual Text Analytics-Task Driven Analytics of Social Media Content*, (pp. 971-980).

Duggan, M., Ellison, N. B., Lampe, C., Lenhart, A., & Madden, M. (2015). *Social media update 2014* Pew Research Center. Retrieved from http://www.pewinternet.org/2015/01/09/social-media-update-2014

Edosomwan, S. P. (2011). The history of social media and its impact on business. *Journal of Applied Management and Entrepreneurship, 16*(3), 79-91.

Egele, M., & Stringhini, G. & Vigna, G. (2013). Detecting compromised accounts on social networks. NDSS, The Internet Society.

Ellison, N. B. (2007). Social network sites: Definition, history, and scholarship. *Journal of Computer-Mediated Communication, 13*(1).

Gattani, A., Lamba, D. S., Garera, N., Tiwari, M., Chai, X., Das, S., & Doan, A. et al. (2013). Entity Extraction, Linking, Classification, and Tagging for Social Media. A Wikipedia-based Approach. In *Proceedings of the VLDB Endow* (Vol. 6, pp.1126-1137). doi:10.14778/2536222.2536237

Gentile, A. L., Lanfranchi, V., Mazumdar, S., & Ciravegna, F. (2011). Extracting semantic user networks from informal communication exchanges. In The Semantic Web–ISWC, (pp. 209-224).

Golbeck, J. A. (2005). *Computing and applying trust in Web-based social networks* (Unpublished Doctoral Dissertation). University of Maryland. Retrieved from http://trust.mindswap.org/papers/GolbeckDissertation.pd

Hamasaki, M., Mtsuo, Y., Ishida, K., Hope, T., Nishimura, T., & Takeda, H. (2006). An integrated method for social network extraction. In *Proceedings of the 15th international conference on World Wide Web* (pp. 845-846).

Harper, F., Moy, D., & Konstan, J. (2009). Facts or friends?: distinguishing informational and conversational questions in social qasites. In *Proceedings of the 27th International conference on Human factors in computing systems*, (pp. 759–768). doi:10.1145/1518701.1518819

Hassan, H., Dahab, M., Bahnassy, K., Idrees, A., & Gamal, F. (2015). Arabic Documents classification method a Step towards Efficient Documents Summarization. *International Journal on Recent and Innovation Trends in Computing and Communication, 3*(1), 351–359. doi:10.17762/ijritcc2321-8169.150171

Hassan, H. A., Dahab, M. Y., Bahnassy, K., Idrees, A. M., & Gamal, F. (2014). Query Answering Approach Based on Document Summarization. *International OPEN ACCESS Journal Of Modern Engineering Research, 4*(12).

Hobbs, J. R., & Riloff, E. (2010). Information extraction. In Handbook of natural language processing. In N. Indurkhya & F. Damerau (Eds.), *Handbook of Natural Language Processing* (pp. 511–532). CRC Press.

Hu, X., & Liu, H. (2012). Text analytics in social media. In C. C. Aggarwal & C. Zhai (Eds.), Mining Text Data (pp. 385-414). doi:10.1007/978-1-4614-3223-4_12

Hu, X., Tang, L., Tang, J., & Liu, H. (2013). Exploiting social relations for sentiment analysis in microblogging. In *Proceedings of the sixth ACM international conference on Web search and data mining*, (pp. 537-546). doi:10.1145/2433396.2433465

Jain, R., & Purohit, D. (2011). Page ranking algorithms for web mining. *International Journal of Computer Applications, 13*(5).

Kaplan, A. M., & Haenlein, M. (2010). Users of the world, unite! The challenges and opportunities of Social Media. *Business Horizons, 53*(1), 59–68. doi:10.1016/j.bushor.2009.09.003

Kontaxis, G., Antoniades, D., Polakis, I., & Markatos, E. P. (2011). An Empirical Study on the Security of Cross-Domain Policies in Rich Internet Applications. In *Proceedings of the 4th European Workshop on System Security (EuroSec)*, (pp. 295-300). doi:10.1145/1972551.1972558

Lee, K., Caverlee, J., & Webb, S. (2010). Uncovering social spammers: social honeypots + machine learning. In *Proceedings of the 33rd international ACM SIGIR conference on Research and development in information retrieval* (pp. 435-442). doi:10.1145/1835449.1835522

Lin, K. Y., & Lu, H. P. (2011). Why people use social networking sites: An empirical study integrating network externalities and motivation theory. *Computers in Human Behavior, 27*(3), 1152–1161. doi:10.1016/j.chb.2010.12.009

Liu, Q., & Eugene, A. (2011). *Modeling answerer behavior in collaborative question answering systems. In Advances in information retrieval* (pp. 67–79). Springer Berlin Heidelberg.

Martinez-Romo, J., & Araujo, L. (2013). Detecting malicious tweets in trending topics using a statistical analysis of language. *Expert System Application, 40*(8), 992–3000. doi:10.1016/j.eswa.2012.12.015

Mobasher, B. (2006). Web Usage Mining. In B. Liu (Ed.), *Web Data Mining: Exploring Hyperlinks, Contents and Usage Data*. Berlin: Springer.

Mooney, R. (1999). Relational learning of pattern-match rules for information extraction. In *Proceedings of the Sixteenth National Conference on Artificial Intelligence*, (pp. 328-334).

Munibalaji, T., & Balamurugan, C. (2012). Analysis of link algorithms for web mining. *International Journal of engineering and Innovative Technology, 1*(2).

Pang, B., & Lee, L. (2008). Opinion mining and sentiment analysis. *Foundations and Trends® in Information Retrieval, 2*(1–2), 1-135.

Punin, J., Krishnamoorthy, M., & Zaki, M. (2002). LOGML: Log markup language for web usage mining. In WEBKDD 2001—Mining Web Log Data Across All Customers Touch Points (pp. 88-112).

Rautio, A. (2012). Social Media ROI as part of Marketing Strategy Work. Observations of Digital Agency Viewpoints (pp. 15-40)

Sakaki, T., Okazaki, M., & Matsuo, Y. (2013). Tweet analysis for real-time event detection and earthquake reporting system development. *IEEE Transactions on Knowledge and Data Engineering, 25*(4), 919–931. doi:10.1109/TKDE.2012.29

Sobkowicz, P., Kaschesky, M., & Bouchard, G. (2012). Opinion mining in social media: Modeling, simulating, and forecasting. *Political Opinions in the Web, 29*(4), 470-479.

Social, M. S. (2015). *How Australian people and businesses are using social media.* Retrieved from: www.sensis.com.au/socialmediareport

Srivastava, T., Desikan, P., & Kumar, V. (2005). Web Mining – Concepts, Applications and Research Directions. *Foundations and Advances in Data Mining: Studies in Fuzziness and Soft Computing, 180*, 275–307. doi:10.1007/11362197_10

Stevenson, M., & Greenwood, M. A. (2006). Learning Information Extraction Patterns Using WordNet. In *Proceeding of The Third International WordNet Conference* (pp. 95-102).

Stringhini, G., Kruegel, C., & Vigna, G. (2010). Detecting spammers on social networks. In *Proceedings of the 26th Annual Computer Security Applications Conference*, (pp. 1–9).

Trant, J. (2009). Studying social tagging and folksonomy: A review and framework. *Journal of Digital Information, 10*(1).

Treem, J. W., & Leonardi, P. M. (2012). Social media use in organizations: Exploring the affordances of visibility, editability, persistence, and association. *Communication Yearbook, 36*, 143-189.

Ventola, C. L. (2014). Social media and health care professionals: Benefits, risks, and best practices. *Pharmacy and Therapeutics, 39*(5), 356–364. PMID:24883008

Vijaya, M. S., & Sudha, V. P. (2013). Research Directions in Social Network Mining with Empirical Study on Opinion Mining. *CSI Communications, 37*(9), 24–27.

Weikum, G., & Theobal, M. (2010). From information to knowledge: harvesting entities and relationships from web sources. In *Proceedings of the twenty-ninth ACM SIGMOD-SIGACT-SIGART symposium on Principles of database systems*, (pp.65-76). doi:10.1145/1807085.1807097

Yang, C., Harkreader, R. C., & Gu, G. (2010). *Recent Advances in Intrusion Detection. In* Lecture Notes in Computer Science: Vol. 6961. *Die free or live hard? empirical evaluation and new design for ghting evolving twitter spammers* (pp. 318–337). Berlin: Springer.

KEY TERMS AND DEFINITIONS

Facebook: Is an American for-profit corporation and online social media and social networking service.

LinkedIn: Is a business and employment-oriented social networking service that operates via websites.

Orkut: Is a social networking website owned and operated by Google to help users meet new and old friends and maintain existing relationships.

OSN: Orbit Showtime Network (stylized as "**osn**")-- Is a direct-broadcast satellite provider serving the Middle East and North Africa (MENA). It offers popular entertainment content such as movies, sporting events and various TV shows from major networks and studios.

Social Media: (Also social networking site or social media) is an online platform that is used by people to build social networks or social relations with other people who share similar personal or career interests, activities, backgrounds or real-life connections, and where can purchase online.

Twitter: is an online news and social networking service where users post and interact with messages, "tweets," restricted to 140 characters. Registered users can post tweets, but those who are unregistered can only read them. Users access Twitter through its website interface, SMS or a mobile device app.

Web 2.0: describes World Wide Web websites that emphasize user-generated content, usability (ease of use, even by non-experts), and interoperability (this means that a website can work well with other products, systems and devices) for end users.

Wikipedia: Is a free online encyclopedia that aims to allow anyone to edit articles. It is the largest and most popular general reference work on the Internet and is ranked among the ten most popular websites.

Section 2
Knowledge Management

Chapter 8
From Personal Knowledge Management to Corporate Knowledge Management

Ayşe Aslı Sezgin
Osmaniye Korkut Ata University, Turkey

Esengül İplik
Osmaniye Korkut Ata University, Turkey

ABSTRACT

The aim of this study is to identify the applications to be used for personal knowledge management, determine their area of use, and specify and analyze the examples obtained for their use at administrative levels in corporations. Within this framework, this study includes the assessment of the workflow of a top manager with the required experience and professionalism in the field of knowledge management. Besides the literature review conducted in line with the content of the subject area in this study, applications that enable personal knowledge management in particular and the similarities between these applications and the features of their social media networks were detected, and their specific purpose of use was clarified. Evernote, chosen as a sample application to be used at corporations, following personal knowledge management, has been assessed within the framework of managers' experiences with the use of depth interview technique.

DOI: 10.4018/978-1-5225-2897-5.ch008

INTRODUCTION

We have been provided with numerous alternatives to make use of knowledge and time efficiently, and to take advantage of opportunities offered by new technologies in the field of knowledge management in an orderly and organized manner in new work environments where time is an important and valuable resource. Individual blogs, micro-blogs, cooperative platforms, content sharing networks, social labeling networks, and text-sound-video-conference sharing devices are some of the numerous examples for the use of social media applications in the field of knowledge management.

These applications that kick in when human mind is not enough seem to undertake a great variety of responsibilities to compensate the drawbacks that are faced with in daily lives as it is impossible to catch up with the speed of the 21st century. Seen from an optimistic angle based on their "facilitating" aspects, these applications have already taken their places in daily life as inevitable applications especially for managers who are in need of reaching them anytime and anywhere even though these applications are sometimes criticized for being too mechanic.

These applications that provide the chance to benefit from in mobiles phones, tablets and notebook computers transfer the past habit of diary keeping to digital environments, through which they have in a sense become the confidants and the most important assistants of modern human beings.

These applications provide us with voice and video note-taking, the possibility to store articles and different internet content with the purpose of reaching them later, making to-do lists, defining business processes and using them from a single point, and ensuring document management. They, in fact, describe the establishment of a new life style based on the ties set up by modern technological humans with the digital world.

The successful adaptation of social media networks and applications with similar features to each daily activity in human life involves the essential fact that they are accessible any time and distributable through storing knowledge from far away by the use of cloud technology.

Today, every organization ranging from state institutions to companies and small-scale businesses seem to comprehend the significance of the use of new technologies and social media for strategically-conducted corporate communication studies and public relations activities. Therefore, it is observed that a dialogue is possible with the target audience in such organizations, and a democratic management mentality, which is open to contribution, has become widespread (Macnamara & Zerfass, 2012).

In a traditional sense, knowledge management systems that carry out the function of constituting knowledge indices and networks, sharing documents and personalization of such knowledge in a central knowledge store (Parise, 2009) have experienced a transformation from individualism to institutionalism via new Internet technologies and social media applications.

The source of change in knowledge management involves important effects of the rich content of social networks in terms of social, organizational and personal knowledge activities and the use of social navigation in setting the related individual links

One of the most important features of social media applications is that they can classify individual content in terms of interests, roles, relationships and activities via formal headings (Parise, 2009).

As web-based knowledge and the transfer of such knowledge within the same environment is possible in our age, it is necessary to develop a viewpoint on how we are perceived in terms of personal and professional aspects. The way we communicate in these networks where we develop an personal knowledge management in a sense, and the sources that we keep in touch with have formed the essential elements of knowledge management (Pfeiffer & Tonkin, 2012). This new stage of personal knowledge management has also reshaped the administrative styles of managers within the context of innovations in the field of corporations. Social media and many applications with similar characteristics to social media have not only facilitated personal knowledge access but also provided advantages for knowledge management, which encourages many corporations to use these applications in administrative level.

These applications, which have the capability of offering all facilities provided by face-to-face relationships, have been preferred in corporations because of their features such as possessing a dynamic structure, establishing large-scale social relationships, gathering people with similar interests, broadcasting knowledge individually, cooperating with foreign people, and having a dynamic structure (Hemsley & Mason, 2013).

Thanks to the new technology network, bonds and effective knowledge sharing has been ensured among geographically scattered groups (Swan, et.al, 1999), leading to a transition from personal success to corporate efficiency through social media applications in new understanding of knowledge management.

In this study, it is aimed to identify the effects of social media applications and similar technologies used in transition from personal knowledge management to corporate knowledge management.

BACKGROUND

Knowledge, which have become the basic power and main capital in human, organizational and social life with the development of communication and technology, is defined as a flexible combination of experiences, values, contextual information and expert opinion, which all constitute a roof for the collection and assessment of new experiences and information. According to the knowledge source classified differently as to a number of criteria, knowledge is divided into two groups, namely explicit and implicit knowledge. The implicit knowledge is defined as the knowledge which is impossible or hard to define clearly in individuals' minds; however, explicit knowledge is defined as sentences, organized data, computer programmes and other specific forms. Explicit knowledge, which is constructed on experiences, is a type of knowledge which involves intuition and foresight and which cannot be visualized and defined. On the other hand, explicit knowledge is obtained through rational thinking and can easily be transferred and shared in the form of universal principles, coded processes, formulas and data (King, 2009; Eskiler, et.al. 2011).

Knowledge which is processed in a specific form, which is meaningful for those who obtain it, which is assumed to be necessary for managerial decisions or which is defined as hard data may be found at various levels ranging from personal levels to corporate levels. Personal knowledge refers to the knowledge kept in an employee's mind whereas corporate knowledge refers to two different levels of knowledge that is the knowledge exiting in each unit of a corporation or in the whole corporation. Accordingly, knowledge kept in a specific unit of a corporation refers to the knowledge that come out as a result of the knowledge kept by the employees of that unit, their communication and the unit's interaction with other units in time. The knowledge kept in the corporation as a whole comprises values, experiences, culture and operation of the whole organization (Gülseçen, 2013).

Knowledge constitutes the basis of personal and administrative decisions, and it is the main resource in economics. However, nowadays people are able to have access to more knowledge easily with each passing day through more varied methods such as voiced, video, electronic, published etc. files than they used to do, and what is important now is not to own the knowledge but to know how to use it. Therefore, it is necessary to possess a sound knowledge management system in order not to lose the existing knowledge, not to waste it and in order to make it productive (Bedük, 2005).

Knowledge management (KM) has been a debatable term with full of incomprehensibility since it was first introduced in early 1990s. In knowledge management literature, many definitions and comments exist to explain this concept from different viewpoints and models. In the most general sense, knowledge management is an integrated and systematic approach including expertise and experiences of individuals as well as database, documents, policies and procedures with the purpose of determining, managing and sharing all information assets of a business (Chatti, 2012; Dur, 2008).

It is also observed that the widely use of new technologies in daily lives lead to economic growth. Advantages of a new invention are experienced through individual utilization, ensuring these technologies to spread. Advantages of adaptation into a new technology, as seen in wireless communication, have been increasing with the facilitating effects of technology (Hall & Khan, 2003).

Knowledge economy requires new types of learning methods and designs. In addition to this, globalization has started to require an attentive and inter-dependent citizenship with a global identity. New technologies, ways of expression and learning methods result in some changes. Social and political unrest against change also causes educational institutions in particular to question their roles in personal development and social development. On the other hand, the use of such technologies in knowledge-based activities, and new developments and new applications in the storage of knowledge continue to draw attention (Atkins, 2005).

New technologies have been used in many fields ranging from education, entertainment and socialization to communication. Especially due to their design-based structures, new technologies have created improvement in young people's attitudes, skills and know-how. Young people who have a command of new technologies in modern societies are able to assess themselves as competent individuals in terms of their knowledge and talents (Bers, 2006). Social media applications also stand out as new technological environments that fit to the structure of modern societies.

Social media, first known as Web 2.0 technology, has been used in every field of life, especially in individual, professional and educational fields. These tools have a cooperative structure that offers many ways to produce projects, share them, discuss on ideas, and set efficient communication environments through brainstorm. Most of these technologies are used in web and mobile environments, which extends their use. Other factors may also be mentioned about the rapid growth of social media. In addition to the possibility of having an access anytime and anywhere, the ability of storing a great amount of data through cloud technology is another advantage of using social media (Claremont Graduate University, n.d.).

Castells (2005) defined the new social outlook as a network society. One of the features of the information era, technology can be shaped in line with needs, values and expectations. Social media enables individuals to contact with other individuals, produce content within the system by making friends' lists, and share, and it is used as a tool for constituting public or semi-public profiles (Boyd & Ellison, 2008).

Social media has started to determine our use of Internet as well as the way we use it. Users are able to contact through popular social media networks, express their opinions and produce content in an interactive environment. Almost all consumers have become online critics and editors in social media networks whose effects are felt in economic life (Smith, 2009).

This study aims to focus on knowledge generation, knowledge management and benefits obtained by users at spots of access to information apart from the fun nature of social media. This study will analyze Evernote, which involves a number of features of social media applications and which is used to benefit from new technologies within information society for the purpose of knowledge generation, access, management and store. In daily life, there is an excessive information flow in which the Internet is utilized as an important means, and social media and similar technologies are used via the Internet and take an active role in information management.

Evernote, which is an important means in information storage, organization and management, is known as one of the most common application used for this purpose. Evernote provides with limitless and creative applications even in its free version. It also offers every kind of possibility for information storage and organization. Information stored on a drive far from Evernote is accessible anywhere with an Internet connection via mobile devices. Evernote contains numerous applications that increase efficiency for everyone using knowledge (Korzaan & Lawrence, 2015).

MAIN FOCUS OF THE CHAPTER

From Personal to Corporate Knowledge Management

In present and past research on knowledge management, there has been a tendency to focus on business levels whereas very little number of empirical studies has been carried out on personal knowledge management, and therefore, it is still not observed and researched sufficiently. Personal knowledge management, which has been better understood in recent years, is a system designed by individuals for their own use in order to manage personal knowledge to ensure that it is accessible, meaningful and valuable for the personal use of individuals in order to organize the information considered important as part of personal knowledge database, and take advantage of personal capital. Personal knowledge management gives answers to questions about what knowledge we have, how we can organize this knowledge to realize our purposes, how we can activate it, how we can use it and how we can continue to generate new knowledge (Cheong & Tsui, 2011; Jain, 2011; Cheong & Tsui, 2010).

An important aspect of personal knowledge management focuses on individuals in their quest for knowledge with the purposes of learning, working more efficiently or socializing is that in allows an individual to manage knowledge processes and mutual interaction, cooperation and information exchange with other individuals in a better way. Initially, personal knowledge management was developed in such a way that it is built as a structure used for organizing knowledge that is of importance for individuals. However, it was then improved so that it could involve the organization of personal knowledge, making sense of information, creating new ideas, developing relationship networks and constituting cooperation in time (Razmerita, et.al., 2009).

A number of applications have been presented for personal knowledge that integrate various data, applications and work flows to help users organize, constitute and utilize their knowledge. Of these applications, Microsoft Access, Filemaker and Protégé provide the possibility of designing both general knowledge models (schemes, ontologies) and constituting some knowledge (tables, samples) related to this. These integrated applications offers the tools that enable users to transfer knowledge through images previously designed to visualize general and personal knowledge (Champin, et.al.,2008).

SaaS (Software-as-a-Servie) and PpcSoft iKnow are other applications to be used for personal knowledge management. SaaS is a computer application serving over the Internet through a web browser. Today, there are many SaaS applications to be used by individuals for supporting personal knowledge management. Moreover, SaaS applications could be mentioned in this context as they can be used over cloud computing. The most appropriate example for SaaS is Gmail. Users can send emails, arrange their documents and back up the files with his service offered by Google. Apart from this, Google Documents (Google Docs) is one of the most attention taking applications as they provide text processing, spreadsheet, presentation and graphic tools for analyzing and integrating the knowledge as well as enabling to prepare HTML documents. However, PpcSoft iKnow is a personal knowledge management tool that stores knowledge and enables to access whenever necessary. PpcSoft iKnow designed to process a number of data helps users to manage excessive information load, save time and work more efficiently. PpcSoft iKnow, which involves inter-related data information providing access to knowledge, constitutes personal knowledge pages on their computers after collecting any type of information. E-mail, calendar, task managers, Weblogs, Online Web Assistants, Wiki, Personal Wiki and Semantic Wiki and Evernote are other personal knowledge management applications that can be used by individuals (Jain, 2011).

Many researchers have tried to set up a personal knowledge management model and explain mutual relationships by focusing on different aspects such as skills, tools, links and societies, and personal knowledge management. The model developed by Frand and Hixon (1999) explained five variables which are seek/find, categorizing/classification, naming/separating, measurement/assessment and combining/relating. According to this, seek/find focuses on the use of different tools such as database selection tools and search engines whereas categorizing/classification includes classification schemes, organizing the information from general to the specific, putting some topics into most specific groups and subdividing when a new category is necessary. Naming/separating involves the selection and use of a meaningful name for individuals. It also focuses on using appropriate terms for different concepts such as names, abbreviations and file extensions. Measuring/assessment is to assess if knowledge is complete and accurate, if it is provided by an expert or authority, and to confirm the provided knowledge and to evaluate if there is a resource to confirm the knowledge. Finally, combining/relating includes the use of obtained knowledge in problem-solving and decision-making process (Cheong & Tsui, 2011).

There is a close relationship between personal knowledge management, which is a tool to make employees gain the necessary skills to manage knowledge, and corporate knowledge management.

Personal knowledge management provides a number of benefits to make efficient use of the information, have corporate productivity and improved performance, continuous innovation, efficient decision-making, ensuring the dissemination of knowledge within the organization and outside the organization to provide information on a number of benefits such as being aware (Jain, 2011).

Due to developments in technology, globalization and the changes taking place as a result of this, society is confronted with rapid change. Despite these changes that bring along a number of challenges, they provide opportunities both for the private sector and the public sector. Most large enterprises in the private sector have adopted new effective management tools, techniques and philosophies in order to be able to survive against environmental change and gain a competitive advantage by gaining competence. One of the approaches emerging in this process is the knowledge management that has started to take its place in literature as the application depends on determining knowledge resources to ensure that they provide competitive advantage by adding high value to the goods or services produced by the company, or taking advantage of these resources effectively (Karakoçak, 2007, Cong & Pandya, 2003).

Knowledge management is a significant element for surviving and ensuring competitive advantage, and it is defined as planning, arranging, activating and controlling people, processes and systems in an institution in order to ensure that the assets of an institution about knowledge are developed and they are made use of effectively. Knowledge and relevant assets available in an institution involves printed information such as patents and manuals, "best practices" database kept in electronic stores, information possessed by the employees for carrying out their tasks in the best way, and information organized by working teams about the solution of certain problems, and other information about the products, processes and relationships of an organization (King, 2009).

Knowledge management includes four stages such as data collection, knowledge organization, filtering and spreading. Accordingly, the first step of knowledge management is data collection, which involves using e-mails, voice files, digital files etc. in order to obtain information. At this stage, what is important is to reach all accessible sources and not to investigate the benefits of information until it is tested in detail. The second stage following the data collection stage requires index forming, clustering, cataloging, filtering and coding methods in an accessible and usable manner in order to transform the data and information obtained into beneficial knowledge. The third stage called filtering involves transforming the open information available within databases into implicit knowledge by the use of data mining. Data mining software is used to predict the behavior based on data available in data warehouses and to warn against problems to be encountered in the future. On filtering the information, the last stage of the knowledge management process is the distribution or transfer of knowledge. This process includes making the knowledge usable by the employees through trainings or guides in order to enable the efficient use of knowledge (Awad & Ghaziri, 2007).

In knowledge management process, the use of knowledge management systems stands out as the most basic drive that determines success or failure in terms of organizations. Knowledge systems refers to technologies (computers, data collection tools, network and communication tools, software development tools) all applications and services (data processing, application software development, data banks and data access services), information on the system and human resources that serve collection, processing, gaining access and distribution of information. Today, information systems used by organizations are classified as follows (Öğüt, 2012; Tutar, 2010):

- **Electronic Data Processing Systems (EDPS):** These systems ensure routine data processing about corporate actions. EDPS is designed to process, store and recall data

- **Office Automation Systems (OAS):** It is a system used to decide on routine decisions that audit operational processes such as automatic stocks, decisions for order and production control. The main aim is to lighten the work load causing paperwork in organizations and carry organizational work onto computers.

- **Management Information Systems (MIS):** They support decision-making process and carrying out the organizational work. They are integrated human-machine systems that offer accurate information to accurate person on time in an economical way. MIS is designed to provide managers with information so that they can examine, analyze, assess and decide on information.

- **Decision Support Systems (DSS):** They provide interactive and active support to the decision making processes of an organization. The system also provides managers with statistical analyses, graphics and models, and software for database and report writing techniques.

- **Top Level Manager Information Systems:** They provide critical information required by top managers in appropriate time zones in a desirable manner from inside or outside the corporation.
- **Expert Systems:** They are header-based information systems with the use of artificial intelligence that provide consultancy support to users in certain fields of specialty (Öğüt, 2012; Tutar, 2010).

The main aim of knowledge management is to inform the organization about the scientific and technological innovations and conceptual improvements in time with the purpose of reflecting them on the organization. Additionally, knowledge management also aims to produce different solutions to problems and keep the sustainability of the solutions, ensure that information and knowledge is delivered to the right person at the right time, increase the employee performance and corporate competition by selecting, separating, storing and organizing the knowledge within the organization, raise the consciousness for innovations, and support cooperation, knowledge exchange, continuous learning and development. The most striking feature of organizations in which there is a dominant understanding of knowledge management in order to fulfill these aims is that they are the leaders in the field of service or products they provide. In this context, knowledge management enables the organizations to become more competitive in decreasing the costs, increasing the speed, meeting customer needs in time, and by using new information. (Celep & Çetin, 2014).

Personal and Corporate Knowledge Management in Social Media

In the information era, in which web-based information and information transfer is dominant, it is necessary to possess a viewpoint about how we are perceived by our environment in personal and professional aspects. Today, many social media networks (from Facebook to LinkedIn) enable us to contact with our families and environment, and interact with our colleagues. These networks play active roles in forming an individual image as well as managing knowledge (Pfeiffer & Tankin, 2012).

Knowledge is engraved in our lives through a variety of systems and social networks we join. Personal knowledge settings have been created through social networks and various information (texts, motion-motionless images, digital objects) can be stored through these settings. Users' requirements and behavior must be understood in developing knowledge settings and services in such situations (Lippincott, 2010).

Social media tools have been used to start and sustain social relationships, which is different from face-to-face communication in terms of quality and quantity. Large groups can have the chance to come together via these networks (Twitter, LinkedIn, Facebook), contents formed individually by people who share the same interests (blogs, Flickr), and information can be produced by cooperating with a foreigner or a friend in any region (Hemsley & Mason, 2013).

Social media offers an interactive setting to the users, enabling them to share information, opinions and knowledge, and it has the necessary features to allow users to contribute to the contents (Solmaz, et. al, 2013). One of the most important advantages of the use of social media is that it is possible to share information and knowledge online among different groups of people. Online exchange of information encourages the communication among people. Social media is also an important means of communication in business life. Its use increases especially during the times of crisis. There are a number of advantages of social media in this respect. Some of the advantages are; first, it is a communication channel, and it is open to sharing opinions, and it is sometimes the source of knowledge (Baruah, 2012).

Social media networks have come into the business life and influence it, leading to the inevitable use of social media applications. Researchers assert that data obtained from social media e-mails, systems on which we save files and share with others especially in business life, online tools with which we prepare projects shape our daily work flow (Blacksmith & Poeppelman, 2013).

Social media will have an important impact on future investments of organizations about knowledge management. Organizations have started to use social media increasingly. Blogs in which technical and organizational problems are discussed, documents are shared, and wikis for which content is formed, applications for which project management is performed, links requiring solutions and expertise are among such social media networks. On observing the studies conducted about knowledge management process, it appears that a different viewpoint towards social media is necessary in knowledge management process of social networks. Social networks signify a setting where sense of reliability and reciprocity is dominant with its inter-human structure (Parise, 2009).

According to Parise (2009), two important features of new knowledge technologies and social media applications used in knowledge management stand out:

1. The content related to knowledge management allows creating rich personal content.
2. It allows finding other individuals who use similar content in that specific field and communicating with them.

Organizations may need to do some changes in their management strategies in line with the changing work conditions of our age and technological innovations. Besides catching the interaction with the their target population with the help of a web page, organizations will also contribute to the work flow and can actively use social knowledge management in social media as social knowledge management is efficient in that there is a consistent knowledge share and content forming is possible. In addition, they may be open to communication and interaction through social media networks (Oracle, 2012).

Inevitable use of the Internet, new media, and social media in daily lives result in the design of future work environment. One of the most important concepts about this setting is putting forward as sense making, defined as possessing a viewpoint towards understanding what is intended to convey or express. Social intelligence, which is used for ensuring desired interactions in communicating with other people, and novel and adaptive thinking, which emphasizes having a solution-oriented thinking and putting it into practice, are required features for being successful in this new environment. On the other hand, computational thinking, which expresses revealing necessary information by summarizing a large quantity of data, and new media literacy, which signifies the ability to read and explain new media content clearly and accurately, are considered as features that could be necessary in such environments (Davies, et. al. 2011). It will be necessary to possess above-mentioned features while taking advantage of social media applications for the purpose of knowledge management in personal sense and applying them into corporate knowledge process.

One of the most popular concepts of the 21st century, personal knowledge management, has started to be evaluated from a new viewpoint in line with the development of social media. Users gain a free or with paid access to applications used personally in storing and organizing a large amount of information. These applications enable their users to communicate with other users, have notes formed by using visual elements, write to-do-lists and tasks lists. These applications enable their users to customize according to the needs, storing and keeping the documents in categories and ensure that information is portable and arrangeable. Information synchronized among different devices becomes easily accessible in different times and places. Given the features of these applications that are used personally, they are important tools for applying knowledge management in corporate terms (Axford & Renfro, 2012).

About Evernote

This study analyzes Evernote, which is used for personal knowledge management, since it has features intended for corporate knowledge management, for chatting and sharing with other users, and has similar features to social media applications.

Used for storing and organizing knowledge, Evernote, allows a number of creative applications in its free served features. Information stored in every setting with Internet connection and via more than one device is possible to gain access over Evernote. Evernote provides its users not only with personally-intended applications but also with innumerable applications for personal and corporate or professional purposes in the field of knowledge management. Evernote has some features about arranging corporate and personal settings as well as the facilities it offers about knowledge management. Important agreements, customer accounts, to-do lists, brainstorm activities and various documents can be stored on Evernote. The most striking applications that users personally take advantage of on Evernote vary from sharing recipes and organizing photographs to following health-sport targets. Evernote can be used as a notepad where digital content can be stored like voices and images, different from traditional notepads (Korzaan & Lawrence, 2015).

Evernote is not only used for note-taking but it is also used for sharing these notes with other users and working together. These notes are recorded on the Evernote content via files and labels with the outlook of a timetable. It also enables the users to add location and make arrangements on notes through common sharing of users (Geyer & Reiterer, 2012).

Axford and Renfro (2012) reached the following conclusions in their studies in which they stated advantages and disadvantages of Evernote. It contains many advantages such as a simultaneous use and synchronization on different devices, working with a large amount of data and the provision of many features free of charge. However, the inability to categorize the information efficiently and inability to add an alarm on the task management section are the disadvantages.

The most important reason why Evernote was chosen as a sample application in this study is primarily the services it provides about personal knowledge management, and the use of these services for corporate purposes results in its assessment as an exemplary application demonstrating the transition from personal knowledge management to corporate knowledge management, and it is appropriate for the scope of the study. Another reason why Evernote was chosen as an example in this study is that it has a structure compatible with social media networks in time. As a proof to this information, it is possible to state that Evernote provides its users with forming public or semi-public profiles as it is in social media networks, as well as sharing information with other Evernote users, forming a friends' list composed of Evernote users, offering the opportunity to chat to these users and tag on shared notes, informing about location, and offering the opportunity to produce content within the system. Evernote was chosen as an exemplary application used for personal and corporate knowledge management.

SOLUTIONS AND RECOMMENDATIONS

In addition to the information transferred within the conceptual framework of the study and the features of Evernote, a comparative table as well as questions and answers were given in line with the data collected as a result of the notes obtained during an in-depth interview with the manager who first used Evernote personally and then for corporate knowledge management purposes for the corporation whose responsibility he took over. The Table showed the use of Evernote by making a comparison between personal knowledge management and corporate knowledge management.

In the study, the manager who was interviewed to be assessed in terms of habits of utilizing Evernote, is a scientist with the title of Professor who has worked as a rector at a university and who applies his expert knowledge about information technologies on personal, corporate and academic fields.

The first column in Table 1 shows some key topics identified among some basic information about knowledge management given within the conceptual framework. The study aims to identify the use of themes related to knowledge management among the information given under Personal Knowledge Management and Corporate Knowledge Management titles. It is aimed to collect information about the use of Evernote in personal and corporate knowledge management by scaling the themes used from 1 to 5. In the scale: 1 is very bad, 2 bad, 3 not bad, 4 good, 5 very good.

The features of Evernote which are used only in personal knowledge management and corporate knowledge management were identified through the comparison made by using the themes in the table.

Given the data in the table, the field where Evernote is the most efficient in corporate knowledge management are team work and in which sharing is increased. It was observed that the application was good or very good for broadcasting the notes for other users, project management and cooperative work. Evernote enables users to make arrangements in the content to the extent permitted, and creates a fast and efficient online work environment in particular.

In the interview, the successful aspects of Evernote were found as follows: It is accessible especially on different devices when used for personal and corporate knowledge management, it has an enabling structure to store a large amount of data and work on them, and notes indicate time and location, it has a social function and a successful query language.

Given the data in the table about personal knowledge management, the most common fields of use are storing the information in particular as well as categorizing and labeling, associating them with other notes whenever necessary, and making back-up.

Table 1. The use of Evernote in personal knowledge management and corporate knowledge management

Themes Related to Knowledge Management	Personal Knowledge Management	Corporate Knowledge Management
Creating a Knowledge Setting	3	4
Distribution the Knowledge	3	4
Project Management	4	5
Joint Work	4	5
Measurement-assessment	3	4
Chat	3	4
Voice, Video Recording and Drawing	4	4
Presentation and Graphic Design	3	3
Making Designs	3	3
Backing Up Files	4	5
Categorizing Files – Tagging	4	5
Searching-Finding the Notes	3	3
Naming-Separating the Notes	4	4
Combining-Associating the Notes	4	4
Broadcasting Notes	4	5
Informing about Time and Location in Notes	5	5
Access from Different Devices	5	5
Working with a Large Amount of Data	5	5
Synchronization	4	5
Free Use	4	-
Query Language	5	5
E-mail Management	2	3

It was concluded that Evernote remained insufficient in e-mail management both in personal use and corporate use.

On analyzing the Table traditionally, it could be concluded that Evernote was graded with higher values in corporate knowledge management whereas it was graded with lower values in personal knowledge management.

During the interview, the manager was asked to answer open-ended questions written in line with the conceptual framework. The questions and the answers given are summarized as follows:

Q1: How long have you been using Evernote?

A1: For five years, but I have been a Premium User for the last two years. I have been doing all my personal and corporate knowledge management on Evernote for three years.

Q2: Do you think Evernote is able to meet users' needs in terms of personal and corporate aspects? (Design, function and accessibility)

A2: It is being developed very fast. However, synchronization and overlapping problems are frequent. Previous and next note options are needed to move faster among notes (along with shortcut function). Search and find functions should also be improved.

Q3: How do you assess users' level of adopting Evernote on the basis of corporate knowledge management?

A3: Adopting Evernote is generally very fast. Ease of use and advantages it provides are effective. Our employees can join cooperative work and project management activities in particular without leaving their desks, which enables to be successful especially in time management.

Q4: Do you think Evernote decreases paperwork at personal and corporate level?

A4: Absolutely. I haven't bought a new printer cartridge in the last three years. I haven't felt the necessity to take a print out for the last year, except for a few pages. Moreover, piled-up documents have almost disappeared in my office.

Q5: Have you used the advantages of Evernote to take efficient decisions during corporate knowledge management?

A5: Partly. It does not result from the inefficiency of Evernote but from the lack of complete use.

Q6: Under what category would you assess Evernote in respect to new technologies?

A6: On Evernote, there is a content in which you form a profile personally, which is shared by other users as much as you allow, which you can use as a chat facility if necessary, where you can use location and time tags, and which includes your personal information. With all these features, Evernote can be said to carry the features of social media networks. However, Evernote can also be considered as an application with these features to be used for knowledge management.

On analyzing the answers given to the questions, it may be concluded that Evernote used for the purpose of personal knowledge management can be successful in corporate knowledge management after gaining relevant experiences, and it can be efficient in fields where cooperative work is required. It is observed that Evernote increases the rate of corporate level operations especially because it decreases paperwork.

CONCLUSION

That information has gained a different value and is regularly managed and communication technology is developed, it has become a necessity for an individual living in the 21st century. Separation and organization of easily accessible information especially through the Internet in particular is as important for an individual as it is to a corporation. New technologies provide users with new applications by considering the needs of users. In modern world, individuals and corporations gain access to knowledge, store it and share it with other individuals and corporations while taking advantage of facilities offered by the digital world. Beyond this sharing, the opportunity to have a joint work is used by new technologies.

Information, which is accessible anytime and anywhere, has become a different structure through social media networks as they attract much attention and through social media networks that have impacts on individuals' daily lives. The rich content of social media networks has prepared a new viewpoint in knowledge management. In this study, Evernote, which has been analyzed and used for the transition from personal knowledge management to corporate knowledge management, may be approached from a different angle because, as a knowledge management application with social media features, Evernote may change the approach towards new technologies as it has information-based content contrary to the fun-based content of social media.

As a result of the introduction of applications used in personal knowledge management to transit to corporate knowledge management, necessary measures will be taken about increasing the paperwork, managing time more efficiently, implementation of the idea of joint working at corporate level, storing and managing large quantities of data, which all will lead to a corporate level success that has already bencaught at individual level.

REFERENCES

Atkins, D. (2005). *University futures and new technologies: Possibilities and issues.* Unpublished discussion paper for an OECD expert meeting.

Awad, E. M. & Ghaziri, H. M. (2007). *Knowledge management.* Delhi: Dorling Kindersley, licenses of Pearson Education in South Asia.

Axford, M., & Renfro, C. (2012). Noteworthy productivity tools for personal knowledge management. *Online, 36*(3), 33–36.

Baruah, T. D. (2012). Effectiveness of social media as a tool of communication and its potential for technology enabled connections: A micro-level study. *International Journal of Scientific and Research Publications, 2*(5), 1–10.

Bedük, A. (2005). *Modern yönetim teknikleri.* Ankara: Gazi Kitabevi.

Bers, U. M. (2006). The role of new technologies to foster positive youth development. *Applied Developmental Science, 10*(4), 200–219. doi:10.1207/s1532480xads1004_4

Blacksmith, N., & Poeppelman, T. (2013). Application of modern technology and social media in the workplace. *The Industrial-Organizational psychologist, 51*(1), 69–73.

Boyd, D., & Ellison, N. (2008). Social network sites: definition, history and scholarship. *Journal of Computer-Mediated Communication, 13*(1), 210–230. doi:10.1111/j.1083-6101.2007.00393.x

Castells, M. (2005). *The network society: from knowledge to policy* (M. Castells & G. Cardoso, Eds.). Washington: Center for Transatlantic Relations.

Celep, C., & Çetin, B. (2014). *Eğitim örgütlerinde bilgi yönetimi.* Ankara: Nobel Akademik Yayıncılık.

Champin, P. A., Prié, Y., & Richard, B. (2008). *Personal knowledge elaboration and sharing: Presentation is knowledge too.* Retrieved from: http://liris.cnrs.fr/Documents/Liris-3437.pdf

Chatti, M. A. (2012). Knowledge management: A personal knowledge network perspective. *Journal of Knowledge Management, 16*(5), 829–844. doi:10.1108/13673271211262835

Cheong, R. K. F., & Tsui, E. (2010). The roles and values of personal knowledge management: An exploratory study. *Vine, 40*(2), 204–227. doi:10.1108/03055721011050686

Cheong, R. K. F., & Tsui, E. (2011). From skills and competencies to outcome-based collaborative work: Tracking a decades development of personal knowledge management (PKM) models. *Knowledge and Process Management, 18*(3), 175–193. doi:10.1002/kpm.380

Cong, X., & Pandya, K. V. (2003). Issues of knowledge management in the public sector. *Electronic Journal of Knowledge Management, 1*(2), 25–33.

Davies, A., Devin, F., & Gorbis, M. (2011). *Future work skills 2020*. Institute for the Future for University of Phoenix Research Institute.

Dur, S. (2008). *Bilgi yönetimi altyapısı ve bilgi yönetimi sürecinin örgütsel performans üzerindeki etkisi. Yüksek Lisans Tezi (Yayımlanmamış)*. Bolu: Abant İzzet Baysal Üniversitesi Sosyal Bilimler Enstitüsü.

Eskiler, E., Özmen, M., & Uzkurt, C. (2011). Bilgi yönetimi pazar odaklılık ve pazarlama newliği ilişkisi: Mobilya sektöründe bir araştırma. *Eskişehir Osmangazi Üniversitesi İİBF Dergisi, 6*(1), 31–69.

Frand, J., & Hixon, C. (1999). *Personal knowledge management: who, what, why, when, where, how?* Retrieved from: http://www.anderson.ucla.edu/faculty/jason. frand/researcher/speeches/PKM.htm

Geyer, F., & Reiterer, H. (2012). Experiences from employing evernote as a tool for documenting collaborative design processes. Proceeding of the DIS'12 workshop on Supporting Reflection in and on Design Processes.

Gülseçen, S. (2013). *Bilgi ve bilginin yönetimi*. İstanbul: Papatya Yayıncılık Eğitim.

Hall, B., & Khan, B. (2003). Adoption of new technology. In J., Derek C.(Ed.), New Economy Handbook. Academic Press. doi:10.3386/w9730

Hemsley, J., & Mason, R. (2013). Knowledge and knowledge management in the social media age. *Journal of Organizational Computing and Electronic Commerce, 23*(1-2), 138–167. doi:10.1080/10919392.2013.748614

Jain, P. (2011). Personal knowledge management: The foundation of organisational knowledge management. *South African Journal of Library and Information Science, 77*(1), 1–14. doi:10.7553/77-1-62

Karakoçak, K. (2007). *Bilgi yönetimi ve verimliliğe etkisi: Türkiye Büyük Millet Meclisi uygulaması. Doktora Tezi (Yayımlanmamış)*. Ankara: Ankara Üniversitesi Sosyal Bilimler Enstitüsü İşletme Anabilim Dalı.

King, W. R. (2009). Knowledge management and organization learning: Annals of knowledge system (4th ed.). Springer. doi:10.1007/978-1-4419-0011-1

Korzaan, M., & Lawrence, C. (2015). Advancing student productivity: An introduction to evernote. *Proceedings of the EDSIG Conference Conference on Knowledge Systems and Computing Education.*

Lippincott, J. (2010). "Benim bilgim": Dijital kütüphaneler, sosyal ağlar ve kullanıcı deneyimi. Bilgi Yönetiminde Teknolojik Yakınsama ve Sosyal Ağlar 2. Uluslararası Değişen Dünyada Bilgi Yönetimi Sempozyumu Bildiriler Kitabı, 22-24 Eylül 2010, Hacettepe Üniversitesi Bilgi ve Belge Yönetimi Bölümü: Ankara.

Macnamara, J., & Zerfass, A. (2012). Social media communication in organizations: The challenges of balancing openness, strategy, and management. *International Journal of Strategic Communication*, *6*(4), 287–308. doi:10.1080/155311 8X.2012.711402

Oracle. (2012). *Is social media transforming your business?* An Oracle White Paper. Retrieved from http://www.oracle.com/us/products/applications/social-trans-bus-wp-1560502.pdf

Parise, S. (2009). Social media networks: What do they mean for knowledge management? *Journal of Knowledge Technology Case and Application Research*, *11*(2), 1–11. doi:10.1080/15228053.2009.10856156

Pfeiffer, H., & Tonkin, E. (2012). Personal and Professional knowledge management. *Bulletin of the American Society for Knowledge Science and Technology*, *38*(2), 22–23.

Razmerita, L., Kirchner, K., & Sudzina, F. (2009). Personal knowledge management: The role of web 2.0 tools for managing knowledge at individual and organisational levels. *Online Knowledge Review*, *33*(6), 1021–1039. doi:10.1108/14684520911010981

Smith, T. (2009). The social media revolution. *International Journal of Market Research*, *51*(4), 559–561. doi:10.2501/S1470785309200773

Solmaz, B., Tekin, G., Herzem, Z., & Demir, M. (2013). İnternet ve social media kullanımı üzerine bir uygulama. *Selçuk İletişim*, *7*(4), 24–32.

Swan, J., Newell, S., Scarbrough, H., & Hislop, D. (1999). Knowledge management and innovation: Networks and networking. *Journal of Knowledge Management*, *3*(4), 262–275. doi:10.1108/13673279910304014

Tutar, H. (2012). *Yönetim bilgi sistemi*. Ankara: Seçkin Yayıncılık.

KEY TERMS AND DEFINITIONS

Corporate Knowledge Management: Process of organizing the corporate information about subjects and everything which are the result of experiences or studies.

Evernote: An application especially for using personel knowledge management. Using for storing, sharing and organizing knowledge with different options.

Information Technologies: Creating, storing, exchanging all forms of data from new technologies.

Knowledge Management: Process of organizing the information about subjects and everything which are the result of experiences or studies.

Knowledge: Information or understanding about subjects and everything, result of experiences or studies.

Personal Knowledge Management: Process of organizing the personal information about subjects and everything which are the result of experiences or studies.

Social Media: New media channels (e.g. Facebook, Twitter, Instagram) which offer *content producing*, unlike traditional media channels (e.g television, radio, printed media products) for its users in digital age at 21st Century.

Chapter 9
The Role of Knowledge Transfer in Modern Organizations

Kijpokin Kasemsap
Suan Sunandha Rajabhat University, Thailand

ABSTRACT

This chapter reveals the overview of knowledge transfer; knowledge transfer, labor mobility, and labor diversity; knowledge transfer and subsidiary perspectives; barriers to knowledge transfer; knowledge transfer and absorptive capacity; knowledge transfer and knowledge acquisition; knowledge transfer and virtual teams; and the advanced issues of knowledge transfer in modern organizations. The process of transferring knowledge is an ongoing progression of learning, adjusting, and improving. At the organizational level, knowledge transfer manifests itself through changes in the knowledge of a unit. Most successful knowledge transfer efforts actively involve both the source of the knowledge and its receiver. Establishing performance expectations for those who will use the knowledge further quantifies the value of the transfer. Companies considering or using knowledge transfer processes, should continuously evaluate their social media readiness. The benefits of knowledge transfer for workplaces include the increases in productivity, speed, agility, profits, and growth.

DOI: 10.4018/978-1-5225-2897-5.ch009

INTRODUCTION

In the era of knowledge-based economy, knowledge has become the most important core competence (Tsai, et al., 2012). Knowledge management (KM) is the process of capturing, organizing, and storing information of workers and groups within an organization (Kasemsap, 2017a). Knowledge transfer is an important issue for KM programs (Herschel & Yermish, 2009) and is the systematic process of sharing knowledge and learning from the experience of others (Henry & Lee, 2009). In order to overcome the challenges posed by globalization, an increasingly complex business world, and the transition to the knowledge-based economy, both academia and practitioners need to reinforce the importance of knowledge transfer activities between universities and other stakeholders and the development of new forms of transfer activities between academia and the external environment (Dima, 2013).

Knowledge management system (KMS) can potentially enhance knowledge transfer by providing the ready access to knowledge across personal, departmental, and organizational boundaries (Fadel, et al., 2011). Effective KM ensures the sustainable infrastructure development through more effective communication across organizations, establishing the awareness of infrastructure needs of present and future generations (Wiewiora, et al., 2012). New knowledge is gained through knowledge acquisition and knowledge transfer processes that can be interpreted as the inbound knowledge flows from the viewpoint of a given organization (Laihonen & Koivuaho, 2011). Knowledge transfer is enhanced by the ready access to a network of assets by the intended knowledge users (Roemer, et al., 2009).

This chapter is based on a literature review of knowledge transfer. The extensive literature of knowledge transfer provides a contribution to practitioners and researchers by revealing the trends and issues of knowledge transfer in order to maximize the impact of knowledge transfer in modern organizations.

BACKGROUND

The rapid proliferation of the Internet and information technology (IT) has dramatically increased the speed of knowledge creation, and information distribution (Hsu, 2009). In the digital economy, the need for managing data, information, and knowledge is ever-increasing (Acar, et al., 2014). During the last decade, improvements in information and communication technology (ICT) have made possible the transformation of knowledge transfer processes from the purely informal communication mechanisms to the formal communication mechanisms that enhance the intra-organizational communication channels (Zapata-Cantú, et al., 2016).

With the complexity of organizations, it is important that organizations must understand how knowledge is created and shared around their core business processes (McLaughlin, 2013). Knowledge can be either tangible or intangible and knowledge transfer is a process responsible for gathering, analyzing, storing, and sharing this knowledge within an organization (Harorimana, 2012). Knowledge sharing is a mechanism to capture, disseminate, transfer, and apply the useful knowledge (Nemati-Anaraki & Heidari, 2016). Knowledge transfer in an organization is the process through which one unit (e.g., group, department, and division) is affected by the experience of another (Kwan & Cheung, 2006). Transferring knowledge leads to the synergistic cost advantages, better implementation of organizational strategies, and competitive advantage (Clinton, et al., 2011).

It is almost impossible for a society to achieve the sustainable growth without constantly creating and transferring knowledge (Khalil & Seleim, 2012). The interpersonal transfer of knowledge-in-use is necessary for individual and organizational learning (Moskaliuk, et al., 2016). Economic development is enhanced through the knowledge-based organizations to create both new market and new industry platforms (Kasemsap, 2016a). Many manufacturing companies have tended to integrate the services into their core product offerings in light of the ongoing transformation from a traditional industrial society to the knowledge-based society (Uchihira, 2014). Companies that are able to strengthen their knowledge transfer ability are in a better position to gain and sustain an advantage over their competitors (Bloodgood, et al., 2014).

Knowledge transfer activities within the university and industry alliance have the positive impact for both universities and industry (Anatan, 2015). A growing interest in the various aspects of knowledge transfer within multinational corporations (MNCs) has been evidenced by a recent surge in empirical research (Haghirian, 2009). The majority of KM research has examined the construct of knowledge transfer (Peachey, et al., 2008). Many policymakers and researchers consider knowledge transfer between academia and industry as one of the most promising measures to strengthen the economic development (Hofer, 2008). Organizations have to base their strategy and competitive advantage on the intangible resources and capabilities (Zapata-Cantú, et al., 2012).

IMPORTANT PERSPECTIVES ON KNOWLEDGE TRANSFER

This section explains the overview of knowledge transfer; knowledge transfer, labor mobility, and labor diversity; knowledge transfer and subsidiary perspectives; barriers to knowledge transfer; knowledge transfer and absorptive capacity; knowledge transfer and knowledge acquisition; knowledge transfer and virtual teams; and the advanced issues of knowledge transfer in modern organizations.

Overview of Knowledge Transfer

Knowledge is one of the most important competitive resources a business can have (Liu, 2008). The term knowledge transfer is often used in a generic sense to include the exchange of knowledge among individuals, teams, groups, and organizations (King, 2008). The understanding of how knowledge is transferred is very important for explaining the evolution and change in institutions, organizations, technology, and economy (Chen, et al., 2008). Knowledge transfer occurs whenever there are a source and a recipient, that is, the source and recipient model of knowledge transfer (Tho & Trang, 2015). Knowledge transfer is about the transfer of tangible resource, expertise, learning, and skills between academia and the non-academic community (Ferreira, et al., 2015).

Knowledge transfer, defined as the transmission of knowledge across organizational boundaries (Easterby-Smith, et al., 2008), is positively related to organizational performance. Knowledge transfer happens for individuals and is conducted by individuals (Haghirian, 2006). Knowledge transfer is a process of transmitting knowledge from the source to the recipient and the recipient acquires and uses the transferred knowledge (Ko, et al., 2005). Knowledge transfer takes place between a source and a recipient and, as posited by theory of knowledge transfer, the success of knowledge transfer depends on the characteristics of both the source and the recipient (Chang, et al., 2012).

The intensity and frequency of tacit knowledge transfer have a positive relationship with operational performance and affect both innovation speed and quality which are related to the long-term performance (Wang & Wang, 2012). Tacit knowledge transfer is positively influenced by four key factors: absorptive capacity of target unit, source unit's motivational disposition to share knowledge, cultural compatibility, and the extent of personal communication between foreign agents (Ismail, 2012). Both the knowledge disseminative capacity of knowledge sender and the knowledge absorptive capacity of knowledge recipient have a great impact on the performance of knowledge transfer (Wu, Liu, et al., 2011).

Knowledge transfer improves the innovative capabilities (Huizingh, 2011), increases the pace of innovation, and strengthens competitive advantage (Foss, et al., 2010). Firms often need to share their own knowledge to gain the access to the external knowledge toward performing the innovation activities (Zhang & Baden-Fuller, 2010). Information system (IS) support for knowledge transfer has a positive direct effect on labor productivity (Zhang, 2007). With the technological uncertainty and complexity, knowledge transfer has become critically important, as firms rely on the open innovation processes to ensure the long-term competitiveness (Chesbrough, 2003). Organizations join the multi-organizational networks to mitigate the environmental uncertainties and to access knowledge (Priestley & Samaddar, 2007).

Knowledge transfer offices (KTOs) in any organization have an important role in consolidating the relationship between researchers and entrepreneurs to ensure an alignment of interests, speeches, and timings in order to promote an effective transfer of knowledge (Pinto, et al., 2016). Firm's accessibility to the broader knowledge-base perspective through external learning has attracted the attention of both practitioners and scholars in strategic management, which have analyzed the knowledge transfer process from both intra-organizational and inter-organizational perspectives (Canestrino & Magliocca, 2016). Transferring knowledge through social media websites has received widespread attention by organizations (Gyamfi, 2016). Transnational knowledge transfer is knowledge transfer across national boundaries (Duan, et al, 2012).

To generate and transmit knowledge, companies develop the effective learning processes (Gil & Mataveli, 2016). In order to improve the level of decision making and competitive advantage, organizations try to develop the new KM techniques that are suited for the evolving global economy (Xia & Gupta, 2008). Knowledge transfer is vital to business success and the transfer of knowledge occurs within organizations whether the process is managed or not (Barrett, et al., 2000). Generating knowledge flows can be viewed as the significant leadership process (Nylund & Raelin, 2015). Collaborative problem-solving and decision-making processes with shared insights can enhance the tacit knowledge transfer in the company (Koskinen, et al., 2003).

Knowledge Transfer, Labor Mobility, and Labor Diversity

Worker flows are related to the organizational outcomes, reflecting the contributions to the organizational productivity of both incoming workers' human capital and knowledge that they carry over from the previous workplaces (Marino, et al., 2016). Through inter-firm labor mobility, an enterprise may gain access to the knowledge pool to which the incoming workers have been exposed in past work environments (Marino et al., 2016). The knowledge pool may partly arise from the learning-by-doing activities as recognized in the early seminal works (Nelson & Winter, 1982) and more recent empirical studies (Gaynor, et al., 2005).

Both ethnic heterogeneity and demographic heterogeneity do not positively correlate with productivity, indicating that the negative effects of the communication and integration costs associated with a more demographically and culturally diverse workforce significantly counteract the positive effects of diversity that arise from the enhanced creativity and knowledge spillover (Alesina & La Ferrara, 2005). Labor mobility can generate the knowledge transfers from the foreign-owned (Poole, 2013), research and development-intensive (Moen, 2005), patenting (Kim & Marschke, 2005), and more productive (Stoyanov & Zubanov, 2012) companies. Labor mobility is a potential channel for knowledge spillover within a broader set of companies in both the manufacturing and service sectors, introducing the generalized process of learning-by-hiring into the economy (Parrotta & Pozzoli, 2012).

Knowledge Transfer and Subsidiary Perspectives

MNC is a differentiated network, in which a focal subsidiary is connected with its headquarters and other subsidiaries across the globe (Nohria & Ghoshal, 1997). The parent MNC possesses the valuable knowledge that subsidiaries can utilize to become more competitive (Ben Hamida, 2016). Social ties are considered as the significant enablers of the MNC-related network and a prerequisite for knowledge transfer within the organization (Ji & Connerley, 2013).

Headquarter knowledge transfer represents a set of knowhow and skills moving from the MNC's headquarters to a focal subsidiary, which can be recognized as the top-down vertical knowledge transfer (Ciabuschi, Dellestrand, & Kappen, 2011). Peer subsidiary knowledge transfer, on the other hand, represents a form of horizontal knowledge that moves from one subsidiary to another (Ciabuschi et al., 2011). Because peer subsidiaries operate in different environmental contexts, their knowledge is likely to be distinct and location-bounded (Rugman & Verbeke, 2001).

The MNCs' headquarters tends to provide their foreign subsidiaries with the firm-specific advantages (Bhanji & Oxley, 2013), often in the form of technological and marketing knowledge that the headquarters acquire from the multiple sources. The parent-driven investment is one of the typical processes through which subsidiaries can develop their own capabilities (Birkinshaw & Hood, 1998). Because of the potential differences in local market conditions, from a focal subsidiary's standpoint, knowledge moving from its headquarters versus peer subsidiaries is likely to execute the different implications (Li & Lee, 2015).

Barriers to Knowledge Transfer

Knowledge transfer is difficult due to the ambiguity and context dependent nature of knowledge (Deng & Mao, 2012). The key challenge is to balance the need for an open knowledge exchange regime with the need to control both knowledge flows and knowledge exchanges to avoid the leakage of knowledge (Oxley & Sampson, 2004). Many organizations deploy technology without due consideration for how their employees access, create, and share both information and knowledge (McLaughlin,

2009). By removing the bottlenecks of knowledge transfer, organizations can increase both their internal efficiency and their external productivity (Laihonen & Lönnqvist, 2011).

MNCs can establish various human resource management (HRM) practices that impact knowledge transfer barriers associated with the behavior of knowledge senders and knowledge receivers (Minbaeva, 2008). Communication barriers, cultural differences, and lack of equivalence in individual competence can slow down the knowledge transfer process (Huong, Katsuhiro, & Chi, 2013). New product development (NPD) is the process of developing a new product or service for the marketplace (Kasemsap, 2016b). NPD teams can reduce barriers by aligning strategies in the four knowledge-creation steps: socialization, externalization, combination, and internalization (Huang, Chang, & Henderson, 2008).

Knowledge Transfer and Absorptive Capacity

Absorptive capacity is an ability to recognize the value of new information, and to assimilate and apply such information for the commercial perspectives (Cohen & Levinthal, 1990). Zahra and George (2002) recognized absorptive capacity as a set of organizational processes, by which firms acquire, transform, and exploit knowledge to generate the organizational capability. Absorptive capacity facilitates knowledge transfer within MNCs (Gupta & Govindarajan, 2000). The role of absorptive capacity in knowledge transfer within the firms is critical in knowledge transfer in joint ventures that have the elements of intra- and inter-firm knowledge transfer (Lane, Salk, & Lyles, 2001).

The changes in the knowledge transfer requirements are considered as the single most important challenge to KM (Solli-Sæther & Gottschalk, 2010). The quality and quantity of knowledge that firms transfer depend on absorptive capacity and trust among firms (Machikita, Tsuji, & Ueki, 2016). Minbaeva (2005) indicated that the employment of HRM practices affects the absorptive capacity of knowledge receivers and positively correlates with the degree of knowledge transfer to the subsidiaries. Among a wide range of HRM practices, human resource development (HRD) practices for enhancing employees' capacity for quality management are fundamental for the success of technology transfer to the manufacturing firms in developing countries (Wu & Hsu, 2001).

Knowledge Transfer and Knowledge Acquisition

The acquisition of tacit knowledge is affected by learning styles (Armstrong & Mahmud, 2008). Firms can achieve the effective performance if they have the idiosyncratic and non-substitutable organizational knowledge that can be utilized for the enhanced value creation (Junni & Sarala, 2012). Knowledge transfer is the acquisition and utilization of new sets of knowledge-based resources (Ranft & Lord, 2002) and plays a significant role in the process of synergy realization in acquisitions (Junni, 2011). Knowledge transfer is important for value creation, both for the acquirer and for the target of a cross-border merger and acquisition (M&A) (Sarala, Junni, Cooper, & Tarba, 2014).

The process of both knowledge transfer and learning is conducive to the performance improvement of international acquisitions (Zou & Ghauri, 2008). Managers at the headquarters should recognize the value of maintaining the embedded relationships with their subsidiaries (Najafi-Tavani, Zaefarian, Naudé, & Giroud, 2015). Organizational culture differences have a negative influence on cross-border acquisition (CBA) performance, but also mediate the relationship between knowledge transfer and CBA performance (Ahammad, Tarba, Liu, & Glaister, 2016). Previous studies have explained several mechanisms facilitating knowledge transfer, such as social community (Bresman, Birkinshaw, & Nobel, 2010), culture as the learning strategy (Zander & Zander, 2010), and dominant logic perspective (Verbeke, 2010).

Knowledge Transfer and Virtual Teams

Globalization and advancing technologies have extended the virtual work arrangements (e.g., virtual teams and virtual communities on the Internet) and have extended the knowledge base upon which individuals can draw while creating, acquiring, sharing, and integrating knowledge (Wan, Haggerty, & Wang, 2015). Virtual team is a group of individuals spread across different time zones, cultures, and languages which are united by a common goal (Kasemsap, 2016c).

Virtual teams can span the time zones, geographies, and cultures toward increasing the efficiency of knowledge transfer (Lyons, 2000). Virtual team can be utilized in every organization to virtually improve productivity, responsiveness, and effectiveness because of the synergy of bringing various expertise, talent, and perspectives together (Jones, 2016). Virtual collaboration, electronic collaboration technologies, and knowledge transfer significantly affect team performance (Ngoma & Lind, 2015).

Advanced Issues of Knowledge Transfer in Modern Organizations

Managing organizational knowledge in alliances implies establishing the best possible strategic design to create, acquire, maintain, transfer, and apply organizational knowledge developed among employees and business partners in order to achieve the strategic business goals (Donate, Guadamillas, & Sánchez de Pablo, 2012).

The importance of identifying the appropriate knowledge transfer mechanisms is paramount (Hasnain, Jasimuddin, & Fuller-Love, 2016). The ability to value and organize the external knowledge is recognized as the basis of competitive advantage (Priestly, 2006).

Enterprise resource planning (ERP) is an accounting-oriented software system for identifying and planning the resource needs of an enterprise (Kasemsap, 2015). The knowledge in the business process from ERP package is transferred into the organization along with business rules inherent in the process due to the process automation, the cross-functional nature of ERP package, and limited flexibility of the package (Lee, Lee, & Sieber, 2002). Organizations that wish to remain successful in the market in this age of globalization, marked by the financial and economic crisis, must be able to adapt to its rapid changes and to fulfill every new demand (Gorela & Biloslavo, 2015). The institutional arrangements deeply affect the outcomes of knowledge transfer (Eom & Fountain, 2013).

Training plays an important role in both knowledge transfer and profession development (Ugolini, Massetti, Sanesi, & Pearlmutter, 2015). Perception of learning positively mediates the relationships between occupational satisfaction and perceived training transfer and between trainee reactions and perceived training transfer (Kasemsap, 2014a). Social capital is the network of relationships among people, firms, and institutions in a society, together with the associated norms of behavior, trust, and cooperation that enable a society to effectively function (Kasemsap, 2014b). Social capital can help increase the economic growth, organizational performance, and KM via the effective social networks by utilizing social media platforms in the digital age (Kasemsap, 2017b). Successful transfer of knowledge within organizations depends on the accumulated social capital embedded within organizational social networks (Sherif & Sherif, 2008).

Technological innovations in the area of digital media have opened up the possibility for a great number of inventive ways to transfer knowledge in online science learning environments (Downing & Holtz, 2008). It is necessary to ensure that the metadata, such as the original creator information, is protected to encourage the transfer of knowledge in a virtual workplace (Rive, 2008). Educational computer games can motivate students to develop the basic competencies and encourage challenging themselves to be better and learn the additional knowledge related to the important tasks (Kasemsap, 2017c). Failing to consider the educational design principles as well as cognitive and motivational support in educational computer games can result in the serious consequences pertaining to learners' cognitive process and motivation in learning (Zheng & Truong, 2017).

The decision regarding strategic alliance choice can affect both the ease of knowledge flow and the intention to share knowledge (Anatan, 2013). The degree of difficulty in knowledge transfer increases for multinational managers and their counterparts because cultural differences affect information processing, management styles, and sense making (Rothberg & Klingenberg, 2010). Knowledge infrastructure capabilities are related to the knowledge transfer success, and more specifically to its effectiveness whereas knowledge processes capabilities are only related to the efficiency of such transfer (Laframboise, Croteau, Beaudry, & Manovas, 2009). The technological and knowledge capability of multinational affiliates systematically enhances the performance of their parent companies (Driffield, Love, & Yang, 2016).

FUTURE RESEARCH DIRECTIONS

The classification of the extensive literature in the domains of knowledge transfer will provide the potential opportunities for future research. Communities of practice (CoPs) can create the valuable opportunities for members to explicitly discuss the productivity of their participation in the group toward sharing knowledge in modern business (Kasemsap, 2016d). Knowledge creation is the formation of new ideas through interactions between explicit and tacit knowledge in the individual's human minds (Kasemsap, 2017d). Talent management is the organization's attempt to recruit, develop, and retain the high-potential people that they can find, afford, and hire (Kasemsap, 2017e).

In knowledge-based organizations (KBOs), career management is a sequential process supported human resource department by that starts from an understanding of oneself and encompasses occupational awareness through KM and organizational learning regarding training and development program and talent management program (Kasemsap, 2017f). An examination of linkages among knowledge transfer, CoPs, knowledge creation, talent management, and career management would seem to be viable for future research efforts.

CONCLUSION

This chapter provided the overview of knowledge transfer; knowledge transfer, labor mobility, and labor diversity; knowledge transfer and subsidiary perspectives; barriers to knowledge transfer; knowledge transfer and absorptive capacity; knowledge transfer and knowledge acquisition; knowledge transfer and virtual teams; and the advanced issues of knowledge transfer in modern organizations. Knowledge transfer is the managerial challenge inside global firms. The process of transferring knowledge is an ongoing progression of learning, adjusting, and improving. At the organizational level, knowledge transfer manifests itself through changes in the knowledge of a unit.

Most successful knowledge transfer efforts actively involve both the source of the knowledge and its receiver. Establishing performance expectations for those who will utilize the knowledge further quantifies the value of the transfer. Companies considering or using knowledge transfer processes, should continuously evaluate their social media readiness. The benefits of knowledge transfer for workplaces include the increases in productivity, speed, agility, profits, and growth.

REFERENCES

Acar, W., Burns, A. T., & Datta, P. (2014). Explicit knowledge transfers in new product development. *International Journal of Strategic Decision Sciences*, *5*(4), 16–50. doi:10.4018/ijsds.2014100102

Ahammad, M. F., Tarba, S. Y., Liu, Y., & Glaister, K. W. (2016). Knowledge transfer and cross-border acquisition performance: The impact of cultural distance and employee retention. *International Business Review*, *25*(1), 66–75. doi:10.1016/j.ibusrev.2014.06.015

Alesina, A., & La Ferrara, E. (2005). Ethnic diversity and economic performance. *Journal of Economic Literature*, *43*(3), 762–800. doi:10.1257/002205105774431243

Aman, A., & Nicholson, B. (2011). Managing knowledge transfer in offshore software development: The role of copresent and ICT-based interaction. In F. Tan (Ed.), *International enterprises and global information technologies: Advancing management practices* (pp. 302–320). Hershey, PA: IGI Global. doi:10.4018/978-1-60960-605-3.ch014

Anatan, L. (2013). A proposed framework of university to industry knowledge transfer. *Review of Integrative Business and Economics Research*, *2*(2), 304–325.

Anatan, L. (2015). Conceptual issues in university to industry knowledge transfer studies: A literature review. *Procedia: Social and Behavioral Sciences*, *211*, 711–717. doi:10.1016/j.sbspro.2015.11.090

Armstrong, S. J., & Mahmud, A. (2008). Experiential learning and the acquisition of managerial tacit knowledge. *Academy of Management Learning & Education*, *7*(2), 189–208. doi:10.5465/AMLE.2008.32712617

Barrett, W., Lau, M. S., & Dew, P. M. (2000). Facilitating knowledge transfer in an R&D environment: A case study. In D. Schwartz, T. Brasethvik, & M. Divitini (Eds.), *Internet-based organizational memory and knowledge management* (pp. 147–169). Hershey, PA: IGI Publishing. doi:10.4018/978-1-878289-82-7.ch008

Ben Hamida, L. (2016). Building R&D capabilities abroad and the role of reverse knowledge transfer in explaining MNCs' productivity. In M. Erdoğdu & B. Christiansen (Eds.), *Handbook of research on comparative economic development perspectives on Europe and the MENA region* (pp. 219–235). Hershey, PA: IGI Global. doi:10.4018/978-1-4666-9548-1.ch011

Bhanji, Z., & Oxley, J. E. (2013). Overcoming the dual liability of foreignness and privateness in international corporate citizenship partnerships. *Journal of International Business Studies, 44*(4), 290–311. doi:10.1057/jibs.2013.8

Birkinshaw, J., & Hood, N. (1998). Multinational subsidiary evolution: Capability and charter change in foreign-owned subsidiary companies. *Academy of Management Review, 23*(4), 773–795.

Bloodgood, J. M., Chilton, M. A., & Bloodgood, T. C. (2014). The effect of knowledge transfer motivation, receiver capability, and motivation on organizational performance. In M. Chilton & J. Bloodgood (Eds.), *Knowledge management and competitive advantage: Issues and potential solutions* (pp. 232–242). Hershey, PA: IGI Global. doi:10.4018/978-1-4666-4679-7.ch013

Bresman, H., Birkinshaw, J., & Nobel, R. (2010). Knowledge transfer in international acquisitions. *Journal of International Business Studies, 41*(1), 5–20. doi:10.1057/jibs.2009.56

Canestrino, R., & Magliocca, P. (2016). Transferring knowledge through cross-border communities of practice. In S. Buckley, G. Majewski, & A. Giannakopoulos (Eds.), *Organizational knowledge facilitation through communities of practice in emerging markets* (pp. 1–30). Hershey, PA: IGI Global. doi:10.4018/978-1-5225-0013-1.ch001

Chang, Y. Y., Gong, Y., & Peng, M. W. (2012). Expatriate knowledge transfer, subsidiary absorptive capacity, and subsidiary performance. *Academy of Management Journal, 55*(4), 927–948. doi:10.5465/amj.2010.0985

Chesbrough, H. (2003). *Open innovation: The new imperative for creating and profiting from technology.* Boston, MA: Harvard Business School Press.

Ciabuschi, F., Dellestrand, H., & Kappen, P. (2011). Exploring the effects of vertical and lateral mechanisms in international knowledge transfer projects. *Management International Review*, *51*(2), 129–155. doi:10.1007/s11575-011-0068-1

Clinton, M. S., Merritt, K. L., & Murray, S. R. (2011). Facilitating knowledge transfer and the achievement of competitive advantage with corporate universities: An exploratory model based on media richness and type of knowledge to be transferred. In M. Jennex (Ed.), *Global aspects and cultural perspectives on knowledge management: Emerging dimensions* (pp. 329–345). Hershey, PA: IGI Global. doi:10.4018/978-1-60960-555-1.ch020

Cohen, W. M., & Levinthal, D. A. (1990). Absorptive capacity: A new perspective on learning and innovation. *Administrative Science Quarterly*, *35*(1), 128–152. doi:10.2307/2393553

Deng, C., & Mao, J. (2012). Knowledge transfer to vendors in offshore information systems outsourcing: Antecedents and effects on performance. *Journal of Global Information Management*, *20*(3), 1–22. doi:10.4018/jgim.2012070101

Dima, A. M. (2013). Knowledge transfer: The innovation side of knowledge management in education. In S. Buckley & M. Jakovljevic (Eds.), *Knowledge management innovations for interdisciplinary education: Organizational applications* (pp. 88–107). Hershey, PA: IGI Global. doi:10.4018/978-1-4666-1969-2.ch005

Donate, M. J., Guadamillas, F., & Sánchez de Pablo, J. D. (2012). Knowledge management for strategic alliances: A case study. *International Journal of Strategic Information Technology and Applications*, *3*(3), 1–19. doi:10.4018/jsita.2012070101

Downing, K. F., & Holtz, J. K. (2008). Knowledge transfer and collaboration structures for online science. In K. Downing & J. Holtz (Eds.), *Online science learning: Best practices and technologies* (pp. 98–119). Hershey, PA: IGI Global. doi:10.4018/978-1-59904-986-1.ch006

Driffield, N., Love, J. H., & Yang, Y. (2016). Reverse international knowledge transfer in the MNE: (Where) does affiliate performance boost parent performance? *Research Policy*, *45*(2), 491–506. doi:10.1016/j.respol.2015.11.004

Duan, Y., Xu, M., & Feng, W. (2012). Transnational knowledge transfer. In *Organizational learning and knowledge: Concepts, methodologies, tools and applications* (pp. 375–387). Hershey, PA: IGI Global. doi:10.4018/978-1-60960-783-8.ch122

Easterby-Smith, M., Lyles, M. A., & Tsang, E. W. K. (2008). Inter-organizational knowledge transfer: Current themes and future prospects. *Journal of Management Studies*, *45*(4), 677–690. doi:10.1111/j.1467-6486.2008.00773.x

Eom, S., & Fountain, J. E. (2013). Enhancing information services through public-private partnerships: Information technology knowledge transfer underlying structures to develop shared services in the U.S. and Korea. In J. Gil-Garcia (Ed.), *E-government success around the world: Cases, empirical studies, and practical recommendations* (pp. 15–40). Hershey, PA: IGI Global. doi:10.4018/978-1-4666-4173-0.ch002

Fadel, K. J., Durcikova, A., & Cha, H. S. (2011). An experiment of information elaboration in mediated knowledge transfer. In M. Jennex (Ed.), *Global aspects and cultural perspectives on knowledge management: Emerging dimensions* (pp. 311–328). Hershey, PA: IGI Global. doi:10.4018/978-1-60960-555-1.ch019

Ferreira, J. J., Fernandes, C., & Raposo, M. L. (2015). Knowledge transfer between universities and knowledge intensive business services: An empirical study. In L. Carmo Farinha, J. Ferreira, H. Smith, & S. Bagchi-Sen (Eds.), *Handbook of research on global competitive advantage through innovation and entrepreneurship* (pp. 320–338). Hershey, PA: IGI Global. doi:10.4018/978-1-4666-8348-8.ch019

Foss, N. J., Husted, K., & Michailova, S. (2010). Governing knowledge sharing in organizations: Levels of analysis, governance mechanisms, and research directions. *Journal of Management Studies*, *47*(3), 455–482. doi:10.1111/j.1467-6486.2009.00870.x

Gaynor, M., Seider, H., & Vogt, W. B. (2005). The volume-outcome effect, scale economies, and learning-by-doing. *The American Economic Review*, *95*(2), 243–247. doi:10.1257/000282805774670329

Gil, A. J., & Mataveli, M. (2016). The knowledge transfer process on the development of dynamic capabilities through industrial networks. In G. Alor-Hernández, C. Sánchez-Ramírez, & J. García-Alcaraz (Eds.), *Handbook of research on managerial strategies for achieving optimal performance in industrial processes* (pp. 562–586). Hershey, PA: IGI Global. doi:10.4018/978-1-5225-0130-5.ch026

Gorela, K., & Biloslavo, R. (2015). Relationship between senior and junior researcher: Challenges and opportunities for knowledge creating and sharing. In P. Diviacco, P. Fox, C. Pshenichny, & A. Leadbetter (Eds.), *Collaborative knowledge in scientific research networks* (pp. 90–125). Hershey, PA: IGI Global. doi:10.4018/978-1-4666-6567-5.ch006

Gupta, A., & Govindarajan, V. (2000). Knowledge flows within multinational corporations. *Strategic Management Journal, 21*(4), 473–496. doi:10.1002/(SICI)1097-0266(200004)21:4<473::AID-SMJ84>3.0.CO;2-I

Gyamfi, A. (2016). The impact of media richness on the usage of Web 2.0 services for knowledge transfer. *International Journal of E-Services and Mobile Applications, 8*(2), 21–37. doi:10.4018/IJESMA.2016040102

Haghirian, P. (2006). International knowledge transfer as a challenge for communities of practice. In E. Coakes & S. Clarke (Eds.), *Encyclopedia of communities of practice in information and knowledge management* (pp. 234–238). Hershey, PA: IGI Global. doi:10.4018/978-1-59140-556-6.ch042

Haghirian, P. (2009). Knowledge transfer within multinational corporations: An intercultural challenge. In J. Girard (Ed.), *Building organizational memories: Will you know what you knew?* (pp. 57–68). Hershey, PA: IGI Global. doi:10.4018/978-1-59904-540-5.ch005

Harorimana, D. (2012). Knowledge, culture, and cultural impact on knowledge management: Some lessons for researchers and practitioners. In *Organizational learning and knowledge: Concepts, methodologies, tools and applications* (pp. 2474–2485). Hershey, PA: IGI Global. doi:10.4018/978-1-60960-783-8.ch701

Hasnain, S. S., Jasimuddin, S. M., & Fuller-Love, N. (2016). Exploring causes, taxonomies, mechanisms and barriers influencing knowledge transfer: Empirical studies in NGOs. *Information Resources Management Journal, 29*(1), 39–56. doi:10.4018/IRMJ.2016010103

Hatak, I., & Roessl, D. (2014). Knowledge transfer strategies within family firm succession. In K. Todorov & D. Smallbone (Eds.), *Handbook of research on strategic management in small and medium enterprises* (pp. 266–281). Hershey, PA: IGI Global. doi:10.4018/978-1-4666-5962-9.ch013

Henry, L. E., & Lee, D. (2009). Transferring knowledge in a knowledge-based economy. In T. Torres-Coronas & M. Arias-Oliva (Eds.), *Encyclopedia of human resources information systems: Challenges in e-HRM* (pp. 862–870). Hershey, PA: IGI Global. doi:10.4018/978-1-59904-883-3.ch127

Herschel, R. T., & Yermish, I. (2009). Knowledge transfer: Revisiting video. In N. Kock (Ed.), *E-collaboration: Concepts, methodologies, tools, and applications* (pp. 151–163). Hershey, PA: IGI Global. doi:10.4018/978-1-60566-652-5.ch013

Hofer, F. (2008). Knowledge transfer between academia and industry. In M. Jennex (Ed.), *Knowledge management: Concepts, methodologies, tools, and applications* (pp. 3086–3095). Hershey, PA: IGI Global. doi:10.4018/978-1-59904-933-5.ch252

Hsu, H. (2009). Managing the information technology: Knowledge transfer in virtual teams. In M. Lytras & P. Ordóñez de Pablos (Eds.), *Knowledge ecology in global business: Managing intellectual capital* (pp. 192–210). Hershey, PA: IGI Global. doi:10.4018/978-1-60566-270-1.ch012

Huang, C. M., Chang, H. C., & Henderson, S. (2008). Knowledge transfer barriers between research and development and marketing groups within Taiwanese small- and medium-sized enterprise high-technology new product development teams. *Human Factors and Ergonomics in Manufacturing & Service Industries, 18*(6), 621–657. doi:10.1002/hfm.20130

Huizingh, E. (2011). Open innovation: State of the art and future perspectives. *Technovation, 31*(1), 2–9. doi:10.1016/j.technovation.2010.10.002

Huong, N. T., Katsuhiro, U., & Chi, D. H. (2013). Knowledge transfer in offshore outsourcing: A case study of Japanese and Vietnamese software companies. In F. Tan (Ed.), *Global diffusion and adoption of technologies for knowledge and information sharing* (pp. 110–128). Hershey, PA: IGI Global. doi:10.4018/978-1-4666-2142-8.ch005

Ismail, K. M. (2012). Theorizing on the role of individualism-collectivism in tacit knowledge transfer between agents in international alliances. *International Journal of Knowledge Management, 8*(1), 71–85. doi:10.4018/jkm.2012010104

Ji, F. X., & Connerley, M. L. (2013). Local embeddedness and expatriates' effectiveness for knowledge transfer within MNCs: A cultural perspective. In B. Christiansen, E. Turkina, & N. Williams (Eds.), *Cultural and technological influences on global business* (pp. 420–436). Hershey, PA: IGI Global. doi:10.4018/978-1-4666-3966-9.ch022

Jones, N. B. (2016). Knowledge transfer and knowledge creation in virtual teams. In C. Graham (Ed.), *Strategic management and leadership for systems development in virtual spaces* (pp. 110–122). Hershey, PA: IGI Global. doi:10.4018/978-1-4666-9688-4.ch007

Junni, P. (2011). Knowledge transfer in acquisitions: Fear of exploitation and contamination. *Scandinavian Journal of Management, 27*(3), 307–321. doi:10.1016/j.scaman.2011.05.003

Junni, P., & Sarala, R. M. (2012). The role of cultural learning and collective teaching initiatives in M&A knowledge transfer. *European Journal of Cross-Cultural Competence and Management, 2*(3/4), 275–298. doi:10.1504/EJCCM.2012.052593

Kasemsap, K. (2014a). Constructing a unified framework and a causal model of occupational satisfaction, trainee reactions, perception of learning, and perceived training transfer. In S. Hai-Jew (Ed.), *Remote workforce training: Effective technologies and strategies* (pp. 28–52). Hershey, PA: IGI Global. doi:10.4018/978-1-4666-5137-1.ch003

Kasemsap, K. (2014b). The role of social capital in higher education institutions. In N. Baporikar (Ed.), *Handbook of research on higher education in the MENA region: Policy and practice* (pp. 119–147). Hershey, PA: IGI Global. doi:10.4018/978-1-4666-6198-1.ch007

Kasemsap, K. (2015). Implementing enterprise resource planning. In M. Khosrow-Pour (Ed.), *Encyclopedia of information science and technology* (3rd ed., pp. 798–807). Hershey, PA: IGI Global. doi:10.4018/978-1-4666-5888-2.ch076

Kasemsap, K. (2016a). Advocating entrepreneurship education and knowledge management in global business. In N. Baporikar (Ed.), *Handbook of research on entrepreneurship in the contemporary knowledge-based global economy* (pp. 313–339). Hershey, PA: IGI Global. doi:10.4018/978-1-4666-8798-1.ch014

Kasemsap, K. (2016b). Creating product innovation strategies through knowledge management in global business. In A. Goel & P. Singhal (Eds.), *Product innovation through knowledge management and social media strategies* (pp. 330–357). Hershey, PA: IGI Global. doi:10.4018/978-1-4666-9607-5.ch015

Kasemsap, K. (2016c). Examining the roles of virtual team and information technology in global business. In C. Graham (Ed.), *Strategic management and leadership for systems development in virtual spaces* (pp. 1–21). Hershey, PA: IGI Global. doi:10.4018/978-1-4666-9688-4.ch001

Kasemsap, K. (2016d). Utilizing communities of practice to facilitate knowledge sharing in the digital age. In S. Buckley, G. Majewski, & A. Giannakopoulos (Eds.), *Organizational knowledge facilitation through communities of practice in emerging markets* (pp. 198–224). Hershey, PA: IGI Global. doi:10.4018/978-1-5225-0013-1.ch011

Kasemsap, K. (2017a). Mastering knowledge management in academic libraries. In B. Gunjal (Ed.), *Managing knowledge and scholarly assets in academic libraries* (pp. 27–55). Hershey, PA: IGI Global. doi:10.4018/978-1-5225-1741-2.ch002

Kasemsap, K. (2017b). The fundamentals of social capital. In G. Koç, M. Claes, & B. Christiansen (Eds.), *Cultural influences on architecture* (pp. 259–292). Hershey, PA: IGI Global. doi:10.4018/978-1-5225-1744-3.ch010

Kasemsap, K. (2017c). Mastering educational computer games, educational video games, and serious games in the digital age. In R. Alexandre Peixoto de Queirós & M. Pinto (Eds.), *Gamification-based e-learning strategies for computer programming education* (pp. 30–52). Hershey, PA: IGI Global. doi:10.4018/978-1-5225-1034-5. ch003

Kasemsap, K. (2017d). Investigating the roles of neuroscience and knowledge management in higher education. In S. Mukerji & P. Tripathi (Eds.), *Handbook of research on administration, policy, and leadership in higher education* (pp. 112–140). Hershey, PA: IGI Global. doi:10.4018/978-1-5225-0672-0.ch006

Kasemsap, K. (2017e). Fundamentals of talent management: Capitalizing on intellectual assets. In M. Mupepi (Ed.), *Effective talent management strategies for organizational success* (pp. 260–282). Hershey, PA: IGI Global. doi:10.4018/978-1-5225-1961-4.ch017

Kasemsap, K. (2017f). Career management in the knowledge-based organizations. *International Journal of Knowledge-Based Organizations, 7*(2), 60–73. doi:10.4018/ IJKBO.2017040105

Khalil, O. E., & Seleim, A. (2012). Culture and knowledge transfer capacity: A cross-national study. In M. Jennex (Ed.), *Conceptual models and outcomes of advancing knowledge management: New technologies* (pp. 305–332). Hershey, PA: IGI Global. doi:10.4018/978-1-4666-0035-5.ch016

Kim, J., & Marschke, G. (2005). Labor mobility of scientists, technological diffusion, and the firm's patenting decision. *The Rand Journal of Economics, 36*(2), 298–317.

King, W. R. (2008). Knowledge transfer. In M. Jennex (Ed.), *Knowledge management: Concepts, methodologies, tools, and applications* (pp. 123–129). Hershey, PA: IGI Global. doi:10.4018/978-1-59904-933-5.ch010

Ko, D. G., Kirsch, L. J., & King, W. R. (2005). Antecedents of knowledge transfer from consultants to clients in enterprise system implementations. *Management Information Systems Quarterly, 29*(1), 59–85.

Koskinen, K. U., Pihlanto, P., & Vanharanta, H. (2003). Tacit knowledge acquisition and sharing in a project work context. *International Journal of Project Management*, *21*(4), 281–290. doi:10.1016/S0263-7863(02)00030-3

Kwan, M. M., & Cheung, P. (2006). The knowledge transfer process: From field studies to technology development. *Journal of Database Management*, *17*(1), 16–32. doi:10.4018/jdm.2006010102

Laframboise, K., Croteau, A., Beaudry, A., & Manovas, M. (2009). Interdepartmental knowledge transfer success during information technology projects. In M. Jennex (Ed.), *Knowledge management, organizational memory and transfer behavior: Global approaches and advancements* (pp. 189–210). Hershey, PA: IGI Global. doi:10.4018/978-1-60566-140-7.ch012

Laihonen, H., & Koivuaho, M. (2011). Knowledge flow audit: Indentifying, measuring and managing knowledge asset dynamics. In B. Vallejo-Alonso, A. Rodriguez-Castellanos, & G. Arregui-Ayastuy (Eds.), *Identifying, measuring, and valuing knowledge-based intangible assets: New perspectives* (pp. 22–42). Hershey, PA: IGI Global. doi:10.4018/978-1-60960-054-9.ch002

Laihonen, H., & Lönnqvist, A. (2011). How knowledge assets are transformed into value: The case of knowledge flows and service productivity. In G. Schiuma (Ed.), *Managing knowledge assets and business value creation in organizations: Measures and dynamics* (pp. 173–187). Hershey, PA: IGI Global. doi:10.4018/978-1-60960-071-6.ch011

Lane, P. J., Salk, J. E., & Lyles, M. A. (2001). Absorptive capacity, learning, and performance in international joint ventures. *Strategic Management Journal*, *22*(12), 1139–1161. doi:10.1002/smj.206

Lee, Z., Lee, J., & Sieber, T. (2002). ERP-based knowledge transfer. In D. White (Ed.), *Knowledge mapping and management* (pp. 79–87). Hershey, PA: IRM Press. doi:10.4018/978-1-931777-17-9.ch009

Li, J., & Lee, R. P. (2015). Can knowledge transfer within MNCs hurt subsidiary performance? The role of subsidiary entrepreneurial culture and capabilities. *Journal of World Business*, *50*(4), 663–673. doi:10.1016/j.jwb.2014.09.004

Liu, S. (2008). Knowledge sharing: Interactive processes between organizational knowledge-sharing initiative and individuals' sharing practice. In E. Bolisani (Ed.), *Building the knowledge society on the Internet: Sharing and exchanging knowledge in networked environments* (pp. 1–23). Hershey, PA: IGI Global. doi:10.4018/978-1-59904-816-1.ch001

Lyons, K. L. (2000). Using patterns to capture tacit knowledge and enhance knowledge transfer in virtual teams. In Y. Malhotra (Ed.), *Knowledge management and virtual organizations* (pp. 124–143). Hershey, PA: Idea Group Publishing. doi:10.4018/978-1-930708-65-5.ch007

Machikita, T., Tsuji, M., & Ueki, Y. (2016). Does Kaizen create backward knowledge transfer to Southeast Asian firms? *Journal of Business Research, 69*(5), 1556–1561. doi:10.1016/j.jbusres.2015.10.016

Marino, M., Parrotta, P., & Pozzoli, D. (2016). Educational diversity and knowledge transfers via inter-firm labor mobility. *Journal of Economic Behavior & Organization, 123*, 168–183. doi:10.1016/j.jebo.2015.10.019

McLaughlin, S. (2009). Improving supply chain performance through the implementation of process related knowledge transfer mechanisms. *International Journal of Knowledge Management, 5*(2), 64–86. doi:10.4018/jkm.2009040105

McLaughlin, S. (2013). Assessing the impact of knowledge transfer mechanisms on supply chain performance. In *Supply chain management: Concepts, methodologies, tools, and applications* (pp. 1477–1491). Hershey, PA: IGI Global. doi:10.4018/978-1-4666-2625-6.ch087

Minbaeva, D. B. (2005). HRM practices and MNC knowledge transfer. *Personnel Review, 34*(1), 125–144. doi:10.1108/00483480510571914

Minbaeva, D. B. (2008). HRM practices and knowledge transfer in multinational companies. In K. O'Sullivan (Ed.), *Strategic knowledge management in multinational organizations* (pp. 1–27). Hershey, PA: IGI Global. doi:10.4018/978-1-59904-630-3.ch001

Moen, J. (2005). Is mobility of technical personnel a source of R&D spillovers? *Journal of Labor Economics, 23*(1), 81–114. doi:10.1086/425434

Moskaliuk, J., Bokhorst, F., & Cress, U. (2016). Learning from others' experiences: How patterns foster interpersonal transfer of knowledge-in-use. *Computers in Human Behavior, 55*, 69–75. doi:10.1016/j.chb.2015.08.051

Najafi-Tavani, Z., Zaefarian, G., Naudé, P., & Giroud, A. (2015). Reverse knowledge transfer and subsidiary power. *Industrial Marketing Management, 48*, 103–110. doi:10.1016/j.indmarman.2015.03.021

Nelson, R. R., & Winter, S. G. (1982). The Schumpeterian tradeoff revisited. *The American Economic Review, 72*(1), 114–132.

Nemati-Anaraki, L., & Heidari, A. (2016). Knowledge sharing for improving effectiveness of university-industry collaborations. In *Business intelligence: Concepts, methodologies, tools, and applications* (pp. 955–972). Hershey, PA: IGI Global. doi:10.4018/978-1-4666-9562-7.ch049

Ngoma, N. S., & Lind, M. (2015). Knowledge transfer and team performance in distributed organizations. *International Journal of Knowledge-Based Organizations, 5*(2), 58–80. doi:10.4018/ijkbo.2015040104

Nohria, N., & Ghoshal, S. (1997). *The differentiated network: Organizing multinational corporations for value creation*. San Francisco, CA: Jossey–Bass.

Nylund, P. A., & Raelin, J. D. (2015). When feelings obscure reason: The impact of leaders' explicit and emotional knowledge transfer on shareholder reactions. *The Leadership Quarterly, 26*(4), 532–542. doi:10.1016/j.leaqua.2015.06.003

Oxley, J. E., & Sampson, R. C. (2004). The scope and governance of international R&D alliances. *Strategic Management Journal, 25*(8/9), 723–749. doi:10.1002/smj.391

Parrotta, P., & Pozzoli, D. (2012). The effect of learning by hiring on productivity. *The Rand Journal of Economics, 43*(1), 167–185. doi:10.1111/j.1756-2171.2012.00161.x

Peachey, T., Hall, D. J., & Cegielski, C. (2008). Knowledge management and the leading information systems journals: An analysis of trends and gaps in published research. In M. Jennex (Ed.), *Knowledge management: Concepts, methodologies, tools, and applications* (pp. 1450–1463). Hershey, PA: IGI Global. doi:10.4018/978-1-59904-933-5.ch119

Pinto, H., Cruz, A. R., & de Almeida, H. (2016). Academic entrepreneurship and knowledge transfer networks: Translation process and boundary organizations. In L. Carvalho (Ed.), *Handbook of research on entrepreneurial success and its impact on regional development* (pp. 315–344). Hershey, PA: IGI Global. doi:10.4018/978-1-4666-9567-2.ch015

Poole, J. P. (2013). Knowledge transfers from multinational to domestic firms: Evidence from worker mobility. *The Review of Economics and Statistics, 95*(2), 393–406. doi:10.1162/REST_a_00258

Priestley, J. L., & Samaddar, S. (2007). The role of ambiguity in the transfer of knowledge within organizational networks. In G. Putnik & M. Cruz-Cunha (Eds.), *Knowledge and technology management in virtual organizations: Issues, trends, opportunities and solutions* (pp. 211–219). Hershey, PA: Idea Group Publishing. doi:10.4018/978-1-59904-165-0.ch009

Priestly, J. L. (2006). Knowledge transfer within interorganizational networks. In E. Coakes & S. Clarke (Eds.), *Encyclopedia of communities of practice in information and knowledge management* (pp. 307–316). Hershey, PA: IGI Global. doi:10.4018/978-1-59140-556-6.ch052

Ranft, A. L., & Lord, M. D. (2002). Acquiring new technologies and capabilities: A grounded model of acquisition implementation. *Organization Science, 13*(4), 420–441. doi:10.1287/orsc.13.4.420.2952

Rive, P. (2008). Knowledge transfer and marketing in second life. In P. Zemliansky & K. St.Amant (Eds.), *Handbook of research on virtual workplaces and the new nature of business practices* (pp. 424–438). Hershey, PA: IGI Global. doi:10.4018/978-1-59904-893-2.ch030

Roemer, L. K., Bigelow, S. M., & Borsato, E. P. (2009). Strategies to meet knowledge transfer needs. In A. Dwivedi (Ed.), *Handbook of research on information technology management and clinical data administration in healthcare* (pp. 564–581). Hershey, PA: IGI Global. doi:10.4018/978-1-60566-356-2.ch035

Rothberg, H. N., & Klingenberg, B. (2010). Learning before doing: A theoretical perspective and practical lessons from a failed cross-border knowledge transfer initiative. In D. Harorimana (Ed.), *Cultural implications of knowledge sharing, management and transfer: Identifying competitive advantage* (pp. 277–294). Hershey, PA: IGI Global. doi:10.4018/978-1-60566-790-4.ch013

Rugman, A. M., & Verbeke, A. (2001). Subsidiary-specific advantages in multinational enterprises. *Strategic Management Journal, 22*(3), 237–250. doi:10.1002/smj.153

Sarala, R. M., Junni, P., Cooper, C. L., & Tarba, S. Y. (2014). A sociocultural perspective on knowledge transfer in mergers and acquisitions. *Journal of Management, 42*(5), 1230–1249. doi:10.1177/0149206314530167

Sherif, K., & Sherif, A. (2008). Think social capital before you think knowledge transfer. In M. Jennex (Ed.), *Current issues in knowledge management* (pp. 53–65). Hershey, PA: IGI Global. doi:10.4018/978-1-59904-916-8.ch005

Solli-Sæther, H., & Gottschalk, P. (2010). Knowledge transfer. In H. Solli-Sæther & P. Gottschalk (Eds.), *Managing IT outsourcing performance* (pp. 132–141). Hershey, PA: IGI Global. doi:10.4018/978-1-60566-796-6.ch007

Stoyanov, A., & Zubanov, N. (2012). Productivity spillovers across firms through worker mobility. *American Economic Journal: Applied Economics, 4*(2), 168–198. doi:10.1257/app.4.2.168

Tho, N. D., & Trang, N. T. M. (2015). Can knowledge be transferred from business schools to business organizations through in-service training students? SEM and fsQCA findings. *Journal of Business Research*, *68*(6), 1332–1340. doi:10.1016/j.jbusres.2014.12.003

Tsai, C., Shen, P., & Chiang, N. (2012). An investigation of the relationship between intellectual capital and knowledge transfer: An exploratory case study of Taiwanese bands. *International Journal of Art, Culture and Design Technologies*, *2*(2), 43–56. doi:10.4018/ijacdt.2012070104

Uchihira, N. (2014). Knowledge transfer in product-based service design. In M. Kosaka & K. Shirahada (Eds.), *Progressive trends in knowledge and system-based science for service innovation* (pp. 258–272). Hershey, PA: IGI Global. doi:10.4018/978-1-4666-4663-6.ch014

Ugolini, F., Massetti, L., Sanesi, G., & Pearlmutter, D. (2015). Knowledge transfer between stakeholders in the field of urban forestry and green infrastructure: Results of a European survey. *Land Use Policy*, *49*, 365–381. doi:10.1016/j.landusepol.2015.08.019

Verbeke, A. (2010). International acquisition success: Social community and dominant logic dimensions. *Journal of International Business Studies*, *41*(1), 38–46. doi:10.1057/jibs.2009.70

Wan, Z., Haggerty, N., & Wang, Y. (2015). Individual level knowledge transfer in virtual settings: A review and synthesis. *International Journal of Knowledge Management*, *11*(2), 29–61. doi:10.4018/IJKM.2015040103

Wang, Z., & Wang, N. (2012). Knowledge sharing, innovation and firm performance. *Expert Systems with Applications: An International Journal*, *39*(10), 8899–8908. doi:10.1016/j.eswa.2012.02.017

Wiewiora, A., Trigunarsyah, B., & Murphy, G. (2012). Knowledge transfer in project-based organisations: The need for a unique approach. In *Organizational learning and knowledge: Concepts, methodologies, tools and applications* (pp. 262–274). Hershey, PA: IGI Global. doi:10.4018/978-1-60960-783-8.ch116

Wu, J., Liu, N., & Xuan, Z. (2011). Simulation on knowledge transfer processes from the perspectives of individuals mentality and behavior. *International Journal of Knowledge and Systems Science*, *2*(4), 1–13. doi:10.4018/jkss.2011100101

Wu, S. H., & Hsu, F. B. (2001). Towards a knowledge-based view of OEM relationship building: Sharing of industrial experiences in Taiwan. *International Journal of Technology Management*, *22*(5), 503–524. doi:10.1504/IJTM.2001.002975

Xia, H., & Gupta, A. (2008). Common knowledge sharing model of 24-hour knowledge factory of grid computing based on case based reasoning. *International Journal of Knowledge Management, 4*(3), 1–18. doi:10.4018/jkm.2008070101

Zahra, S. A., & George, G. (2002). Absorptive capacity: A review, reconceptualization, and extension. *Academy of Management Review, 27*(2), 185–203.

Zander, U., & Zander, L. (2010). Opening the grey box: Social communities, knowledge and culture in acquisitions. *Journal of International Business Studies, 41*(1), 27–37. doi:10.1057/jibs.2009.76

Zapata-Cantú, L., Ramírez, J., & Pineda, J. L. (2012). HRM adaptation to knowledge management initiatives: Three Mexican cases. In *Human resources management: Concepts, methodologies, tools, and applications* (pp. 170–190). Hershey, PA: IGI Global. doi:10.4018/978-1-4666-1601-1.ch012

Zapata-Cantú, L., Treviño, T., Morton, F., & Monterrubio, E. L. (2016). Digital technologies as media to transfer knowledge in IT firms. In A. Goel & P. Singhal (Eds.), *Product innovation through knowledge management and social media strategies* (pp. 204–217). Hershey, PA: IGI Global. doi:10.4018/978-1-4666-9607-5.ch009

Zhang, J., & Baden-Fuller, C. (2010). The influence of technological knowledge base and organizational structure on technology collaboration. *Journal of Management Studies, 47*(4), 679–704. doi:10.1111/j.1467-6486.2009.00885.x

Zhang, M. J. (2007). An empirical assessment of the performance impacts of IS support for knowledge transfer. *International Journal of Knowledge Management, 3*(1), 66–85. doi:10.4018/jkm.2007010105

Zheng, R. Z., & Truong, T. N. (2017). A framework for promoting knowledge transfer in SNS game-based learning. In R. Zheng & M. Gardner (Eds.), *Handbook of research on serious games for educational applications* (pp. 66–91). Hershey, PA: IGI Global. doi:10.4018/978-1-5225-0513-6.ch004

Zou, H., & Ghauri, P. N. (2008). Learning through international acquisitions: The process of knowledge acquisition in China. *Management International Review, 48*(2), 207–226. doi:10.1007/s11575-008-0012-1

ADDITIONAL READING

Adam, A., Prostean, G., Badea, A., & Prostean, O. (2015). Knowledge transfer in educational projects. *Procedia: Social and Behavioral Sciences*, *191*, 1460–1466. doi:10.1016/j.sbspro.2015.04.346

Aerts, G., Dooms, M., & Haezendonck, E. (2017). Knowledge transfers and project-based learning in large scale infrastructure development projects: An exploratory and comparative ex-post analysis. *International Journal of Project Management*, *35*(3), 224–240. doi:10.1016/j.ijproman.2016.10.010

Azagra-Caro, J. M., Barberá-Tomás, D., Edwards-Schachter, M., & Tur, E. M. (2017). Dynamic interactions between university-industry knowledge transfer channels: A case study of the most highly cited academic patent. *Research Policy*, *46*(2), 463–474. doi:10.1016/j.respol.2016.11.011

Chen, C. J., Hsiao, Y. C., & Chu, M. A. (2014). Transfer mechanisms and knowledge transfer: The cooperative competency perspective. *Journal of Business Research*, *67*(12), 2531–2541. doi:10.1016/j.jbusres.2014.03.011

del Chiappa, G., & Baggio, R. (2015). Knowledge transfer in smart tourism destinations: Analyzing the effects of a network structure. *Journal of Destination Marketing & Management*, *4*(3), 145–150. doi:10.1016/j.jdmm.2015.02.001

Fang, Y., Wade, M., Delios, A., & Beamish, P. W. (2013). An exploration of multinational enterprise knowledge resources and foreign subsidiary performance. *Journal of World Business*, *48*(1), 30–38. doi:10.1016/j.jwb.2012.06.004

Ivanov, E., & Liebowitz, J. (2011). Commentary: Research needed on cross-cultural generational knowledge flows. In E. Coakes (Ed.), *Knowledge development and social change through technology: Emerging studies* (pp. 177–184). Hershey, PA: IGI Global. doi:10.4018/978-1-60960-507-0.ch013

Kalid, K. S. (2012). Transfer knowledge using stories: A Malaysian university case study. In *Organizational learning and knowledge: Concepts, methodologies, tools and applications* (pp. 2998–3010). Hershey, PA: IGI Global. doi:10.4018/978-1-60960-783-8.ch812

Kimmerle, J., Moskaliuk, J., Oeberst, A., & Cress, U. (2015). Learning and collective knowledge construction with social media: A process-oriented perspective. *Educational Psychologist*, *50*(2), 120–137. doi:10.1080/00461520.2015.1036273 PMID:26246643

Lepik, K., Krigul, M., & Terk, E. (2012). Problems of initiating international knowledge transfer: Is the Finnish living lab method transferable to Estonia? In A. Zolait (Ed.), *Knowledge and technology adoption, diffusion, and transfer: International perspectives* (pp. 154–165). Hershey, PA: IGI Global. doi:10.4018/978-1-4666-1752-0.ch012

Liao, H., Liu, X., & Wang, C. (2012). Knowledge spillovers, absorptive capacity and total factor productivity in China's manufacturing firms. *International Review of Applied Economics*, *26*(4), 533–547. doi:10.1080/02692171.2011.619970

Mariano, S. (2013). Understanding the nature of knowledge: An empirical study of knowledge sharing in a knowledge intensive organisation. *International Journal of Learning and Intellectual Capital*, *10*(2), 151–164. doi:10.1504/IJLIC.2013.052908

Matschke, C., Moskaliuk, J., & Cress, U. (2012). Knowledge exchange using Web 2.0 technologies in NGOs. *Journal of Knowledge Management*, *16*(1), 159–176. doi:10.1108/13673271211199007

Moshonsky, M., Serenko, A., & Bontis, N. (2014). Examining the transfer of academic knowledge to business practitioners: Doctoral program graduates as intermediaries. *International Journal of Knowledge Management*, *10*(3), 70–95. doi:10.4018/ijkm.2014070105

Mudambi, R., Piscitello, L., & Rabbiosi, L. (2014). Reverse knowledge transfer in MNEs: Subsidiary innovativeness and entry modes. *Long Range Planning*, *47*(1/2), 49–63. doi:10.1016/j.lrp.2013.08.013

Nair, S. R., Demirbag, M., & Mellahi, K. (2016). Reverse knowledge transfer in emerging market multinationals: The Indian context. *International Business Review*, *25*(1), 152–164. doi:10.1016/j.ibusrev.2015.02.011

Najafi-Tavani, Z., Giroud, A., & Sinkovics, R. R. (2012). Mediating effects in reverse knowledge transfer processes. *Management International Review*, *52*(3), 461–488. doi:10.1007/s11575-011-0097-9

Pan, W., Liu, Z., Ming, Z., Zhong, H., Wang, X., & Xu, C. (2015). Compressed knowledge transfer via factorization machine for heterogeneous collaborative recommendation. *Knowledge-Based Systems*, *85*, 234–244. doi:10.1016/j.knosys.2015.05.009

Park, B. I. (2011). Knowledge transfer capacity of multinational enterprises and technology acquisition in international joint ventures. *International Business Review*, *20*(1), 75–87. doi:10.1016/j.ibusrev.2010.06.002

Patnayakuni, N., Patnayakuni, R., & Gupta, J. N. (2017). Towards a model of social media impacts on cybersecurity knowledge transfer: An exploration. In R. Chugh (Ed.), *Harnessing social media as a knowledge management tool* (pp. 249–271). Hershey, PA: IGI Global. doi:10.4018/978-1-5225-0495-5.ch012

Pla-Barber, J., & Alegre, J. (2014). The role of knowledge and learning in internationalization. *International Business Review*, *23*(1), 1–3. doi:10.1016/j.ibusrev.2013.09.005

Rabbiosi, L., & Santangelo, G. D. (2013). Parent company benefits from reverse knowledge transfer: The role of the liability of newness in MNEs. *Journal of World Business*, *48*(1), 160–170. doi:10.1016/j.jwb.2012.06.016

Ranucci, R. A., & Souder, D. (2015). Facilitating tacit knowledge transfer: Routine compatibility, trustworthiness, and integration in M&As. *Journal of Knowledge Management*, *19*(2), 257–276. doi:10.1108/JKM-06-2014-0260

Rodgers, W., Mubako, G. N., & Hall, L. (2017). Knowledge management: The effect of knowledge transfer on professional skepticism in audit engagement planning. *Computers in Human Behavior*, *70*, 564–574. doi:10.1016/j.chb.2016.12.069

Sawada, A., Yoshida, T., Horii, H., Horii, M., & Hayashi, M. (2015). Reducing costs of knowledge transfer in tourism development using historical materials. In *Hospitality, travel, and tourism: Concepts, methodologies, tools, and applications* (pp. 1299–1309). Hershey, PA: IGI Global. doi:10.4018/978-1-4666-6543-9.ch074

Spears, J. L., & San Nicolas-Rocca, T. (2015). Knowledge transfer in information security capacity building for community-based organizations. *International Journal of Knowledge Management*, *11*(4), 52–69. doi:10.4018/IJKM.2015100104

Zhao, Y., & Tan, J. (2015). Knowledge transfer model within strategic alliance in telecommunication industries. *International Journal of Interdisciplinary Telecommunications and Networking*, *7*(1), 1–12. doi:10.4018/ijitn.2015010101

KEY TERMS AND DEFINITIONS

Communication: The exchange of thoughts, messages, or information, as by speech, signals, writing, or behavior.

Information: The act of informing or the condition of being informed.

Information Technology: The development, installation, and implementation of computer systems and applications.

Knowledge: The familiarity, awareness, or understanding gained through experience or study.

Knowledge Management: The range of practices used by organizations to identify, create, represent, and distribute the knowledge.

Learning: The process or experience of gaining knowledge or skill.

Technology: The science or knowledge put into the practical use to solve the problems or invent the useful tools.

Training: The process of learning and being conditioned.

Chapter 10
Expert Knowledge in the University–Industry Cooperation:
The Cases of Germany and Russia

Oxana Karnaukhova
Southern Federal University, Russia

Oliver Hinkelbein
University of Bremen, Germany

ABSTRACT

The idea of the chapter is to make a cross-cultural analysis of the various knowledge management processes, with the aim of identifying advantages and disadvantages, perspectives and obstacles for knowledge management (KM) within the boundaries between university and industry. KM strategies revealed the importance of institutionalization and legitimation processes of practitioners' knowledge. In the contemporary networking world with blurring boundaries between professional and non-professional knowledge the position of expert is changing. It immediately influences knowledge flows between university and industry. The chapter will provide a comparative analysis of two KM cases in the field of university-industry relations – Germany and Russia with emphasis on difficulties and advantages of KM implementation for enhancing decision-making process on both sides; evolving stakeholders to participate in activities, building efficient societal capabilities and developing knowledge-based communities.

DOI: 10.4018/978-1-5225-2897-5.ch010

INTRODUCTION

There are some critical remarks on the matter of the role and functioning of expert knowledge in the university-industry cooperation. The first one concerns the idea of so-called expert knowledge, or 'expert systems' – as well as it affects the expert term itself. As Anthony Giddens suggested, in the contemporary networking world with blurring boundaries between professional and non-professional knowledge the position of expert is changing. It immediately influences knowledge flows between university and industry. 'Though we may think we consult specific experts irregularly, many aspects of our lives are influenced by them, because you cannot know about all the things that you must trust in, e.g. engineering systems, airplanes, internet security, surgeons/therapists, financial controllers – when we can't deal with people personally we must trust systems, protocols & security measures; has there recently been a questioning of experts in some fields?' (Giddens, 1990). The critical point of this kind of definitions is that 'the expert' is considered very narrow and grouped around special technical skills. With the result that knowledge itself is conceptualized very technocratic. From an anthropological perspective an expert is defined "as an actor who has developed skills in, semiotic-epistemic competence for, and attentional concern with, some sphere of practical activity" (Boyer, 2008, p. 39). Taking into account 'practical activity' opens the opportunity to investigate knowledge management (KM) in a more complex way. This is an absolutely necessary aspect when such different 'cultures' as universities and industries are compared.

The second remark concerns digitalization and networking as core mottos and practices in knowledge management today. The digital expertise can prompt new reading of the guiding media (such as written culture), and is reconfigured in new techniques. Intrusions and intervention into the mainstream corpus of interpretations and discourses takes the form of critical approach, revealing dimensions of the knowledge concealed in the fact of its creation. In this case virtual expert spaces are the places of circulating online narratives, which imply a specific form of knowledge via certain channels. Considering these new forms of knowledge and practices implies 'new mediators' (Hinkelbein, 2014) who are able to manage knowledge in contemporary networked and mediated cultures. So the aim of our chapter is to compare role and shape of these actors in KM strategies in Russia and Germany.

Finally, knowledge is not about direct information circulation. Culture takes the role of moderator in effective and smooth knowledge share. It is clear that at the organization level knowledge management system has to match culture through diverse approaches: solving day-to-day business problems, adopting a knowledge parcel to pre-existing cultural patterns, reformulating KM initiatives in line with culturally specific communication style, creating a KM system on the existing networks of people, building institutional environment welcoming KM hierarchy. Also a fundamental change in knowledge flow – from very hierarchical to a more rhizomatic movement of knowledge – has to be taken into account in KM (strategies).

The chapter will provide a comparative analysis of two KM cases in the field of university-industry relations – Germany and Russia with emphasis on difficulties and advantages of KM implementation for enhancing decision-making process on both sides; evolving stakeholders to participate in activities, building efficient societal capabilities and developing knowledge-based communities.

THEORETICAL BACKGROUND

The notion of social capital has originated from 1960s, when J. Jacobs (1961) described it as a resource of relations in families and communities. Today social capital gains much interest from different disciplines, including knowledge transfer. Although it is placed in the list of intangible resources, social capital is distinctive from human capital since it exists in the framework of relationships between actors, and so jointly owned. For this reason benefits of social capital are debatable. As Kwon and Adler (2014) assume that it fragments broad collectivities in the name of local identities. In the case of supplier-buyer relations fragmentation hurts organization performance and influences decision-making process. Moreover, while facilitating a certain social actions, like targeted solidarization, social capital could neglect others. The strong norms and framed identification may have a powerful influence on milieu performance, at the same time limiting access to information and knowledge datasets. Moreover, shared norms dictate expectations of accepted behavior, so may cause problems with free flowing and denial to experiment beyond the network. This aspect can produce a specific collective blindness toward certain sides of community activities (Perrow, 1984; Inkpen & Tsang, 2005; Payne et al., 2011; Kindred et al., 2015).

Since the end of 1990s social capital is labeled as having dimensions (Nahapiet, 1998). The first dimension is structural, representing series of ties and connections that communities or individuals have with others. These ties serve as channels for knowledge flow. The second, relational dimension is about resources created within interactive relationships of actors. These resources are trust, obligations, and shared norms. Facilitation of transactions in communities with further reciprocity on a mutual dependency basis can result in more intense ties, which in their turn influence effectiveness of cooperation and knowledge assimilation. The cognitive dimension has the means of common interest that facilitates opportunities to recombine and exchange knowledge on the common ground (Al-Tabbaa, 2016).

The idea of common interest serves as the background of the clusterization concept, where clusters are geographically concentrated groups of interconnected companies, specialized service providers, firms and institutions connected with their activities in certain areas, competing, and at the same time, seeking for collaboration (Proter, 1990). The inclusion of clusters in global chains of creating added cost can significantly increase the level of technological base, speed and quality of economic growth by strengthening international competitiveness of enterprises and institutions included in a cluster, by:

- Implementing the best available technologies, using the up-to-date equipment;
- Gaining access to modern management techniques, and special knowledge;
- Receiving opportunities to enter highly competitive international markets.

There are two main divisions of clusters: vertical clusters of enterprises and industries, which are connected by the relations "buyer-seller"; and horizontal clusters, involving enterprises and institutions which can share a common market for manufacturing products to use the same or similar technology, comparable professional qualifications and skills labour and other shared resources. The essence of the cluster theory presented by M. Porter is that competitiveness of economy is based on the so-called "determinants", including factors, demands, related and supporting industry, and strategy of enterprises, their structure and rivalry. According to this theory, competition can occur only at maturity and asset of the interaction of these factors.

The theory of regional cluster follows the clusterization paradigm and demonstrates that competitive advantage is created not at the national level, but at the regional, where the main role is played by historical preferences, and shortcuts development of regions, the diversity of cultures in conducting business, production and education. Thus, the concept of regional cluster is considered as an industrial cluster in which member-organizations are located in geographical proximity to each other.

With the expansion of knowledge-based industries throughout the world and innovation promotion policy as an economic and social strategy the formation of expert communities plays a crucial role. In this case universities assume to play a broad-set "third role" in the regional development; while the function of teaching serves as a predictor of employment, the impact of being engaged in real world research and knowledge transfer (including expertising) is more sensitive to the institutional environment, structural characteristics and the regional economic context. Possible explanations could be found in differences in the roles performed by universities in diverse regional and international settings and perceiving these roles by business environment.

MAIN FOCUS OF THE CHAPTER

The millennium shift nearly 20 years ago laid an important ground for this chapter. Metaphorically the first decade of the new century was like a gold-rush mood to integrate new media and technologies within a wider transformation of society, politics and economy. Following the famous predictions of D. Bell (Bell, 1973) modern universities experienced three consequent phases. The first one concerns transformations of society from capitalist-industrial to knowledge-post-industrial condition, so universities appeared as a new generation of capitalists. Intellectual technologies unfold the second shift. The third phase supposed to be superseding industrial enterprises by universities with a specific form of organization.

European Union demonstrates that the European education system is located within the third 'entrepreneurial' phase of its development. The Lisbon Agenda became a turning point in the new trend. In the German case study it is explored how the Lisbon Agenda as well as the Excellence Initiative triggered the change of German universities and their self-conceptions. Both are very powerful policies set up by the European Commission respective the German Government. It will be shown that within the goal of the Lisbon Agenda to make the EU the most competitive economic area in the world, based on the knowledge society, the universities changed a lot.

At the same time the Russian case demonstrates a significant delay in the so-called 'catch-up development" of Russian universities. Russia entered the Bologna process in 2003, and in 2005 UNESCO announced the transfer toward the knowledge society with a brand-new type of organization. Since that time paths of education systems approach.

For the universities as organizations this was a challenge, as they had to start an organizational change. The specific tasks and functions the universities should play within the creation of a knowledge based society were to serve as a key actor to educate experts for the development of new digital infrastructure as well as for all socio-cultural, economic and political fields. As will be shown the result was that the universities pushed themselves to a more entrepreneurial environment while competing at the same time with other universities on the global level for best scientific production of knowledge. In the German case study it will get evident that German universities lost track in the global competition. For that reason there will be a focus on the German Excellence Initiative, that is one of the biggest policies in education and science since decades.

The Russian case is chosen to demonstrate that 'entrepreneurial' turn as well as social media intervention into the 'academic capitalism' (the term coined by B. Jessop, 2017) in the university development was perceived as artificial in relation to the nature of highly intelligent and even spiritual knowledge production and pulldown from the longstanding cultural context.

Coming from an anthropological background within this chapter it will be shown how important it is to know the cultural practices and implications within the organizational change of the universities. While being pushed to be more active on the cross links between the universities and social, political and economic organizations new fields of expertise emerged. The change of culture within the universities gets most evident when focusing on the use of social media practices. Within our chapter we focus on how social media are used and how this connects to a changing role of expert knowledge and KM.

ANALYTICAL METHODS

In the contemporary era of globalization the complexities of culture and society are manifested in many different contexts (Hannerz, 1992). Thus, doing research about and analysis of knowledge management processes, expert communities and conflicting roles of experts in contemporary university-industry landscapes are challenging. The research field is not only provoking because of its complexities but also because of the fact that we are far away of a common understanding in the humanities what an expert is (Boyer, 2008; Holmes & Marcus 2005). "I would suggest that we define an expert as an actor who has developed skills in, semiotic-epistemic competence for, and attentional concern with, some sphere of practical activity" (Boyer, 2008, p. 39).[1] Focusing on experts and their practices in empirical research also needs to be problematized in the scope of action. We argue that the boundary between university and (social-) industry and the development of knowledge channels are grounded in various advanced processes that are currently being challenged by sustainability issues. From a research point of view we substantiate that cultural practices matter and can't be neglected when focusing on experts and knowledge production. According to anthropological approaches ethnography is the only way to grasp the actor's point of view in this complex setting of knowledge production, expert communities and networks – online and offline. According to Shore and Wright "the anthropologist is seeking a method for analysing connections between levels and forms of social process and action, and exploring how those processes work in different sites – local, national and global" (Shore & Wright, 1997, p. 14). It is therefore necessary to develop a way of working which is able to collect and analyse ethnographic material in the different fields that constitute the subject matter.

The anthropologist Marcus (1995) developed multi-sited ethnography for heterogeneous research fields, which consist of many different places. This is a research approach that follows the complex interrelationships that constitute the object. Starting from a certain problem or context, the networks of relationships of the actors and their meanings are understood for the cultural practice that radiates to other places, and are closely linked by manifold links. Doing empirical research on the transition between university and (social) industry makes it necessary to apply such a complex method like multi-sited ethnography. As in the contemporary era cultural practices also take place in the virtual realm approaches of the virtual ethnography have to be taken into account (Hine, 2000; Miller & Slater 2000).

Furthermore, it is important to underline that ethnography is ambiguous as such. On the one hand, according to the research topic, it contains a certain set of single methods like expert interviews and participant observation. On the other hand, it is a certain way of analyzing the data and writing (Emerson, et al., 2011). When it comes to analysis the anthropological approach is clearly based in the hermeneutic and interpretive tradition (Geertz, 1973). Single analytical methods like coding and content analysis are used to analyze the data gained for example by expert interviews and participant observation for each case studied. In the further process of analysis the results are compared to each other, opening up the opportunity of cross cultural analysis – between Russia and Germany as in our example of expert knowledge in the university-industry cooperation.

The Case: Germany

In 2005 the Excellence Initiative passed by the German federal and state governments to promote research and improve the quality of German universities until 2017. This was a reaction to the fact that "at the turn of the millennium, Germany's research system was not in the best state" (Weigmann, 2015, p. 142). At the core of one of the biggest funding programs in German history are three funding lines:

1. Graduate schools to promote early career researchers,
2. Clusters of excellence to promote top-level research and,
3. Institutional strategies to promote top-level university research (DFG, 2016).

Since the beginning of the program 11 universities were chosen to be an excellent university. Still the "excellence titles" of some of the universities show the importance of knowledge and its transfer beyond the university world itself: "International Network University" (Freie Universität Berlin), "The Synergetic University" (Dresden University of Technology), "Model Konstanz: Towards a Culture of Creativity" (University of Konstanz), "LMUexcellent: Working Brains – Networking Minds – Living Knowledge" (Ludwig Maximilian University of Munich) or "TUM. The Entrepreneurial University" (Technical University of Munich). The political decision to reform and the focus on knowledge transfer is also embedded in a broader policy of the European Union. It was in 2000 when the European Commission launched the Lisbon Agenda to transform the EU to a knowledge-based economy within 10 years. "The strategy attributed high priority to research and set target of spending 3% of gross domestic product (GDP) for research by 2010" (Weigmann, 2015, p. 142). A higher and more stable funding of research and knowledge production was considered as a basis to make knowledge a driving force within economy and the European societies itself. By the help of information and communication technologies and live long learning programs within EU countries knowledge should be transferred to all parts of society, economy and politics to make it one of the basic resources of innovation and change (Hinkelbein, 2014).

The fundamental change provoked by strategies like the above-mentioned was and still is a challenge for German universities. One of the reasons is that academic knowledge production for a very long time took place in an ivory tower. But, close cooperation between universities and companies is by no means new in Germany. Even though Humboldt's ideas of teaching, learning, and research, which are central to German universities, are frequently criticized as ivory-tower ideology and practice-far, many cooperative relations already arose in the last third of the nineteenth century – especially in chemistry and electrical engineering (Kloke & Krücken, 2010; Szöllosi-Janse, 2004). Nevertheless, in general, scientific experts, among other university actors, had only few connections to the non-academic world like to economic, political and cultural actors. While highly connected to other experts in the academic world the self-conception of connecting oneself to fields outside the academic world was not widespread because of the dominant general principal of a contract between science and society, according to which only the provision of scientific knowledge was expected from science (Krücken et al., 2007). This concept was the case for the traditional universities until tremendous political changes and new demands towards the academic world started within the last two decades. Nevertheless the idea of reform universities that goes back to the 1960ies and 70ies conceptualized knowledge production and communication in a much more open way. A good example is the University of Bremen that was founded in 1971. Compared to the traditional universities like Heidelberg, Freiburg or Tübingen the self-conception always has been to be an institution connected to the public.

The change in the traditional universities as well as the open concept of the reform universities raised a lot of questions. What do universities do in order to connect to the non-academic world? How does this process change the role of academic experts and how are processes of knowledge management influenced? One of the main problems is that academic experts in practice-oriented fields often are not perceived as experts but as theorists. Within the neoliberal trend the universities have been confronted with a dilemma. At the one hand they are under the pressure to be more open to contribute to value production and at the other hand academic expert communities tend to have symbolic boundaries with experts from other fields like industry, economy and politics.

Remarkable examples that show that within the last two decades the situation in university-industry cooperation changed tremendously. So-called clusters emerged in the field of renewable energies, space technology and biotechnology, to mention just a few. Within those fields the role of the academic expert changed dramatically. It was not any longer that scientific experts remained in the academic ivory tower and learned to translate their knowledge into the realm of application. Knowledge production no longer takes place in the university itself but is more and more connected with technology development in industry itself. According to a study conducted by Kloke and Krücken (2010) joint knowledge production and transfer takes place on a personal level. This means that cooperation between scientific experts and experts from industry and economy are based on personal linkages between them and include personal trust. Nevertheless, regarded from and organisational level, universities have institutionalised knowledge transfer in the last decades (Kloke & Krücken, 2010; Reinhard & Schmalholz, 1996). This resulted in the fact that a vast majority of German universities now have centres of technology transfer as well as further education to transfer knowledge to the public and the private sector (ELFI, 2016). But also industry and business changed their policies and connected themselves much closer to the universities. Remarkable physical symbols are industry parks that have emerged around university campuses. The German Research Foundation considers this development as an effect of the Excellence Initiative: "The success has been evident in significantly more productive research, the emergence of centres and regions with strong research capacity and much more scientific knowledge transferred to business and society" (DFG, 2014).

According to Wilkesmann and Würmseer (2007) knowledge management has been a popular discourse in the re-organisation of companies but can't be applied to universities in the same way because of the structural difference between the two types of organisation. While in companies there is much more focus on the question what can be transferred to the public and which knowledge is kept within the organisation universities per se have a much more open knowledge management. Scientist from all disciplines have always shared knowledge on conferences and through publications and since the rise of new media and communication technologies they also started to use this channels for knowledge transfer. This shows that there is a natural affinity within the academic world to share knowledge and compared to companies there is a much more democratic way of governance in the process of sharing knowledge. Differing to companies in universities the power which knowledge is shared is in the hand of the scientist himself or herself and not determined by the management of the university. Within that culture of knowledge management university cooperation with industry and business, especially within the natural sciences and technology based disciplines have been emerging. This also was leading to a stable infrastructure that finds its expression in non-university research institutes like the Frauenhofer

Society, the Max Planck Society or the Leibniz Society. Within that realm the role of the scientific expert changed tremendously in the last two decades. While scientist have been known as non-understandable theorists today they work on a cooperative basis with experts in industry, bio-technology, energy production and logistics – to mention just a few. In the slipstream of those developments knowledge management itself changed a lot. Science communication, public relation departments, social media and other tools of knowledge communication are used for transfer. This changed the role of the scientific expert a lot. Today a scientist is not only a researcher any longer but also works as consultant, university and non-university team member and capitalistic value producer – as well as he is more open to accept non-academic experts to produce and share knowledge. In other words the scientific expert is much more open not only to communicate research results to the public but to "translate" (Callon, 2006, pp. 135-174) it into applied fields of economy and technology.

While new forms of knowledge management and a change of the meaning of the expert in the above-mentioned fields of the university context emerged, within the humanities the change in knowledge production, transfer and management is much more a challenge. Although there are a rising number of cooperation's within humanity departments with schools, NGO's, health care institutions, public administration, other institutions of the civil societies and private companies the move towards social industry and social entrepreneurship is still difficult. One of the reasons might be the fact that within a neoliberal climate the production of social value is not rated that high like capitalistic value production. But a much more important cause is the self-conception of expert knowledge within the humanities itself. Independency, the adherence to Humboldt's ideas of teaching, learning, and research and a critical perspective on utilisation of academic expert knowledge outside academia makes it more difficult for scientists from the humanities to change their self-conceptions what an expert is. When it comes to the above-mentioned social and cultural fields the humanities expert self-concept still is based on the idea to be a consultant instead of being involved in shared knowledge production with non-academic experts. There is still an imbalance of power between academic and non-academic actors and the ones who break up those power relations are seen as going to be applied and loose reputation within the academic community. The challenge for the humanities towards a changing self-conception of what an expert is and who should have the power over knowledge itself gets evident when looking on how knowledge management is done in practice. While in the natural sciences and technology based disciplines there are more and more public relations departments to be found, with a new class of science communication experts that use tools like social media and work together with media or are the connecting links between different groups of academic and non-academic experts, within the humanities those developments are still at the beginning.

The Case: Russia

Information on innovation clusters in Russia is weakly presented, and the study of economic, infrastructural, institutional, and socio-cultural conditions and their impact on the activities effectiveness is not sufficient. The discrepancy between the pace of change in business and education, the delay in the application received in academic knowledge, the rapid obsolescence, and more are fixed as the most divisive obstacles in the Russian context of university-industry relations. Both sides speak different professional languages. However, the demonstration of some tendencies could be possible on the basis of regional cases. Since innovation is one of the integrative indicators of successful university-industry cooperation and knowledge flow, it is important to look at extra-economic factors influencing regional development. The South Russian agglomeration is chosen as a feasible example of the regional clusterization and innovation indicators located below the state average (Yagolnitser, 2015).

In order to implement the state program of the Rostov region "Economic development and innovative economy" in 2015 the Concept of cluster development of the Rostov region in 2015 – 2020 has been approved (Cluster, 2015). The Russian experience and samples known abroad demonstrates that in the conditions of aggravation competition between regions for investment, employment and other resources require new tools to maintain and improving the competitiveness of territories, including on the basis to use the cluster approach – cluster support in the priority areas of the regional economy as groups of geographically close and interrelated enterprises and organizations, which are characterized by common activities and complementary to each other. The result application of the cluster approach will be of maximum use of competitive advantages presented by a region and, as a result, the overall economic growth. As it was mentioned, cluster is considered as an instrument of business and power interactions.

In 2013 a regional business cluster maintained by the relevant Centre has been created as a key element of innovation infrastructure, implementing policies for cluster development, and the founders invited Rostov region and the leading educational organizations in the region to participate: Southern Federal University, South-Russian State Polytechnic University, Don State Technical University. The main objective of the Centre is the effective interaction of all participants of innovative processes, including subjects of innovative activity, members of the territorial clusters, institutions of education and science, non-profit and public organizations, bodies of state power and local self-government, investors, innovators, inventors.

The tasks of the Center for cluster development of the Rostov region are following:

- Consulting and marketing services to members clusters;
- Organizing and conducting training seminars, conferences in the field cluster development;
- Methodical and information support of development programs (strategies) development of clusters;
- Development and implementation of joint cluster projects involving the participants of the cluster, institutions of education and science, bodies state power, bodies of local self-government municipal entities Rostov region, financial organizations and institutions development;
- Organization of training, retraining and advanced training personnel;
- Assisting the cluster members in raising funds of state support;
- Assisting the cluster members in promotion of new products (services);
- Identification of the potential development of clusters, including innovative, scientific, industrial, financial and economic.

There is a network of small and medium innovative companies associated with universities and providing commercialization of results of scientific and technical activities. For instance, enterprises of the "innovation belt" lead by Southern Federal University annually produce products with the cost more than 2.5 billion rubles (Cluster, 2015).

One of the priority directions in the development of Southern Federal University is its integration into the regional innovation and technology clusters created with participation of SFedU. Currently, SFedU has created a set of centres for better knowledge management, such as: "Unified regional center of innovative development of the Rostov region", "Rostov technology transfer centre", "Innovation cluster of biotechnology, Biomedicine and environmental security". This set of clusters was called "Southern Constellation".

In 2014 the brand new "The South Start-Up" aimed at creating an effective communication platform for interaction between Southern Federal University and regional business communities for solving problems of commercialization of research results and further development; development of student inter-faculty and interdisciplinary cooperation for implementation of new and ambitious projects, as well as formation of practice-oriented competences of students from different educational programs. The analysis of the university-industry cooperation in the South Russian agglomeration has demonstrated the delayed development of the region.

In 2016 the South Start-Up has presented the results of the recent survey on interactions of business communities and universities with more than 100 private and mixed public-private enterprises as well as academics took part. This survey gave light on the regional specifics of the knowledge management and university-industry mutual misunderstanding. Education, research and commercialization are considered as potentially important spheres for university-industry cooperation, at the same time the real effectiveness of current activities is estimated as extremely low. Among factors influencing mutual distrust there are following: the lack of information on current applied research, weak participation of the business communities in business-parks and other university projects, absence of initiatives coming from the academic side, so business communities are excluded from the decision-making process. At the same time universities appear to be the only knowledge keepers, while enterprises are left the role of financial support. Finally, the state is mentioned by participants, even though the state, in addition to its traditional legislative and regulatory functions can act as a co-investor and customer of innovations based on the needs and level of socio-economic development of the region.

FUTURE RESEARCH DIRECTIONS

Recent studies on university-industry relations demonstrate that innovation is considered as the most expected result of this marriage. Organizations increasingly rely on external sources of innovation via inter-organizational network relationships. At the same time the anxiety around technologization of academy results in some cases (like Russia, for instance) in mistrust toward an effective dialogue and network of entrepreneurs and knowledge producing universities.

On the basis of the comparative case-study, the role of practices such as collaborative research, R&D centres, and academic expertise is analyzed. The cases suggest that such university–industry relationships are widely practiced, whereby cultural differences in understanding interactive, non-professional innovation exist.

Our case studies clearly show that the university-industry link became stronger within the last decade. Especially within the humanities there is a lack of knowledge on the connection between universities and social industry. For further research it is necessary to do basic research on the cross links of those very different organizational cultures. By using in depth ethnographic research, such as qualitative interviews, long term participant observation and doing research on- and offline, the practices of experts need to be unfolded. Having a focus on how, where and why social media tools are used for communication there must also be shed light on the experts themselves and their practices of KM.

The fundamental change of the self-conception of universities and their links to (social) industry must be considered as global phenomenon. Today, university-industry clusters and networks are composed by universities, organizations and businesses on a global scale. As a consequence cross-cultural research and comparison allows to get knowledge on the high potential of digital infrastructure in organizational change. Goal of such basic research on the edge of academic and industrial organization is to find indicators for good practice use of social media and other communication technologies on a global scale. At the same time this allows to consider the cultural diversity that is an important research target too.

While existing research focuses on the effects of university–industry links on innovation-specific variables such as firm innovativeness, the dynamics of university-social business relationships remain under-researched.

The future research agenda addresses needs in two main directions: deep analysis of cultural practices of search and match collaboration between universities and industry, and the organization and management of socially-oriented relationships with possible implications of social media.

CONCLUSION

In our chapter we focused on the changing culture of expert knowledge and knowledge management in the university-industry cooperation in the German-Russian context. As members of the scientific community in both countries we are experts in an anthropological sense and at the same time we are influenced by a tremendous change in the global academic landscape. Fundamental change, triggered by the global economic and financial crisis, brought up the idea that a new knowledge based society and economy could be the answer to new demands in different realms like education, research, politics and economy. While we have shown in the theoretical background and the case studies of our chapter social capital plays a crucial role in university-industry cooperation. It structures the relation between scientific and industry experts on the level of the actors itself. In the methods part we argued that only qualitative ethnographic research on the micro-level could gain knowledge on knowledge management culture at the interface between universities and industry. Using our case studies we demonstrated how new global demands to knowledge production are implemented in two very different academic cultures. According to Appadurai (2013) globalization is not leading to same practices on the national, regional and local level but creates different approaches. In that sense we have been choosing the German-Russian context because the new global demands are resulting in very different approaches in the respective academic cultures and could therefore be used as contrasting and illustrating examples.

The South Russian agglomeration exhibits the slow innovation progress. As it was mentioned, innovative activity of the region corresponds to the developed educational complex in both quantitative and qualitative aspect, as well as institutions of socio-cultural sphere (Yagolnitser, 2015).

In the Russian context the existing clusters have the following problems:

- The lack of qualified personnel;
- Low susceptibility of enterprises to innovations, the slow pace updates range of products, insufficient level competitiveness;
- The lack of quality of separate elements of transport, social and engineering infrastructure;
- Insufficient level of organizational development of clusters;
- Insufficient level of cooperation and mechanisms subcontracting, characterized by a relatively low share of the components produced by external suppliers;
- Financial and other barriers (sanctions, restrictions related to legislation in the sphere of export control, the instability in the currency financial market) to expensive production equipment, materials and technologies;
- The low intensity of research activities at the some of the directions of development of clusters;
- The low efficiency of the process of technology commercialization.

Compared to the Russian context university-industry corporation in Germany has a long tradition and goes back to the last third of the nineteenth century, when the first corporations between universities and the chemistry industry and electrical engineering emerged. Nevertheless until the last third of the 20th century German universities were working in Humboldt's ideas of teaching, learning, and research. From the 1970s this has been frequently criticized as ivory-tower ideology and practice-far. As a result of diverse economic crisis's and political changes new demands from economy and society towards universities and knowledge transfer emerged. Embedded in a broader EU-strategy (Lisbon Agenda) towards a knowledge based economy and society the Excellence Initiative (2005-2017) is the most recent funding program for German universities. The idea of this strategy is not only to promote research and improve the quality of German universities but also to prepare them for new forms of knowledge production and transfer. Knowledge should no longer be kept in the academic ivory tower but serve as a resource of value production on the market. In the slipstream of those developments a tremendous change of organisational culture in German universities started and gave much more importance to knowledge management.

While in the past knowledge was transferred on personal linkages of scientific experts on conferences and in publications in the last three decades new organisational infrastructure like technology transfer units and further education centres at German universities emerged. The digital revolution also was leading to new tools like social media, websites and electronic databases to be used in a still changing culture of knowledge management. Compared to the past the interface between universities and industry is much more permeable today and can be seen as a reaction of the universities towards new demands from the market and society. But for academic experts, especially from the humanities it is still a challenge to serve "the market" with knowledge as a resource for social industry. In order to understand those challenges and to gain more information on knowledge management culture much more qualitative data is needed.

REFERENCES

Al-Tabbaa, O., & Ankrah, S. (2016). Social capital to facilitate engineered university–industry collaboration for technology transfer: A dynamic perspective. *Technological Forecasting and Social Change, 104*, 1–15. doi:10.1016/j.techfore.2015.11.027

Appadurai, A. (2013). *The Future as Cultural Fact. Essays on the Global Condition.* London, New York: Verso.

Bell, D. (1973). *The coming of post-industrial society.* London: Heinemann.

Boyer, D. (2008). Thinking through the Anthropology of Experts. *Anthropology in Action, 15*(2), 38–46. doi:10.3167/aia.2008.150204

Callon, M. (1986). Some Elements of a Sociology of Translation: Domestication of the Scallops and the Fishermen of St Brieuc Bay. In J. Law (Ed.), *Power, Action and Belief: A New Sociology of Knowledge?* (pp. 196–233). London: Routledge.

Cluster. (2015). *Conception of the cluster development in Rostov region – 2015.* Retrieved at: http://inno.sfedu.ru/sites/default/files/doc/164%D0%9F%20 %D0%BE%D1%82%2012.03.2015.pdf

DFG – German Research Foundation (2014). Excellence Initiative Institutions Call for Swift Decision on Future Development. *Press Release, 42*(10).

DFG – German Research Foundation. (2016). Excellence Initiative (2005-2017). General Information. Retrieved from http://www.dfg.de/en/research_funding/ programmes/excellence_initiative/general_information/index.html

ELFI. (2016). *Servicestelle für Eletronische Forschungsförderinformationen.* Retrieved from www.elfi.info

Elsner, W. (1998). An industrial policy agenda 2000 and beyond: Experience, Theory and Policy. In Theory and Policy. Bremen Contributions to Institutional and Social-Economics. Academic Press.

Emerson, R. M., Fretz, R. I., & Shaw, L. L. (2011). *Writing Ethnographic Fieldnotes*. Chicago: The University of Chicago Press. doi:10.7208/chicago/9780226206868.001.0001

Giddens, A. (1990). *The Consequences of Modernity*. Cambridge, UK: Polity.

Groth, K. (2013). *Using Social Networks for Knowledge Management*. Stockholm, Sweden: Royal Institute of Technology.

Hinkelbein, O. (2014). *Digitale Integration von Migranten? Ethnographische Fallstudien zur digitalen Spaltung in Deutschland*. Bielefeld: Transcript Verlag.

Inkpen, A., & Tsang, E. (2005). Social capital, networks, and knowledge transfer. *Academy of Management Review, 30*(1), 146–165. doi:10.5465/AMR.2005.15281445

Jacobs, J. (1961). *The Death and Life of Great American Cities*. New York: Penguin Books.

Jennex, M. E. (2008). *Knowledge Management: Concepts, Methodologies, Tools, and Applications*. Hershey, PA: IGI Global. doi:10.4018/978-1-59904-933-5

Jessop, B. (2017). Varieties of academic capitalism and entrepreneurial universities: On past research and three thought experiments. *Higher Education*, 1–18.

Kindred, J., & Petrescu, C. (2015). Expectations versus reality in a university–community partnership: A case study. *Voluntary International Journal of Voluntary Nonprofit Organizations, 26*(3), 823–845. doi:10.1007/s11266-014-9471-0

Kloke, K., & Krücken, G. (2010). Grenzstellungsmanager zwischen Wissenschaft und Wirtschaft? Eine Studie zu Mitarbeiterinnen und Mitarbeitern in Einrichtungen des Technologietransfers und der wissenschaftlichen Weiterbildung. In Beiträge zur Hochschulforschung, 32. Jahrgang, 3, 32-52.

Krucken, G., Meier, F., & Muller, A. (2007). Information, Cooperation, and the Blurring of Boundaries – Technology Transfer in German and American Discourses. *Higher Education, 53*(6), 675–696. doi:10.1007/s10734-004-7650-4

Kwon, S. W., & Adler, P. S. (2014). Social capital: Maturation of a field of research. *Academy of Management Review, 39*(4), 412–422. doi:10.5465/amr.2014.0210

McDermott, R., & ODell, C. (2001). Overcoming cultural barriers to sharing knowledge. *Journal of Knowledge Management, 5*(1), 76–85. doi:10.1108/13673270110384428

Nahapiet, J., & Ghoshal, S. (1998). Social capital, intellectual capital, and the organizational advantage. *Academy of Management Review, 23*, 242–266.

Payne, G. T., Moore, C. B., Griffis, S. E., & Autry, C. W. (2011). Multilevel challenges and opportunities in social capital research. *Journal of Management, 37*(2), 491–520. doi:10.1177/0149206310372413

Perrow, C. (1984). *Normal Accidents, Living with High-Risk Technology.* New York: Basic Books.

Porter, M. E. (1990). *The Competitive Advantage of Nations.* New York: Free Press. doi:10.1007/978-1-349-11336-1

Reinhard, M., & Schmalholz, H. (1996). Technologietransfer in Deutschland: Stand und Reformbedarf. Berlin: Academic Press.

Stenius, M., Hankonen, N., Ravaia, N., & Haukkala, A. (2016). Why share expertise? A closer look at the quality of motivation to share or withhold knowledge. *Journal of Knowledge Management, 20*(2), 181–198. doi:10.1108/JKM-03-2015-0124

Szöllosi-Janse, M. (2004). Wissensgesellschaft in Deutschland: Überlegungen zur Neubestimmung der deutschen Zeitgeschichte uber Verwissenschaftlichungsprozesse. *Geschichte und Gesellschaft (Vandenhoeck & Ruprecht), 30*, 277–313.

UNESCO. (2005). *Towards knowledge societies.* Paris: UNESCO.

Weigmann, K. (2015). Lessons learned in germany. *EMBO Reports, 16*(2), 142–145. doi:10.15252/embr.201440011 PMID:25582450

Wilkesmann, U. & Würmseer, G. (2007). *Wissensmanagement an Universitäten.* Discussion papers des Zentrums für Weiterbildung Universität Dortmund, 03.

Yagolnitser, M. A. (2015). Diagnosis of Conditions for the Formation of Innovation Clusters in Russian Regions: Mathematical and Statistical Approach. *International Journal of Econometrics and Financial Management, 3*(1), 38–43.

Yesina, J. L., Stepanenkova, N. M., & Agaphonova, E. E. (2015). Forms and Mechanisms of Integration of Science, Education and Business-Community in the Context of Innovative Changes in the Regional Economy. *Creative Economy, 9*(12), 1491–1508.

KEY TERMS AND DEFINITIONS

Clusterization: Or cluster analysis or clustering is the task of grouping a set of objects in such a way that objects in the same group (called a cluster) are more similar (in some sense or another) to each other than to those in other groups (clusters).

Expert System: Is a computer system that emulates the decision-making ability of a human expert. Expert systems are designed to solve complex problems by reasoning about knowledge, represented mainly as if–then rules rather than through conventional procedural code.

Expert: Is defined as an actor who has developed skills in, semiotic-epistemic competence for, and attentional concern with, some sphere of practical activity.

Graduate School: Is a school that awards advanced academic degrees (i.e. master's and doctoral degrees) with the general requirement that students must have earned a previous undergraduate (bachelor's) degree.

Knowledge Management: (KM) Is the process of creating, sharing, using and managing the knowledge and information of an organization. It refers to a multidisciplinary approach to achieving organisational objectives by making the best use of knowledge.

Knowledge Transfer: Refers to sharing or disseminating of knowledge and providing inputs to problem solving. In organizational theory, knowledge transfer is the practical problem of transferring knowledge from one part of the organization to another.

Mediator: Is engaged between two business parties that have required the services of the other and are deadlocked in an acrimonious debate.

ENDNOTE

[1]   Another important and often underestimated problem is the question where to draw the line between the researcher as an expert and the observed as an expert (Boyer 2005, Holmes & Marcus 2008).

Chapter 11
Employee Wellbeing English Language Proficiency a Key to Knowledge Sharing and Social Interaction

Muhammad Khaleel
Universiti Sains Malaysia, Malaysia

Shankar Chelliah
Universiti Sains Malaysia, Malaysia

ABSTRACT

This chapter discusses the significance of employee wellbeing at the workplace and self-perceived English language proficiency as a predictor variable. The importance of employee wellbeing has been recognized all around the world. To generalize the findings of previous literature this study has examined the proposed model in the context of telecom MNCs in Pakistan. This chapter starts with what is wellbeing at the workplace? And moves towards it significance in the context of developed and underdeveloped countries. Further, this chapter explains the empirical findings of the proposed model. The results revealed a strong correlation between self-perceived English language proficiency and dimensions of employee wellbeing at the workplace. This is a very important chapter for both researchers and managers.

DOI: 10.4018/978-1-5225-2897-5.ch011

INTRODUCTION

The key objective in this chapter is highlighting the challenges of employee wellbeing at workplace in telecom MNCs in Pakistan. In the same time will also explore how human capital able affect MNCs to be successful in international business with the international market's environment, there is full of uncertainty impact that may affect the telecom sector's international performance, with comparing with example from other country. The last part of this chapter will be able to have clear idea how to handle human capital and outcome all challenges. The chapter enable manager and student to discover more about Pakistani culture, value and firm behaviour. Over the last few decades, many changes have been taken place in the working environment. However, the most fundamental development is the increased psychological work load. The growing international competition and globalization that organizations are facing now days have compelled them to increase their interest in core elements of the organizational success such as human resource. That is why employees are the most valuable assets for their organizations. Employees who are not satisfied from their work or lives tend to decrease their job performance, job commitment, and devotion to their work and family. Numbers of studies have connected employees' well-being with: decline in turnover; high performance and improved physical health Low level of employees' well-being adversely affects worker and their organizations; a clear identification of workers well-being predictors is needed in order to frame an effective theoretical framework for understanding employees' well-being at workplace. Constantly growing competition in the telecommunication industry in Pakistan has compelled the companies to focus on every aspect that contributes in the success of the company. For instance, human capital plays important role for the organizations. Therefore, it is important for the telecom MNCs operating in Pakistan to be aware of the psychological demands of their human capital. This chapter tries to extend the knowledge on employee wellbeing and English language proficiency by including empirical studies from telecom sector of Pakistan.

BACKGROUND: EMPLOYEE WELLBEING AT WORKPLACE

Employees' well-being is also an important constituent for an employee to make decision for his future in the organization. Thus, there is extensive amount of evidence to point out the correlation between employees' well-being and performance. Meanwhile, importance of employees' well-being is also noticed by the policy makers in Pakistan. They have highlighted the importance of employees' well-being by ensuring the welfare of the worker, job security and good working conditions as key element in the Fifth Labor Policy, 2010. It is argued that environments should be created in a way, in which employees and employers are dedicated in enhancing the labor productivity (Fifth Labor Policy, 2010).

Definition

The term employee well-being refers to *"the mental and physical health of the workers"* (Currie, 2001; Eatough, 2013). Which means that employee should be working in such environment where he feels safe both physically and mentally. Mental health refers to the presence of wellness rather than the absence of illness. Well-being is a broader topic that covers so many organizational and workplace factors. Page and Vella-Brodrick (2009) operationalizes employee wellbeing and covers all the aspects of employee's wellbeing including psychological wellbeing, subjective wellbeing and wellbeing at workplace. Figure below explains the idea of Page and Vella-Brodrick. As shown in Figure 1.

SIGNIFICANCE OF EMPLOYEE WELLBEING AT WORKPLACE

This chapter on employee wellbeing at workplace will promote:

- The health and safety of work, working methods and the work environment.
- Employees' physical, psychological and social well-being.
- The meaningfulness of work.
- Healthy and safe ways of organizing work.
- Risk assessment and management.
- The control of exposure, strain and stress.

Figure 1. Model of Employee Mental Health

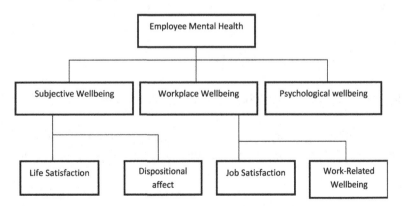

- The development of occupational health care and rehabilitation.
- The balance between work and leisure.
- The role of occupational health and safety at work as a productive factor, and its role in business.
- Information and influencing attitudes.
- The impact of work as a health-promoting factor.
- The dissemination of good practices.

GLOBAL OVERVIEW OF EMPLOYEE WELLBEING AT WORKPLACE

The topic of employee wellbeing at workplace has been under discussion since many decades. Number of authors and managers have emphasized on employees' wellbeing and related it to the world's economy. It is represented by the topic and the study included in this chapter is based on the employees working in developing country like Pakistan. It is needed over here to discuss the global perspective of employees' wellbeing at workplace. As discussed earlier, human capital is the backbone of business organizations and wellness of employees is favorable for both business and the employees themselves. Starting from the developed countries, HR departments have mainly focused on the development of healthy labor including front line employees to top management. Not only the companies themselves, Government have also put emphasize on the companies to recruit and maintain the healthy staff. For example, The Ministry of Social Affairs and Health (Finland) has started a Forum for well-being at work in order to expand co-operation in the promotion of wellbeing at workplace. The Forum provides a natural and reliable foundation for extensive co-operation by all actors. Social partners, insurance and research organizations, and ministries are all represented in the steering group of the forum. It provides a platform to which these and other organizations can bring their ideas and proposals and promote new initiatives.

MAIN FOCUS OF THE CHAPTER

Employee Wellbeing at Workplace in the Context of Pakistan

Employees' well-being is also an important constituent for an employee to make decision for his future in the organization. Thus, there is extensive amount of evidence to point out the correlation between employees' well-being and performance (Bryson & Stokes, 2014). Meanwhile, importance of employees' well-being is also noticed by the policy makers in Pakistan. They have highlighted the importance of employees' well-being by ensuring the welfare of the worker, job security and good working conditions as key element in the Fifth Labor Policy, 2010. It is argued that environments should be created in a way, in which employees and employers are dedicated in enhancing the labor productivity (Fifth Labor Policy, 2010). But even after five years, desired goals set by the fifth labor policy and favorable conditions for the workers are not achieved. Decrease in the well-being of the employees directly and indirectly effect the performance of the organization. Evidences shows that due to less productivity and profitability, multi-national telecommunication companies are pulling out their business from Pakistan. It is needed to maintain the well-being of the existing employees through well-organized strategies to overcome such organizational hazards. Therefore, this study provides the predictors of workers well-being that helps in making well planned strategies to overcome the situation if the employees' well-being is low.

Dimensions of Employee Wellbeing at Workplace

Employee wellbeing at workplace is a broader topic; many scientists have worked on this particular construct using different dimensions based on the context and theories. There are no empirically proved common dimensions of employee wellbeing at workplace. For example studies from 1998-2016 authors have conceptualized the construct wellbeing with different dimensions whereas job satisfaction is considered as most common dimension of employee wellbeing at workplace. As shown in Table 1.

Warr (1990) has conceptualized employee wellbeing at three axis as shown in the figure 2 below. This chapter has utilized Warr's (1990) model as a basic foundation in understanding employees' well-being at work. This model operationalizes employees' well-being at work as it comprises of three main axis pleasure - displeasure, depression – enthusiasm and anxiety – comfort. Warr's model provides a comprehensive over view of employees' well-being at workplace, including job satisfaction as a key element of employees' well-being at work (Sparr & Sonnentag, 2008). His model includes cognitive and affective judgments of the individuals that show the overall employees' well-being at work appropriately to the aims of this study investigation.

Four dimensions have been extracted based on the model and prior studies. Job satisfaction from pleased-displeased, job depression from enthusiastic-depressed, job anxiety from anxious-contented and turnover intention is selected as it is behavioral outcome of negative effects at the workplace.

Table 1. Dimensions of Employees' Well-Being at Work (1998-2016)

Author	Country	Employees' well-being at Work Indicators	Participants
De Jonge and Schaufeli (1998)	Netherland	• Job satisfaction • Job related anxiety • Occupational burnout	1437 Dutch health workers
Richter et al. (2013)	Sweden	• Subjective job Satisfaction • Mental health	553 Swedish accounting firm employees
Duygulu, Ciraklar, Guripek, and Bagiran (2013)	Turkey	• Work related happiness • Professional self –acceptance • Occupational growth	180 sales representatives
Sparr and Sonnentag (2008)	Germany	• Job satisfaction • Turnover intention • Job anxiety • Job Depression	260 R&D and Public administer employees
Meier, Semmer, and Gross (2014)	Switzerland	• job satisfaction • Somatic complaints • Job-related depressive mood.	127 employees with different jobs
Zacher, Jimmieson, and Bordia (2014)	Australia	• Emotional exhaustion • Job Satisfaction	771 white and blue collar employees
Noor (2004)	United Kingdom	• Job satisfaction • Distress	Not stated.
Mattern and Bauer (2014)	Germany	• Emotional exhaustion • Job Satisfaction	664 German secondary mathematics teachers
Narainsamy and Van Der Westhuizen (2013)	South Africa	• Occupational stress • Job Satisfaction • Work Engagement • Burnout	202 Medical Laboratory Staff
Horn, Taris, Schaufeli, and Schreurs (2004)	Netherland	• Social well-being • Affective Well-being • Professional Well-being	1200 Dutch teachers
Anaby, Jarus, Backman, and Zumbo (2010)	Israel	Life Satisfaction	288 Working Adults
Ibrahim (2012)	Malaysia	• Job satisfaction • Job affective well-being • Life satisfaction • Positive affect • Negative affect • Psychological well-being	1125 assembly workers, supervisors and managers from the manufacturing sector in Malaysia
Singh and Kaur (2005)	Malaysia	• Job Satisfaction • Physical well-being • Psychological well-being	197 respondents from manufacturing Industries
Eatough (2013)	America	• State self-esteem • Discrete emotions. • Fatigue • Job satisfaction • Sleep quality • Trait self-esteem	90 participants filled questionnaire for two weeks (daily dairy studies)
Elovainio et al. (2015)	Finland	• Psychological distress • Perceived Stress	1545 finish employees working in elderly care centers.
Hansen (2016)	New Zealand	Psychological wellbeing	181 managers working in various companies

Job Satisfaction

Job satisfaction of the individual has both intrinsic and extrinsic aspects. The intrinsic components are work with colleagues, task accomplishment, educational opportunities, social support and personal need of recognition. The extrinsic aspects include promotion and salary given by the organization.

Spector (1997) has given the most comprehensive definition of the job satisfaction. He describes that job satisfaction is comprise of nine aspects: promotion, benefits provided, operating procedures and policies, pay, supervision, contingent rewards as a means of recognition and appreciation, dealing with coworkers, nature of the work, communication within the organization and nature of the work (Spector, 1997). As per those nine aspects, job satisfaction is considered strongly associated with individual and organizational outcomes.

Job satisfaction has influence on individual's life satisfaction. The researchers have examined three possible relationships between job satisfaction and life satisfaction: (1) spillover, where work life influence individuals non work life or vice versa; (2) Compensation, where dissatisfying job is compensated by looking for happiness in his or her non work life and vice versa; (3) segmentation, where job and life involvements are separated and have no concern with each other (Saari & Judge, 2004).

Klassen and Chiu (2010) have conducted a study on educators in which they have mentioned low level of self-efficacy produces high level of job stress and decreases the job satisfaction. Another study examining constant predictors of job stress, job satisfaction, and employee retention between New Zealand Customs Services workers also supported these factors and gathered that satisfied employees enjoy decision-making latitude or autonomy (Mansell, Brough, & Cole, 2006). There are number of factors of job satisfaction have been recognized in previous studies. They are job security, organizational reward systems, centralization, and power distribution, the need for achievement, job resources and self-esteem. Various studies have observed job satisfaction along with other variables, therefore job satisfaction is normally considered as critical outcomes construct. Job satisfaction has a negative relation with absenteeism, and has a positive relation with productivity. For that reason, it is very effective to know which job provisions and characteristics raise job satisfaction.

Studies showed that job satisfaction produces high consumer satisfaction and decreases hiring and training costs. Fleet Boston Financial Corp. assessed in 1999 that only 1% increase in employee commitment could produce $11 million a year and reduce over expense for hiring and training up to $15 million to $19 million a year (Costanzo, 2003). In past few decades, researchers have found various variables that contribute to job satisfaction. Glisson and Durick (1988) roughly organized thee variables in to three groups: (1) variables that explain characteristics of the organizations; (2) variable that explain characteristics of the task; (3) variables that explain characteristics of the worker.

In determining the job satisfaction and evaluating the level of satisfaction of the individuals, three different approaches are proposed. First approach explains the job characteristic and known as "Information Processing Model" (Hackman & Oldham, 1976). As per this model, individual gather the information related to their work place and task and by these elements, they perceive their job satisfaction (Jex, 2002). Second approach explains that job satisfaction depend on the mood or characteristics of the individuals. These moods and characteristics of the individuals are generally associated with genetic heritage or experience or on both. Third approach explains that the evaluation of job satisfaction based on "Social Information"- how other thinks about the workplace. This approach is called "social information processing model".

Job satisfaction has been distinguished as an important predictor of critical work outcome thereby researcher's interest in this variable is higher than any other. Highly motivated, loyal and satisfied workforce is the element of success for the organizations to compete in the corporate world. Job satisfaction is a key component in maintaining high performance and efficiency of the work which directly influences the productivity of the organization. In order to increase the job satisfaction of the individuals, they should be trusted and provided with autonomy to their concerned departments. Leaders from successful organizations understand that to create positive work environment employee's job satisfaction have a great importance.

EMPLOYEES' TURN OVER INTENTIONS

Job satisfaction have significant role in turnover of the employee and is main factor in most of the turnover models (Farooq & Farooq, 2014; Naumann, 1993). Turnover of the employee is among great interesting topics for organizations, professional and researchers in the discipline of economics, management and organization behaviors (Chan & Mai, 2015; Koh & Goh, 1995). Tett and Meyer (1993) have defined turnover intention as the deliberate readiness to leave an organization. Most of the studies showed, that turnover intention is developed as dissatisfaction of; (1) individual from organization; (2) organization from individual. Turnover intention develops when an employee interested to leave his current job, based on his own desire (Khatri, Budhwar, & Fern, 1999). No matter the size of organization, turnover intention is the main concern for every organization. However part time working industries such as hotels and fast food does not have issue with turnover intention (Cascio, 2006).

Turnover intention is considered as an element of determining actual turnover. Turnover theory develops from attitude – behavior theory by supposing intention to carry out certain behavior defines that behavior. Intentions to leave the organization show the level of dissatisfaction from the current job. Generally, people believe that if someone gets dissatisfied from his job he or she starts finding alternatives, compare the other options with their job and then use the decision power to quit or not to quit (Chan & Mai, 2015).

There is a strong relationship between turnover intention and turnover (Udo, Guimãrães, & Igbaria, 1997). Researchers recommended studying turnover intention instead of actual turnover as it is difficult to calculate the actual turnover (McBey & Karakowsky, 2001). It is likely to ask individuals regarding to their intention to leave than to find and ask individuals on their actual turnover by longitudinal study. Turnover intensions have relationship between commitment, job dissatisfaction and work- life conflict. The significance of studying intentional turnover is based on several organizational consequences that are financial, reputational, loss of customer and scheduling difficulties (Lee, et al., 2004; Mishra & Morrissey, 1990). High rates of turnover intentions provide alarming situation to organizations so they can discourage intentions to leave organization by providing training and compensation to the employees (Wong, et al., 2001). There is no specific reason or goal for the turnover and turnover intention (Percy & Kostere, 2006).

Those employees who want to leave can be costly to the organization. Halpern (2005) in his study found that individuals whom intention is to leave the organization reduce their efficiency prior to quitting. The cost incurred due to turnover can be high containing cost of temporary help or overtime to complete certain project, loss of productivity, sign-on bonuses, time spent in orientation, lost business and hiring costs. Hom, Caranikas-Walker, Prussia, and Griffeth (1992) distributed the cost incurred due to turnover in to three categories: cost of separation, cost of replacement and cost of training. Cost of separation includes paper work and leaving interview; cost of replacement comprises of filling the vacancy by new candidate; cost of training includes training of newly hired candidate.

Turnover is a problem for the organizations but not all turnovers are problem for the organizations. If low performers leave the organization, it is in the beneficial of the organization. As the main concern is to retain the high performing workers. Previous studies recommend that one way to retain and reduce intentional turnover is to offer individual for work life balanced practices. Offering reduced hours, flexible scheduling and onsite daycare are important in reducing turnover.

To be successful in today's era of high competition, the retention of skilled and competent employees are significant for the organizations (Shah et al., 2011). Keeping the high quality skilled employees are more important today than ever before (Holtom, et al., 2008). Without valuable workers, a business cannot be successful and prosper. Every individual has its own importance and share in achievement of the goals, elimination of one individual makes difficult to achieve the desired results. Retaining the workers is the key target for the organization because sometimes high salaries and designations cannot successfully retain the employees that is, what happening in the telecom industry of Pakistan (Shoaib, et al., 2009).

JOB DEPRESSION

In clinical settings depression is defined as a period of intense, often continuous feeling of hopelessness and sadness followed by somatic and cognitive symptoms that usually require treatment (Wells & Sturm, 1995). There are various clinical and non-clinical symptoms of depression. Usually depression affects the way one eats and sleeps, the way a person perceive about things and the way a person thinks about himself (Shani & Pizam, 2009). According to Nolen-Hoeksema and Girgus (1994) most common symptoms of depression are lessen interest in daily activities, depressive moods, feelings of worthlessness, significant increase or decrease in weight, fatigue, sleep problems, and loss of energy, indecisiveness, less focus, and suicidal thoughts and in extreme case suicidal attempts.

Job related depression is defined as intense feelings and depressive moods originated from work environment. Work related depression produces serious economic consequences for the organization. US faces $23 billion loss due to depressed work force. The direct costs of depression comprises of primary care, hospitalization, pharmaceuticals, outpatient care and rehabilitation. Still, the major financial loss due to depression stems from indirect costs, which include loss of productivity and absenteeism.

Sometimes outcomes of work related depressions are not directly observed. With the increase in competition around the world organizations are focusing on creative and innovative workforce. Dunnagan, Peterson, and Haynes (2001) argued that this creativity and innovativeness "can be stymied if the individual's mind is clouded with maladaptive stress, anger, and depression." The work environment itself is the common element in developing depression among employees. Zagorski (2007) associated several work environment aspects such as low level of social support within the workplace, increased psychological demands, high job strain and low employment security with the development of job related depression. One of the prominent cause of workplace depression is job related stress which develops from negative work climate, culture or both.

Most of the studies on depression have been conducted on clinical settings. Moreover it has also been studies in organizational settings but they are very few in numbers. For example Kahill (1988) and Maslach, Schaufeli, and Leiter (2001) in their studies have examined antecedents of workplace depression, they found burnout, a state of physical, mental and emotional exhaustion and resulting from interpersonal and chronic emotional stressors on the job as the main predictors of job related depression. Warr (1990) and (Sparr & Sonnentag, 2008) in their studies have conceptualized job depression using depressed, gloomy and miserable situations at workplace and related it with the individual's wellbeing at workplace. Thus job depression is the key component of individual's wellbeing.

Shani and Pizam (2009) conducted a study on 151 hotel employees. The results of the study show that job burnout, work related stress are positively related to job depression whereas job satisfaction is negatively related to job depression. Similarly Wang et al. (2012) has also examined job depression by commencing study on 1436 employees, he found that effort reward imbalance, job strain and work family conflict are strongly associated with job related depression. In another study by Cho et al. (2008) shows that organizational injustice, job demands, inadequate social support and job control are the significant predictor of job depression. In line with Warr (1990) this study further examines job depression as a dimension of wellbeing at workplace.

JOB ANXIETY

Anxiety is part of everyday life. It is the provocation of inferiority feelings. Job Anxiety refers to a psychological state that arises when a person feels threat towards his job (Mishra & Yadav, 2013). Negative and positive responses are followed by the anxiety on the job. It can leads to the productive and motivated behavior of the employee. However, anxiety may also result in to harmful effects such as physical, psychological and emotional problems like heart diseases, infection, and depression(Jones, et al., 2011). Mishra and Yadav (2013) argued that job anxiety is an anxiety towards one's job, anxiety which is described as an extromoly threatening sensation of danger. It is such a common trend in the world that almost everybody has experienced it at times, at least to a mild degree.

The workplace is an important part of individuals' lives and thus exerts a strong influence on general wellbeing and health. Muschalla, Heldmann, and Fay (2013) observed the significance of job-anxiety in workplace settings and found it related to the sickness and the absence from the workplace. Furthermore they collected response from 249 employees working in different organizations and distinguished between job anxiety and trait- anxiety. Also Muschalla and collegues (2013) suggested to researchers and practitioners to identify the difference among both forms of anxieties. Thus, work can be a source of potentially anxiety-provoking stimuli and because of its complexity different dimensions of anxiety can be provoked at work.

Most of the studies on job anxiety have been investigated in clinical studies. Whereas Warr (1990) has conceptualized job anxiety as dimension of wellbeing at workplace. Data from 1686 employees revealed that job anxiety is negatively related to occupational levels and positively related to work load and job uncertainty. There are various organizational factors that are influencing job anxiety in the workplace. For example Sowmya and Panchanatham (2014) examined job anxiety by conducting study on 100 public bank employees in Chennai. Results of the study showed that organizational politics is the predictor of job anxiety. De Jonge and Schaufeli (1998) studied Warr vitamin model using three dimensions of employee wellbeing at workplace (job satisfaction, job anxiety and emotional exhaustion) and job characteristics (Job demands, job autonomy and workplace social support). It was found in the study that job anxiety is negatively related to job characteristics.

To the best of present study authors' knowledge whether and to what degree job-anxiety occurs in a non-clinical working population, and whether job-anxiety is influenced by the organizational factors. Similar to Sparr and Sonnentag (2008), the present study examines job anxiety with the organizational factors as one of the dimension of employee wellbeing at workplace.

PREDICTORS OF EMPLOYEE WELLBEING AT WORKPLACE

Various studies have examined various predictors of employee wellbeing at workplace. These predictors are both from positive stand points and negative stand points. For example Ibrahim (2012) has conducted a study on Malaysian manufacturing company employees and considered organizational justice as a predictor of employee wellbeing at workplace. Results from the study showed that if there is high justice in the organization employee's wellbeing at workplace will be also high. Similarly other scientist has chosen trust, organizational support, workplace deviance, workplace flexibility, leadership styles and etc. as strong predictors of employee wellbeing at workplace. In this chapter the main focus of the study is on employees' wellbeing in telecom MNCs in Pakistan. MNCs are facing global challenges due to various challenges and on the top of those challenges is demographic issue. Pakistan is a country where different cultures are combined together. MNCs who are interested to do their business in Pakistan face many demographic challenges. Language is one of the most common issues that are faced by MNCs. Now a days 4 telecom MNCs are operating in Pakistan. These companies have been working since 10 years and even after high competition in the market these companies reaches the revenue of more than 500 billion. It is because of managing all the issues faced by these MNCs. This chapter discusses the role of English language proficiency on employee wellbeing at workplace.

SELF-PERCEIVED ENGLISH LANGUAGE PROFICIENCY

Globalization and increased level of a firm's involvement in exchanging goods and commodities, information, finance, and personnel across national borders (Rugman & Verbeke, 2004), creates challenges for its employees. One such challenge is an increased use of a foreign language at work (Marschan-Piekkari, Welch, & Welch, 1999). Adopting a foreign language in an environment where this language is not the native language of the majority of the local people and where the local language is the predominant. In such an environment, the levels of foreign-language proficiency by employees tend to vary increasingly, which becomes an obstacle for interpersonal communication and may affect an individuals' task performance (Fredriksson, Barner-Rasmussen, & Piekkari, 2006; Harzing & Pudelko, 2013).

Language is considered as the most common aspect to categorize the group of people than any other acquired characteristic in the people and hence considered as a powerful sign for identity of individual (Linguists Giles & Johnson, 1981). Keeping in the view of Linguists and Johnson (1981), a French author said *"In the universal process of cultural homogenization, the role of language will remain intact as a key cultural differentiator, while other sources of cultural differentiation will progressively disappear."* (Usunier, 1998). According to Anxiety and Uncertainty Management theory (1995), interpersonal interaction is positively associated with the language capability and increases the propensity to over-estimate the significance of group members on the behaviors (Gudykunst, 1995). Gudykunst (1995) also argued that uncertainty in the relationship leads to negative consequences in the relationship between people.

English is the de facto global language (Crystal, 2003) and it is often recognized as the global business language for firms involved in international business (Crystal, 2003; Harzing & Pudelko, 2013). There is significant pressure and motivation for employees who speak English as a foreign language to improve their English language proficiency. Indeed, a number of studies (e.g., Harzing et al., 2011; Neeley et al., 2012) have reported negative emotional responses by non-native English speakers toward their English native colleagues' sense of superiority and their complacency for learning foreign languages. Harzing and Pudelko (2013) developed a model proposing the competency of English language in multinational subsidiaries around the world. In his model he has distributed the regions on the basis of language speaking in the subsidiaries as shown in the figure below. Asian countries have less English speaking labor and are characterized in to low English speaking zone. Multinational organizations in this region usually operate in the local language (Harzing & Pudelko, 2013). See the Figure 3 below.

Figure 2. Warr's Vitamins Model

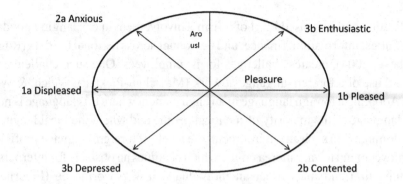

Figure 3. English language skill based on demography

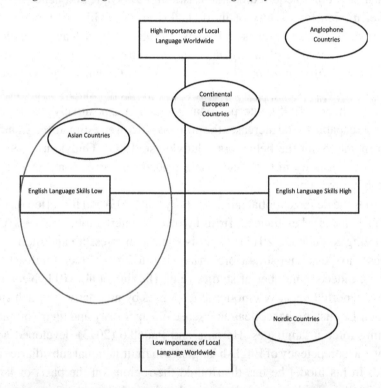

Among the educated individuals in Pakistan, only one out of 10 can read write and speak English proficiently remain 90% cannot even speak or write 2 sentences of correct English (Dar, 2013). In such environment where individuals are not proficient in English tends to misunderstand the information provided to them in

Figure 4. Model of the study

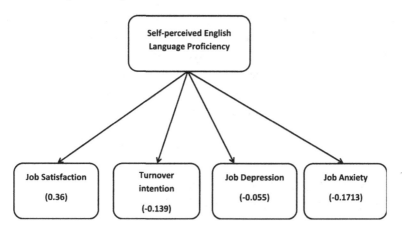

English. Present study explores the effect of English language in the employees working in telecommunication industry in Pakistan.

Based on self-efficacy theory, the self-perceived English-language proficiency of employees who speak English as a foreign language influence their commitment to their organization. Self-efficacy is essentially about a person's confidence in their ability to achieve a goal in a given circumstance (Bandura, 1977, 1982). Self-efficacy is known as a buffer for adverse conditions at work and it is an important predictor of the attitudes of employees to their jobs (e.g., (Saks, 1995) including turnover intention and job satisfaction (Tojjari, et al., 2013; Troutman, et al., 2011).

Applied linguistics research on foreign language acquisition suggests that self-perceived foreign-language proficiency influences a person's confidence in coping with an environment in which the foreign language is used. For instance, recent empirical studies has suggested that the higher a person's self-perceived foreign-language proficiency, the less anxious he or she becomes when communicating in this language (Dewaele, et al., 2008). Therefore, employees who are proficient in speaking English as a foreign language may be more committed to their organizations.

Language is considered as most significant way of communication as (Charles, 2007) said: "only language can enable individuals and companies (and countries) to communicate". Now days multinational companies are using not only local languages but also single corporate language to communicate with the headquarters, subsidiaries and other stakeholders in information sharing (Feely & Harzing, 2003; Lauring & Selmer, 2010). However all employees are not capable to speak the corporate language effectively, which lead individual to avoid to communicate in the organization. Different authors have explained language barrier as obstacle in effective communication (Tenzer, et al., 2013). Impediments in communication also depend on the language differences. Jablin (1987) have anticipated communication factor as antecedents of several individual responses in the organization (i.e. job satisfaction and organizational commitment). Communication avoidance is topic of interest by numerous researchers in psychology and communication literature. Communication avoidance can be defined as unwilling to verbally communicate with other people (McCroskey, et al., 1985). Communication is also antecedent of job satisfaction and turnover intention. There is direct and indirect relationship between the communication, job satisfaction and turnover (Mohamad, 2008).

SELF-PERCEIVED LANGUAGE PROFICIENCY AND EMPLOYEE WELLBEING AT WORK

English language proficiency is referred as the competencies in general English and professional English (Xu & Du-Babcock, 2012). Barner-Rasmussen and Aarnio (2011) in his study mentioned that lack of language proficiency leads to negative consequences in the organization such as low density of communication, lack of information sharing and trustworthiness. Therefore presence of English language proficiency in individual working in the multinational organization in Asian countries (such as Pakistan) leads to effective communication, proper information sharing and trustworthiness. For example Jablin (1987) in his study showed that communication is antecedent of job satisfaction and organizational commitment.

As discussed earlier language differences produce negative consequences in the organization such as isolation and disconnection of the subsidiary manager with the head quarter (Björkman & Piekkari, 2009). Since there are very few reports available on English language proficiency, this study explores whether this is issue in organizational settings. Language proficiency is part of effective organizational communication system. So the presence of self- perceived English language proficiency may influence employee well-being at workplace.

English language is highlighted as an issue in multinational organizations in Asian countries (Harzing & Pudelko, 2013). Procedures defined to the employee working in multinational organizations in Pakistan are in English. Individuals, who have good expertise in English, understand the procedures more effectively than those who have less proficiency in English. Individuals who can effectively speak foreign language influence their commitment to their organization (Yamao & Sekiguchi, 2015). Furthermore a recent study conducted by Shafaei and Razak (2016) revealed positive relationship between psychological wellbeing and self-perceived English language proficiency Therefore presence of high perceived English language proficiency produces positive consequences in the organization. Hence based on prior studies this chapter explores the relationship between self-perceived English language proficiency and employee wellbeing at work.

WHAT IS ROLE OF SELF-PERCEIVED ENGLISH LANGUAGE PROFICIENCY ON EMPLOYEE WELLBEING AT WORKPLACE IN TELECOM MNCS IN PAKISTAN?

To test the role of self-perceived English Language in Pakistan, a quantitative survey based study was conducted. Managers working in telecom MNCs were selected as the respondents of the study. The results from the study revealed that self-perceived English language Proficiency is significantly related to employee wellbeing at workplace.

A total 300 survey questionnaires was distributed to the respondents and 240 questionnaires were returned. Only 5 out of 240 questionnaires were unusable. The final usable questionnaires were 235 with a response rate of 78.3%. most of the respondents of the study were male participants 68.5% whereas female participants were consisted of 31.5% out of overall total respondents of 235. Majority of the respondents fall under the age range between 26 to 30 years old 42.1%. Respondents at the age of 25 and less years old were 20.4% followed by the age group of 31-35 years old 18.3%. Only 6.0% of the respondents were more than 41 years old. Further for the educational background, most of the respondents had degree 86.0% followed by the diploma holders 12.3%. There was no respondent under diploma level or form high school degree. In terms of respondents' organization, majority of the respondents were from Mobilink 35.7% followed by respondents working in Zong 32.3%. Respondents working in Telenor were 17.9% and the least were respondents working in Warid 14.0%. As per experience, majority of the respondents had 1 to 5 year experience 67.2%. Respondent with 6 to 10 year experience were 19.1% followed by the respondents with less than 1 year experience 7.2%. Only 1.3% of the respondents had more than 15 year of experience. With regard to organizational position, all of the respondents were managers.

PLS is generally used for the prediction, the goodness of theoretical model is acknowledged by the variance explained (R2) of the indigenous constructs and the substance of all the path estimates (Hair et al. 2014). After estimation of the path estimates in the structural model, a bootstrap analysis was used to measure the statistical significance of the path coefficient. Chin (1998) advocates 500 re-sampling when operating bootstrapping to estimate a parameter. Therefore, in this study the bootstrapping procedures with 500 re-sampling was used.

The bootstrapping results of the study revealed that all the direct hypothesis are supported in this study. Self-perceived English Language Proficiency is a significant predictor of employee's wellbeing at workplace. As shown in the Table 2.

Review of the literature suggests that self-perceived English language proficiency is a significant predictor of various job outcomes such as job commitment and psychological wellbeing (Yamao & Sekiguchi, 2015). In line with previous literature, it was found that there is a strong relationship between self-perceived English language proficiency and employee's wellbeing at work place (i.e., job satisfaction, turnover intention and job anxiety). English language proficiency is the key job prerequisite in most of the telecommunication companies because most of the verbal communication is processed in English language. Employees with high proficiency in English language are able to understand and communicate in English language leading to a positive job outcome such as job satisfaction, commitment and less anxiety. Also, employees who are proficient in English language understand their job roles and perform accordingly that makes them satisfied, less anxious and committed to their organization. See Figure 4.

Moreover, Yamao and Sekiguchi (2015) explained that self-perceived English language proficiency is one of the key components of an individual to survive in his organization by showing a strong commitment with his organization. The results of this study support the findings of Shafaei and Razak (2016). They have argued that individual's wellbeing at the job is correlated with self-perceived English language proficiency. Therefore, the findings of this study showed a strong correlation between self-perceived English language proficiency and wellbeing at workplace.

Table 2. Hypothesis Testing

Hypothesis	Path	Std. Beta	Std. Error	t-value	Result
H1	Self-Perceived Language Proficiency -> Job Anxiety	-0.1713	0.0861	**1.9894**	**Supported**
H2	Self-Perceived Language Proficiency -> Job Depression	-0.055	0.0792	**1.6944**	**Supported**
H3	Self-Perceived Language Proficiency -> Job Satisfaction	0.3612	0.08	**4.5163**	**Supported**
H4	Self-Perceived Language Proficiency -> Turnover Intention	-0.1396	0.0738	**1.8921**	**Supported**

CONCLUSION AND RECOMMENDATION

Employees' wellbeing at workplace is critically significant for the organizations, to survive in highly competitive market. In connection with the point mentioned what organizations should do to enhance employee's wellbeing at workplace is limited in research. How to enhance employee's wellbeing at workplace must be a focus of the organization since it specifies organizational responsibility for workers' health. Furthermore, organizational efforts to enhance wellbeing at workplace will increase its reputation to use human capital for business operations. Though individual research effort was made to identify the predictors of employee's wellbeing at workplace, research based on these grounds is still limited in the developing countries such as Pakistan, particularly in telecommunication sectors. Thus, this study explored four dimensions of employee's wellbeing at workplace in telecommunication MNCs in the context of developing countries.

English language is not the first language in Pakistan, but the official communication in the multinational organizations in Pakistan is carried out in English. Individuals who are proficient in English language shows positive attitude towards their organization. That is why, this study has found that employees' perception of their English language skill has a key role in their job satisfaction, turnover intention and job anxiety.

REFERENCES

Alex Bryson, J. F. a., & Stokes, L. (2014). *Does Worker Wellbeing Affect Workplace Performance?* Academic Press.

Bandura, A. (1977). Self-efficacy: Toward a unifying theory of behavioral change. *Psychological Review*, *84*(2), 191–215. doi:10.1037/0033-295X.84.2.191 PMID:847061

Bandura, A. (1982). Self-efficacy mechanism in human agency. *The American Psychologist*, *37*(2), 122–147. doi:10.1037/0003-066X.37.2.122

Barner-Rasmussen, W., & Aarnio, C. (2011). Shifting the faultlines of language: A quantitative functional-level exploration of language use in MNC subsidiaries. *Journal of World Business*, *46*(3), 288–295. doi:10.1016/j.jwb.2010.07.006

Björkman, A., & Piekkari, R. (2009). Language and foreign subsidiary control: An empirical test. *Journal of International Management, 15*(1), 105–117. doi:10.1016/j.intman.2008.12.001

Cascio, W. F. (2006). The high cost of low wages. *Harvard Business Review, 84*(12), 23.

Chan, S. H. J., & Mai, X. (2015). The relation of career adaptability to satisfaction and turnover intentions. *Journal of Vocational Behavior, 89,* 130–139. doi:10.1016/j.jvb.2015.05.005

Charles, M. (2007). Language Matters in Global Communication Article Based on ORA Lecture, October 2006. *Journal of Business Communication, 44*(3), 260–282. doi:10.1177/0021943607302477

Cho, J. J., Kim, J. Y., Chang, S. J., Fiedler, N., Koh, S. B., Crabtree, B. F., & Choi, Y. H. (2008). Occupational stress and depression in Korean employees. *International Archives of Occupational and Environmental Health, 82*(1), 47–57. doi:10.1007/s00420-008-0306-4 PMID:18301911

Costanzo, C. (2003). Shutting Out Fraud. *Banking Strategies,* 28-35.

Crystal, D. (2003). *English as a global language.* Cambridge University Press. doi:10.1017/CBO9780511486999

Currie, D. (2001). *Managing employee well-being.* Chandos Publishing.

Dar, H. (2013). *The importance of education: Economics of the English language in Pakistan.* Tribune.

De Jonge, J., & Schaufeli, W. B. (1998). Job characteristics and employee well-being: A test of Warrs Vitamin Model in health care workers using structural equation modelling. *Journal of Organizational Behavior, 19*(4), 387–407. doi:10.1002/(SICI)1099-1379(199807)19:4<387::AID-JOB851>3.0.CO;2-9

Dewaele, J. M., Petrides, K. V., & Furnham, A. (2008). Effects of trait emotional intelligence and sociobiographical variables on communicative anxiety and foreign language anxiety among adult multilinguals: A review and empirical investigation. *Language Learning, 58*(4), 911–960. doi:10.1111/j.1467-9922.2008.00482.x

Dunnagan, T., Peterson, M., & Haynes, G. (2001). Mental health issues in the workplace: A case for a new managerial approach. *Journal of Occupational and Environmental Medicine, 43*(12), 1073–1080. doi:10.1097/00043764-200112000-00009 PMID:11765678

Eatough, E. M. (2013). *Illegitimate tasks and employee well-being: A daily diary study*. Academic Press.

Farooq, M., & Farooq, O. (2014). Organizational justice, employee turnover, and trust in the workplace: A study in South Asian telecommunication companies. *Global Business and Organizational Excellence, 33*(3), 56–62. doi:10.1002/joe.21539

Feely, A. J., & Harzing, A.-W. (2003). Language management in multinational companies. *Cross Cultural Management: An International Journal, 10*(2), 37–52. doi:10.1108/13527600310797586

Fredriksson, R., Barner-Rasmussen, W., & Piekkari, R. (2006). The multinational corporation as a multilingual organization: The notion of a common corporate language. *Corporate Communications: An International Journal, 11*(4), 406–423. doi:10.1108/13563280610713879

Glisson, C., & Durick, M. (1988). Predictors of job satisfaction and organizational commitment in human service organizations. *Administrative Science Quarterly, 33*(1), 61–81. doi:10.2307/2392855

Gudykunst, W. B. (1995). Anxiety/Uncertainty Management (AUM) Theory: Current Status. In *Intercultural Communication Theory*. Sage.

Hackman, J. R., & Oldham, G. R. (1976). Motivation through the design of work: Test of a theory. *Organizational Behavior and Human Performance, 16*(2), 250–279. doi:10.1016/0030-5073(76)90016-7

Halpern, D. F. (2005). How time flexible work policies can reduce stress, improve health, and save money. *Stress and Health, 21*(3), 157–168. doi:10.1002/smi.1049

Harzing, A.-W., Köster, K., & Magner, U. (2011). Babel in business: The language barrier and its solutions in the HQ-subsidiary relationship. *Journal of World Business, 46*(3), 279–287. doi:10.1016/j.jwb.2010.07.005

Harzing, A.-W., & Pudelko, M. (2013). Language competencies, policies and practices in multinational corporations: A comprehensive review and comparison of Anglophone, Asian, Continental European and Nordic MNCs. *Journal of World Business, 48*(1), 87–97. doi:10.1016/j.jwb.2012.06.011

Holtom, B. C., Mitchell, T. R., Lee, T. W., & Eberly, M. B. (2008). 5 turnover and retention research: A glance at the past, a closer review of the present, and a venture into the future. *The Academy of Management Annals, 2*(1), 231–274. doi:10.1080/19416520802211552

Hom, P. W., Caranikas-Walker, F., Prussia, G. E., & Griffeth, R. W. (1992). A meta-analytical structural equations analysis of a model of employee turnover. *The Journal of Applied Psychology*, *77*(6), 890–909. doi:10.1037/0021-9010.77.6.890

Ibrahim, R. Z. A. R. (2012). *Psychosocial work environment, organisational justice and work family conflict as predictors of Malaysian worker wellbeing*. Melbourne, Australia: Victoria University.

Jablin, F. M. (1987). Organizational entry, assimilation, and exit. In F. M. Jablin, L. L. Putnam, K. H. Roberts, & L. W. Porter (Eds.), *Handbook Organizational and communication* (pp. 389–419). Newbury Park, CA: Sage.

Jex, S. (2002). *Organizational Psychology: A Scientist-Practitioner Approach*. New York: John Wiley & Sons.

Jones, M. K., Latreille, P. L., & Sloane, P. J. (2011). *Job anxiety, work-related psychological illness and workplace performance*. NILS, Flinders University and IZA.

Kahill, S. (1988). Symptoms of professional burnout: A review of the empirical evidence. *Canadian Psychology*, *29*(3), 284–297. doi:10.1037/h0079772

Khatri, N., Budhwar, P., & Fern, C. (1999). *Employee turnover: bad attitude or poor management*. Singapore: Nanyang Technological University.

Klassen, R. M., & Chiu, M. M. (2010). Effects on teachers self-efficacy and job satisfaction: Teacher gender, years of experience, and job stress. *Journal of Educational Psychology*, *102*(3), 741–756. doi:10.1037/a0019237

Koh, H. C., & Goh, C. T. (1995). An analysis of the factors affecting the turnover intention of non-managerial clerical staff: A Singapore study. *International Journal of Human Resource Management*, *6*(1), 103–125. doi:10.1080/09585199500000005

Lauring, J., & Klitmøller, A. (2015). Corporate language-based communication avoidance in MNCs: A multi-sited ethnography approach. *Journal of World Business*, *50*(1), 46–55. doi:10.1016/j.jwb.2014.01.005

Lauring, J., & Selmer, J. (2010). Multicultural organizations: Common language and group cohesiveness. *International Journal of Cross Cultural Management*, *10*(3), 267–284. doi:10.1177/1470595810384587

Lee, T. W., Mitchell, T. R., Sablynski, C. J., Burton, J. P., & Holtom, B. C. (2004). The effects of job embeddedness on organizational citizenship, job performance, volitional absences, and voluntary turnover. *Academy of Management Journal*, *47*(5), 711–722. doi:10.2307/20159613

Mansell, A., Brough, P., & Cole, K. (2006). Stable Predictors of Job Satisfaction, Psychological Strain, and Employee Retention: An Evaluation of Organizational Change Within the New Zealand Customs Service. *International Journal of Stress Management, 13*(1), 84–107. doi:10.1037/1072-5245.13.1.84

Marschan-Piekkari, R., Welch, D., & Welch, L. (1999). Adopting a common corporate language: IHRM implications. *International Journal of Human Resource Management, 10*(3), 377–390. doi:10.1080/095851999340387

Maslach, C., Schaufeli, W. B., & Leiter, M. P. (2001). Job burnout. *Annual Review of Psychology, 52*(1), 397–422. doi:10.1146/annurev.psych.52.1.397 PMID:11148311

McBey, K., & Karakowsky, L. (2001). Examining sources of influence on employee turnover in the part time work context. *Career Development International, 6*(1), 39–48. doi:10.1108/13620430110381025

McCroskey, J. C., Fayer, J. M., & Richmond, V. P. (1985). Dont speak to me in English: Communication apprehension in Puerto Rico. *Communication Quarterly, 33*(3), 185–192. doi:10.1080/01463378509369597

Mishra, J., & Morrissey, M. A. (1990). Trust in employee/employer relationships: A survey of West Michigan managers. *Public Personnel Management, 19*(4), 443–463. doi:10.1177/009102609001900408

Mishra, & Yadav, B. (2013). Job Anxiety And Personality Adjustment Of Secondary School Teachers In Relation Of Gender And Types Of Teacher. *Educational Research International, 1*(1), 105-126.

Mohamad, S. F. (2008). Effects of communication on turnover intention: a case of hotel employees in Malaysia. *Graduate Theses and Dissertations.* 11164. Retrieved from http://lib.dr.iastate.edu/etd/11164

Muschalla, B., Heldmann, M., & Fay, D. (2013). The significance of job-anxiety in a working population. *Occupational Medicine, 63*(6), 415–421. doi:10.1093/occmed/kqt072 PMID:23771887

Naumann, E. (1993). Antecedents and consequences of satisfaction and commitment among expatriate managers. *Group & Organization Management, 18*(2), 153–187. doi:10.1177/1059601193182003

Neeley, T. B., Hinds, P. J., & Cramton, C. D. (2012). The (un) hidden turmoil of language in global collaboration. *Organizational Dynamics, 41*(3), 236–244. doi:10.1016/j.orgdyn.2012.03.008

Nolen-Hoeksema, S., & Girgus, J. S. (1994). The emergence of gender differences in depression during adolescence. *Psychological Bulletin, 115*(3), 424–443. doi:10.1037/0033-2909.115.3.424 PMID:8016286

Page, K. M., & Vella-Brodrick, D. A. (2009). The what,whyand howof employee well-being: A new model. *Social Indicators Research, 90*(3), 441–458. doi:10.1007/s11205-008-9270-3

Percy, W., & Kostere, K. (2006). *Qualitative research approaches in psychology.* Capella University.

Policy, T. L. (2010). *Fifth Pakistan Labour policy.* Pakistan: Academic Press.

Rugman, A. M., & Verbeke, A. (2004). A perspective on regional and global strategies of multinational enterprises. *Journal of International Business Studies, 35*(1), 3–18. doi:10.1057/palgrave.jibs.8400073

Saari, L. M., & Judge, T. A. (2004). Employee attitudes and job satisfaction. *Human Resource Management, 43*(4), 395–407. doi:10.1002/hrm.20032

Saks, A. (1995). Viewpoints: A symposium on the usefulness of literacy research. *Research in the Teaching of English,* 326–348.

Shafaei, A., & Razak, N. A. (2016). International Postgraduate Students' Cross-Cultural Adaptation in Malaysia: Antecedents and Outcomes. *Research in Higher Education,* 1–29.

Shah, S. S., Aziz, J., Jaffari, A. R., Ejaz, M. W., Khattak, A., & Rehman, K. R. A. (2011). Mentoring and its effects on turnover intentions in perspective of Pakistan's telecom sector. *Information Management and Business Review, 3*(3), 133–138.

Shani, A., & Pizam, A. (2009). Work-related depression among hotel employees. *Cornell Hospitality Quarterly, 50*(4), 446–459. doi:10.1177/1938965509344294

Shoaib, M., Noor, A., Tirmizi, S. R., & Bashir, S. (2009). Determinants of employee retention in telecom sector of Pakistan. *Proceedings of the 2nd CBRC,* 14.

Sowmya, K., & Panchanatham, N. (2014). Job Anxiety as an Outcome of Organizational Politics in Banking Sector-Chennai. *International Journal of Management & Innovation, 6*(2).

Sparr, J. L., & Sonnentag, S. (2008). Fairness perceptions of supervisor feedback, LMX, and employee well-being at work. *European Journal of Work and Organizational Psychology, 17*(2), 198–225. doi:10.1080/13594320701743590

Spector, P. E. (1997). *Job satisfaction: Application, assessment, causes, and consequences* (Vol. 3). Sage publications.

Tenzer, H., Pudelko, M., & Harzing, A.-W. (2013). The impact of language barriers on trust formation in multinational teams. *Journal of International Business Studies*, *45*(5), 508–535. doi:10.1057/jibs.2013.64

Tett, R. P., & Meyer, J. P. (1993). Job satisfaction, organizational commitment, turnover intention, and turnover: Path analyses based on meta analytic findings. *Personnel Psychology*, *46*(2), 259–293. doi:10.1111/j.1744-6570.1993.tb00874.x

Tojjari, F., Esmaeili, M. R., & Bavandpour, R. (2013). The effect of self-efficacy on job satisfaction of sport referees. *European Journal of Experimental Biology*, *3*(2), 219–225.

Troutman, C. S., Burke, K. G., & Beeler, J. D. (2011). The Effects Of Self-Efficacy, Assertive-ness, Stress, And Gender On Intention To Turnover In Public Accounting. *Journal of Applied Business Research*, *16*(3). doi:10.19030/jabr.v16i3.2043

Udo, G. J., Guimãrães, T., & Igbaria, M. (1997). An investigation of the antecedents of turnover intention for manufacturing plant managers. *International Journal of Operations & Production Management*, *17*(9), 912–930. doi:10.1108/01443579710171280

Usunier, J. C. (1998). *International and cross-cultural management research*. SAGE Publications Ltd.

Wang, J., Smailes, E., Sareen, J., Schmitz, N., Fick, G., & Patten, S. (2012). Three job-related stress models and depression: A population-based study. *Social Psychiatry and Psychiatric Epidemiology*, *47*(2), 185–193. doi:10.1007/s00127-011-0340-5 PMID:21234534

Warr, P. (1990). The measurement of well being and other aspects of mental health. *Journal of Occupational Psychology*, *63*(3), 193–210. doi:10.1111/j.2044-8325.1990.tb00521.x

Wells, K. B., & Sturm, R. (1995). Care for depression in a changing environment. *Health Affairs*, *14*(3), 78–89. doi:10.1377/hlthaff.14.3.78 PMID:7498906

Wong, C.-S., Wong, Y., Hui, C., & Law, K. S. (2001). The significant role of Chinese employees organizational commitment: Implications for managing employees in Chinese societies. *Journal of World Business*, *36*(3), 326–340. doi:10.1016/S1090-9516(01)00058-X

Xu, X., & Du-Babcock, B. (2012). Impact of English-language Proficiency on Chinese Expatriates' Adjustment to Overseas Assignments. *Global Advances in Business Communication*, *1*(1), 4.

Yamao, S., & Sekiguchi, T. (2015). Employee commitment to corporate globalization: The role of English language proficiency and human resource practices. *Journal of World Business*, *50*(1), 168–179. doi:10.1016/j.jwb.2014.03.001

Zagorski, B. (2007). Major depressive episodes and work stress: Results from a national population survey. *American Journal of Public Health*, *97*(11), 2088–2093. doi:10.2105/AJPH.2006.104406 PMID:17901431

KEY TERMS AND DEFINITIONS

Anxiety: Is an emotion characterized by an unpleasant state of inner turmoil, often accompanied by nervous behavior, such as pacing back and forth, somatic complaints, and rumination.

Comfort: (Or being comfortable) Is a sense of physical or psychological ease, often characterized as a lack of hardship.

Depression: Is a state of low mood and aversion to activity that can affect a person's thoughts, behavior, feelings, and sense of well-being.

Displeasure: Or pain in a broad sense, may be an experience of unpleasantness and aversion associated with the perception of harm or threat of harm in an individual.

Enthusiasm: Is intense enjoyment, interest, or approval. The word was originally used to refer to a person possessed by a god, or someone who exhibited intense piety.

Human Resource: Are the people who make up the workforce of an organization, business sector, or economy.

Turnover Intention: Is the act of replacing an employee with a new employee. Partings between organizations and employees may consist of termination, retirement, death, interagency transfers, and resignations.

Well-Being: Is a general term for the condition of an individual or group, for example their social, economic, psychological, spiritual or medical state; a high level of well-being means in some sense the individual or group's condition is positive, while low well-being is associated with negative happenings.

Section 3
Information Technology

Chapter 12

Demystifying the Power of Digital to Become a Cleverer Enterprise:
The Concept of "Digital Quotient"

Murat Yaslioglu
Istanbul University, Turkey

Duygu Toplu Yaslioglu
Istanbul University, Turkey

ABSTRACT

New challenge in all industries is to catch up with the digital revolution. There are some pioneers and some followers in all industries but it is inevitable that digits catch every company by its claws. Our research aims to put forward the dynamics of the digital era or in other words new economy. Companies with a good level of digital maturity and thus high digital quotient become the leaders of their industries. Of course it is in some sectors digitization has become more obvious compared to others, but it is a rising trend in every industry, one can appoint. Banking sector is casts a great example how digital quotient and its factors come into play. Our research tries to define the new concept of digital quotient and illustrate a good practice by evaluating the strategies of a leading bank in Turkey.

DOI: 10.4018/978-1-5225-2897-5.ch012

INTRODUCTION

The word digital refers to numbers, however the digitization and its effect on business and industrialization have altered the way we work and produce entirely. Digital business has begun with the internet in the early 90s. It was never expected that this network would expand globally and would even connect "things" in our lives (Kopetz, 2011; Bughin, et.al., 2015). Increased connectivity, new technical opportunities and more "knowledge power" helps us to discover and share even more. Contemporary meaning of digital hence refers to technological foundations that allow humans and things to share information among each other (EY, 2014).

Today's most of the known enterprises such as Facebook, Google, Twitter, Amazon, e.g. can be said to be "born digital". However, digitization has its own eras in it; information technologies' craftsmanship or so called "ITsmiths" focused on the technology's development itself. Their capabilities included but not limited to mostly programming and system management. These ITsmiths were isolated and disengaged. Most of the outputs were inordinate and ragged automation with every problem. Second era followed immediately with IT's rapid industrialization through process focused IT and service management. CIOs and information workers whom treat colleagues as valuable customers have emerged, however this era had its deficiencies such as their very low engagement with external environment and especially customers. Outcome of this era were high tech services and solutions focused to efficiency and effectiveness (Taylor, & Todd, 1995). We can account ourselves at the end of this era, because drivers of digital intelligence such as cloud services, mobile engagement, social networking, social media and its analytics has already started to force us think out of the clichés and paradigm shift for the new digital enterprise. Change is not an isolated event, but a constantly evolving way of being. Leaders must embed a capability to adapt and react to change within their organizational fabric, including cultures, business models and strategies, value propositions, processes, and, crucially, their internal and external communication strategies and channels. (Tapscott, & Caston, 1993; Veling, et.al, 2014). Businesses will be forced to think on platform models which interlocks and connects everything; not just our computers to the mobile phones but smart things in our life, including our milieu and us. Yesterday's ITsmiths have started to evolve into "digital leaders" with deep knowledge of IT and its necessary use; treat their colleagues as partners and also engage with external customers. The result will be digital business innovation, new types of value and higher "digital quotient".

The term digital transformation is perhaps one of the most frightening words in contemporary corporate lexicon. Stakes are high and new technology with new business models are tipping and turning over entire industries. Threatening all officials with an atypical billow of disruptive forces. Leaders acknowledge they somehow have to rise their Digital Quotient, but many don't know how to do it. Digitization is a consummating transformation. When a global bank has transformed its processes for their clients, the results were dramatic decrease in costs, ground breaking customer experience on the commercial side. As attractive as it looks, it also leaves an exhausted organization behind, wondering if it can redo what it did and went through for the remaining parts of its business. It is even harder to accomplish the same thing for more than one at the same time. Companies that has achieved to do the transformation at the scale should have found a better way. They knew they had to start the conversion process in their structure to enable them to digitize at scale and fast. This distinct structure enabled them to transform in a more consistent way, with consistent resources (Rickards et.al, 2015). These companies not only acknowledge the high stakes daring them, they also act on knowledge. Knowledge about how customers behave and want to be treated. Many of us download an app from the store to our mobile phones, try that new application once or twice, then if we fail to get it work in the way we do, we simply leave it aside. The same applies to the companies striving to digitize. Customers give companies one or two chances for their digital offerings, if those attempts fail implementation fails. This chapter tries to outline the digital transformation towards a higher "Digital Quotient" and for this the necessary capabilities are enlisted together with a supportive industry case.

BACKGROUND

Digital Quotient

When we refer to human intelligence the first thing strikes our minds is the measurement of it by the help of systematic and standardized tests, which is popularly called "Intelligence Quotient", or in abbreviation "IQ". McKinsey's recent research has first implied the concept of DQ with a well-formed metric for digital maturity of a company (Catlin et.al, 2014). Here we aim to conceptualize the digital quotient and create a foundation for further research with a more theoretical basis. Increasing maturity of digitization and therefore reaching a higher level of digital quotient a company must perform certain capabilities at scale (Desmet, 2015; Dörner & Meffert, 2015; Catlin et.al., 2014).

MAIN FOCUS OF THE CHAPTER

Big Data Empowered Decision Making and Data Analytics

Data is raw information, which is processed into knowledge. Relentless and ever-ending collection of data from all over the internet search engines, mobile phones, broadcasts, applications, web sites, social media, blogs, wikis and so on, has created an opportunity and a great deal of knowledge source in the form of raw data. However, this data has piled up unimaginably after the digital revolution and recently this repository has increased its pace more than an exponential function. This vast repository can also be harnessed by analytics, and therefore eventually used for decision making in various areas. The US department of labor predicts 4.4 million job opportunities on data analytics by 2018 (Henry, & Venkatraman, 2015). According to SINTEF (2013) research, raw data created in 2011 and 2012 was accounted for %90 of all outstanding data ever created. Problem with the big data and its analytics is that it is not a database, which is organized and structured to be used conveniently. Data could have been produced and reproduced several times by humans, machines or both; examples of people generated data are text messages, Facebook posts, tweets, web content, blogs, forum messages. Machines generate logs, GPS data, sensor backups, surveillance, satellite data e.g. The reproduction occurs when both parties use data generated with either party to regenerate new data or information, this is a never ending cycle. Some applications of the analytics are (Schneider, 2006); business performance monitoring through web and social media, anomaly and crisis detection, estimation of possibilities, business process uplift, optimizations, customer trends and CRM as well as demand forecasting. According to and because of aforementioned reasons traditional tools for big data handling are obsolete, there are several software working with different logics. The ones based on NoSQL (Not only SQL) are Cassandra, Hbase, Apache CouchDB, MongoDB, Dynamo and Neo4J. And also there is Hadoop which is very light and cost efficient (Henry, & Venkatraman, 2015).

Traditional sources of data such as reports, excel files, SQL were the tools of traditional managers, or as mentioned before "ITsmiths" and information workers; contemporary managers or so-called "digital leaders" need and harness their information from analytics tools and depend on a real-time source of information. This, hence, gives less chance of success to managers. To keep the digital quotient on a base level, every organization should have "digital leaders" with great deal of expertise in this area. This implementation requires some technological and organizational considerations in addition to the bottom-line: "digital leaders". Some technological considerations are (Dobrev & Hart, 2015):

- **Integration:** Multiple systems, distributed systems, difficulty in changing infrastructure, legacy systems integration, migration and data consolidation.
- **Message-Bus Data:** Combination of a common data model, a common command set, and a messaging infrastructure to allow different systems to communicate through a shared set of interfaces (Hohpe & Woolf, 2004). Structured and unstructured data, master and historic data, data latency and data management hardware.
- Architecture.

The organizational considerations are (Dobrev & Hart, 2015);

- **Requirements:** To be defined, incorporated to business strategies.
- Costs.
- **Rules and Regulations:** To be defined in all cases and monitoring should be solid and ethical.
- **Business Process Reengineering:** Absolutely mandatory enterprise-wide.
- **IT Skills and Support:** Education and training in new tools and tech., management of skilled "knowledge workers" require digital leaders.
- **Build vs. Buy:** Build the skills and maturity but buy the configuration and vendor assessment.
- **Change Management:** Necessary to overcome resistance to total BPR.

Connectivity and Information Technology

Data empowered decision making is a desire which goes through the usage of information and communication technologies (ICT) which brings great opportunities; however un-planned and unsystematic use of these technologies often ends up with frustration because of the costs accompanied with them. ICT has both internal and external use; internal use of ICT gives the opportunity of decentralization in the means of data flow, which enables decisions to be made on operational level where data is created and consumed. Decentralization brings the necessity of more skilled and expert "knowledge workers"; monitoring costs, residual loss, information processing deficit and cost related to the knowledge transfers (Bhatnagar & Schware, 2000; Gurbaxani & Whang, 1991). However, usage of ICT has also positive impact on the knowledge transfer costs. Priority of ICT usage has changed according to McKinsey (Khan & Sikes, 2014) survey results. Priority shifted from reducing costs to improving effectiveness of business processes drastically. However, the cost of ICT structure itself still consists of mostly the infrastructure and core application investment and in the upcoming years executives expect less investment in these areas. The solution seems to improve business's accountability for IT related projects and reallocate

ICT budgets to focus on critical drivers of business value rather than sole use of the technology for nothing but easing the pain of business life. Therefore, this requires a great change in mind-set and addresses talent challenges for companies (Melville et.al, 2004; Schreyer, 2000). Using WhatsApp or Skype for meetings, padding to latest tech laptops and tablets with great connectivity among each other is a good way of working, however if this infrastructure costs are not transferred to create "real" value, it is a dead end for the company. Talent challenge requires improved and agile culture, use of cutting-edge technology in the means of automation, more competitive salary, benefits and incentives.

If challenges are overcome by the help of new talents, digital leaders, agile culture then ICT has and will show its benefits in operational, tactical and strategic means and will become the key tool for success. Some operational benefits are; improved data management and communication, faster and flexible decision making, relocation of work and talent, reduced paperwork and labor costs, improved ability to exchange and analyze data, improved response time and improved control over cash-flow, oversight on quality and just in time production, improved efficiency, faster and more reliable, operationally integrated procurement (Thorp, 2003). Tactical benefits include; improved response to changes, improved service quality and teamwork, proactive culture, improved planning times, reduced time to compile tenders, improved integration among functions. And finally strategic benefits are; improved growth and reduced marketing costs, access to new technology, opportunity to take benefit of big data, more agile and improved relations with customers, reaching more relevant and valuable information to create strategies and most importantly integration of customer/supplier and operation needs to better strategic decisions (Kosakowski, 1998; Ion, & Andreea, 2008).

Recent technological changes that fosters digital quotient by altering the way we do business are (Holtgrewe, 2014):

- The convergence of telecommunications and IT;
- The increasing omnipresence not just of 'chips' but of Internet connectivity and consequently, the diffusion of web-based services and functionalities into increasingly diverse spaces and spheres of activity;
- The increasing independence of computing capacity from local hardware equipment and software ('cloud computing')
- The utilization of the resulting amounts of data and meta-data for various commercial and public purposes and business models ('big data').

ICT's impact on working conditions are somewhat liquid employment implying flexible and mobile working conditions and possibility of relocation; more benefit from outsourcing employees and crowdsourcing; virtual collaboration (AWPA, 2013).

Automation

Automation or automatic control, is the use of various control systems for operating equipment such as machinery, processes in factories, boilers and heat treating ovens, switching on telephone networks, steering and stabilization of ships, aircraft and other applications with minimal or reduced human intervention. Some processes have been completely automated (Wikipedia - Automation, 2016; Rifkin, 1995). Businesses tend to use automation for the business processes to increase efficiency, reduce the costs, improve quality and lead times, and to decrease the amount of errors caused by humans. Especially business process automation has become a very high priority for companies to improve efficiency initially. The first phase of business process automation was within the companies' processes, however second phase hit with the emergence and rise of e-commerce. There is recently a very great deal of interest in automation technologies for coordination and automation of intra-firm and inter-firm business processes. For instance; using automation in business processes and interconnecting with the connectivity of every step in wide and local area, banks have shortened their account opening processes from two-tree days to less than 10 minutes (Bunz, 2009). Credit applications are also automated with integration to credit scores from the government to give opportunity to the customers to get provisions in a few minutes.

Automation, besides business processes, is also used for some level of decision making. The goal of this automation in critical decision-making contexts like intensive care units, nuclear power plants and aircraft cockpits is to reduce human error. Human brain is not capable of comprehending to much of information at once and therefore need to use tech support, if these info gets larger and gets more complex at the level of inter and intra-connectivity; automation takes an important role. Therefore, we can redefine automation as define automation as a device or system that accomplishes (partially or fully) a function that was previously, or conceivably could be, carried out (partially or fully) by a human operator (Parasuraman & Riley, 1997).

There are contradicting research on the effect of automation on decision quality and erroneousness, for example various problems with automated decision aids have been identified, including mode misunderstandings and mode errors; failures to understand automation behavior; confusion or lack of awareness concerning what automated aids are doing and why; and difficulty associated with tracing the reasoning processes and functioning of automated agents (Sarter & Woods, 1993; Billings, 1996). Therefore, the excessive, unplanned, undescribed and unintegrated exercise of automation in the hands of unskilled, inadequately educated utilizers may create obstacles rather than reducing errors (Skitka & Mosier, 1999).

Digitally mature organizations, or organizations with high level of "digital quotient" should be in a stage where necessary implementation of automation is set and levelled. There are various levels of automation, if well implemented, should benefit the enterprise. Throughout the decision process, automation may add value to information acquisition, information analysis, decision selection, action implementation (Parasuraman & Riley, 1997). First thing to decide is what to automate, then it is pretty important to decide the level of automation. After the initial execution, it is crucial to evaluate the performance outcomes real-time; otherwise the consequences may be severe if misuse or inadequacies discovered late. First evaluation should be to check whether the mental workload of the operator decreased or not. If the automation increases the mental workload rather than decreasing it, there is something seriously wrong with it (Wiener, 1981; Landauer, 1995). Home automation systems, if poorly invested and set up, is a good example of this. If the user has to click many applications, then has to make some more clicks to turn on the heat and the lights; it is always better to operate manually by turning the wall switch and heater on. However; automation such as library search systems, ATMs, databases, chart representations of raw financials cast good examples of decreased mental workload. Secondly, oversimplification of decision-making process may make the position/job either obsolete or unsatisfying/demotivating (Endsley & Kiris, 1995; Kirlik, 1993). Thirdly, if the operator spends much of his/her time controlling the decisions made by automata, then this represent increased mental workload but most importantly lack of applicability and feasibility (Endsley, 1996). And finally, completeness of the automation system throughout all the process must be gradually checked. For example, automated payments or digital signatures are convenient to use, but if the following process requires wet signature or could not integrate digital payments/signatures to the system then there is no added value. If one considers the digital evolution of e-governments can easily come up with un-integrated parts of the process even though many parts of it is already automated. The other criteria to account for are the reliability of the automation against the failures and therefore its ability to get trusted by the operators and the company; and the cost for value to the automation investment (Lee, & Moray, 1992; Masalonis, &. Parasuraman, 1999; Swets, 1998; Kuchar, 1996; Wickens et al, 1999). However, these criteria are our less concern within the context of digital quotient.

The aforementioned levels of automation of decision and action selection from 1 (low) to 10 (high) are (Parasuraman et al., 2000);

1. The computer decides everything, acts autonomously, ignoring the human.
2. Informs the human only if it, the computer, decides to.
3. Informs the human only if asked.
4. Executes automatically, then necessarily informs the human.
5. Allows the human a restricted time to veto before automatic execution.
6. Executes that suggestion if the human approves.

7.   Suggests one alternative.
8.   Narrows the selection down to a few.
9.   The computer offers a complete set of decision/action alternatives.
10. The computer offers no assistance; the human must make all decisions and actions.

Agile Culture and Organization

Executives need a framework for making informed decisions about IT infrastructure. An agile organization and as its antecedent an agile culture forms the foundation and bottom-line for any kind of digital implementation, innovation and eventually higher digital quotient. Such culture will compensate for missing skills and implementation and moreover will help enterprise to cover all kind of knowledge processing, automation and connectivity through ICT (Catlin, et al., 2014). Enterprises with the highest degree of agility have more services in each cluster and broader implementations of each service. Strategic agility requires time, money, leadership and focus — and an understanding of which distinct patterns of high-capability infrastructures are needed where (Subramani, & Broadbent, 2002).

Agile culture is formed through and contributed with learning orientation, skilled knowledge workers, collaboration and communication, shared vision and balanced allocation of resources (Adler, 2014). Learning orientation refers to capability of organizations to learn, learn how to learn and renew themselves in a timely manner (Argyris, 1999; Senge, 1998). First is to continuously assess what skills and innovations are needed for organization goal achievement and successful strategy execution and to develop them in a timely manner. Second, is to reflect in an effective manner on the entire process that is occurring in the first three capabilities (the assessment, direction and execution) and make adjustments as needed (Adler, 2014). Skilled knowledge workers imply the human resources to align its planning, selection, evaluation and education functions to the level of digital maturity (Lang, 2001). Shared vision is the shared dedication to the organization's goals by the leadership and employees across the organization (Beer, & Eisenstat, 2000; Doz & Kosonen, 2008). Subunits' differences and requirements should have been reconciled with more dialogue and attempts to collaborate and communicate in line with vision. Therefore, a basis of communication and collaboration should be founded throughout the entire enterprise. Resource Allocation Planning includes forecasting and decision making about how to allocate resources for strategy execution. Such resources include the people, time and budget. Doz and Kosonen (2008) describe several organizational conditions that influence the Resource Allocation Planning process. These include the pace of such allocations, collaboration and inclusion, maintaining a systems view, and perceived fairness as central to the effectiveness of resource planning (Adler, 2014).

They relate perceived fairness of the process to the ensuring the process is open and transparent and the decision-making is based on shared values of collaboration and system thinking of the good for the entire company.

Role of Social Media in Rising the Digital Quotient

In many of the companies, marketers were the ones who were the first to be aware of social media's power. However, as organizations digital involvement and technology maturity increases, the social media takes a more comprehensive and extended role. This role is about supplying and supporting information for competitive strategy. Especially web 2.0 technology has changed the traditional one-way communication of the internet and thanks to web 2.0, the internet has become a social and interactive platform that users can involve into digital process of companies (Rad & Benyoucef, 2010). Conventional ways of data and information gathering gets reshaped with the force of social media and now involves gathering intelligence from a wider range of public and sources, using analytics to clarify insights. This isn't to suggest a total replacement of traditional ways of intelligence gathering, but social media should emerge as a strong complement. There are two traditional sources of information to support competitive analyses; first is the primary sources information such as managers, competitors, suppliers, department reports, customer data within the company e.g. and the other is the secondary resources such as published journals, articles, market researches (e.g. Hox & Boeije, 2005). Social media acts on a different plane, it operates on social spaces with peoples' real time conversations and behaviours. If you can find vital and accurate information and right experts and analytics to make use of that information, then there isn't much need of traditional databases and published work. For this, the process of mapping sources of information becomes and evolves into mapping people and their conversations; gathering data becomes engaging a mapped network of experts and online community and tracking through on-time basis; synthesizing and analysing becomes structuring complex and mining relevant data; and simply communicating that information becomes embedding new ways of thinking into strategic processes simultaneously and preaching appropriate information via micro publications (Harrysson et al., 2012).

Once businesses realized that they would contribute to gaining competitive advantage, they turned to web 2.0 applications within their own businesses, namely to social media applications. Thus, questions such as; "what are the benefits of social media to active users and employees?" and "what are the factors that are necessary for using social media tools in the business?" have come into the agenda. Businesses have differentiated their orientation towards social media applications in order to gain and sustain competitive advantage and to establish a closer relationship with the customer compared to other businesses (Paroutis & Saleh, 2009). Accordingly, social media is a component of all the capabilities enlisted in this chapter. First of all, as discussed, if used properly it is the all-for-one source of input to all processes. The best example of the use of social media is observable in big data empowered decision making. Obviously, big data is not limited to social media, but the voice of the customers is mostly on the social media side of it. The networks of social media have no direct impact on connectivity and automation, but indirect effects. The effectiveness and efficiency of both can easily be observed with the social conversations, and this input or feedback should immediately be used for continuous improvement of the processes. Thus, social media is a mirror for companies' capabilities. Moreover, it is kind of right to say both connectivity and automation also involves social media.

Today's customers do not simply want the digital versions of current bureaucratic processes. So, the transformation should delicately involve continuous learning and feedback. Being digitally intelligent, and eventually having a greater Digital Quotient should begin with understanding the needs of customers and continuously involving them in the process. Hence, we can simply say that social media is all an enabler, source and force for digital transformation.

DIGITIZATION, DIGITAL STRATEGY AND BANKING ON DIGITAL

Digitization of information is considered as an economy base, digital economy. The developments in the digital economy have critical impacts on economic systems and how economic values are created. Main mechanisms of the digital economy are structures, processes, products, infrastructures and services (Zimmermann, 2000). The most aspects of the new economy, is not about getting your products or services to be the best, or producing your products as efficiently as possible but is about owning your customer, fulfilling their needs and demands, having the best strategy and business model that can base that (van Eijsden, 2000). Digitization isn't just another incremental change that can be adapted to fit an existing business model. Besides, it is a new paradigm that demands an entire revision of the ways in which business compete for customers. Digitization of business processes, products and services are trending in business world and businesses are beginning or have already begun to make investments to information technology (IT). IT is used as a tool to help people doing their work and also it is immersed as part of the business environment and cannot be separated from work and the systemic properties of inter-, intra-organizational relationships. Moreover, firms can gain a competitive advantage and differentiate from their competitors and create demands to fit with competitive norms. Thus they have to integrate their digital quotient to digital business strategies (Mithas et al., 2013; Oestreicher-Singer & Zalmanson, 2013).

Contemporary business environment necessitates companies to implement digital strategies since digitization in every aspect of business offers significant opportunities to businesses to enhance their competitiveness. Business strategists argue that pioneering high digital capabilities and implementing digital content to their products and especially services, offer companies a first mover advantage (Grover & Kohli, 2013).

Digital business alters the definition of value, even though the forces are the same, it is not solely a function of products and services' utilities. It is somewhat under less control of producers' abilities to present things. Value is relative and shifting and it is an output of creativity, diversity combined with digital capabilities (Keen & Williams, 2013). Connection is the key to new economic system yet digital world allows it more easily and cheaply. Economic value behaves differently compared to traditional ways of doing business. Connectivity requires companies' digital business strategies to be aligned with their core values, identity and core competences (Pagani, 2013; Oestreicher-Singer & Zalmanson, 2013).

In the last few decades, firms have integrated their business strategies according to the development of technology. This is already apparent in many industries such as automotive, textiles and services. Development of interactive digital technology, internet of services and other IT developments alter the rules of the practice in many industries since digital economy is a growing ecosystem, which contains rapid changes of information and communication technologies (Pagani, 2013). These changes in the last decade have unleashed new functionalities, thus the post-dotcom decade has global connectivity through standard protocols to adapt business strategy infrastructures to the new digital era. Digital Technologies are also transforming the structure of social relationships of both the consumers and the businesses with social networking/media. Social media is a result of social networking, and it is both source and execution area of feedback and information. While it is a knowledge base for new technology and process development, it is the biggest arena for application of digital strategy.

Digital strategy is distinct from traditional IT strategy because it is much more than a cross-functional use of resources. In other words, one can say that digital strategy can be viewed as being inherently trans-functional and independent. It should not be positioned as a sub-strategy but treated as the strategy itself. Table 1. indicates four key themes that could guide the future thinking on digital business strategy (Bharadwaj, et. al., 2013):

Because of immense connection opportunities, digitization is becoming more important and affecting all industries. Publishing, music, tourism and IT industries have transformed beyond expectations over the past two decades. Firms that are early digitization pioneers are now harvesting the added-value on increased performance and rising stakeholder value (Accenture Digital, 2015). For the time being, just a

Table 1. Key Questions on Digital Business Strategy Themes

Scope of Digital Business Strategy; - What is the extent of fusion and integration between IT strategy and business strategy? - How encompassing is digital business strategy? - How well does digital business strategy exploit the digitization of products and services, and the information around them? - How well does digital business strategy exploit the extended business ecosystem?
Scale of Digital Business Strategy; - How rapidly and cost effectively can the IT infrastructure scale up and down to enable a company's digital business strategy to bolster a strategic dynamic capability? - How well does digital business strategy leverage network effects and multisided platforms? - How well does digital business strategy take advantage of data, information and knowledge abundance? - How effective is digital business strategy in scaling volume through alliances and partnerships?
Speed of Digital Business Strategy; - How effective is digital business strategy in accelerating new product launches? - How effective is digital business strategy in speeding up learning for improving strategic and operational decision making? - How quickly does digital business strategy enable the formation of new business networks that provide complementary capabilities? - How effectively does the digital business strategy speed up the sense and respond cycle?
Sources of Value Creation and Capture; - How effective is digital business strategy in leveraging value from information? - How effective is digital business strategy in capturing value through coordinated business models in networks? - How effective is digital business strategy in appropriating value through the control of the company's digital architecture?

few of the companies are following a structured strategy towards digitization and building consistent digital business models. Some of them prefer to implement their digital strategies over time, constantly digitizing their processes and infrastructures.

Accenture Mobility Research 2015 puts forward a research done through interviews with senior decision makers about new digital trends in business. Research is based on the emergence and application of digital technologies shaping and transforming businesses, governmental institutions and sectors around the globe. Mobile technologies, their possibilities and contributions to mobility has altered the business transactions among consumers and firms. Digital strategy allows companies to combine multiple platforms together for a wider business transformation. According to the research, there are five outcomes of combination which are; opportunities to create more revenues, increased product and service development, exploitation of new markets, more customer engagement and faster responses to customer demands. The research also indicates that the companies have made a leap toward becoming digital enterprises, however their concerns on the security side of the digital transactions are, challenges to keep up with technological change pace. Research showed a correlation among companies' profitability and their approach to and capacity on digital tech. Companies with less profitability see technological advancement as a threat rather than an opportunity. Despite all concerns, managers recognize the possibilities offered with digital technologies and admit their companies have made a huge progress in adapting to and applying them both for themselves and their consumers (Accenture Digital, 2015b).

Banking on Digital

Customer satisfaction tools change day to day and it has become more difficult for businesses to maintain customer satisfaction. Information and communication technologies encourage people to engage with the firms and people can easily contact and communicate through them. Online service platforms such as social media creates a favorable environment for customers and competitors to observe businesses' applications in online world (Mucan & Özeltürkay, 2014). Information and communication technologies play a major role across many industries and affect both economic development and growth in societies. Banking sector is one of them. In this sector, especially internet banking is a cost saving tool for banks and it is a new focus because of the developments in information and communication technology. Development of the information and communication technology can facilitate improvement of customer satisfaction and affect customer attitudes positively towards banking (Hajli, 2015). Banking sector is a good example which IT infrastructures have had implications on the economic development of nations. There are many examples of IT applications in the banking sector that have helped building new markets and force the economy forward. For instance, ATM technology has increased community efficiency and led to a reduction in costs, improvement in quality and increase in the added value to and satisfaction of customers (Kamel, 2005). Nowadays, every bank has an online presence for their customers to look at their account information and transfer money right from their devices. In Europe digitization in the banking industry is between %20 and %40, moreover the banks keep on spending a vast amount of money on their digitization reaching to %90 new investment for some. Also, recent analyses indicate that over the next five to ten years, more than two-thirds of Europe's banking customers will become online customers with self-management of their accounts. (http://www.mckinsey.com/ business-functions/business-technology/our-insights/the-rise-of-the-digital-bank).

Digital banking helps firms combine customer experience on an efficient and effective model. This model is a combination of benefits such as a fairer price, transparent transactions and service comparable to rivals. With digital banking, customers have the opportunity to have immediate and high quality interaction, they are more in control and therefore they feel more secure. Digital banking offers wider range of products and services with faster and cheaper response. Banks, by the help of digitization, have a leaner channel of operations and an organizational structure. Transparent governance and agile culture, more effective and efficient operations, better developed revenue system can be accounted as some other benefits of digital banking (Kearney, 2013) Banks that successfully implement internal and external digital strategies can potentially increase revenues by up to 55% over the following five years and reduce their costs by up to 30%. A true understanding of digital economies and implementing economic capabilities can help banks achieve these types of results. Digital banking winners adopt a continuous cycle of planning, target-setting, experimenting with or optimizing digital programs and tracking outcomes (Accenture Strategy, 2015). Digital disruption has the potential to shrink the role and relevance of today's banks, and help them create better, faster, cheaper services that make them an even more essential part of everyday life for institutions and individuals. Accenture's "The Future of Fintech and Banking" report demonstrates results about financial technology (Fintech) and banking sectors' digitization improvements. According to the report, investment in financial technology companies grew by 201% globally in overall venture-capital investments. It is obvious that the digital development and improvement in financial services is going further (Accenture, 2015).

A research was done by Accenture in Switzerland in 2015 and 101 Swiss companies were chosen to investigate their progress on the digital agenda. Companies were investigated according to their digitization strategy, digitization servicing and digitization enablement criteria. Table 2. enlists the Accenture's Digitization Index Criteria. Results of the research show the best sectors in the digital maturity are IT and communication, media and entertainment, banking. Banking and insurance sector have the highest results on three of the criteria in research. Banking sector is put forward as the best at digital strategy (Accenture Digital, 2015b).

Adoption of digital banking around the globe forces banks to be more digitally skillful. Ones failing this, is in the risk of loosing customers and eventually their business. Digital banking comes with vast opportunities, but also has threats for banks. Revenue and quantity increases from new products and services also supported by cheaper and more efficient business models, easier and quicker sales, opportunities of cross-selling using gathered date, lower operational costs with automation are among potential opportunities. Its most common potential risks can be counted as; higher operational risks, compressed profit margins, loss of human resources, and finally because of losing face contact with customers a lower conduct and innovational opportunities by customers.

Comparing its threats to opportunities offered, it is without doubt worth the benefits (http://www.mckinsey.com/industries/financial-services/our-insights/strategic-choices-for-banks-in-the-digital-age).

Table 2. Accenture's Digitization Index Criteria (Accenture Digital, 2015a; Accenture, 2015b)

Dimension	Criteria	Explanation
Digitization Strategy	Trend	Extent to which the company's strategic objectives reflects "digital" as a relevant industry trend
	Objective	Extent to which the company's strategic objectives reflect "digital"
Digitization Servicing	Product and Solutions	Extent to which the company offers intelligent, smart and digitalized products or solutions.
	Services	Extent to which the company offers client-facing internet-based services.
	Interaction	Extent to which the company offers digital interaction functionalities.
	Sales Functionality	Extent to which the company offers client-facing sales or order specific digital functionalities.
	Service Functionality	Extent to which the company offers client-facing, service specific digital or online functionalities.
Digitization Enablement	Resources and Organization	Extent to which "digital" is referred to in context of the company's internal processes, programs, initiatives.
	Workflow	Extent to which the company applies "digital" to organizing and perform its daily operations.

Financial services and banking have been highest investors on IT and communication technologies. The traditional retail and face to face banking supported with call center activities has shifted to fully automatized smart ATMs and online banking. And banking industry still heavily invests in new digital capabilities, information technologies, digital safety, social media and leaner operations (Friedrich, et al., 2011).

Accenture Digitization Index Turkey, was prepared in 2015 and determines Turkey's best digital companies. Accenture Digitization Index's conceptual context has differences from other studies because it has 10 criteria with 91 indicators through digital strategies. These indicators provide companies a digitization checklist to evaluate their strengths and weaknesses in their digital strategies and help them prepare a digital transformation strategy map. Accenture invites 350 companies to this research and 104 companies accept to participate. So according to collect to data and Accenture's digitization criteria interviews were conducted with IT managers of the companies which participate. Other data sources are open public sources like company's web sites, annual reports, investor relations reports, brochures, presentations and news. In Accenture Digitization Index Turkey's average score is 60, which indicates that in digitization area Turkey has remarkable progress so far. Furthermore, companies' scores differ among each other, these differences imply that different industries have different digital needs. Best industries in digitization in Turkey are financial services, service operations, retailing and commerce. Chemicals, manufacturing of chemical products and construction industries are below the average according to the index. Financial services are the most digitized ones in Turkey, with the score of 76% and the leader of the sector is the "Garanti Bank" which has the highest digitization score with 93%. According to methodology, companies whose digitization score higher than 80% are called "Digitization Pioneers". Only 14 companies are classified as digitization pioneers and 4 of them are from financial sector, and all of these four are successful banks in Turkey. All digitization pioneers have best digital strategy scores (over 90%) and also they reported digitization has the highest impact on their corporate business strategy (Accenture, 2015).

Banking on Digital: The Case of Garanti Bank of Turkey

Garanti Bank is Turkey's second largest private bank which was established in 1946. It is mentioned by the company that it builds its strategy on the principles of; always approaching its customers in a transparent, clear and responsible manner, improving customer experience continuously by offering products and services that are tailored to their needs. Furthermore, it is pointed out that Garanti aims to ease its customers' lives by integrating the most recent developments in technology to its banking services (https://www.garantiinvestorrelations.com/en/about-garanti/detay/History/4/14/0). Main pillars of Garanti Bank's corporate strategy are on; customer centricity, focus on the continuity of technological innovation, focus on competent human resources, focus on operational efficiency, focus on disciplined growth, focus on strong delivery channels, focus on sustainable banking and focus on risk management and audit. It is remarked that the best and the fastest technological equipment is upgraded and integrated with business segments and IT infrastructure is highly important for them to be up to date. Table 3. summarizes Garanti's digital strategy's milestones and their relations with its digital quotient capabilities.

Online banking plays an important role on Garanti Bank's corporate strategy. Because, Internet banking usage is increasing with the growing use of the internet in households. According to Internet Banking Statistics of the Banks Association of Turkey, total number of customers logged in internet banking at least once in the past 3 months is around 16,2 million, and to mobile banking is 10,4 million. As previously discussed, Garanti Bank, the "Digitization Index" study found Garanti Bank as the "Most Digitized Company in Turkey" and it has the most awards regarding to its digital channels, and digital strategy. Garanti Bank has more awards which are related with its digitization;

- Garanti Bank's website won the "IMA-Best in Class" award in "Banking" and "Financial Services" categories at the Interactive Media Awards.
- "Best Corporate/Institutional Digital Bank in Western Europe" in the World's Best Corporate Bank Websites

- In Felis Awards' Mobile category Garanti Bank won the "Interface and Website Navigation" and "User Experience" subcategory awards.
- It has quite a few awards for its social media projects and campaigns, from Crystal Apple, Summit Creative Awards and "Best use of Existing Social Media Platforms" award from Digital Impact Awards.

These tables offer remarkable clues about the digital quotient of Garanti Bank. Accordingly, Garanti aims to increase its number of digital customers' day by day. Furthermore, Garanti Bank also denotes it's digitally related competitive advantages in its 2015 Annual Report that, it has business integrated IT, fully in-house developed, custom-fit IT solutions, dynamic and advanced technology enabling customer service time, multi-channel CRM tools offering effective and timely solutions, operational efficiency and digitalization, leading position in internet and mobile banking. Accordingly, Garanti Bank has nearly 4 million digital banking customers, 2,5 million mobile banking customers and the total customers are numbered as nearly 14 million.

CONCLUSION AND FURTHER RESEARCH DIRECTIONS

Digitization is becoming more important with every passing day. Digital tech is impacting everyone and everywhere more than ever. The impact on various industries has been massive. Industries such as publishing, travel, music and IT have transformed beyond recognition over the past 20 years. Leading firms embracing digitization early on are now harvesting the benefits of increased company performance and growing value. For the time being, few companies are setting up digital business models consistently of following a structured digitization plan. Some companies choose to deploy their digital strategies over time, continuously digitizing their internal, external processes and infrastructure.

Digital business strategies offer significant opportunities for businesses to heighten their competitiveness against to their rivals in the industry. Today's competitive advantage is based on a digital economy, which necessitates implementing business strategies for firms. According to business strategists by pioneering digital content products and services firms still can gain the first mover advantage (Grover & Kohli, 2013). The paper demonstrates how good use of correct digital strategies enhance digital quotient with a case study. Components of digital quotient are illustrated on the best example of Turkey and shows how important they are on the foundation of strategic success. Further research may aim to measure the factors of digital quotient empirically and create a survey for every company to measure its DQ and hence enhance its missing position in the digital savvy.

Table 3. Garanti Bank's digital strategy's milestones and their relation with its digital quotient capabilities 1

Implementations	Relation to DQ
Garanti quickly positioned social media as a digital channel and introduced creative applications.	Data analytics and connectivity
Active on more than 10 networks with over 40 social media accounts.	Connectivity
It has become the first Turkish bank facilitating money transfer via Facebook and Twitter.	Automation
"Digital customers" transacting via internet banking and mobile banking number 4 million at Garanti, it is a leader of online banking.	Automation and connectivity
91% of all non-cash financial transaction occur through digital channels at the bank.	Automation
Pioneers the mobile banking in Turkey with its applications. Garanti was the first bank in the World to launch quick money transfer via mobile phones with its mobile banking application.	Automation and connectivity
First bank in Turkey to offer web-based transaction on The Turkish Derivatives Exchange via online banking.	Automation and connectivity
Turkey's first bank to offer "e-government" payments.	Connectivity and automation
Offered Western Union transactions via Internet branch as a first in the World.	Automation
In 2012 introduced an application, which offers special campaigns to social media users as a first in Turkey.	Big data empowered decisions
Launched world's first banking application for Windows 8.	Automation
First bank in the World to offer web-based solution to the working capital needs of car dealers for the purchase of second hand cars via Exchange Finance.	Automation and connectivity
In 2013, launched with a telecommunication company in Turkey, contactless payment by mobile phones a first in the world.	Agile culture and organization
In 2013 it began receiving general-purpose loan applications with the secure form made available on Facebook.	Automation and big data empowered decision making
Introduced another digital transaction banking service iGaranti, it is a first in the mobile World.	Connectivity and automation
In 2013 it became the first Turkish bank to have a presence on all of the leading platforms with the Mobile Phone Branch.	Agile culture and organization
The first in the World in the use of banking products/services on social media with the application forms receive via Facebook, "Insurance at Garanti", "Pension at Garanti" and "Net Savings with Garanti".	Big data empowered decision making and connectivity
The first bank in Turkey offering payment services via its corporate web site using it's cards for Bill Payments, Government/Tax Payments and GSM top-ups.	Connectivity
The first bank in Turkey that enables loan applications received via any channel to be finalized on the internet banking.	Automation
iGaranti Glass application become the world's first financial application developed for Google Glass.	Automation and connectivity
In 2015 authored a first among large-scale banks in Turkey by introducing "iPad Banking Application" enabling Customer Relationship Managers in branches to offer service to customers from outside the branches.	Connectivity
First in Turkey by initiating iTunes Code sales from Internet Banking and Mobile Banking platforms.	Connectivity and automation
First in Turkey to add money withdrawal with QR code feature to login page preceding the password field in Mobile Banking so as to permit Money withdrawal from an ATM without logging in.	Automation
In 2015 launched a new credit card which giving access to all cards and a large number of transactions unavailable on mobile applications and it also analyses spending habits and sends push notifications regarding the campaigns that best suit the customers.	Automation and data analytics
First bank to launch an enterprise-wide social network initiative and first to apply and integrate social media links to its corporate web site	Data analytics and big data empowered decisions
Awarded talent programs, 14,500 employee suggestion & ideas collected, 86% of employees are university graduates, 54 hours/employee training per annum, 226,000 hours of trainings are delivered through technological methods.	Agile culture and organization
Reputation as "innovator", Conducting market research and listening to customers, Encouraging employees to share their suggestion and innovative ideas	Agile culture and organization
Systems enabling profitability & propensity analysis and product development, Multi-channel CRM tools offering effective & timely solutions	Big data empowered decision making and data analytics
Centralized Management Reporting, enabling management to take timely actions, Warehousing all data electronically	Automation and Data empowered decisions
First bank to set up centralized operations in Turkey, 99% centralization ratio	Automation
81% of all financial transactions occur via digital channels	Automation
First bank to provide applications in all major operating platforms, 4,003 ATMs facilitating >180 transactions	Automation

REFERENCES

Accenture Digital. (2015a). (pp. 3–32). Amsterdam, Netherlands: Digital High Performance Research- Are AEX Listed Companies Keeping Up with The Pace of Digital Disruption.

Digital, A. (2015b). Digital High Performance Research. *Digital Index Switzerland, 2015*, 2–30.

Strategy, A. (2015). Banking on Digital-Three actions banks can take to generate more value from their digital investments. Academic Press.

Adler, N. (2014). *The Strategically agile organization: Development of a measurement instrument* (Doctoral dissertation). Alliant International University, California School of Professional Psychology, San Francisco, CA.

Aite Group. (2015). *The Current and Future Sales of Corporate Mobile Banking Around the Globe*. Author.

Argyris, C. (1999). *On Organizational learning* (2nd ed.). Blackwell Publishers Inc.

Eistert, T., Deighton, J., Marcu, S., Gordon, F., & Ullrich, M. (2013). *Banking in a Digital World*. AT Kearney.

AWPA. (2013). *Information and Communications Technology Workforce Study*. Retrieved from http://awpa.gov.au/ publications/Documents/ICT-STUDY-FINAL-28-JUNE-2013.pdf

Beer, M., & Eisenstat, R. A. (2000). The silent killers of strategy implementation and learning. *Sloan Management Review, 41*(4), 29

Bharadwaj, A., El Sawy, O., Pavlou, P. A., & Venkatraman, N. (2013). Digital Business Strategy: Toward Next Generation of Insights. *Management Information Systems Quarterly, 37*(2), 471–482.

Bhatnagar, S., & Schware, R. (2000). *Information and communication technology in rural development. Case Studies from India*. World Bank Institute.

Billings, C. E. (1996). *Human-centered aircraft automation: Principles and guidelines. National Aeronautics and Space Administration*. Ames Research Center.

Dughin, J., Chui, M., & Manyika, J. (2015). *An executive's guide to the Internet of Things*. McKinsey & Company.

Bunz, M. (2009, November 9). Burberry checks out crowdsourcing with The Art of the Trench. *Guardian*.

Business Wire. (2015). *CitiConnect ERP Integrator Wins 2015 Celent Model Bank Award*. Retrieved from http://www.businesswire.com/news/home/20150326005072/en/CitiConnect%C2%AE-ERP-Integrator-Wins-2015-Celent-Model

Catlin, T., Scanlan, J., & Willmott, P. (2014). *Raising Your Digital Quotient: Making Sense of Digital Landscape*. McKinsey Quarterly Digital.

Citi Group Treasury and Trade Solutions. (2015). *Managing Innovation in a World of Risk*. Author.

Citi Group. (2013). *Annual Report*. Retrieved from www.citigroup.com/citi/investor/quarterly/2014/ar13c_en.pdf

Citi Group. (2014). *Annual Report*. Retrieved from www.citigroup.com/citi/investor/quarterly/2014/ar14c_en.pdf

Citi Group. (2015). *Annual Report*. Retrieved from www.citigroup.com/citi/investor/quarterly/2016/ar15c_en.pdf

Desmet, D., Duncan, E., Scanlan, J., & SingerSix, M. (2015). Building blocks for creating a highperforming digital enterprise. *McKinsey Quarterly*.

Dobrev, K., & Hart, M. (2015). Benefits, Justification and Implementation Planning of Real-Time Business Intelligence Systems. *Electronic Journal of Information Systems Evaluation, 18*(2).

Doz, Y. & Kosonen, M. (2008). How agile is your strategy process? *Strategy Magazine, 15*.

Dörner, K., & Meffert, J. (2015). *Nine questions to help you get your digital transformation right*. McKinsey & Company.

Endsley, M. R., & Kiris, E. O. (1995). The out-of-the-loop performance problem and level of control in automation. Human Factors. *The Journal of the Human Factors and Ergonomics Society, 37*(2), 381–394. doi:10.1518/001872095779064555

EY. (2014). *Born to be Digital: How leading CIOs are preparing for a digital transformation*. EY.

Finextra. (2016). *Trends in Global Digital Banking Drive Citi's Digital Strategy*. Retrieved from https://www.finextra.com/blogposting/10708/trends-in-global-digital-banking-drive-citis-digital-strategy

Friedrich, R., Merle, M., Gröne, F., & Koster, A. (2011). *Measuring Industry Digitization: Leaders and Laggards in the Digital Economy*. Strategy & Pwc.

Grover, V., & Kohli, R. (2013). Revealing Your Hand: Caveats In Implementing Digital Business Strategy. *Management Information Systems Quarterly*, *37*(2), 655–662.

Gurbaxani, V., & Whang, S. (1991). The impact of information systems on organizations and markets. *Communications of the ACM*, *34*(1), 59–73. doi:10.1145/99977.99990

Harrysson, M., Metayer, E., & Sarrazin, H. (2012). How "social intelligence" can guide decisions. *The McKinsey Quarterly*, *4*, 81–89.

Hajli, N. (2015). *Handbook of Research on Integrating Social Media into Strategic Marketing*. IGI Global. doi:10.4018/978-1-4666-8353-2

Henry, R., & Venkatraman, S. (2015). Big Data Analytics the Next Big Learning Opportunity. *Journal of Management Information and Decision Sciences*, *18*(2), 17.

Hohpe, G., & Woolf, B. (2004). *Enterprise integration patterns: Designing, building, and deploying messaging solutions*. Addison-Wesley Professional.

Holtgrewe, U. (2014). New new technologies: The future and the present of work in information and communication technology. *New Technology, Work and Employment*, *29*(1), 9–24. doi:10.1111/ntwe.12025

Hox, J. J., & Boeije, H. R. (2005). Data collection, primary vs. secondary. Encyclopedia of Social Measurement, 1(1), 593-599.

Ion, P., & Andreca, Z. (2008). Use of ICT in SMES management within the sector of services. *Faculty of Economics*, *4*(1), 481–487.

Kamel, S. (2005). The Use of Information Technology to Transform the Banking Sector In Developing Nations: Editorial Introduction. *Information Technology for Development*, *11*(4), 305–312. doi:10.1002/itdj.20023

Khan, N., & Sikes, J. (2014). *IT under pressure: McKinsey Global Survey results*. McKinsey & Company.

Kirlik, A. (1993). Modeling strategic behavior in human-automation interaction: Why an" aid" can (and should) go unused. *Human Factors: The Journal of the Human Factors and Ergonomics Society*, *35*(2), 221–242. PMID:8349287

Kopetz, H. (2011). Internet of things. In Real-time systems. Springer US.

Kosakowski, J. (1998). *The Benefits of Information Technology*. ERIC Digest.

Kuchar, J. K. (1996). Methodology for alerting-system performance evaluation. *Journal of Guidance, Control, and Dynamics, 19*(2), 438–444. doi:10.2514/3.21637

Landauer, T. K. (1995). *The trouble with computers: Usefulness, usability, and productivity*. Cambridge, MA: MIT Press.

Lee, J., & Moray, N. (1992). Trust, control strategies and allocation of function in human-machine systems. *Ergonomics, 35*(10), 1243–1270. doi:10.1080/00140139208967392 PMID:1516577

Masalonis, A. J., & Parasuraman, R. (1999). Trust as a construct for evaluation of automated aids: Past and future theory and research. *Proceedings of the Human Factors and Ergonomics Society Annual Meeting, 43*(3), 184-187. doi:10.1177/154193129904300312

Melville, N., Kraemer, K., & Gurbaxani, V. (2004). Review: Information technology and organizational performance: An integrative model of IT business value. *Management Information Systems Quarterly, 28*(2), 283–322.

Mithas, S., Tafti, A., & Mitchell, W. (2013). How A Firm's Competitive Environment And Digital Strategic Posture Influence Digital Business Strategy. *Management Information Systems Quarterly, 37*(2), 511–536.

Mucan, B., & Özeltürkay, E. Y. (2014). Social Media Creates Competitive Advantages: How Turkish Banks Use This Power? A Content Analysis of Turkish Banks Through Their Webpages. *Procedia-Social and Behavioral Sciences, 2nd International Conference on Strategic Innovative Marketing, 148,* 137-145.

Oestreicher-Singer, G., & Zalmanson, L. (2013). Content or Community? A Digital Business Strategy For Content Providers in the Social Age. *Management Information Systems Quarterly, 37*(2), 591–616.

Pagani, M. (2013). Digital Business Strategy and Value Creation: Framing The Dynamic Cycle of Control Points. *Management Information Systems Quarterly, 37*(2), 617–632.

Parasuraman, R., & Riley, V. (1997). Humans and automation: Use, misuse, disuse, abuse. *Human Factors: The Journal of the Human Factors and Ergonomics Society, 39*(2), 230–253. doi:10.1518/001872097778543886

Parasuraman, R., Sheridan, T. B., & Wickens, C. D. (2000). A model for types and levels of human interaction with automation. Systems, Man and Cybernetics, Part A: Systems and Humans. *IEEE Transactions on, 30*(3), 286–297.

Paroutis, S., & Saleh, A. A. (2009). Determinants of Knowledge Sharing Using Web 2.0 Technologies. *Journal of Knowledge Management, 13*(4), 52–63. doi:10.1108/13673270910971824

Rad, A. A., & Benyoucef, M. (2010). A Model for Understanding Social Commerce. *Conference on Information Systems Applied Research, 3*, 12-25.

Rickards, T., Smaje, K., & Sohoni, V. (2015, September). Transformer in chief: The new chief digital officer. *McKinsey Digital,* 1-6.

Rifkin, J. (1995). *The End of Work: The Decline of the Global Labour Force and the Dawn of the Post-Market Era.* Putnam Publishing Group.

Sarter, N. R., & Woods, D. D. (1993). *Cognitive engineering in aerospace application: Pilot interaction with cockpit automation.* Mofferr Field, CA: Nasa Ames Research Centre.

Schneider, D. A. (2006). Practical Considerations for Real-Time Business Intelligence. *BIRTE Workshop, Business Intelligence for the Real-Time Enterprises* (1-3). Seoul, Korea: Springer.

Schreyer, P. (2000). *The contribution of information and communication technology to output growth.* STI Working Paper.

Senge, P. M. (1998). The leader's new work. *Leading Organizations,* 439-457.

SINTEF. (2013). Big data, for better or worse: 90% of world's data generated over last two years. *Science Daily.* Retrieved January 13, 2015 from www.sciencedaily.com/releases/2013/05/130522085217.htm

Skitka, L. J., Mosier, K. L., & Burdick, M. (1999). Does automation bias decision-making? *International Journal of Human-Computer Studies, 51*(5), 991–1006. doi:10.1006/ijhc.1999.0252

Swets, J. A. (1998). Measuring the accuracy of diagnostic systems. *Science, 240*(4857), 1285–1293. doi:10.1126/science.3287615 PMID:3287615

Tapscott, D., & Caston, A. (1993). Paradigm Shift: The New Promise of Information Technology. McGraw Hill, Inc.

Taylor, S., & Todd, P. A. (1995). Understanding information technology usage: A test of competing models. *Information Systems Research*, 6(2), 144–176. doi:10.1287/isre.6.2.144

Thorp, J. (2003). *The information paradox: realizing the business benefits of information technology*. McGraw-Hill Ryerson.

Van Eijsden, G. A. (2000). *Banking in the Digital Economy* (Doctoral Dissertation). Technical University Eindhoven.

Veling, L., Murnane, S., Carcary, M., & Zlydareva, O. (2014). *The Digital Imperative*. IVI White Paper Series.

Weill, P., Subramani, M., & Broadbent, M. (2002). Building IT infrastructure for strategic agility. *MIT Sloan Management Review*, 44(1), 57.

Wickens, C. D., Conejo, R., & Gempler, K. (1999). Unreliable automated attention cueing for air-ground targeting and traffic maneuvering. *Proceedings of the Human Factors and Ergonomics Society Annual Meeting*, 43(1), 21-25. doi:10.1177/154193129904300105

Wiener, E. I. (1981). Complacency: Is the term useful for air safety. *Proceedings of the 26th Corporate Aviation Safety Seminar*.

Zimmermann, H. (2000). *Understanding the Digital Economy: Challenges for new Business Models*. SSRN Electronic Journal.

KEY TERMS AND DEFINITIONS

Automation: The use or introduction of automatic equipment in a manufacturing or other process or facility.

Agile Culture: The capability of a company to rapidly change or adapt in response to changes in the market.

Big Data: Extremely large data sets that may be analysed computationally to reveal patterns, trends, and associations, especially relating to human behaviour and interactions.

Connectivity: Capacity for the interconnection of platforms, systems, and applications.

Digital Quotient: A company's ability and capacity to benefit and exploit information technologies, apply automation, use big data for decision making.

Digitization: The conversion of text, pictures, or sound into a digital form that can be processed by a computer.

Information Technology (IT): The study or use of systems (especially computers and telecommunications) for storing, retrieving, and sending information.

Intelligence Quotient (IQ): A person's reasoning and learning ability (measured using problem-solving tests) as compared to the statistical norm or average for their age, taken as 100.

ENDNOTE

[1]   Information on the table is acquired from the company's corporate web site and investor relations page.

Chapter 13
Freelancing in the Economy 4.0:
How Information Technology Can (Really) Help

Simone Scalabrino
University of Molise, Italy

Remo Pareschi
University of Molise, Italy

Salvatore Geremia
University of Molise, Italy

Marcello Bogetti
University of Turin, Italy

Rocco Oliveto
University of Molise, Italy

ABSTRACT

In the last years social media are increasing their importance in the context of digital freelancing by letting companies offer projects to external professionals through the Web. However, the available platforms for digital freelancing are still far from supporting the ecosystem of companies and professionals during the implementation of complex projects through an accurate definition of the required skills, roles, interdependencies and responsibilities. This chapter presents a roundup of the available systems of support to freelancers. The goal is to identify the essential features and structure of a comprehensive social media able to effectively manage and support the potential of an "economy 4.0" characterized by a free and flexible circulation of highly skilled professionals, that can be aggregated to support the needs of organizations.

DOI: 10.4018/978-1-5225-2897-5.ch013

INTRODUCTION

The Digital Transformation is an epochal phenomenon that goes well beyond the integration through information technology of corporate processes. Indeed, it crucially touches the very essence of the life of organizations, namely their human resources. Among the many ways in which this trend is materializing, one of the most noticeable is digital freelancing, which lets companies offer projects to external professionals through the Web. On the economical and societal side, digital freelancing is responding to two converging demands: on one hand, the preference of many skilled workers from the new "professions 4.0" to self-manage one's source of economic livelihood, thus escaping the traditional schemes of wage employment; on the other, the requirement of nowadays organizations to rely on a streamlined core kernel of basic competencies, to be enriched dynamically according to needs with further skills so as to meet the ever changing market conditions.

However, the keywords here are "projects" and "teams", meaning that both aspects need to be supported in order to engage freelancers 4.0 into serious work for the enterprises, but neither one appears currently within the reach of the platforms underlying the numerous commercial initiatives (such as Guru, Freelance.com, and many others) aimed to intercept the trend. Indeed, these platforms manage a simple auction mechanism with the objective to level down the cost of projects that do not necessarily require high skills and that can be typically executed by a single worker. For example, it is easy to find a proliferation of offers for jobs of translation and of technical writing. By contrast, it is much rarer to find offers for complex projects that require complementary high skills owned by multiple workers, such as the development of a Web presence with e-commerce capabilities for a traditional distribution company, or a digital manufacturing activity, where design capabilities are coupled with the technical mastery of 3D printing and scanning.

There is therefore need to support the ecosystem of companies and professionals with effective tools that can dynamically implement complex projects through an accurate definition of the required skills, roles, interdependencies and responsibilities. They must also be capable to source the appropriate professionals, thus building up highly performing teams, as well as to monitor the progress of the projects up to their conclusions. Finally, they should maintain and upgrade a knowledge base of ratings of the professionals throughout the projects they participate, so as to consolidate their reputations on the basis of shared parameters from the community.

In this article, the authors do a roundup of the available systems of support to professionals through the digital cloud, both commercially, as exemplified in the above initiatives, and in the broader frame of recommending systems applicable in this area. This analysis is then evaluated with respect to an array of requirements that must be met to finalize effectively the potential of an "economy 4.0" characterized by a free and flexible circulation of highly skilled professionals, that can be aggregated to support the needs of organizations. From here, the authors identify the essential features and structure of a software architecture for systems effectively fulfilling the full gamut of requirements arising from this new ecosystem.

BACKGROUND

This section provides background information on both the use of information technology for freelancing and recommendation systems, a vital ingredient to improve the effectiveness of social media in the freelancing economy.

Social Media for Freelancing

There is a plethora of social media designed with the aim to create a bridge between freelancers and project managers or companies that want to hire them. In this chapter the authors make a roundup of the most popular ones. In order to assess their popularity, a search was performed and the first results provided by the Google search engine were analysed (Caramela, 2016; Johansson, 2015; Lingel, 2016; Rampton, 2016). The 10 most cited social media were taken into account. A result (i.e., College Recruiter) was discarded, because it does not specifically address freelancers.

Table 1 summarizes the features (on the rows) provided by the most popular social media (on the columns). Upwork, Guru and 99designs are the social media with the highest number of features (equal to 7). 99design targets, however, a very specialized market and does not address every kind of freelancer. Therefore, Upwork and Guru can be considered as the most complete platforms. For each social medium a brief description is given here below.

Freelancer (FL)

Through Freelancer.com, project managers can offer a project and receive bids from freelancers proposing themselves for specific roles. One of the key-features is the integrated payment platform, which guarantees correct transactions to both freelancers and project managers. This platform allows project managers to pay employees step-by-step, when specific goals are achieved.

Table 1. A Comparison Among the Most Popular Social Media for Freelancing

	FL	UW	Guru	TT	99D	CS	PPH	LI	iFL	FRR
Public project/job proposal	X	X	X		X		X	X	X	
Feedbacks about freelancers		X	X		X	X	X	X	X	
Payment support	X	X	X				X			X
Bids from freelancers	X				X			X	X	
Generic	X	X	X				X	X	X	X
Skill-based freelancer recommendation		X		X				X		
In-project communication		X	X		X		X		X	
In-project file sharing		X	X		X					
Project management			X			X				
Freelancers quality assurance				X		X				
Freelancers contest					X					
Feedback on the product					X	X				
Product quality assurance						X				

Upwork (UW)

Upwork.com has the same key-features of Freelancer, except for the fact that it does not let freelancers make bids. On the other hand, Upwork suggests project managers the most appropriate candidates to fulfil the roles required by the proposed project. Upwork also provides their users with a platform for file sharing and communication, which can be used throughout the project

Guru.

Guru.com is very similar to Upwork, except for the lack of freelancer recommendation. On the other hand, Guru offers a schedule and cost management tool together with file sharing and chat features.

Toptal (TT)

Toptal.com is completely different from the other social media for freelancers shown so far. It focuses on the quality of freelancer, by claiming to connect project managers with the "top 3% of freelance talents". Toptal also provides an automated recommendation system for freelancers.

99design (99D)

99design.it is a platform specifically dedicated to designers. It allows customers to ask for a specific design (e.g., a logo) associated with a prize that will be won by the author(s) of the chosen logo. Freelancers interested in the work can participate to a contest in which the customer is the judge. The winner gets the whole prize. 99design also allows freelancers to create drafts and enables customers to give them an intermediate feedback. Finally, this platform lets customers memorize favourite designers for future contact.

CrowdSource (CS)

CrowdSource.com is also very different from the other platforms. It provides a first phase of "training and testing" of workers on a specific task. Then, workers can choose the tasks they wish to complete among a set of available tasks. CrowdSource provides a quality assurance process, in which all the task results are reviewed multiple times before they are delivered. The platform offers promotion and reward based on results.

PeoplePerHour (PPH)

PeoplePerHour.com is specifically designed for short jobs, from 1 hour to 4 days. In terms of features, it is very similar to Guru, except for the lack of file-sharing and project management.

LinkedIn Pro Finder (LI)

LinkedIn Pro Finder is the LinkedIn platform dedicated to freelancers. It has many features in common with Freelancer. LinkedIn Pro Finder also lets employers release feedbacks to employees who worked for them.

iFreelance (iFL)

iFreelance.com is quite similar to LinkedIn Pro Finder. A distinctive feature is that it does not recommend potentially interesting freelancers, but offers a chat feature to facilitate the communication between freelancers and project managers.

Fiverr (FRR)

Fiverr is very similar to PeoplePerHour, except for some missing features, i.e. project proposals, chat and feedbacks on freelancers.

Recommendation Systems

Recommendation systems are software products capable to suggest items of possible interest to specific users (Ricci, Rokach, & Shapira, 2001). They are widespread in many contexts, such as e-commerce (e.g., Amazon.com), entertainment (e.g., Netflix or Youtube) and travel (e.g., Tripadvisor). The following section describes the most common kinds of recommender systems.

Content-Based

Content-based (CB) recommendation systems "try to recommend items similar to those a given user has liked in the past" (Lops, De Gemmis, & Semeraro, 2011). On the basis of the characteristics of an item previously evaluated by a user, a CB system creates a user profile. Such a user profile contains preferences of the user and is a structured representation of the user interests. The recommendation process matches the attributes of each item with the user profile, suggesting items with higher degrees of similarity with the user profile, by taking into account both the attributes and the interests of the user. The more details are contained in the user's profile, the more likely that the suggestions match the real interests of the user (Pazzani, & Billsus, 2007). Moreover, all this is of huge benefit to the effectiveness of the process of information access (Lops et al., 2011).

Another key element for CB recommendation systems is the reaction of the user after the suggestion, i.e., its feedback. Two different techniques can be adopted for recording user's feedback: explicit feedback and implicit feedback. The feedback is *explicit* when the system asks the user to evaluate one or more items, through the use of like/dislike, ratings or textual comments. On the other hand, an *implicit* feedback can be acquired by observing the user activity.

Collaborative Filtering-Based

Collaborative filtering (CF)-based recommendation techniques help people make choices based on the opinions of other people who share similar interests (Deshpande, & Karypis, 2004).

The goal of a CF algorithm is to suggest new items for a particular user based on the user's previous likings and the opinion of other like-minded users. In a typical CF scenario, there is a list of m users $U = \{u_1, u_2,.., u_m\}$ and a list of n items $I = \{i_1, i_2, ..., i_n\}$. Each user u_i has a list of items I_{ui}, over which the user has expressed his/her opinions (Sarwar, Karypis, Konstan, & Riedl, 2001).

The different CF-based algorithms can be divided into two categories: memory-based (also known as user-based) algorithms and model-based (also known as item-based) algorithms. The difference between the two categories of algorithms is that user-based algorithms identify a set of users, called neighbours, who have similar interests with respect to the target user. On the other hand, item-based algorithms make use of a model of user ratings to provide recommendation items. The potential drawback of item-based CF algorithms is to select only the most similar items/users.

Knowledge-Based (KB)

KB recommendation techniques recommend items according to the knowledge about the users, items and/or their relationships. This approach uses a functional knowledge base that highlights "how a particular item meets a specific user's need, which can be performed based on inferences about the relationship between a user's need and a possible recommendation" (Lu, Wu, Mao, Wang, & Zhang, 2015).

Hybrid

A hybrid recommendation technique combines two or more different techniques in order to exploit the best features of each technique. At the same time, this approach aims to improve performance of traditional techniques by mutually limiting their drawbacks. Burke (2002) suggests seven different types of hybrids defined as:

- **Weighted:** the score of different recommendation components are combined numerically;
- **Switching:** the system chooses among recommendation components and applies the select one;
- **Mixed:** recommendation from different recommenders are presented together;
- **Feature Combination:** features derived from different knowledge sources are combined together and given to a single recommendation algorithm;
- **Feature Augmentation:** one recommendation technique is used to compute a feature or set of features, which is then part of the input to the next technique;
- **Cascade:** recommenders are given strict priority, with the lower priority ones breaking ties in the scoring of the higher ones;

- **Meta-Level:** one recommendation technique is applied and produces some sort of model, which is then used by the next technique.

Computational Intelligence-Based

CI-based approaches use a variety of techniques of computational intelligence techniques to build the recommendation model, such as:

- **Artificial Neural Network (Ann) (Zurada, 1992):** Tries to replicate the power and flexibility of the human brain by the use of nodes (artificial neurons) which are interconnected through weighted links;
- **Bayesian Network:** Is a probabilistic graphical model in which each item is represented by a node and a set of parent items corresponds to its best predictors;
- **Clustering Techniques:** Groups the items so that items in the same cluster are more similar to each other than to those in other clusters;
- **Fuzzy Set Theory:** Is based on fuzzy sets which are a natural extension of the classical set theory;
- **Genetic Algorithms:** Are heuristic algorithms based on the principle of natural selection and biological evolution.

Social Network-Based

Social network-based recommendation systems (SNRS) are based on explicit social relations. These techniques investigate how user preferences and/or user ratings are related to those of friends and how this information can be used to provide a recommendation. In practice, when we want to make a decision on or we want to buy an item that is unknown, we are inclined (we tend) to ask friends who have already had experience with the item. Usually, the choice is influenced by friends' suggestions. In other words, the concept of trust (Ben-Shimon, 2007) plays a key role in the SNRS. He and Chu (2010) explain what are the three factors that have an impact on the customer decisions:

- User preferences;
- Information from the public media;
- Feedback from friends.

These last two factors make up the *knowledge about the target item*.

Context Awareness-Based

Usually, recommender systems consider two types of entities: user and items. As suggested by Adomavicius and Tuzhilin (2015), in many applications it may not be sufficient to consider only these two entities, however it is also important to "incorporate the contextual information into the recommendation process in order to recommend items to user in certain circumstances". For example, a travel recommender system should use the temporal context to provide useful recommendations. To this end, the rating function R as a two-dimensional function (*R: User* x *Item -> Rating*) becomes a multi-dimensional function (*R: User* x *Item* x *Context -> Rating*). According to Adomavicius and Tuzhilin (2015), it is possible to "*apply the information about the current or desired context at various stages of the recommendation process*". In particular, the context-aware recommendation process can implement three different paradigms:

- Contextual pre-filtering;
- Contextual post-filtering;
- Contextual modelling.

Group

Usually, recommender systems are used to recommend items to individual users. However, there are cases in which a group of users participate together in a single activity. So, "group recommendation aims at identify items that are welcomed by the group as a whole, rather than by individual group members" (Shabib, Gulla, & Krogstie, 2013). The key components of GRS are:

- **Group:** A variable number of users who explicitly choose to be part of a group or users implicitly aggregate based on some similarity function;
- **Aggregation Strategies:** Aggregation of individual preferences into a single recommendation list or aggregation of individual recommendation lists to the group recommendation list (Berkovsky, & Freyne, 2010);
- **Aggregation Function:** It is used to get the highest group-value item recommendation for a user group.

A COMPREHENSIVE SOCIAL MEDIUM FOR FREELANCERS

Social media described in the previous section provide a very basic support to freelancers. Specifically, such solutions are mainly showcases for freelancers and can support project managers that actively look for freelancers, also keeping into account their salary, which has to fit the project budget. Nevertheless, failing the selection of the right candidate could lead to increased costs for the project and, given the short-term nature of the collaboration between the employer and the employee, even to the failure of the entire project. Of course, these problems are mitigated when people know each other. But this is not always the case.

Web platforms dedicated to freelancers fail in taking into account the complexity of team building and they leave this burden to the project manager. Moreover, once the choice of the freelancer is done, only few platforms offer some kind of support for the management of the project and there is no tracking about the project activities.

This happens because currently available social media for freelancers focus on the freelancer rather than on the project. Furthermore, skills of freelancers needed for the project are self-claimed, and they are mostly subjective, which means that project managers have to almost blindly trust them, except for some platform designed with the specific aim of providing high quality freelancers (e.g., Toptal).

In this section the authors introduce a comprehensive social medium for freelancers, so as to provide many tools to both project managers and freelancers with one basic aim: making the project succeed. To fulfil this purpose, the focus is shifted to the project itself: project managers can publish a brief description about the project in order to attract freelancers but can also add a private and more detailed version of the project description, which is addressed to the team. This key aspect is at the base of a complete project management platform, that will be provided to project managers so as to help them to handle not only the team, but also the budget and the schedule of the project.

At the end of the project, all the co-workers have to provide a feedback about each other on different aspects: through this mechanism, all the skills shown and acquired on the field by freelancers will be recorded and certified by the system.

Using data recorded from previous projects, a recommendation system will suggest project managers the most suitable team needed for a new project, based on the specific kind of proposed project, thus suggesting not only the most fitting freelancers for a specific role, but also the roles and the number of people needed for that project.

This comprehensive social medium is also a social network of freelancers, such that the more people work together the stronger is the connection between them. This aspect is also taken into account by the recommender system when suggesting freelancers: often it is better to have two medium-skilled freelancers that already worked together many times than having two experts that may create a risk if put together for the first time.

The following subsections provide details about all the main features of this comprehensive social medium for freelancers.

Certification of Skills

Many forms of official certification for specific skills exist. Nevertheless, they are not widespread, and often project managers have to trust what freelancers say about them. Among freelancers, these official certifications are highly expensive, in terms of both money and time, and while traditional employees may be supported by their company, this does not happen for freelancers. In this respect, freelancers would highly benefit from a form of certification derived from their work for projects they took part in. But also project managers would benefit from this kind of recognition, because they would have a clear indication about the skills of a human resource. Ultimately, also project managers may have their own certifications, in order to attract more freelancers to join their project.

An automatic system of certification of skills requires a sort of feedback, which should be released in a two-directional way from project manager to freelancer and from freelancer to project manager. This kind of feedback is very common in e-commerce systems, such as eBay. In the case of freelancing, the feedback would be linked to the specific project in which both the freelancer and the manager were involved. This aspect is very important, because it is possible to acquire information about the skills used by participants also from the project specification.

Another advantage of using an automatic certification system for skills is that the certification, which usually has a binary nature (either "I *have* the certification" or "I *do not have* it"), could also have a percentage of acquisition. The more a freelancer is involved in projects that need a specific skill, the more the percentage of acquisition is increased, until the certification is acquired.

Furthermore, the system should support also different levels of certifications, and for each level should report the percentage of acquisition achieved by the freelancer.

Example: Consider a project about a new Android app for events notifications. This project is under high time pressure, and needs indeed to be delivered within 1 month. Among the required professionals, there are are two Java developers with Android development skills. There are three candidates:

1. John, 100% @ Level 5 Java developer, 10% @ Level 1 Android developer
2. Jean, 90% @ Level 2 Java developer, 90% @ Level 2 Android developer
3. Jim, 90% @ Level 4 Java developer, 20% @ Level 2 Android developer

In this case the two candidates selected would be, most likely, Jean and Jim. Both of them have a decent Java level but, most important, they both have good skills in Android development. Instead, John just started to learn about Android, and he would be a burden, even if he has excellent Java skills. In a longer-term project, instead, John would have been preferred over Jean, because his java skills are better and could help him to acquire also Level 2 Android developer certification in little time, providing the project with an excellent resource, which could be used also in other contexts.

While people have skills, projects usually do not require a set of skills that can be covered by everyone in the team; instead, projects usually require persons able to cover specific roles, that complement each other in the fulfilment of the project requirements. A role consists of a set of skills that are desirable for a candidate in order to fill it satisfactorily. Furthermore, for each skill required by a role, the following features are defined: defined (i) the weight of such a skill for the role and (ii) the target level required for such a skill. Formally, a role *r* is defined as triple of vectors (*S*, *W*, *T*), where w_i indicates the weight and t_i indicates the target level of s_i, *i.e.,* the i-th skill required for *r*. Using this notation, it is possible to compute an index that indicates, how much a specific person is suitable for a role required by a project, i.e., an *adequacy index*. An adequacy index can be defined as the weighted sum of the fitting of single skills and computed using the formula depicted in Figure 1, where *t* is a vector of levels required by the role *r*, *w* is the vector of weights of skills of the role *r* (i.e., W), *p* is a vector in which the i-th skill required by *r* has the value of the level of the skill acquired by a candidate and *n* is the total number of skills required by *r*. Skill targets and levels acquired by candidates are expressed in decimal form, keeping into account also the completing percentage: it is computed by summing the current highest certified level plus the percentage of the next level of the same skill expressed in the interval [0, 1). For example, if a person has a Level 4 for a specific skill and she already acquired the 80% of Level 5, the decimal expression of the level will be 4.8.

Through the function *fitting* it is possible to decide how to (i) increase the index when a user has a higher level compared to the one required by the role and (ii) decrease the index when a user has a lower level compared to the level required by *r*. The constraints of function *fitting* are:

1. *fitting(x) > 0* when $x \geq 0$; this insures that the index is increased when a user has a highest level compared to the one required by the role.
2. *fitting(x) < 0* when *x < 0;* this insures that the index is decreased when a user has a highest level compared to the one required by the role.

Figure 1. Adequacy Index

$$A(t, w, p) = \sum_{i=1}^{n} w_i \cdot fitting(p_i - t_i)$$

3.   Given a positive integer x, $|fitting(x)| < |fitting(-x)|$; this insures that a surplus in a skill do not balance alone the dearth in another skill.

Example: A project requires the role "Android developer", which requires the following skills:

1.   Java programming, with a weight equals to 0.3 and a target level equals to 4;
2.   Android programming, with a weight equals to 0.5 and a target level equals to 4;
3.   Databases, with a weight equals to 0.2 and a target level equals to 3.

The vectors *required skills* depicted in Figure 2 represent the role "Android developer". Now, let us suppose that there are two candidates, *John* and *Jim*, having the skills formalized by the vectors *candidate human resources* in Figure 2. An example of *fitting* function is given in Figure 3. Hence, for each candidate we will have the fitting values and the weighted fitting values reported in Figure 2.

Based on the above fitting values, the adequacy index for John is -0.60, while for Jim is -0.88. Thus, Jim has a lower adequacy index because he has a lower level in android development, which is the most important skill for the Android developer role. Nevertheless, the lack of two levels in "Database" for John also strongly penalizes him, even if this skill has a limited importance. This is reasonable, because two levels are quite hard to acquire, and even if it is not a core skill, there will be problems. This is reflected by the fact that the adequacy index is negative.

Building and Exploiting the Social Network of Freelancers

A social network is a representation of the relationships between single actors, which are people in most of the cases. Examples of social networks are Facebook, Twitter or the aforementioned LinkedIn. Social networks use a graph representation in order to model social interactions between people, group of persons or organizations.

A graph $G = (V, E)$ is an ordered couple of two sets: V, the set of vertices and E, the set of edges. A vertex is a node in the graph, which can be connected to other vertices through an edge. E is a subset of V^2; thus, an edge is represented as a couple of vertices (v_1, v_2). A graph can be either *directed* or *undirected*: in the first case, the order of vertices in edges is important, while this is not true for undirected graphs, in which the same edge can be represented both as (v_1, v_2) and as (v_2, v_1). Finally, a graph is *weighted* if there exists a function f: $E \rightarrow R$ that maps each edge to a real number, which can represent a weight of the relationship; a graph is *unweighted* if such a function is not defined.

Figure 2. Computation of fitting values

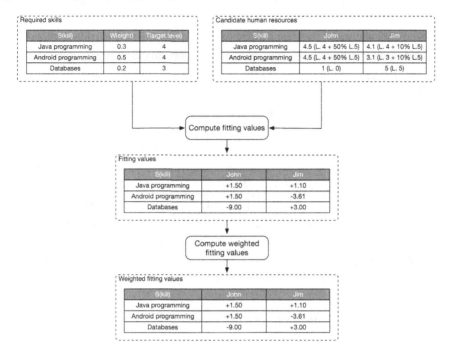

Figure 3. Example of fitting function

$$fitting(x) \begin{cases} 1 + x & if \ x \geq 0 \\ -(1 - x)^2 & otherwise \end{cases}$$

Facebook, for example, uses a graph to represent its social network. Specifically, the graph used is a *unweighted undirected graph*: people are represented as vertices of a graph, while the friendship between them can be represented as edges. In its basic representation, this graph is *undirected*, because the relationship represented (i.e., friendship) is commutative, in the sense that "*a* is a friend of *b*" is equal to say that "*b* is a friend of *a*" and, at the same time, it is *unweighted*, because there is no need to weigh the "friendship" between two persons.

A social network of freelancers aims at tracking working relationships between people. Therefore, it is very different from other social networks, because the actors (i.e., freelancers or project managers) do not explicitly declare their relationships; these are inferred from the social network itself on the basis of the actions executed by the actors. The graph used is a weighted undirected graph. While the relationship "works with" is commutative, and, thus, there is no need to track its direction, it would be important to understand the strength of the collaboration between two people.

In an initial scenario, the graph just contains unconnected vertices representing registered users, without any edge. When a project starts, an edge created between each pair of components of the team. Each edge has weight 1, indicating that the collaboration is present, but is still weak. After the project is over, it is possible to reassess the relationship between two people through a questionnaire about each other that both the members will answer. If both the members have a good perception of their collaboration, the weight of the edge between them is boosted; on the other hand, if the questionnaire shows that the collaboration was negative and both the actors have a bad perception of the colleague, the weight may be reduced.

The weight of the edges representing collaborations is increased or decreased by using an algorithm which decides, for each collaboration between two people on a project P_i, the total increment $T_i = I_i + B_i$, where I_i is the basic increment due to the collaboration to the i-th project and B_i is the boost given to the increment at the end of the project. Such an algorithm has to respect the following constraints:

1. Given the collaboration on the i-th project P_i the increment of the weight I_i has to be major than the increment $I_{i\,j}$. This rule insures that the weight grows in a nonlinear fashion, modelling the fact that the more people collaborate the more their harmony grows.

2. The value of the boost B_i given by the algorithm at the end of the i-th collaboration in project P_i must be major than $-W_i$. This rule reflects the fact that a bad collaboration can potentially destroy the harmony between two persons. In this case B_i would be $-W_i$, resetting the weight to 0. A weight minor than 1 always indicates that there is a conflict between two persons and, therefore, that these person should never work together. It is worth noting that when there is no collaboration there is no edge, and thus the weight is not present at all, but is not 0.

3. The value of the boost B_i given by the algorithm at the end of the i-th collaboration in project P_i has to be minor than $I_{i+1} - I_i$. This rule insures that $T_i < I_{i+1}$. In other words, the total increment of the weight due to a collaboration should always be minor than the basic increment of the hypothetical next collaboration, ensuring that the boost is just a refinement of the relationship given by the collaboration itself and is not too influent if there is a new collaboration.

Table 2 shows an example of the growing of weights in five positive collaborations. In the reported example, I_i is just equal to i, which respect the constraint 1. Therefore, in order to respect constraint 3, B_i is always minor than 1, because the difference between I_{i+1} and I_i is always equal to 1. The choice of the function I_i affects the

Table 2. How the weight of an edge in the social network increases due to positive collaborations

Collaboration i	Basic Increment I_i	Boost Increment B_i	Total Weight W_i
1	1	0.8	1.8
2	2	0.7	4.5
3	3	0.3	7.8
4	4	0.9	12.7
5	5	0.4	18.1

steepness of the growth of the weight when multiple collaborations are performed; on the other hand, the way in which the final questionnaire is mapped to a specific boost has a strong effect on the way in which a negative collaboration affects the resulting weight.

For a candidate team, *i.e.,* a set C of users, it can be defined a subgraph T of G, where G is the social network. T contains only the vertices that represent the users in C. The edges in G that connect users in C with users not belonging to C are removed from T. Using such subgraph it is possible to define the *degree of cohesiveness* Λ of T as the sum of a specific node influence metric computed for each node (see formula in Figure 4).

A node influence metric (Lawyer, 2014) allows ranking the influence that each user has on other users. If users have low influence on each other or there are few users that have a high influence, than the graph represents a team with relatively low cohesive members; otherwise, when users have a high influence, it means that each user is strongly connected to many other users in the same graph; this means that the graph represents a cohesive team. The degree of cohesiveness is used by recommenders (described in the next section) to compare candidate teams and to recommend the most cohesive one.

Figure 4. Degree of cohesiveness

$$\Lambda(T) = \frac{\sum_{x \in C} influence(x)}{|C|}$$

Recommendations for Freelancers

Recommendation systems described in the background section can be used in the context of freelancing in order to help (i) freelancers finding the best project for their interests and (ii) project managers creating the best team for their project.

The recommendation of the most interesting projects to freelancers can be made through a set of data gathered from previous experiences both of a specific freelancer and of similar freelancers. If a user has many past experiences tracked by the platform, such experiences weighs more than all other factors for the recommendation. For example, consider *John,* a Java developer that was involved in three projects: two of them were about career management and the other one were about Artificial Intelligence (AI). At the end of these projects, John expressed a high interest for the project about AI, while he was neutral about the other two projects. In this case, it can be inferred the rule that John prefers projects about AI rather than projects about career management. In the case in which the freelancer is new and, therefore, there is no previous data to exploit to make a meaningful recommendation, the system will identify a set of users similar in terms of skills and will exploit their data to infer preference rules and thus the most interesting projects for the newcomer. Therefore, a mixed technique can be used, a collaborative filtering-based approach for new users, and a content-based approach for freelancers with many past experiences.

The recommendation of the best team for a specific project is a more difficult to perform, because it involves many technical, social and economical aspects.

A given project P requires a set of roles R; each role $r \in R$ requires a proper set of skills S_r. A number of people needed to cover each role can be estimated and, from there, a total number of people to allocate to the project (N). The recommendation should respect the following constraints:

1. A set of $N \pm \varepsilon$ people must be recommended, where ε should be a very small fraction of N. As an outcome of the recommendation process, a team of $N - \varepsilon$ people can be recommended, if composed by members with high experience. In this case, some roles will need fewer employees. On the other hand, a team of $N + \varepsilon$ persons can be recommended, if it is convenient to add some specific members for cohesiveness reasons (constraint 3) and it is not possible to remove others.
2. All the required skills necessary to carry out the project should be covered proportionally to the effort required for the role that provides such skills.

3. The team should be as cohesive as possible. The platform should prefer pre-existing collaborations, so that the risk of failure due to this aspect is minimum.

It is possible to exploit the social network of freelancers for recommendations. For each role, a set of candidates is identified. The adequacy index previously described is used, in this context, to sort candidates for each role. Among the possible combinations of candidates which respect to the skill/role constraint, the one will be selected which respects the budget constraint of the project and has the highest degree of cohesiveness.

Freelancers may also be interested in classical job opportunities, rather than participating in single projects. Therefore, freelancers should also have the opportunity to actively search for a job. The main problem faced by freelancers when searching for a job opportunity is that there are many places in which such opportunities are exposed. Moreover, it is difficult to find a job opportunity that actually fits the user in terms of the required skills.

A comprehensive social medium should offer to freelancers the opportunity to search for job opportunities; but, also, it should integrate a recommender system that indicates precisely the most suitable job opportunities for each candidate. Such a feature offers a great advantage also to companies: indeed, there is a preliminary selection made by the recommender system, which saves time to recruiters. Freelancers are saved from announcements about jobs they are not interest in or jobs that require a lower profile candidate; on the other hand, they are able to see in a specific section the jobs that they cannot apply for at the moment for lack of skills. This could serve as an incentive to acquire new skills. The recommender should also be able to suggest the most important skills to acquire in order to become more appealing to companies.

Usually, e-recruiting platforms use trivial information retrieval techniques (e.g., boolean search and filtering) in order to make users perform searches (Al-Otaibi, & Ykhlef, 2012). Literature about recommendation systems for job opportunities confirms that such systems need information about skills required by the job and skills acquired by the candidate (Al-Otaibi, & Ykhlef, 2012). The comprehensive social medium stores this information. As said beforehand, skills acquired by candidates are certified and there are formal levels of skill achievement: this feature improves the accuracy of the recommendation, which makes the recommendation itself more reliable, because less biased by subjectivity (e.g., auto-assessment of skills). The approaches most used to automatically suggest job opportunities are content-based (Paparrizos, Cambazoglu, & Gionis, 2011; Singh, Rose, Visweswariah, Chenthamarakshan, & Kambhatla, 2010; Yu, Liu, & Zhang, 2011) and hybrid (Chen, 2009; Färber, Weitzel, & Keim, 2003; Fazel-Zarandi, & Fox, 2009; Keim, 2007;

Lee, & Brusilovsky, 2007; Malinowski, Keim, Wendt, & Weitzel, 2006; Malinowski, Weitzel, & Keim, 2008).

While companies should be able to manually insert job opportunities on the platform, the platform itself should be able to automatically and systematically search for job opportunities in the web, adding them to a global board. The system should be able to automatically extract structured and unstructured information, using Natural Language Processing techniques. While this kind of feature reduces the accuracy of the recommendation for jobs announcements, which do not contain many details, it can extend the context of the search for freelancers and provide them with more opportunities, when the ones directly added on the platform are not sufficient.

Supporting Project and Resource Management

Project managers have to deal with many aspects of management: they have to handle team, costs and schedule issues. While team building is important to them in order to have a good set of participants, they still have to manage the team during the project itself. Also, project costs should be kept low, according to the available budget, and the product should be released in time. Therefore, project managers would highly benefit from a complete project and resource management platform within the comprehensive social medium. Such a platform should provide, at least, the following groups of features:

- **Project Resource Management:** Team building, complete team management.
- **Project Schedule Management:** Activities/Tasks management, schedule management/monitoring, release date prediction.
- **Project Cost Management:** Costs monitoring, remaining budget monitoring, final cost prediction.

The most interesting part of a resource management tool is the team building capability. A detailed description was provided above of the team builder of the comprehensive social medium for freelancers. On the other hand, project managers should also be able to add new resources when possible, as well as to remove resources and to assign team members to tasks. The platform tracks the resource allocation activity of project managers, in order to evaluate on a more objective basis both the manager and the members. For example, if a member does not respect the task deadline, it could be inferred that he/she do not have a sufficient level of skills for that specific task. On the other hand, if many members show this kind of problem, it could be inferred that the manager is not able to estimate a proper deadline for tasks. Finally, when there are serious risks of release delay, the system could also suggest to add a specific resource to the project.

In order to provide this kind of information, the platform should also provide a project schedule management tool, through which one can create activities and tasks, assign them to team members and define deadlines. This tool should also provide capabilities for Gantt and/or Pert chart creation and management, these representations being commonly used by project managers in order to define the temporal evolution of the project. Delays in specific tasks or activities could also delay the final release date of the product. Therefore, the platform should provide a feature enabling project managers to reassess the release date, to re-schedule future activities, possibly assigning critical tasks to members that have proved to be more punctual.

The other dimension that should be taken into account is the cost of a project. Cost management is a key activity carried out by project managers, for which a comprehensive social medium should provide support. The part of cost management already described beforehand is the one related to team building, which should respect specific budget constraints. Anyhow, the project can have other costs, related to hardware, software, facilities and other aspects. Furthermore, a schedule delay could imply a higher final cost, due, for example, to the team salary. The platform should provide the managers with a cost management tool, through which they can monitor costs and also forecast the final cost of the project, considering modifications in the schedule, in the team and all the related factors.

All the fine-grained data gathered during this phase should be used to profile team members and project managers, in order to improve the confidence of skill certification.

FUTURE RESEARCH DIRECTIONS

Future research involve in the first an implementation of the model proposed and described here and its testing and refinement through its adoptions by freelancers and companies. Beyond that, one relevant focus will be the capability of the model to provide effective support for institutional infrastructures fpor innovative product development such as the Digital Innovation Hubs launched by the European Union as building blocks for the realization of the Industry 4.0 program. The role of human resources is paramount for the effectiveness of Digital Information Hubs, and this fits with our purpose to go beyond a broad inspiration from the driving principles and statements of Industry 4.0 and make our model fully usable within concrete implementations of the Industry 4.0 paradigm. Last but not least, the integration of the project management and team building of freelancers with a decentralized self-management of their payments through peer-to-peer transactional platforms such as the blockchain (well-known for their use in cryptocurrencies such as Bitcoin but usable in a large variety of other contexts) will be a further step in the support of freelancers in the Economy 4.0.

CONCLUSION

The title of this chapter recalls clearly the Industry 4.0 program proposed by the German government as the basis for a fourth industrial revolution in the context of cloud computing and global digitization, and pursued under other names in other contexts (Manufacturing USA, Industrie du Futur, Industria 4.0). The flexible and adaptive management of human resources is one of the key points of this program, and to these ends it can not ignore the contribution of skills and competencies given by the new professions, in contexts such as open-source software engineering, app development, 3d printing. Platforms and existing recommender system for freelancers have led the way in that direction, but in their current state of the art are bound to get into a blind constraint, and thus will be unable to meet the required needs for Economy 4.0 to grow and flourish as a result of the effective realization of an Industry 4.0. In fact, they are mostly focused on individual professionals that act as fillers for organizations that do not want to hire new resources on a permanent basis to meet occasional needs.

The authors have thus argued that the point of view must be radically reversed, by conceiving projects to be permanently implemented through the systematic use of external resources endowed with the required advanced skills, because most of such skills are indeed available externally and because the speed of technological change does not allow organizations to keep pace except by using these external human resources. The authors have then shown what are the design prerequisites to create IT platforms supporting this change of perspective, by identifying the necessary technological building blocks and by evolving and differentiating what has been made available through the technological background underlying social networks, recommender systems and project management tools. The implementation of the comprehensive social medium presented in this chapter is part of the authors' agenda of future work.

REFERENCES

Adomavicius, G., & Tuzhilin, A. (2015). Context-aware recommender systems. In Recommender systems handbook (pp. 191-226). Springer US. doi:10.1007/978-1-4899-7637-6_6

Al-Otaibi, S. T., & Ykhlef, M. (2012). A survey of job recommender systems. *International Journal of Physical Sciences*, *7*(29), 5127–5142. doi:10.5897/IJPS12.482

Ben-Shimon, D., Tsikinovsky, A., Rokach, L., Meisles, A., Shani, G., & Naamani, L. (2007). Recommender system from personal social networks. In *Advances in Intelligent Web Mastering* (pp. 47–55). Springer Berlin Heidelberg. doi:10.1007/978-3-540-72575-6_8

Berkovsky, S., & Freyne, J. (2010, September). Group-based recipe recommendations: analysis of data aggregation strategies. In *Proceedings of the fourth ACM conference on Recommender systems* (pp. 111-118). ACM. doi:10.1145/1864708.1864732

Burke, R. (2002). Hybrid recommender systems: Survey and experiments. *User Modeling and User-Adapted Interaction*, *12*(4), 331–370. doi:10.1023/A:1021240730564

Caramela, S. (2016, Sep 28). *Attention Freelancers! 15 Great Websites for Finding Works*. Retrieved from http://www.businessnewsdaily.com/6965-freelance-job-websites.html

Chen, P. C. (2009). A fuzzy multiple criteria decision making model in employee recruitment. *IJCSNS International Journal of Computer Science and Network Security*, *9*(7), 113–117.

Deshpande, M., & Karypis, G. (2004). Item-based top-n recommendation algorithms. *ACM Transactions on Information Systems*, *22*(1), 143–177. doi:10.1145/963770.963776

Färber, F., Weitzel, T., & Keim, T. (2003). An automated recommendation approach to selection in personnel recruitment. *AMCIS 2003 Proceedings*, 302.

Fazel-Zarandi, M., & Fox, M. S. (2009). Semantic matchmaking for job recruitment: an ontology-based hybrid approach. In *Proceedings of the 8th International Semantic Web Conference* (Vol. 525).

He, J., & Chu, W. W. (2010). *A social network-based recommender system* (pp. 47–74). Springer, US.

Johansson, A. (2015, May 12). *The 15 Best Freelance Websites to Find Jobs.* Retrieved from https://www.entrepreneur.com/article/245953

Keim, T. (2007, January). Extending the applicability of recommender systems: A multilayer framework for matching human resources. In *System Sciences, 2007. HICSS 2007. 40th Annual Hawaii International Conference on* (pp. 169-169). IEEE. doi:10.1109/HICSS.2007.223

Lawyer, G. (2014). *Understanding the spreading power of all nodes in a network: a continuous-time perspective.* arXiv preprint arXiv:1405.6707

Lee, D. H., & Brusilovsky, P. (2007, June). Fighting information overflow with personalized comprehensive information access: A proactive job recommender. In *Autonomic and Autonomous Systems, 2007. ICAS07. Third International Conference on* (pp. 21-21). IEEE. doi:10.1109/CONIELECOMP.2007.76

Lingel, G. (2016). *The Best Freelancing Sites of 2016.* Retrieved from http://www. lifehack.org/368286/the-best-freelancing-sites-2016

Lops, P., De Gemmis, M., & Semeraro, G. (2011). Content-based recommender systems: State of the art and trends. In Recommender systems handbook (pp. 73-105). Springer US.

Lu, J., Wu, D., Mao, M., Wang, W., & Zhang, G. (2015). Recommender system application developments: A survey. *Decision Support Systems, 74,* 12–32. doi:10.1016/j.dss.2015.03.008

Malinowski, J., Keim, T., Wendt, O., & Weitzel, T. (2006, January). Matching people and jobs: A bilateral recommendation approach. In *Proceedings of the 39th Annual Hawaii International Conference on System Sciences (HICSS'06)* (Vol. 6, pp. 137c-137c). IEEE. doi:10.1109/HICSS.2006.266

Malinowski, J., Weitzel, T., & Keim, T. (2008). Decision support for team staffing: An automated relational recommendation approach. *Decision Support Systems, 45*(3), 429–447. doi:10.1016/j.dss.2007.05.005

Paparrizos, I., Cambazoglu, B. B., & Gionis, A. (2011, October). Machine learned job recommendation. In *Proceedings of the fifth ACM Conference on Recommender Systems* (pp. 325-328). ACM. doi:10.1145/2043932.2043994

Pazzani, M. J., & Billsus, D. (2007). Content-based recommendation systems. In *The adaptive web* (pp. 325–341). Springer Berlin Heidelberg. doi:10.1007/978-3-540-72079-9_10

Rampton, J. (2016, Mar 16). *Top 10 Freelance Job Sites in 2016*. Retrieved from http://www.johnrampton.com/top-10-freelance-job-sites-in-2016/

Ricci, F., Rokach, L., & Shapira, B. (2011). *Introduction to recommender systems handbook*. Springer, US. doi:10.1007/978-0-387-85820-3_1

Sarwar, B., Karypis, G., Konstan, J., & Riedl, J. (2001, April). Item-based collaborative filtering recommendation algorithms. In *Proceedings of the 10th international conference on World Wide Web* (pp. 285-295). ACM.

Shabib, N., Gulla, J. A., & Krogstie, J. (2013). On the Intrinsic Challenges of Group Recommendation. In *RSWeb*. RecSys.

Singh, A., Rose, C., Visweswariah, K., Chenthamarakshan, V., & Kambhatla, N. (2010, October). PROSPECT: a system for screening candidates for recruitment. In *Proceedings of the 19th ACM international conference on Information and knowledge management* (pp. 659-668). ACM. doi:10.1145/1871437.1871523

Yu, H., Liu, C., & Zhang, F. (2011). Reciprocal recommendation algorithm for the field of recruitment. *Journal of Information & Computational Science*, 8(16), 4061–4068.

Zurada, J. M. (1992). *Introduction to artificial neural systems* (Vol. 8). St. Paul: West.

KEY TERMS AND DEFINITIONS

Project Management: Is the discipline of initiating, planning, executing, controlling, and closing the work of a team to achieve specific goals and meet specific success criteria. A project is a temporary endeavor designed to produce a unique product, service or result with a defined beginning and end (usually time-constrained, and often constrained by funding or deliverables) undertaken to meet unique goals and objectives, typically to bring about beneficial change or added value.

Recommendation Systems: (Sometimes replacing "system" with a synonym such as platform or engine) are a subclass of information filtering system that seek to predict the "rating" or "preference" that a user would give to an item.

Resource Management: In organizational studies, resource management is the efficient and effective development of an organization's resources when they are needed. Such resources may include financial resources, inventory, human skills, production resources, or information technology (IT).

Skill Assessment: The process of documenting knowledge, skills, attitudes, and beliefs Health assessment, a plan of care that identifies the specific needs.

Social Media: Are computer-mediated technologies that allow the creating and sharing of information, ideas, career interests and other forms of expression via virtual communities and networks.

Social Network Analysis: Is the process of investigating social structures through the use of network and graph theories. It characterizes networked structures in terms of nodes (individual actors, people, or things within the network) and the ties, edges, or links (relationships or interactions) that connect them.

Survey: A field of applied statistics, survey methodology studies the sampling of individual units from a population and the associated survey data collection techniques, such as questionnaire construction and methods for improving the number and accuracy of responses to surveys.

Compilation of References

Acar, W., Burns, A. T., & Datta, P. (2014). Explicit knowledge transfers in new product development. *International Journal of Strategic Decision Sciences, 5*(4), 16–50. doi:10.4018/ijsds.2014100102

Accenture Digital. (2015a). (pp. 3–32). Amsterdam, Netherlands: Digital High Performance Research- Are AEX Listed Companies Keeping Up with The Pace of Digital Disruption.

Adamic, L., Zhang, J., Bakshy, E., & Ackerman, M. (2012). Knowledge sharing and yahoo answers: everyone knows something. *17th international conference on World Wide Web,* (pp. 665–674).

Adamic, L., Zhang, J., Bakshy, E., & Ackerman, M. (2008). Knowledge sharing and yahoo answers: everyone knows something. In *Proceeding of the 17th international confrerence on world wide web*, (pp. 665-674). doi:10.1145/1367497.1367587

Adler, N. (2014). *The Strategically agile organization: Development of a measurement instrument* (Doctoral dissertation). Alliant International University, California School of Professional Psychology, San Francisco, CA.

Adomavicius, G., & Tuzhilin, A. (2015). Context-aware recommender systems. In Recommender systems handbook (pp. 191-226). Springer US. doi:10.1007/978-1-4899-7637-6_6

Agnihotri, R., Kothandaraman, P., Kashyap, R., & Singh, R. (2012). Bringing social into sales: The impact of salespeoples social media use on service behaviors and value creation. *Journal of Personal Selling & Sales Management, 22*(3), 333–348. doi:10.2753/PSS0885-3134320304

Agrawal, R. (2003). Mining newsgroups using Networks arising from social behavior. *Proceedings of 12th international Conference on WWW*.

Agrifoglio, R. (2015). *Knowledge Preservation Through Community of Practice. Theoretical Issues and Empirical Evidence. Information Systems Series*. Springer. doi:10.1007/978-3-319-22234-9

Ahammad, M. F., Tarba, S. Y., Liu, Y., & Glaister, K. W. (2016). Knowledge transfer and cross-border acquisition performance: The impact of cultural distance and employee retention. *International Business Review, 25*(1), 66–75. doi:10.1016/j.ibusrev.2014.06.015

Aiken, K. D., & Boush, D. M. (2006). Trustmarks, objective-source ratings, and implied investments in advertising: Investigating online trust and the context-specific nature of internet signals. *Journal of the Academy of Marketing Science, 34*(3), 308–323. doi:10.1177/0092070304271004

Aite Group. (2015). *The Current and Future Sales of Corporate Mobile Banking Around the Globe*. Author.

Ajzen, I. (1991). The theory of planned behavior. *Organizational Behavior and Human Decision Processes, 50*(2), 179–211. doi:10.1016/0749-5978(91)90020-T

Al Saifi, S. A., Dillon, S., & McQeen, R. (2016). The relationship between face to face social networks and knowledge sharing: An exploratory study of manufacturing firms. *Journal of Knowledge Management, 20*(2), 308–326. doi:10.1108/JKM-07-2015-0251

Alavi, M., & Leidner, D. E. (2001). Review: Knowledge Management and Knowledge Management Systems: Conceptual Foundations and Research Issues. *Management Information Systems Quarterly, 25*(1), 107–136. doi:10.2307/3250961

Alduaij, S., Chen, Z., & Gangopadhyay, A. (2016). Using crowd sourcing to analyze consumers response to privacy policies of online social network and financial institutions at micro level. *International Journal of Information Security and Privacy, 10*(2), 41–63. doi:10.4018/IJISP.2016040104

Alesina, A., & La Ferrara, E. (2005). Ethnic diversity and economic performance. *Journal of Economic Literature, 43*(3), 762–800. doi:10.1257/002205105774431243

Alex Bryson, J. F. a., & Stokes, L. (2014). *Does Worker Wellbeing Affect Workplace Performance?* Academic Press.

Alim, S., Abdulrahman, R., Neagu, D., & Ridley, M. (2011). Online social network profile data extraction for vulnerability analysis. *International Journal of Internet Technology and Secured Transactions, 3*(2), 194–209. doi:10.1504/IJITST.2011.039778

Almandoz, J. (2014). Founding teams as carriers of competing logics: When institutional forces predict banks risk exposure. *Administrative Science Quarterly, 59*(3), 442–473. doi:10.1177/0001839214537810

Al-Otaibi, S. T., & Ykhlef, M. (2012). A survey of job recommender systems. *International Journal of Physical Sciences, 7*(29), 5127–5142. doi:10.5897/IJPS12.482

Al-Tabbaa, O., & Ankrah, S. (2016). Social capital to facilitate engineered university–industry collaboration for technology transfer: A dynamic perspective. *Technological Forecasting and Social Change, 104*, 1–15. doi:10.1016/j.techfore.2015.11.027

Aman, A., & Nicholson, B. (2011). Managing knowledge transfer in offshore software development: The role of copresent and ICT-based interaction. In F. Tan (Ed.), *International enterprises and global information technologies: Advancing management practices* (pp. 302–320). Hershey, PA: IGI Global. doi:10.4018/978-1-60960-605-3.ch014

Anatan, L. (2013). A proposed framework of university to industry knowledge transfer. *Review of Integrative Business and Economics Research, 2*(2), 304–325.

Anatan, L. (2015). Conceptual issues in university to industry knowledge transfer studies: A literature review. *Procedia: Social and Behavioral Sciences*, *211*, 711–717. doi:10.1016/j.sbspro.2015.11.090

Anderson, P. (2007). *What is Web 2.0? Ideas, technologies and implications for education*. JISC reports. Available: http://www.jisc.ac.uk/media/documents/techwatch/tsw0701b.p

Appadurai, A. (2013). *The Future as Cultural Fact. Essays on the Global Condition*. London, New York: Verso.

Argyris, C. (1999). *On Organizational learning* (2nd ed.). Blackwell Publishers Inc.

Armstrong, S. J., & Mahmud, A. (2008). Experiential learning and the acquisition of managerial tacit knowledge. *Academy of Management Learning & Education*, *7*(2), 189–208. doi:10.5465/AMLE.2008.32712617

Arsal, I., Woosnam, K. M., Baldwin, E. D., & Backman, S. J. (2010). Residents as Travel Destination Information Providers: An Online Community Perspective. *Journal of Travel Research*, *49*(4), 400–413. doi:10.1177/0047287509346856

Atkins, D. (2005). *University futures and new technologies: Possibilities and issues*. Unpublished discussion paper for an OECD expert meeting.

Avram, G. (2006). At the crossroads of knowledge management and social software. *Electronic Journal of Knowledge Management*, *4*(1), 1–10.

Awad, E. M. & Ghaziri, H. M. (2007). *Knowledge management*. Delhi: Dorling Kindersley, licenses of Pearson Education in South Asia.

AWPA. (2013). *Information and Communications Technology Workforce Study*. Retrieved from http://awpa.gov.au/ publications/Documents/ICT-STUDY-FINAL-28-JUNE-2013.pdf

Axford, M., & Renfro, C. (2012). Noteworthy productivity tools for personal knowledge management. *Online*, *36*(3), 33–36.

Baggio, R., & Cooper, C. (2010). Knowledge transfer in a tourism destination: The effects of a network structure. *Service Industries Journal*, *30*(10), 1757–1771. doi:10.1080/02642060903580649

Bagozzi, R. P. (2000). On the concept of intentional social action in consumer research. *The Journal of Consumer Research*, *27*(3), 388–396. doi:10.1086/317593

Bagozzi, R. P., & Dholakia, U. (1999). Goal Setting and Goal Striving in Consumer Behavior. *Journal of Marketing*, *63*, 19–32. doi:10.2307/1252098

Bai, L., Tang, J., Yang, Y., & Gong, S. (2014). Hygienic food handling intention: An application of the theory of planned behavior in the Chinese cultural context. *Food Control*, *42*, 172–180. doi:10.1016/j.foodcont.2014.02.008

Bandura, A. (1977). Self-efficacy: Toward a unifying theory of behavioral change. *Psychological Review*, *84*(2), 191–215. doi:10.1037/0033-295X.84.2.191 PMID:847061

Bandura, A. (1982). Self-efficacy mechanism in human agency. *The American Psychologist*, *37*(2), 122–147. doi:10.1037/0003-066X.37.2.122

Barbara, C., Elena, F., & Raymond, H. (2011). Semantic web-based social network access control. *Computers & Security*, *30*(2), 108–115.

Barner-Rasmussen, W., & Aarnio, C. (2011). Shifting the faultlines of language: A quantitative functional-level exploration of language use in MNC subsidiaries. *Journal of World Business*, *46*(3), 288–295. doi:10.1016/j.jwb.2010.07.006

Barreto, A. M. (2014). The word-of-mouth phenomenon in the social media era. *International Journal of Market Research*, *56*(5), 631–654.

Barrett, W., Lau, M. S., & Dew, P. M. (2000). Facilitating knowledge transfer in an R&D environment: A case study. In D. Schwartz, T. Brasethvik, & M. Divitini (Eds.), *Internet-based organizational memory and knowledge management* (pp. 147–169). Hershey, PA: IGI Publishing. doi:10.4018/978-1-878289-82-7.ch008

Bartol, K. M., & Srivastava, A. (2002). Encouraging Knowledge Sharing: The Role of Organizational Reward Systems. *Journal of Leadership & Organizational Studies*, *9*(1), 64–76. doi:10.1177/107179190200900105

Baruah, T. D. (2012). Effectiveness of social media as a tool of communication and its potential for technology enabled connections. A micro-level study. *International Journal of Scientific and Research Publications*, *2*(5), 1–10.

Ba, S., & Pavlou, P. A. (2002). Evidence of the effect of trust building technology in electronic markets: Price premiums and buyer behavior. *Management Information Systems Quarterly*, *26*(3), 243–268. doi:10.2307/4132332

Battaglino, C., Bosco, C., Cambria, E., Damiano, R., Patti, V., & Rosso, P. (2013). *Emotion and Sentiment in Social and Expressive Media. Proceedings of the workshop of AIIA 2013 - 25th Year Anniversary.*

Baum, J. A. C., & Ingram, P. (1997). Chain affiliation and the failure of Manhattan hotels, 1898-1980. *Administrative Science Quarterly*, *42*(1).

Bazerman, M. H., Tenbrunsel, A. E., & Wade-Benzoni, K. (1998). Negotiating with Yourself and Losing: Making Decisions with Competing Internal Preferences. *Academy of Management Review*, *23*(2), 225–241. doi:10.2307/259372

Bebensee, T., Helms, R., & Spruit, M. (2011). Exploring Web 2.0 applications as a means of bolstering up knowledge management. *Electronic Journal of Knowledge Management*, *9*(1), 1–9.

Becerra-Fernandez, I., & Sabherwal, R. (2010). *Knowledge management: systems and processes.* Armonk, NY: M.E. Sharpe, Inc.

Becker, P. H. (1993). Common pitfalls in published grounded theory research. *Qualitative Health Research*, *3*(2), 254–260. doi:10.1177/104973239300300207

Compilation of References

Bedük, A. (2005). *Modern yönetim teknikleri*. Ankara: Gazi Kitabevi.

Beer, M., & Eisenstat, R. A. (2000). The silent killers of strategy implementation and learning. *Sloan Management Review*, *41*(4), 29.

Behringer, N., & Sassenberg, K. (2015). Introducing social media for knowledge management: Determinants of employees intentions to adopt new tools. *Computers in Human Behavior*, *48*, 290–296. doi:10.1016/j.chb.2015.01.069

Bell, D. (1973). *The coming of post-industrial society*. London: Heinemann.

Ben Hamida, L. (2016). Building R&D capabilities abroad and the role of reverse knowledge transfer in explaining MNCs' productivity. In M. Erdoğdu & B. Christiansen (Eds.), *Handbook of research on comparative economic development perspectives on Europe and the MENA region* (pp. 219–235). Hershey, PA: IGI Global. doi:10.4018/978-1-4666-9548-1.ch011

Benbasat, I., & Weber, R. (1996). Research Commentary: Rethinking Diversity in Information System Research. *Information Systems Research*, *7*(4), 389–399. doi:10.1287/isre.7.4.389

Benevenuto, F., Magno, G., & Rodrigues, T., & Almeida. (2014). Detecting spammers on twitter, Collaboration, Electronic messaging. *Anti-Abuse and Spam Conference (CEAS)*.

Ben-Shimon, D., Tsikinovsky, A., Rokach, L., Meisles, A., Shani, G., & Naamani, L. (2007). Recommender system from personal social networks. In *Advances in Intelligent Web Mastering* (pp. 47–55). Springer Berlin Heidelberg. doi:10.1007/978-3-540-72575-6_8

Beritelli, P., Strobl, A., & Peters, M. (2013). Interlocking directorships against community closure: A trade-off for development in tourist destinations. *Tourism Review*, *68*(1), 21–34. doi:10.1108/16605371311310057

Berkovsky, S., & Freyne, J. (2010, September). Group-based recipe recommendations: analysis of data aggregation strategies. In *Proceedings of the fourth ACM conference on Recommender systems* (pp. 111-118). ACM. doi:10.1145/1864708.1864732

Bers, U. M. (2006). The role of new technologies to foster positive youth development. *Applied Developmental Science*, *10*(4), 200–219. doi:10.1207/s1532480xads1004_4

Bhanji, Z., & Oxley, J. E. (2013). Overcoming the dual liability of foreignness and privateness in international corporate citizenship partnerships. *Journal of International Business Studies*, *44*(4), 290–311. doi:10.1057/jibs.2013.8

Bharadwaj, A. S. (2000). A resource-based perspective on information technology capability and firm performance: An empirical investigation. *Management Information Systems Quarterly*, *24*(1), 169–196. doi:10.2307/3250983

Bharadwaj, A., El Sawy, O., Pavlou, P. A., & Venkatraman, N. (2013). Digital Business Strategy: Toward Next Generation of Insights. *Management Information Systems Quarterly*, *37*(2), 471–482.

Bharati, P., Zhang, W., & Chaudhury, A. (2015). Better knowledge with social media? Exploring the roles of social capital and organizational knowledge management. *Journal of Knowledge Management, 19*(3), 456–475. doi:10.1108/JKM-11-2014-0467

Bhatnagar, S., & Schware, R. (2000). *Information and communication technology in rural development. Case Studies from India.* World Bank Institute.

Bhisikar, P., & Sahu, P. (2013). Overview on Web Mining and Different Technique for Web Personalisation. *International Journal of Engineering Research and Applications, 3,* 2.

Bianchi, C., & Andrews, L. (2015). Investigating marketing managers perspectives on social media in Chile. *Journal of Business Research, 68*(12), 2552–2559. doi:10.1016/j.jbusres.2015.06.026

Bickart, B., & Schindler, R. M. (2001). Internet forums as influential sources of consumer information. *Journal of Interactive Marketing, 15*(3), 31–40. doi:10.1002/dir.1014

Bilgihan, A. (2016). Gen Y customer loyalty in online shopping: An integrated model of trust, user experience, and branding. *Computers in Human Behavior, 61,* 103–113. doi:10.1016/j.chb.2016.03.014

Billings, C. E. (1996). *Human-centered aircraft automation: Principles and guidelines. National Aeronautics and Space Administration.* Ames Research Center.

Birkinshaw, J., & Hood, N. (1998). Multinational subsidiary evolution: Capability and charter change in foreign-owned subsidiary companies. *Academy of Management Review, 23*(4), 773–795.

Björkman, A., & Piekkari, R. (2009). Language and foreign subsidiary control: An empirical test. *Journal of International Management, 15*(1), 105–117. doi:10.1016/j.intman.2008.12.001

Blacksmith, N., & Poeppelman, T. (2013). Application of modern technology and social media in the workplace. *The Industrial-Organizational psychologist, 51*(1), 69–73.

Bloodgood, J. M., Chilton, M. A., & Bloodgood, T. C. (2014). The effect of knowledge transfer motivation, receiver capability, and motivation on organizational performance. In M. Chilton & J. Bloodgood (Eds.), *Knowledge management and competitive advantage: Issues and potential solutions* (pp. 232–242). Hershey, PA: IGI Global. doi:10.4018/978-1-4666-4679-7.ch013

Bock, G. W., Zmud, R., Kim, Y. G., & Lee, J. N. (2005). Behavioral intention formation in knowledge sharing: Examining the roles of extrinsic motivators, social-psychological forces, and organizational climate. *Management Information Systems Quarterly, 29*(1), 87–111.

Bonson, E., & Flores, F. (2011). Social media and corporate dialogue: The response of the global financial institutions. *Online Information Review, 35*(1), 34–49. doi:10.1108/14684521111113579

Bouncken, R. B. (2002). Knowledge management for quality improvements in hotels. *Journal of Quality Assurance in Hospitality & Tourism, 3*(3-4), 25–59. doi:10.1300/J162v03n03_03

Bowley, R. C. (2009). A comparative case study: Examining the organizational use of social networking sites (Thesis). Hamilton: The University of Waikato. Available http://researchcommons. waikato.ac.nz/bitstream/handle/10289/3590/thesis.pdf?sequence=1&isAllowed=y

Boyd, D., & Ellison, N. (2008). Social network sites: definition, history and scholarship. *Journal of Computer-Mediated Communication, 13*(1), 210–230. doi:10.1111/j.1083-6101.2007.00393.x

Boyer, D. (2008). Thinking through the Anthropology of Experts. *Anthropology in Action, 15*(2), 38–46. doi:10.3167/aia.2008.150204

Bradley, A. J., & McDonald, M. P. (2011). Social media versus knowledge management. *Harvard Business Review*, 1–4. Retrieved from https://hbr.org/2011/10/social-media-versus-knowledge

Bresman, H., Birkinshaw, J., & Nobel, R. (2010). Knowledge transfer in international acquisitions. *Journal of International Business Studies, 41*(1), 5–20. doi:10.1057/jibs.2009.56

BrightLocal. (2015). *Local Consumer Review Survey*. Retrieved from https://www.brightlocal. com/learn/local-consumer-review-survey/

Briones, R. L., Kuch, B., Liu, B. F., & Jin, Y. (2011). Keeping up with the digital age: How the American Red Cross uses social media to build relationships. *Public Relations Review, 37*(1), 37–43. doi:10.1016/j.pubrev.2010.12.006

Brodie, R. J., Ilic, A., Juric, B., & Hollebeek, L. (2013). Consumer engagement in a virtual brand community: An exploratory analysis. *Journal of Business Research, 66*(1), 105–114. doi:10.1016/j.jbusres.2011.07.029

Brown, J. S., & Duguid, P. (2000). Mysteries of the region: knowledge dynamics in Silicon Valley. *The Silicon Valley Edge*, 16-45.

Brown, A. L. (1988). Motivation to learn and understand: On taking charge of ones own learning. *Cognition and Instruction, 5*(4), 311–321. doi:10.1207/s1532690xci0504_4

Brown, J. S., & Duguid, P. (1998). Organizing knowledge. *California Management Review, 40*(3), 90–111. doi:10.2307/41165945

Bruhn, M., Schoenmueller, V., & Schafer, D. B. (2012). Are social media replacing traditional media in terms of brand equity creation? *Management Research Review, 35*(9), 770–790. doi:10.1108/01409171211255948

Budapest Open Access Initiative. (2016). *Read the Budapest open access initiative*. Retrieved October 10, 2016, from http://www.budapestopenaccessinitiative.org/read

Bughin, J. (2015). Taking the measure of the networked enterprise. *McKinsey Quarterly Survey*. Retrieved from http://www.mckinsey.com/business-functions/business-technology/our-insights/ taking-the-measure-of-the-networked

Bughin, J., Chui, M., & Manyika, J. (2015). *An executive's guide to the Internet of Things*. McKinsey & Company.

Buhalis, D., & Schertler, W. (1999). Information and Communication Technologies in tourism. *ENTER 99 Conference Proceedings*.

Buhalis, D. (1998). Strategic use of information technologies in the tourism industry. *Tourism Management, 19*(5), 409–421. doi:10.1016/S0261-5177(98)00038-7

Buhalis, D., & Law, R. (2008). Progress in information technology and tourism management: 20 years on and 10 years after the Internet—The state of eTourism research. *Tourism Management, 29*(4), 609–623. doi:10.1016/j.tourman.2008.01.005

Buhalis, D., & Licata, M. C. (2002). The future eTourism intermediaries. *Tourism Management, 23*(3), 207–220. doi:10.1016/S0261-5177(01)00085-1

Bunz, M. (2009, November 9). Burberry checks out crowdsourcing with The Art of the Trench. *Guardian*.

Buonocore, F., & Metallo, C. (2004). Tourist Destination Networks, Relational Competencies and "Relationship Builders"–the Central Role of Information Systems and Human Resource Management. In *Networking and partnerships in destination development and management: Proceedings of the ATLAS annual conference* (pp. 377-398).

Burke, R. (2002). Hybrid recommender systems: Survey and experiments. *User Modeling and User-Adapted Interaction, 12*(4), 331–370. doi:10.1023/A:1021240730564

Business Wire. (2015). *CitiConnect ERP Integrator Wins 2015 Celent Model Bank Award*. Retrieved from http://www.businesswire.com/news/home/20150326005072/en/CitiConnect%C2%AE-ERP-Integrator-Wins-2015-Celent-Model

BusinessDictionary.com. (2016). *Tacit knowledge*. Retrieved September 30, 2016, from http://www.businessdictionary.com/definition/tacit-knowledge.html

Cabrera, A., & Cabrera, E. F. (2002). Knowledge-Sharing Dilemmas. *Organization Studies, 23*(5), 687–710. doi:10.1177/0170840602235001

Cabrera, Á., Collins, W. C., & Salgado, J. F. (2006). Determinants of individual engagement in knowledge sharing. *International Journal of Human Resource Management, 17*(2), 245–264. doi:10.1080/09585190500404614

Cai, K., Spangler, S., Chen, Y., & Zhang, L. (2008). Leveraging sentiment analysis for topic detection. *Proceedings of the 2008 IEEE/WIC/ACM International Conference on Web Intelligence and Intelligent Agent Technology*, 265-271.

Callon, M. (1986). Some Elements of a Sociology of Translation: Domestication of the Scallops and the Fishermen of St Brieuc Bay. In J. Law (Ed.), *Power, Action and Belief: A New Sociology of Knowledge?* (pp. 196–233). London: Routledge.

Canestrino, R., & Magliocca, P. (2016). Transferring knowledge through cross-border communities of practice. In S. Buckley, G. Majewski, & A. Giannakopoulos (Eds.), *Organizational knowledge facilitation through communities of practice in emerging markets* (pp. 1–30). Hershey, PA: IGI Global. doi:10.4018/978-1-5225-0013-1.ch001

Cao, Q., Sirivianos, M., Yang, X., & Pregueiro, T. (2012). Aiding the detection of fake accounts in large scale social online services. In *Proceedings of the 9th USENIX Conference on Networked Systems Design and Implementation.* USENIX Association.

Caramela, S. (2016, Sep 28). *Attention Freelancers! 15 Great Websites for Finding Works.* Retrieved from http://www.businessnewsdaily.com/6965-freelance-job-websites.html

Casaló, L. V., Flaviàn, C., & Guinlalìu, M. (2010). Determinants of the intention to participate in firm-hosted online travel communities and effects on consumer behavioural intentions. *Tourism Management, 31*(6), 898–911. doi:10.1016/j.tourman.2010.04.007

Cascio, W. F. (2006). The high cost of low wages. *Harvard Business Review, 84*(12), 23.

Castells, M. (2005). *The network society: from knowledge to policy* (M. Castells & G. Cardoso, Eds.). Washington: Center for Transatlantic Relations.

Catlin, T., Scanlan, J., & Willmott, P. (2014). *Raising Your Digital Quotient: Making Sense of Digital Landscape.* McKinsey Quarterly Digital.

Celep, C., & Çetin, B. (2014). *Eğitim örgütlerinde bilgi yönetimi.* Ankara: Nobel Akademik Yayıncılık.

Champin, P. A., Prié, Y., & Richard, B. (2008). *Personal knowledge elaboration and sharing: Presentation is knowledge too.* Retrieved from: http://liris.cnrs.fr/Documents/Liris-3437.pdf

Chang, Y. Y., Gong, Y., & Peng, M. W. (2012). Expatriate knowledge transfer, subsidiary absorptive capacity, and subsidiary performance. *Academy of Management Journal, 55*(4), 927–948. doi:10.5465/amj.2010.0985

Chang, Y., Yu, H., & Lu, H. (2015). Persuasive messages, popularity cohesion, and message diffusion in social media marketing. *Journal of Business Research, 68*(4), 777–782. doi:10.1016/j.jbusres.2014.11.027

Chan, K. W., & Li, S. Y. (2010). Understanding consumer-to-consumer interactions in virtual communities: The salience of reciprocity. *The Journal of Business, 63*, 1033–1040.

Chan, S. H. J., & Mai, X. (2015). The relation of career adaptability to satisfaction and turnover intentions. *Journal of Vocational Behavior, 89*, 130–139. doi:10.1016/j.jvb.2015.05.005

Charband, Y., & Navimipour, N. J. (2016). Online knowledge sharing mechanisms: A systematic review of the state of the art literature and recommendations for future research. *Information Systems Frontiers*, 1–21.

Charles, M. (2007). Language Matters in Global Communication Article Based on ORA Lecture, October 2006. *Journal of Business Communication, 44*(3), 260–282. doi:10.1177/0021943607302477

Chathoth, P. K., Ungson, G. R., Harrington, R. J., & Chan, E. S. (2016). Co-creation and higher order customer engagement in hospitality and tourism services: A critical review. *International Journal of Contemporary Hospitality Management, 28*(2), 222–245. doi:10.1108/IJCHM-10-2014-0526

Chatti, M. A. (2012). Knowledge management: A personal knowledge network perspective. *Journal of Knowledge Management, 16*(5), 829–844. doi:10.1108/13673271211262835

Chatti, M. A., Klamma, R., Jarke, M., & Naeve, A. (2007). The Web 2.0 driven SECI model based learning process. In *Seventh IEEE International Conference on Advanced Learning Technologies (ICALT 2007)* (Vol. 5, pp. 780–782). IEEE. doi:10.1109/ICALT.2007.256

Cheng, M. Y., Ho, J. S. Y., & Lau, P. M. (2009). Knowledge sharing in academic institutions: A study of Multimedia University Malaysia. *Electronic Journal of Knowledge Management, 7*(3), 313–324.

Chen, I.Y., & Chen, N.S., & Kinshuk. (2009). Examining the Factors Influencing Participants' Knowledge Sharing Behavior in Virtual Learning Communities. *Journal of Educational Technology & Society, 12*(1), 134–148.

Chen, P. C. (2009). A fuzzy multiple criteria decision making model in employee recruitment. *IJCSNS International Journal of Computer Science and Network Security, 9*(7), 113–117.

Cheong, R. K. F., & Tsui, E. (2010). The roles and values of personal knowledge management: An exploratory study. *Vine, 40*(2), 204–227. doi:10.1108/03055721011050686

Cheong, R. K. F., & Tsui, E. (2011). From skills and competencies to outcome-based collaborative work: Tracking a decades development of personal knowledge management (PKM) models. *Knowledge and Process Management, 18*(3), 175–193. doi:10.1002/kpm.380

Chesbrough, H. (2003). *Open innovation: The new imperative for creating and profiting from technology*. Boston, MA: Harvard Business School Press.

Cheung, C. M. K., & Lee, M. K. O. (2012). What drives consumers to spread electronic word of mouth in online consumer-opinion platforms. *Decision Support Systems, 53*(1), 218–225. doi:10.1016/j.dss.2012.01.015

Cheung, M. F. Y., & To, W. M. (2015). Do task- and relation-oriented customers co-create a better quality of service? An empirical study of customer-dominant logic. *Management Decision, 53*(1), 179–197. doi:10.1108/MD-05-2014-0252

Chevalier, J. A., & Mayzlin, D. (2006). The effect of word of mouth on sales: Online book reviews. *JMR, Journal of Marketing Research, 43*(3), 345–354. doi:10.1509/jmkr.43.3.345

Childers, T. L., Carr, C. L., Peck, J., & Carson, S. (2002). Hedonic and utilitarian motivations for online retail shopping behavior. *Journal of Retailing*, *77*(4), 511–535. doi:10.1016/S0022-4359(01)00056-2

Chitturi, R., Raghunathan, R., & Mahajan, V. (2008). Delight by design: The role of hedonic versus utilitarian benefits. *Journal of Marketing*, *72*(3), 48–63. doi:10.1509/jmkg.72.3.48

Choi, B., & Lee, I. (2016). *Trust in open versus closed social media: The relative influence of user- and marketer generated content in social network services on customer trust.* Telematic Information. doi:10.1016/j.tele.2016.11.005

Choi, S. M., Lee, W. N., & Kim, H.-J. (2005). Lessons from the Rich and Famous: A Cross-Cultural Comparison of Celebrity Endorsement in Advertising. *Journal of Advertising*, *34*(2), 85–98. doi:10.1080/00913367.2005.10639190

Choi, S. M., & Rifon, N. J. (2012). It is a match: The impact of congruence between celebrity image and consumer ideal self on endorsement effectiveness. *Psychology and Marketing*, *29*(9), 639–650. doi:10.1002/mar.20550

Cho, J. J., Kim, J. Y., Chang, S. J., Fiedler, N., Koh, S. B., Crabtree, B. F., & Choi, Y. H. (2008). Occupational stress and depression in Korean employees. *International Archives of Occupational and Environmental Health*, *82*(1), 47–57. doi:10.1007/s00420-008-0306-4 PMID:18301911

Choo, C. (1998). *The Knowing Organization: How Organizations Use Information for Construct Meaning, Create Knowledge and Make Decisions.* New York: Oxford Press.

Cho, S. H., Chang, K. L., Yeo, J. H., Head, L. W., Zastrow, M., & Zdorovtsov, C. (2015). Comparison of fruit and vegetable consumption among Native and non-Native American population in rural communities. *International Journal of Consumer Studies*, *39*(1), 67–73. doi:10.1111/ijcs.12153

Christensen, P. H. (2007). Knowledge sharing: Moving away from the obsession with best practices. *Journal of Knowledge Management*, *11*(1), 36–47. doi:10.1108/13673270710728222

Chu, S. C., & Kim, Y. (2011). Determinants of consumer engagement in electronic word-of-mouth (eWOM) in social networking sites. *International Journal of Advertising*, *30*(1), 47–75. doi:10.2501/IJA-30-1-047-075

Ciabuschi, F., Dellestrand, H., & Kappen, P. (2011). Exploring the effects of vertical and lateral mechanisms in international knowledge transfer projects. *Management International Review*, *51*(2), 129–155. doi:10.1007/s11575-011-0068-1

Citi Group Treasury and Trade Solutions. (2015). *Managing Innovation in a World of Risk.* Author.

Citi Group. (2013). *Annual Report.* Retrieved from www.citigroup.com/citi/investor/quarterly/2014/ar13c_en.pdf

Citi Group. (2014). *Annual Report.* Retrieved from www.citigroup.com/citi/investor/quarterly/2014/ar14c_en.pdf

Citi Group. (2015). *Annual Report*. Retrieved from www.citigroup.com/citi/investor/quarterly/2016/ar15c_en.pdf

Clark, S. S., Berardy, A., Hannah, M. A., Seager, T. P., Selinger, E., & Makanda, J. V. (2015). Group tacit knowledge and globally distributed virtual teams: Lessons learned from using games and social media in the classroom. *Connexions - International Professional Communication Journal, 3*(1), 113–151.

Clifford, C. (2015). Instagram Is Crushing Twitter and Facebook Brand Engagement. *Entrepreneur*. Retrieved from https://www.entrepreneur.com/article/253838

Clinton, M. S., Merritt, K. L., & Murray, S. R. (2011). Facilitating knowledge transfer and the achievement of competitive advantage with corporate universities: An exploratory model based on media richness and type of knowledge to be transferred. In M. Jennex (Ed.), *Global aspects and cultural perspectives on knowledge management: Emerging dimensions* (pp. 329–345). Hershey, PA: IGI Global. doi:10.4018/978-1-60960-555-1.ch020

Cluster. (2015). *Conception of the cluster development in Rostov region – 2015*. Retrieved at: http://inno.sfedu.ru/sites/default/files/doc/164%D0%9F%20%D0%BE%D1%82%2012.03.2015.pdf

Cohen, W. M., & Levinthal, D. A. (1990). Absorptive capacity: A new perspective on learning and innovation. *Administrative Science Quarterly, 35*(1), 128–152. doi:10.2307/2393553

Cong, X., & Pandya, K. V. (2003). Issues of knowledge management in the public sector. *Electronic Journal of Knowledge Management, 1*(2), 25–33.

Constant, D., Sproull, L. S., & Kiesler, S. B. (1996). The kindness of strangers: The usefulness of electronic weak ties for technical advice. *Organization Science, 7*(2), 119–135. doi:10.1287/orsc.7.2.119

Cook, S. D. N., & Brown, J. S. (1999). Bridging Epistemologies: The Generative Dance Between Organizational Knowledge and Organizational Knowing. *Organization Science, 10*(4), 381–400. doi:10.1287/orsc.10.4.381

Cooper, C. (2006). Knowledge management and tourism. *Annals of Tourism Research, 33*(1), 47–64. doi:10.1016/j.annals.2005.04.005

Cooper, C. (2015). Managing tourism knowledge. *Tourism Recreation Research, 40*(1), 107–119. doi:10.1080/02508281.2015.1006418

Costanzo, C. (2003). Shutting Out Fraud. *Banking Strategies*, 28-35.

Costa, R. A., Silva, E. M., Neto, M. G., Delgado, D. B., Ribeiro, R. A., & Meira, S. R. L. (2009). Social knowledge management in practice: A case study. In L. Carriço, N. Baloian, & B. Fonseca (Eds.), *Groupware: Design, Implementation, and Use* (Vol. 5784, pp. 94–109). Springer Berlin Heidelberg. doi:10.1007/978-3-642-04216-4_8

Cross, R., & Sproull, L. (2004). More than an answer: Information relationships for actionable knowledge. *Organization Science, 15*(4), 446–462. doi:10.1287/orsc.1040.0075

Crystal, D. (2003). *English as a global language*. Cambridge University Press. doi:10.1017/CBO9780511486999

Cuccia, T., & Cellini, R. (2007). Is cultural heritage really important for tourists? A contingent rating study. *Applied Economics*, *39*(2), 261–271. doi:10.1080/00036840500427981

Culnan, M., McHugh, P., & Zubillaga, J. (2010). How large U.S. companies can use twitter and other social media to gain business value. *MIS Quarterly Executive*, *9*(4), 243–259.

Cummings, J. (2003). *Knowledge sharing: A review of the literature*. Washington, DC: The World Bank.

Cummings, J. L., & Teng, B. S. (2006). The keys to successful knowledge sharing. *Journal of General Management*, *31*(4), 1–18. doi:10.1177/030630700603100401

Cummings, J. N. (2004). Work groups, structural diversity, and knowledge sharing in a global organization. *Management Science*, *50*(3), 352–364. doi:10.1287/mnsc.1030.0134

Curran, J., & Lennon, R. (2011). Participating in the conversation: Exploring usage of social media. *Academy of Marketing Studies Journal*, *15*(1), 21–38.

Currie, D. (2001). *Managing employee well-being*. Chandos Publishing.

Cutillo, L. A., Manulis, M., & Strufe, T. (2010). Security and privacy in online social networks. In *Handbook of Social Network, Technologies and Applications*. Springer. doi:10.1007/978-1-4419-7142-5_23

Czepiel, J. A. (1975). Patterns of interorganizational communications and the diffusion of a major technological innovation in a competitive industrial community. *Academy of Management Journal*, *18*(1), 6–24. doi:10.2307/255621

Dahab, M. Y., & Edrees, A., & Rafea, A. (2010). Pattern Based Concept Extraction for Arabic Documents. *International Journal of Intelligent Computing and Information Sciences*, *10*(2).

Dar, H. (2013). *The importance of education: Economics of the English language in Pakistan*. Tribune.

Dave, B., & Koskela, L. (2009). Collaborative knowledge management - A construction case study. *Automation in Construction*, *18*(7), 894–902. doi:10.1016/j.autcon.2009.03.015

Davenport, T. H. (1999). Groups and teams. In *Organisational behaviour*. London: Financial Times Pitman Publishing.

Davenport, T. H., & Prusak, L. (1998). *Working Knowledge*. Boston: Harvard Business School Press.

Davenport, T. H., & Prusak, L. (1998). *Working knowledge: How organizations manage what they know*. Boston, MA: Harvard Business School Press.

Davenport, T. H., & Prusak, L. (1998). *Working Knowledge: How Organizations Manage What They Know*. Boston: Harvard Business School Press.

Davidavičienė, V., & Raudeliūnienė, J. (2010). ICT in Tacit Knowledge Preservation. In *The 6th International Scientific Conference "Business and Management 2010"* (pp. 822-828).

Davies, A., Devin, F., & Gorbis, M. (2011). *Future work skills 2020*. Institute for the Future for University of Phoenix Research Institute.

Davis, F. D., Bagozzi, R. P., & Warshaw, P. R. (1989). User acceptance of computer technology: A comparison of two theoretical models. *Management Science*, *35*(8), 982–1003. doi:10.1287/mnsc.35.8.982

Dawson, R. (2007). *Future of Media Report 2007*. Available at: www.rossdawsonblog.com/Future_of_Media_Report2007.pdf

Dawson, S. (2008). A study of the relationship between student social networks and sense of community. *Journal of Educational Technology & Society*, *11*(3), 224–238.

De Bruyn, A., & Lilien, G. L. (2008). A multi-stage model of word-of-mouth influence through viral marketing. *International Journal of Research in Marketing*, *25*(3), 151–163. doi:10.1016/j.ijresmar.2008.03.004

De Jonge, J., & Schaufeli, W. B. (1998). Job characteristics and employee well-being: A test of Warrs Vitamin Model in health care workers using structural equation modelling. *Journal of Organizational Behavior*, *19*(4), 387–407. doi:10.1002/(SICI)1099-1379(199807)19:4<387::AID-JOB851>3.0.CO;2-9

De Wever, B., Mechant, P., Veevaete, P., & Hauttekeete, L. (2007). E-learning 2.0: Social software for educational use. *Ninth IEEE International Symposium on Multimedia Workshops (ISMW 2007)*, 511–516. doi:10.1109/ISM.Workshops.2007.91

Deal, T. E., & Kennedy, A. A. (1982). *Corporate Cultures*. Reading, MA: Addison-Wesley.

Deloitte, L. L. P. (2015). *Travel Consumer 2015. Engaging the empowered holidaymaker*. Retrieved from http://www2.deloitte.com/content/dam/Deloitte/uk/Documents/consumer-business/deloitte-uk-travel-consumer-2015.pdf

Deng, C., & Mao, J. (2012). Knowledge transfer to vendors in offshore information systems outsourcing: Antecedents and effects on performance. *Journal of Global Information Management*, *20*(3), 1–22. doi:10.4018/jgim.2012070101

Deshpande, M., & Karypis, G. (2004). Item-based top-n recommendation algorithms. *ACM Transactions on Information Systems*, *22*(1), 143–177. doi:10.1145/963770.963776

Desmet, D., Duncan, E., Scanlan, J., & SingerSix, M. (2015). Building blocks for creating a highperforming digital enterprise. *McKinsey Quarterly*.

Dewaele, J. M., Petrides, K. V., & Furnham, A. (2008). Effects of trait emotional intelligence and sociobiographical variables on communicative anxiety and foreign language anxiety among adult multilinguals: A review and empirical investigation. *Language Learning*, *58*(4), 911–960. doi:10.1111/j.1467-9922.2008.00482.x

DFG – German Research Foundation (2014). Excellence Initiative Institutions Call for Swift Decision on Future Development. *Press Release, 42*(10).

DFG – German Research Foundation. (2016). Excellence Initiative (2005-2017). General Information. Retrieved from http://www.dfg.de/en/research_funding/programmes/excellence_initiative/general_information/index.html

Dhar, R., & Kim, E. Y. (2007). Seeing the forest or the trees: Implications of construal level theory for consumer choice. *Journal of Consumer Psychology, 17*(2), 96–100. doi:10.1016/S1057-7408(07)70014-1

Dhar, R., & Wertenbroch, K. (2000). Consumer choice between hedonic and utilitarian goods. *JMR, Journal of Marketing Research, 37*(1), 60–71. doi:10.1509/jmkr.37.1.60.18718

Dhouioui, Z., Ali, A. A., & Akaichi, J. (2016). Social networks security policies. *Proceedings of 9th KES International Conference on Intelligent Interactive Multimedia Systems and Services,* 395–403.

Di Maggio, P. J. (1997). Culture and cognition. *Annual Review of Sociology, 23*(1), 263–287. doi:10.1146/annurev.soc.23.1.263

Di Pietro L., Di Virgilio F. & Pantano E. (2013). Negative eWOM in user-generated contents: recommendations for firms and organizations. *International Journal of Digital Content Technology and its Applications, 7*(5), 1-8.

Di Pietro, L., Di Virgilio, F. & Pantano, E (2013). Negative eWOM in user-generated contents: recommendations for firms and organizations. *International Journal of Digital Content Technology and its Applications, 7*(5), 1-8.

Di Pietro, L., Di Virgilio, F., & Pantano, E. (2012). Social network for the choice of tourist destination: Attitude and behavioural intention. *Journal of Hospitality and Tourism Technology, 3*(1), 60–76. doi:10.1108/17579881211206543

Di Virgilio, F., Camillo, A. A., & Camillo, I. (2017). The Impact of Social Network on Italian Users Behavioural Intention for the Choice of a Medical Tourist Destination. *International Journal of Tourism and Hospitality Management in the Digital Age, 1*(1), 36–49. doi:10.4018/IJTHMDA.2017010103

DiGangi, P. M., & Wasko, M. (2016). Social media engagement theory: Exploring the influence of user engagement on social media usage. *Journal of Organizational and End User Computing, 28*(2), 53–73. doi:10.4018/JOEUC.2016040104

Digital, A. (2015b). Digital High Performance Research. *Digital Index Switzerland, 2015*, 2–30.

Dima, A. M. (2013). Knowledge transfer: The innovation side of knowledge management in education. In S. Buckley & M. Jakovljevic (Eds.), *Knowledge management innovations for interdisciplinary education: Organizational applications* (pp. 88–107). Hershey, PA: IGI Global. doi:10.4018/978-1-4666-1969-2.ch005

Dobrev, K., & Hart, M. (2015). Benefits, Justification and Implementation Planning of Real-Time Business Intelligence Systems. *Electronic Journal of Information Systems Evaluation, 18*(2).

Donate, M. J., Guadamillas, F., & Sánchez de Pablo, J. D. (2012). Knowledge management for strategic alliances: A case study. *International Journal of Strategic Information Technology and Applications, 3*(3), 1–19. doi:10.4018/jsita.2012070101

Dörner, K., & Meffert, J. (2015). *Nine questions to help you get your digital transformation right.* McKinsey & Company.

Dou, W., Wang, K., & Ribarsky, W., & Zhou. (2012). Event detection in social media data. In *Proceedings IEEE VisWeek Workshop on Interactive Visual Text Analytics-Task Driven Analytics of Social Media Content,* (pp. 971-980).

Downing, K. F., & Holtz, J. K. (2008). Knowledge transfer and collaboration structures for online science. In K. Downing & J. Holtz (Eds.), *Online science learning: Best practices and technologies* (pp. 98–119). Hershey, PA: IGI Global. doi:10.4018/978-1-59904-986-1.ch006

Doz, Y. & Kosonen, M. (2008). How agile is your strategy process? *Strategy Magazine, 15.*

Dretske, F. (1981). *Knowledge and the Flow of information.* MIT Press.

Driffield, N., Love, J. H., & Yang, Y. (2016). Reverse international knowledge transfer in the MNE: (Where) does affiliate performance boost parent performance? *Research Policy, 45*(2), 491–506. doi:10.1016/j.respol.2015.11.004

Duan, Y., Xu, M., & Feng, W. (2012). Transnational knowledge transfer. In *Organizational learning and knowledge: Concepts, methodologies, tools and applications* (pp. 375–387). Hershey, PA: IGI Global. doi:10.4018/978-1-60960-783-8.ch122

Duggan, M., Ellison, N. B., Lampe, C., Lenhart, A., & Madden, M. (2015). *Social media update 2014.* Pew Research Center. Retrieved from http://www.pewinternet.org/2015/01/09/social-media-update-2014

Dumbrell, D., & Steele, R. (2014). Social Media Technologies for Achieving Knowledge Management Amongst Older Adult Communities. *Procedia: Social and Behavioral Sciences, 147,* 229–236. doi:10.1016/j.sbspro.2014.07.165

Dunnagan, T., Peterson, M., & Haynes, G. (2001). Mental health issues in the workplace: A case for a new managerial approach. *Journal of Occupational and Environmental Medicine, 43*(12), 1073–1080. doi:10.1097/00043764-200112000-00009 PMID:11765678

Dur, S. (2008). *Bilgi yönetimi altyapısı ve bilgi yönetimi sürecinin örgütsel performans üzerindeki etkisi. Yüksek Lisans Tezi (Yayımlanmamış).* Bolu: Abant İzzet Baysal Üniversitesi Sosyal Bilimler Enstitüsü.

Dwivedi, A., McDonald, R. E., & Johnson, L. W. (2014). The impact of a celebrity endorsers credibility on consumer self-brand connection and brand evaluation. *The Journal of Brand Management, 21*(7-8), 559–578. doi:10.1057/bm.2014.37

Easterby-Smith, M., Lyles, M. A., & Tsang, E. W. K. (2008). Inter-organizational knowledge transfer: Current themes and future prospects. *Journal of Management Studies*, *45*(4), 677–690. doi:10.1111/j.1467-6486.2008.00773.x

Eatough, E. M. (2013). *Illegitimate tasks and employee well-being: A daily diary study*. Academic Press.

Edosomwan, S. P. (2011). The history of social media and its impact on business. *Journal of Applied Management and Entrepreneurship, 16*(3), 79-91.

Egele, M., & Stringhini, G. & Vigna, G. (2013). Detecting compromised accounts on social networks. NDSS, The Internet Society.

Eijkman, H. (2011). Dancing with Post Modernity: Web 2.0+ as a New Epistemic Learning Space. IGI Global.

Eistert, T., Deighton, J., Marcu, S., Gordon, F., & Ullrich, M. (2013). *Banking in a Digital World*. AT Kearney.

El Azab, Amira, M., Idrees, A. A., Mahmoud, M. A., & Hefny, H. (2016). Fake Accounts Detection in Twitter based on Minimum Weighted Feature. World Academy of Science, Engineering and Technology. *International Journal of Computer, Electrical, Automation, Control and Information Engineering, 10*(1).

ELFI. (2016). *Servicestelle für Eletronische Forschungsförderinformationen*. Retrieved from www.elfi.info

Ellison, N. B. (2007). Social network sites: Definition, history, and scholarship. *Journal of Computer-Mediated Communication*, *13*(1).

Elsner, W. (1998). An industrial policy agenda 2000 and beyond: Experience, Theory and Policy. In Theory and Policy. Bremen Contributions to Institutional and Social-Economics. Academic Press.

Emerson, R. M., Fretz, R. I., & Shaw, L. L. (2011). *Writing Ethnographic Fieldnotes*. Chicago: The University of Chicago Press. doi:10.7208/chicago/9780226206868.001.0001

Endsley, M. R., & Kiris, E. O. (1995). The out-of-the-loop performance problem and level of control in automation. Human Factors. *The Journal of the Human Factors and Ergonomics Society*, *37*(2), 381–394. doi:10.1518/001872095779064555

Engel, R. J., & Schutt, R. K. (2005). *The practice of research in social work*. Thousand Oaks, CA: Sage Publications.

Eom, S., & Fountain, J. E. (2013). Enhancing information services through public-private partnerships: Information technology knowledge transfer underlying structures to develop shared services in the U.S. and Korea. In J. Gil-Garcia (Ed.), *E-government success around the world: Cases, empirical studies, and practical recommendations* (pp. 15–40). Hershey, PA: IGI Global. doi:10.4018/978-1-4666-4173-0.ch002

Erdogan, B. Z. (1999). Celebrity endorsement: A literature review. *Journal of Marketing Management, 15*(4), 291-314.

Ertimur, B., & Gilly, M. C. (2012). So whaddya think? Consumers create ads and other consumers critique them. *Journal of Interactive Marketing, 26*(3), 115–130. doi:10.1016/j.intmar.2011.10.002

Eskiler, E., Özmen, M., & Uzkurt, C. (2011). Bilgi yönetimi pazar odaklılık ve pazarlama newliği ilişkisi: Mobilya sektöründe bir araştırma. *Eskişehir Osmangazi Üniversitesi İİBF Dergisi, 6*(1), 31–69.

EY. (2014). *Born to be Digital: How leading CIOs are preparing for a digital transformation.* EY.

Fadel, K. J., Durcikova, A., & Cha, H. S. (2011). An experiment of information elaboration in mediated knowledge transfer. In M. Jennex (Ed.), *Global aspects and cultural perspectives on knowledge management: Emerging dimensions* (pp. 311–328). Hershey, PA: IGI Global. doi:10.4018/978-1-60960-555-1.ch019

Färber, F., Weitzel, T., & Keim, T. (2003). An automated recommendation approach to selection in personnel recruitment. *AMCIS 2003 Proceedings*, 302.

Farooq, M., & Farooq, O. (2014). Organizational justice, employee turnover, and trust in the workplace: A study in South Asian telecommunication companies. *Global Business and Organizational Excellence, 33*(3), 56–62. doi:10.1002/joe.21539

Fazel-Zarandi, M., & Fox, M. S. (2009). Semantic matchmaking for job recruitment: an ontology-based hybrid approach. In *Proceedings of the 8th International Semantic Web Conference* (Vol. 525).

Featherman, M. S., & Hajli, N. (2015). Self-service technologies and e-services risks in social commerce era. *Journal of Business Ethics*, 1–19.

Feely, A. J., & Harzing, A.-W. (2003). Language management in multinational companies. *Cross Cultural Management: An International Journal, 10*(2), 37–52. doi:10.1108/13527600310797586

Ferreira, J. B., da Rocha, A., & Ferreira da Silva, J. (2014). Impacts of technology readiness on emotions and cognition in Brazil. *Journal of Business Research, 67*(5), 865–873. doi:10.1016/j.jbusres.2013.07.005

Ferreira, J. J., Fernandes, C., & Raposo, M. L. (2015). Knowledge transfer between universities and knowledge intensive business services: An empirical study. In L. Carmo Farinha, J. Ferreira, H. Smith, & S. Bagchi-Sen (Eds.), *Handbook of research on global competitive advantage through innovation and entrepreneurship* (pp. 320–338). Hershey, PA: IGI Global. doi:10.4018/978-1-4666-8348-8.ch019

Fesenmaier, D., Klein, S., & Buhalis, D. (2000). *Information and Communication Technologies in Tourism*. Vienna: Springer.

Fetters, M. D., Curry, L. A., & Creswell, J. W. (2013). Achieving integration in mixed methods design principles and practices. *Health Services Research, 48*(6.2), 2134-2156.

Finextra. (2016). *Trends in Global Digital Banking Drive Citi's Digital Strategy*. Retrieved from https://www.finextra.com/blogposting/10708/trends-in-global-digital-banking-drive-citis-digital-strategy

Fishbein, M., & Ajzen, I. (1975). *Belief, attitude, intention and Behavior: An introduction to theory and research*. Reading, MA: Addison-Wesley.

Fogues, R., Such, J. M., Espinosa, A., & Garcia-Fornes, A. (2015). Open challenges in relationship-based privacy mechanisms for social network services. *International Journal of Human-Computer Interaction*, *31*(5), 350–370. doi:10.1080/10447318.2014.1001300

Ford, D. P., & Mason, R. M. (2013a). A multilevel perspective of tensions between knowledge management and social media. *Journal of Organizational Computing and Electronic Commerce*, *23*(1–2), 7–33. doi:10.1080/10919392.2013.748604

Ford, D. P., & Mason, R. M. (2013b). Knowledge management and social media: The challenges and benefits. *Journal of Organizational Computing and Electronic Commerce*, *23*(1–2), 1–6. doi:10.1080/10919392.2013.748603

Foss, N. J., Husted, K., & Michailova, S. (2010). Governing Knowledge Sharing in Organizations: Levels of Analysis, Governance Mechanisms, and Research Directions. *Journal of Management Studies*, *47*(3), 455–482. doi:10.1111/j.1467-6486.2009.00870.x

Foss, N. J., Minbaeva, D. B., Pedersen, T., & Reinholt, M. M. (2009). Encouraging knowledge sharing among employees: How job design matters. *Human Resource Management*, *48*(6), 871–893. doi:10.1002/hrm.20320

Fotis, J., Buhalis, D., & Rossides, N. (2012). *Social media use and impact during the holiday travel planning process*. Springer-Verlag. doi:10.1007/978-3-7091-1142-0_2

Frand, J., & Hixon, C. (1999). *Personal knowledge management: who, what, why, when, where, how?* Retrieved from: http://www.anderson.ucla.edu/faculty/jason.frand/researches/speeches/PKM.htm

Freberg, K., Graham, K., McGaughey, K., & Freberg, L. A. (2011). Who are the social media influencers? A study of public perceptions of personality. *Public Relations Review*, *37*(1), 90–92. doi:10.1016/j.pubrev.2010.11.001

Fredriksson, R., Barner-Rasmussen, W., & Piekkari, R. (2006). The multinational corporation as a multilingual organization: The notion of a common corporate language. *Corporate Communications: An International Journal*, *11*(4), 406–423. doi:10.1108/13563280610713879

French, A. M., & Read, A. (2013). My moms on Facebook: An evaluation of information sharing depth in social networking. *Behaviour & Information Technology*, *32*(10), 1049–1059. doi:10.1080/0144929X.2013.816775

Friedland, R., & Alford, R. R. (1991). Bringing society back in: Symbols, practices, and institutional contradictions. In W. Powell & P. J. DiMaggio (Eds.), *The New Institutionalism in Organizational Analysis* (pp. 232–263). Chicago: University of Chicago Press.

Friedrich, R., Merle, M., Gröne, F., & Koster, A. (2011). *Measuring Industry Digitization: Leaders and Laggards in the Digital Economy.* Strategy & Pwc.

Gaál, Z., Szabó, L., & Obermayer-Kovács, N. (2014). Personal knowledge sharing: Web 2.0 role through the lens of Generations. *ECKM 2014 – Conference Proceedings, 15th European Conference on Knowledge Management*, 362-370.

Gaál, Z., Szabó, L., Kovács, Z., Obermayer-Kovács, N., & Csepregi, A. (2008). Knowledge Management Profile Maturity Model. *ECKM 2008 - Conference Proceedings, 9th European Conference on Knowledge Management*, 209-216.

Gaál, Z., Szabó, L., Obermayer-Kovács, N., & Csepregi, A. (2015). Exploring the role of social media in knowledge sharing. *Electronic Journal of Knowledge Management, 13*(3), 185–197.

García, J., Amescua, A., Sánchez, M. I., & Bermón, L. (2011). Design guidelines for software processes knowledge repository development. *Information and Software Technology, 53*(8), 834–850. doi:10.1016/j.infsof.2011.03.002

Gattani, A., Lamba, D. S., Garera, N., Tiwari, M., Chai, X., Das, S., & Doan, A. et al. (2013). Entity Extraction, Linking, Classification, and Tagging for Social Media. A Wikipedia-based Approach. In *Proceedings of the VLDB Endow* (Vol. 6, pp.1126-1137). doi:10.14778/2536222.2536237

Gaynor, M., Seider, H., & Vogt, W. B. (2005). The volume-outcome effect, scale economies, and learning-by-doing. *The American Economic Review, 95*(2), 243–247. doi:10.1257/0002828054577429

Gefen, D. (2002). Reflections on the dimensions of trust and trustworthiness among online consumers. *The Data Base for Advances in Information Systems, 33*(3), 38–53. doi:10.1145/569905.569910

Gefen, D., Karahanna, E., & Straub, D. W. (2003). Trust and TAM in online shopping: An integrated model. *Management Information Systems Quarterly, 27*(1), 51–90.

Gefen, D., & Straub, D. (2000). The relative importance of perceived ease of use in IS adoption: A study of E-commerce adoption. *Journal of the Association for Information Systems, 1*, 1–30.

Gefen, D., & Straub, D. W. (2004). Consumer trust in B2C e-commerce and the importance of social presence: Experiments in e-products and e-services. *Omega, 32*(6), 407–424. doi:10.1016/j.omega.2004.01.006

Gentile, A. L., Lanfranchi, V., Mazumdar, S., & Ciravegna, F. (2011). Extracting semantic user networks from informal communication exchanges. In The Semantic Web–ISWC, (pp. 209-224).

Geyer, F., & Reiterer, H. (2012). Experiences from employing evernote as a tool for documenting collaborative design processes. Proceeding of the DIS'12 workshop on Supporting Reflection in and on Design Processes.

Gherardi, S., Nicolini, D., & Odella, F. (1998). Toward a social understanding of how people learn in organizations: The notion of situated curriculum. *Management Learning, 29*(3), 273–297. doi:10.1177/1350507698293002

Giddens, A. (1990). *The Consequences of Modernity*. Cambridge, UK: Polity.

Gil, A. J., & Mataveli, M. (2016). The knowledge transfer process on the development of dynamic capabilities through industrial networks. In G. Alor-Hernández, C. Sánchez-Ramírez, & J. García-Alcaraz (Eds.), *Handbook of research on managerial strategies for achieving optimal performance in industrial processes* (pp. 562–586). Hershey, PA: IGI Global. doi:10.4018/978-1-5225-0130-5.ch026

Gillin, P., & Moore, G. A. (2009). *The new influencers: A marketer's guide to the new social media*. Linden Publishing.

Giuffrida, R., & Dittrich, Y. (2013). Empirical studies on the use of social software in global software development - A systematic mapping study. *Information and Software Technology, 55*(7), 1143–1164. doi:10.1016/j.infsof.2013.01.004

Glaser, B. G., & Strauss, A. L. (1967). *The discovery of grounded theory*. Chicago, IL: Aldine Pub. Co.

Glisson, C., & Durick, M. (1988). Predictors of job satisfaction and organizational commitment in human service organizations. *Administrative Science Quarterly, 33*(1), 61–81. doi:10.2307/2392855

Gloet, M. (2006). Knowledge management and the links to HRM. *Management Research News, 29*(7), 402–413. doi:10.1108/01409170610690862

Gloet, M., & Terziovski, M. (2004). Exploring the relationship between knowledge management practices and innovation performance. *Journal of Manufacturing Technology Management, 15*(5), 402–409. doi:10.1108/17410380410540390

Goh, S. K., & Sandhu, M. S. (2013). Knowledge sharing among Malaysian academics: Influence of affective commitment and trust. *Electronic Journal of Knowledge Management, 11*(1), 38–48.

Golbeck, J. A. (2005). *Computing and applying trust in Web-based social networks* (Unpublished Doctoral Dissertation). University of Maryland. Retrieved from http://trust.mindswap.org/papers/GolbeckDissertation.pd

Goodman, P. S., & Darr, E. D. (1998). Computer-aided systems and communities: Mechanisms for organizational learning in distributed environment. *Management Information Systems Quarterly, 22*(4), 417–440. doi:10.2307/249550

Gorela, K., & Biloslavo, R. (2015). Relationship between senior and junior researcher: Challenges and opportunities for knowledge creating and sharing. In P. Diviacco, P. Fox, C. Pshenichny, & A. Leadbetter (Eds.), *Collaborative knowledge in scientific research networks* (pp. 90–125). Hershey, PA: IGI Global. doi:10.4018/978-1-4666-6567-5.ch006

Gottschalk, P. (2007). *CIO and corporate strategic management: changing role of CIO to CEO.* Hershey, PA: Idea Group Publication. doi:10.4018/978-1-59904-423-1

Graham, I. D., Logan, J., Harrison, M. B., Straus, S. E., Tetroe, J., Caswell, W., & Robinson, N. (2006). Lost in knowledge translation: Time for a map? *The Journal of Continuing Education in the Health Professions, 26*(1), 13–24. doi:10.1002/chp.47 PMID:16557505

Grant, R. M. (1996). Prospering in dynamically-competitive environments: Organizational capability as knowledge integration. *Organization Science, 7*(4), 375–387. doi:10.1287/orsc.7.4.375

Grant, R. M. (1996). Toward a Knowledge-Based Theory of the Firm. *Strategic Management Journal, 17*(2), 109–122. doi:10.1002/smj.4250171110

Greenwood, R., Raynard, M., Kodeih, F., Micelotta, E. R., & Lounsbury, M. (2011). Institutional Complexity and Organizational Responses. *The Academy of Management Annals, 5*(1), 317–371. doi:10.1080/19416520.2011.590299

Grizelj, F. (2003). Collaborative knowledge management in virtual service companies-approach for tourism destinations. *Tourism, 51*(4), 371–385.

Groth, K. (2013). *Using Social Networks for Knowledge Management.* Stockholm, Sweden: Royal Institute of Technology.

Grover, V., & Davenport, T. (2001). General Perspectives on Knowledge Management: Fostering a Research Agenda. *Journal of Management Information Systems, 18*(1), 5–22.

Grover, V., & Kohli, R. (2013). Revealing Your Hand: Caveats In Implementing Digital Business Strategy. *Management Information Systems Quarterly, 37*(2), 655–662.

Gruenfeld, D. H., Mannix, E. A., Williams, K. Y., & Neale, M. A. (1996). Group composition and decision making: How member familiarity and information distribution affects process and performance. *Organizational Behavior and Human Decision Processes, 67*(1), 1–15. doi:10.1006/obhd.1996.0061

GSM Association. (2015). *The mobile economy.* Retrieved October 1, 2016, from http://www.gsmamobileeconomy.com/GSMA_Global_Mobile_Economy_Report_2015.pdf

Gudykunst, W. B. (1995). Anxiety/Uncertainty Management (AUM) Theory: Current Status. In *Intercultural Communication Theory.* Sage.

Guerar, M., Migliardi, M., & Merlo, A. (2016). Using screen brightness to improve security in mobile social network access, IEEE Trans. *Dependable Secure Computer, 99*, 1545–5971.

Gülseçen, S. (2013). *Bilgi ve bilginin yönetimi.* İstanbul: Papatya Yayıncılık Eğitim.

Gupta, A., & Govindarajan, V. (2000). Knowledge flows within multinational corporations. *Strategic Management Journal, 21*(4), 473–496. doi:10.1002/(SICI)1097-0266(200004)21:4<473::AID-SMJ84>3.0.CO;2-I

Gurbaxani, V., & Whang, S. (1991). The impact of information systems on organizations and markets. *Communications of the ACM, 34*(1), 59–73. doi:10.1145/99977.99990

Gyamfi, A. (2016). The impact of media richness on the usage of Web 2.0 services for knowledge transfer. *International Journal of E-Services and Mobile Applications, 8*(2), 21–37. doi:10.4018/IJESMA.2016040102

Haas, M. R., & Hansen, M. T. (2007). Different knowledge, different benefits: Toward a productivity perspective on knowledge sharing in organizations. *Strategic Management Journal, 28*(11), 1133–1153. doi:10.1002/smj.631

Hackman, J. R., & Oldham, G. R. (1976). Motivation through the design of work: Test of a theory. *Organizational Behavior and Human Performance, 16*(2), 250–279. doi:10.1016/0030-5073(76)90016-7

Haghirian, P. (2006). International knowledge transfer as a challenge for communities of practice. In E. Coakes & S. Clarke (Eds.), *Encyclopedia of communities of practice in information and knowledge management* (pp. 234–238). Hershey, PA: IGI Global. doi:10.4018/978-1-59140-556-6.ch042

Haghirian, P. (2009). Knowledge transfer within multinational corporations: An intercultural challenge. In J. Girard (Ed.), *Building organizational memories: Will you know what you knew?* (pp. 57–68). Hershey, PA: IGI Global. doi:10.4018/978-1-59904-540-5.ch005

Hajli, N. (2015). *Handbook of Research on Integrating Social Media into Strategic Marketing.* IGI Global. doi:10.4018/978-1-4666-8353-2

Hajli, N. et al.. (2016). A social commerce investigation of the role of trust in a social networking site on purchase intentions. *Journal of Business Research.* doi:10.1016/j.jbusres.2016.10.004

Hakami, Y., Tam, S., Busalim, A. H., & Husin, A. R. C. (2014). A review of factors affecting the sharing of knowledge in social media. *Science International, 26*(2), 679–688.

Hall, B., & Khan, B. (2003). Adoption of new technology. In J., Derek C.(Ed.), New Economy Handbook. Academic Press. doi:10.3386/w9730

Hallin, C. A., & Marnburg, E. (2008). Knowledge management in the hospitality industry: A review of empirical research. *Tourism Management, 29*(2), 366–381. doi:10.1016/j.tourman.2007.02.019

Halpern, D. F. (2005). How time flexible work policies can reduce stress, improve health, and save money. *Stress and Health, 21*(3), 157–168. doi:10.1002/smi.1049

Hamasaki, M., Mtsuo, Y., Ishida, K., Hope, T., Nishimura, T., & Takeda, H. (2006). An integrated method for social network extraction. In *Proceedings of the 15th international conference on World Wide Web* (pp. 845-846).

Hansen, M. T., Nohria, N. & Tierney, T. (1999, March). What is your strategy for managing knowledge. *Harvard Business Review,* 106-116.

Harorimana, D. (2012). Knowledge, culture, and cultural impact on knowledge management: Some lessons for researchers and practitioners. In *Organizational learning and knowledge: Concepts, methodologies, tools and applications* (pp. 2474–2485). Hershey, PA: IGI Global. doi:10.4018/978-1-60960-783-8.ch701

Harper, F., Moy, D., & Konstan, J. (2009). Facts or friends?: distinguishing informational and conversational questions in social qasites. In *Proceedings of the 27th International conference on Human factors in computing systems*, (pp. 759–768). doi:10.1145/1518701.1518819

Harrysson, M., Schoder, D., & Tavakoli, A. (2016). *The evolution of social technologies.* McKinsey Quarterly Survey. Retrieved from http://www.mckinsey.com/industries/high-tech/our-insights/the-evolution-of-social-technologies

Harrysson, M., Metayer, E., & Sarrazin, H. (2012). How "social intelligence" can guide decisions. *The McKinsey Quarterly*, *4*, 81–89.

Harzing, A.-W., Köster, K., & Magner, U. (2011). Babel in business: The language barrier and its solutions in the HQ-subsidiary relationship. *Journal of World Business*, *46*(3), 279–287. doi:10.1016/j.jwb.2010.07.005

Harzing, A.-W., & Pudelko, M. (2013). Language competencies, policies and practices in multinational corporations: A comprehensive review and comparison of Anglophone, Asian, Continental European and Nordic MNCs. *Journal of World Business*, *18*(1), 87 97. doi:10.1016/j.jwb.2012.06.011

Hasnain, S. S., Jasimuddin, S. M., & Fuller-Love, N. (2016). Exploring causes, taxonomies, mechanisms and barriers influencing knowledge transfer: Empirical studies in NGOs. *Information Resources Management Journal*, *29*(1), 39–56. doi:10.4018/IRMJ.2016010103

Hassan, H. A., Dahab, M. Y., Bahnassy, K., Idrees, A. M., & Gamal, F. (2014). Query Answering Approach Based on Document Summarization. *International OPEN ACCESS Journal Of Modern Engineering Research, 4*(12).

Hassandoust, F., & Perumal, V. (2011). Online knowledge sharing in institutes of higher learning: A Malaysian perspective. *Journal of Knowledge Management Practice, 12*(1). Retrieved October 1, 2016, from http://www.tlainc.com/articl247.htm

Hassan, H., Dahab, M., Bahnassy, K., Idrees, A., & Gamal, F. (2015). Arabic Documents classification method a Step towards Efficient Documents Summarization. *International Journal on Recent and Innovation Trends in Computing and Communication, 3*(1), 351–359. doi:10.17762/ijritcc2321-8169.150171

Hatak, I., & Roessl, D. (2014). Knowledge transfer strategies within family firm succession. In K. Todorov & D. Smallbone (Eds.), *Handbook of research on strategic management in small and medium enterprises* (pp. 266–281). Hershey, PA: IGI Global. doi:10.4018/978-1-4666-5962-9.ch013

Hau, Y. S., Kim, B., Lee, H., & Kim, Y. G. (2013). The effects of individual motivations and social capital on employees tacit and explicit knowledge sharing intentions. *International Journal of Information Management*, *33*(2), 356–366. doi:10.1016/j.ijinfomgt.2012.10.009

Hays, S., Page, S. J., & Buhalis, D. (2013). Social media as a destination marketing tool: Its use by national tourism organisations. *Current Issues in Tourism*, *16*(3), 211–239. doi:10.1080/13 683500.2012.662215

Heider, F. (2013). *The psychology of interpersonal relations*. Psychology Press.

Heinonen, K., & Strandvik, T. (2015). Customer-dominant logic: Foundations and implications. *Journal of Services Marketing*, *29*(6/7), 472–484. doi:10.1108/JSM-02-2015-0096

Heinonen, K., Strandvik, T., Mickelsson, K. J., Edvardsson, B., Sundström, E., & Andersson, P. (2010). A customer-dominant logic of service. *Journal of Service Management*, *21*(4), 531–548. doi:10.1108/09564231011066088

He, J., & Chu, W. W. (2010). *A social network-based recommender system* (pp. 47–74). Springer, US.

Hemsley, J., & Mason, R. (2013). Knowledge and knowledge management in the social media age. *Journal of Organizational Computing and Electronic Commerce*, *23*(1-2), 138–167. doi:1 0.1080/10919392.2013.748614

Hemsley, J., & Mason, R. M. (2011). The nature of knowledge in the social media age: Implications for knowledge management models. *Proceedings of the Annual Hawaii International Conference on System Sciences*, 3928–3937.

Henry, L. E., & Lee, D. (2009). Transferring knowledge in a knowledge-based economy. In T. Torres-Coronas & M. Arias-Oliva (Eds.), *Encyclopedia of human resources information systems: Challenges in e-HRM* (pp. 862–870). Hershey, PA: IGI Global. doi:10.4018/978-1-59904-883-3. ch127

Henry, R., & Venkatraman, S. (2015). Big Data Analytics the Next Big Learning Opportunity. *Journal of Management Information and Decision Sciences*, *18*(2), 17.

Herschel, R. T., & Yermish, I. (2009). Knowledge transfer: Revisiting video. In N. Kock (Ed.), *E-collaboration: Concepts, methodologies, tools, and applications* (pp. 151–163). Hershey, PA: IGI Global. doi:10.4018/978-1-60566-652-5.ch013

Hinkelbein, O. (2014). *Digitale Integration von Migranten? Ethnographische Fallstudien zur digitalen Spaltung in Deutschland*. Bielefeld: Transcript Verlag.

Hislop, D. (2013). *Knowledge management in organisations: A critical introduction*. Oxford, UK: Oxford University Press.

Hobbs, J. R., & Riloff, E. (2010). Information extraction. In Handbook of natural language processing. In N. Indurkhya & F. Damerau (Eds.), *Handbook of Natural Language Processing* (pp. 511–532). CRC Press.

Hofer, F. (2008). Knowledge transfer between academia and industry. In M. Jennex (Ed.), *Knowledge management: Concepts, methodologies, tools, and applications* (pp. 3086–3095). Hershey, PA: IGI Global. doi:10.4018/978-1-59904-933-5.ch252

Hohpe, G., & Woolf, B. (2004). *Enterprise integration patterns: Designing, building, and deploying messaging solutions*. Addison-Wesley Professional.

Hollebeek, L. D., Glynn, M. S., & Brodie, R. J. (2014). Consumer brand engagement in social media: Conceptualization, scale development and validation. *Journal of Interactive Marketing*, *28*(2), 149–165. doi:10.1016/j.intmar.2013.12.002

Holtgrewe, U. (2014). New new technologies: The future and the present of work in information and communication technology. *New Technology, Work and Employment*, *29*(1), 9–24. doi:10.1111/ntwe.12025

Holtom, B. C., Mitchell, T. R., Lee, T. W., & Eberly, M. B. (2008). 5 turnover and retention research: A glance at the past, a closer review of the present, and a venture into the future. *The Academy of Management Annals*, *2*(1), 231–274. doi:10.1080/19416520802211552

Hom, P. W., Caranikas-Walker, F., Prussia, G. E., & Griffeth, R. W. (1992). A meta-analytical structural equations analysis of a model of employee turnover. *The Journal of Applied Psychology*, *77*(6), 890–909. doi:10.1037/0021-9010.77.6.890

Hox, J. J., & Boeije, H. R. (2005). Data collection, primary vs. secondary. Encyclopedia of Social Measurement, *1*(1), 593-599.

Hsu, H. (2009). Managing the information technology: Knowledge transfer in virtual teams. In M. Lytras & P. Ordóñez de Pablos (Eds.), *Knowledge ecology in global business: Managing intellectual capital* (pp. 192–210). Hershey, PA: IGI Global. doi:10.4018/978-1-60566-270-1.ch012

Hsu, M., Ju, T. L., Yen, C., & Chang, C. (2007). Knowledge sharing behavior in virtual communities: The relationship between trust, self-efficacy, and outcome expecta- tions. *International Journal of Human-Computer Studies*, *65*(2), 153–169. doi:10.1016/j.ijhcs.2006.09.003

Hu, X., & Liu, H. (2012). Text analytics in social media. In C. C. Aggarwal & C. Zhai (Eds.), Mining Text Data (pp. 385-414). doi:10.1007/978-1-4614-3223-4_12

Hu, Y., Manikonda, L., & Kambhampati, S. (2014). What we instagram: A first analysis of instagram photo content and user types. In *Proceedings of the 8th International Conference on Weblogs and Social Media, ICWSM 2014* (pp. 595-598). The AAAI Press.

Huang, C. M., Chang, H. C., & Henderson, S. (2008). Knowledge transfer barriers between research and development and marketing groups within Taiwanese small- and medium-sized enterprise high-technology new product development teams. *Human Factors and Ergonomics in Manufacturing & Service Industries*, *18*(6), 621–657. doi:10.1002/hfm.20130

Huber, G. (1991). Organizational Learning: The Contributing Processes and the Literatures. *Organization Science*, *2*(1), 88–115. doi:10.1287/orsc.2.1.88

Huizingh, E. (2011). Open innovation: State of the art and future perspectives. *Technovation, 31*(1), 2–9. doi:10.1016/j.technovation.2010.10.002

Huong, N. T., Katsuhiro, U., & Chi, D. H. (2013). Knowledge transfer in offshore outsourcing: A case study of Japanese and Vietnamese software companies. In F. Tan (Ed.), *Global diffusion and adoption of technologies for knowledge and information sharing* (pp. 110–128). Hershey, PA: IGI Global. doi:10.4018/978-1-4666-2142-8.ch005

Hu, X., Tang, L., Tang, J., & Liu, H. (2013). Exploiting social relations for sentiment analysis in microblogging. In *Proceedings of the sixth ACM international conference on Web search and data mining,* (pp. 537-546). doi:10.1145/2433396.2433465

Huzita, E. H. M., Leal, G. C. L., Balancieri, R., Tait, T. F. C., Cardoza, E., Penteado, R. R. D. M., & Vivian, R. L. (2012). Knowledge and contextual information management in global software development: challenges and perspectives. In *2012 IEEE Seventh International Conference on Global Software Engineering Workshops* (pp. 43–48). IEEE. doi:10.1109/ICGSEW.2012.12

Hyman, P. (2012). In the year of disruptive education. *Communications of the ACM, 55*(12), 20–22. doi:10.1145/2380656.2380664

Iacono, M. P., De Nito, E., Esposito, V., Martinez, M., & Moschera, L. (2014). Investigating the relationship between coordination mechanisms and knowledge in a wine firm. *Knowledge and Process Management, 21*(4), 280–291. doi:10.1002/kpm.1436

Ibrahim, R. Z. A. R. (2012). *Psychosocial work environment, organisational justice and work family conflict as predictors of Malaysian worker wellbeing.* Melbourne, Australia: Victoria University.

Ingram, P., & Roberts, P. W. (2000). Friendships among competitors in the Sydney Hotel Industry1. *American Journal of Sociology, 106*(2), 387–423. doi:10.1086/316965

Inkinen, H. (2016). Review of empirical research on knowledge management practices and firm performance. *Journal of Knowledge Management, 20*(2), 230–257. doi:10.1108/JKM-09-2015-0336

Inkpen, A., & Tsang, E. (2005). Social capital, networks, and knowledge transfer. *Academy of Management Review, 30*(1), 146–165. doi:10.5465/AMR.2005.15281445

Ion, P., & Andreea, Z. (2008). Use of ICT in SMES management within the sector of services. *Faculty of Economics, 4*(1), 481–487.

Ip, C., Lee, H., & Law, R. (2010). Profiling the users of travel websites for planning and online experience sharing. *Journal of Hospitality & Tourism Research (Washington, D.C.), 36*(3), 418–426. doi:10.1177/1096348010388663

Ipe, M. (2003). Knowledge sharing in organizations: A conceptual framework. *Human Resource Development Review, 2*(4), 337–359. doi:10.1177/1534484303257985

Ismail, K. M. (2012). Theorizing on the role of individualism-collectivism in tacit knowledge transfer between agents in international alliances. *International Journal of Knowledge Management, 8*(1), 71–85. doi:10.4018/jkm.2012010104

Jablin, F. M. (1987). Organizational entry, assimilation, and exit. In F. M. Jablin, L. L. Putnam, K. H. Roberts, & L. W. Porter (Eds.), *Handbook Organizational and communication* (pp. 389–419). Newbury Park, CA: Sage.

Jackall, R. (1988). *Moral Mazes: The World of Corporate Managers.* New York: Oxford University Press.

Jacobsen, J. K. S., & Munar, A. M. (2012). Tourist information search and destination choice in a digital age. *Tourism Management Perspectives, 1*, 39–47. doi:10.1016/j.tmp.2011.12.005

Jacobs, J. (1961). *The Death and Life of Great American Cities.* New York: Penguin Books.

Jain, R., & Purohit, D. (2011). Page ranking algorithms for web mining. *International Journal of Computer Applications, 13*(5).

Jain, P. (2011). Personal knowledge management: The foundation of organisational knowledge management. *South African Journal of Library and Information Science, 77*(1), 1–14. doi:10.7553/77-1-62

Jakubik, M. (2008). Experiencing collaborative knowledge creation processes. *The Learning Organization, 15*(1), 5–25. doi:10.1108/09696470810842475

Jalonen, H. (2014). Social media and emotions in organisational knowledge creation. *Conference Proceedings, Federated Conference on Computer Science and Information Systems*, 1371–1379. doi:10.15439/2014F39

Jamhawi, M. M., & Hajahjah, Z. A. (2016). It-Innovation and Technologies Transfer to Heritage Sites: The Case of Madaba, Jordan. *Mediterranean Archaeology and Archaeometry, 16*(2), 41–46.

Jasimuddin, S. M., & Zhang, Z. (2014). Knowledge management strategy and organizational culture. *The Journal of the Operational Research Society, 65*(10), 1490–1500. doi:10.1057/jors.2013.101

Jennex, M. E. (2008). *Knowledge Management: Concepts, Methodologies, Tools, and Applications.* Hershey, PA: IGI Global. doi:10.4018/978-1-59904-933-5

Jessop, B. (2017). Varieties of academic capitalism and entrepreneurial universities: On past research and three thought experiments. *Higher Education*, 1–18.

Jex, S. (2002). *Organizational Psychology: A Scientist-Practitioner Approach.* New York: John Wiley & Sons.

Jiang, C., Zhao, W., Sun, X., Zhang, K., Zheng, R., & Qu, W. (2016). The effects of the self and social identity on the intention to microblog: An extension of the theory of planned behavior. *Computers in Human Behavior, 64*, 754–759. doi:10.1016/j.chb.2016.07.046

Ji, F. X., & Connerley, M. L. (2013). Local embeddedness and expatriates' effectiveness for knowledge transfer within MNCs: A cultural perspective. In B. Christiansen, E. Turkina, & N. Williams (Eds.), *Cultural and technological influences on global business* (pp. 420–436). Hershey, PA: IGI Global. doi:10.4018/978-1-4666-3966-9.ch022

Johansson, A. (2015, May 12). *The 15 Best Freelance Websites to Find Jobs*. Retrieved from https://www.entrepreneur.com/article/245953

Jones, M. B. (1974). Regressing group on individual effectiveness. *Organizational Behavior and Human Performance*, *11*(3), 426–451. doi:10.1016/0030-5073(74)90030-0

Jones, M. K., Latreille, P. L., & Sloane, P. J. (2011). *Job anxiety, work-related psychological illness and workplace performance*. NILS, Flinders University and IZA.

Jones, N. B. (2016). Knowledge transfer and knowledge creation in virtual teams. In C. Graham (Ed.), *Strategic management and leadership for systems development in virtual spaces* (pp. 110–122). Hershey, PA: IGI Global. doi:10.4018/978-1-4666-9688-4.ch007

Joshi, P., & Kuo, C. C. (2011). Security and privacy in online social networks: A survey. *Proceedings of IEEE International Conference on Multimedia and Expo*. doi:10.1109/ICME.2011.6012166

Junni, P. (2011). Knowledge transfer in acquisitions: Fear of exploitation and contamination. *Scandinavian Journal of Management*, *27*(3), 307–321. doi:10.1016/j.scaman.2011.05.003

Junni, P., & Sarala, R. M. (2012). The role of cultural learning and collective teaching initiatives in M&A knowledge transfer. *European Journal of Cross-Cultural Competence and Management*, *2*(3/4), 275–298. doi:10.1504/EJCCM.2012.052593

Kahill, S. (1988). Symptoms of professional burnout: A review of the empirical evidence. *Canadian Psychology*, *29*(3), 284–297. doi:10.1037/h0079772

Kahle, L. R., & Homer, P. M. (1985). Physical Attractiveness of the Celebrity Endorser: A Social Adaptation Perspective. *The Journal of Consumer Research*, *11*(4), 954–961. doi:10.1086/209029

Kaiser, S., & Müller-Seitz, G. (2008). Leveraging lead user knowledge in software development: The case of weblog technology. *Industry and Innovation*, *15*(2), 199–221. doi:10.1080/13662710801954542

Kakabadse, N. K., Kakabadse, A., & Kouzmin, A. (2003). Reviewing the knowledge management literature: Towards a taxonomy. *Journal of Knowledge Management*, *7*(4), 75–91. doi:10.1108/13673270310492967

Kalkan, V. D. (2008). An overall view of knowledge management challenges for global business. *Business Process Management Journal*, *14*(3), 390–400. doi:10.1108/14637150810876689

Kamel, S. (2005). The Use of Information Technology to Transform the Banking Sector In Developing Nations: Editorial Introduction. *Information Technology for Development*, *11*(4), 305–312. doi:10.1002/itdj.20023

Kane, G. C. (2015). Enterprise social media: Current capabilities and future possibilities. *MIS Quarterly Executive, 14*(1), 1–16.

Kane, G. C., Labianca, G., & Borgatti, S. P. (2014). What's different about social media networks? A framework and research agenda. *Management Information Systems Quarterly, X*(X), 1–30.

Kang, J., Rhee, M., & Kang, K. H. (2010). Revisiting knowledge transfer: Effects of knowledge characteristics on organizational effort for knowledge transfer. *Expert Systems with Applications, 37*(12), 8155–8160. doi:10.1016/j.eswa.2010.05.072

Kang, M., & Schuett, M. A. (2013). Determinants of sharing travel experiences in social media. *Journal of Travel & Tourism Marketing, 30*(1-2), 93–107. doi:10.1080/10548408.2013.751237

Kaplan, A. M., & Haenlein, M. (2009). Consumers, companies, and virtual social worlds: A qualitative analysis of Second Life. *Advances in Consumer Research. Association for Consumer Research (U. S.), 36*(1), 873–874.

Kaplan, A. M., & Haenlein, M. (2010). Users of the world, unite! The challenges and opportunities of social media. *Business Horizons, 53*(1), 59–68. doi:10.1016/j.bushor.2009.09.003

Karakoçak, K. (2007). *Bilgi yönetimi ve verimliliğe etkisi: Türkiye Büyük Millet Meclisi uygulaması. Doktora Tezi (Yayımlanmamış)*. Ankara: Ankara Üniversitesi Sosyal Bilimler Enstitüsü İşletme Anabilim Dalı.

Kasemsap, K. (2014a). Constructing a unified framework and a causal model of occupational satisfaction, trainee reactions, perception of learning, and perceived training transfer. In S. Hai-Jew (Ed.), *Remote workforce training: Effective technologies and strategies* (pp. 28–52). Hershey, PA: IGI Global. doi:10.4018/978-1-4666-5137-1.ch003

Kasemsap, K. (2014b). The role of social capital in higher education institutions. In N. Baporikar (Ed.), *Handbook of research on higher education in the MENA region: Policy and practice* (pp. 119–147). Hershey, PA: IGI Global. doi:10.4018/978-1-4666-6198-1.ch007

Kasemsap, K. (2015). Implementing enterprise resource planning. In M. Khosrow-Pour (Ed.), *Encyclopedia of information science and technology* (3rd ed., pp. 798–807). Hershey, PA: IGI Global. doi:10.4018/978-1-4666-5888-2.ch076

Kasemsap, K. (2016a). Advocating entrepreneurship education and knowledge management in global business. In N. Baporikar (Ed.), *Handbook of research on entrepreneurship in the contemporary knowledge-based global economy* (pp. 313–339). Hershey, PA: IGI Global. doi:10.4018/978-1-4666-8798-1.ch014

Kasemsap, K. (2016b). Creating product innovation strategies through knowledge management in global business. In A. Goel & P. Singhal (Eds.), *Product innovation through knowledge management and social media strategies* (pp. 330–357). Hershey, PA: IGI Global. doi:10.4018/978-1-4666-9607-5.ch015

Kasemsap, K. (2016c). Examining the roles of virtual team and information technology in global business. In C. Graham (Ed.), *Strategic management and leadership for systems development in virtual spaces* (pp. 1–21). Hershey, PA: IGI Global. doi:10.4018/978-1-4666-9688-4.ch001

Kasemsap, K. (2016d). Utilizing communities of practice to facilitate knowledge sharing in the digital age. In S. Buckley, G. Majewski, & A. Giannakopoulos (Eds.), *Organizational knowledge facilitation through communities of practice in emerging markets* (pp. 198–224). Hershey, PA: IGI Global. doi:10.4018/978-1-5225-0013-1.ch011

Kasemsap, K. (2017a). Mastering knowledge management in academic libraries. In B. Gunjal (Ed.), *Managing knowledge and scholarly assets in academic libraries* (pp. 27–55). Hershey, PA: IGI Global. doi:10.4018/978-1-5225-1741-2.ch002

Kasemsap, K. (2017b). The fundamentals of social capital. In G. Koç, M. Claes, & B. Christiansen (Eds.), *Cultural influences on architecture* (pp. 259–292). Hershey, PA: IGI Global. doi:10.4018/978-1-5225-1744-3.ch010

Kasemsap, K. (2017c). Mastering educational computer games, educational video games, and serious games in the digital age. In R. Alexandre Peixoto de Queirós & M. Pinto (Eds.), *Gamification-based e-learning strategies for computer programming education* (pp. 30–52). Hershey, PA: IGI Global. doi:10.4018/978-1-5225-1034-5.ch003

Kasemsap, K. (2017d). Investigating the roles of neuroscience and knowledge management in higher education. In S. Mukerji & P. Tripathi (Eds.), *Handbook of research on administration, policy, and leadership in higher education* (pp. 112–140). Hershey, PA: IGI Global. doi:10.4018/978-1-5225-0672-0.ch006

Kasemsap, K. (2017e). Fundamentals of talent management: Capitalizing on intellectual assets. In M. Mupepi (Ed.), *Effective talent management strategies for organizational success* (pp. 260–282). Hershey, PA: IGI Global. doi:10.4018/978-1-5225-1961-4.ch017

Kasemsap, K. (2017f). Career management in the knowledge-based organizations. *International Journal of Knowledge-Based Organizations*, *7*(2), 60–73. doi:10.4018/IJKBO.2017040105

Katz, E., & Lazarsfeld, P. F. (1955). *Personal Influence: The Part of Played by People in The Flow of Mass Communications*. Free Press.

Keim, T. (2007, January). Extending the applicability of recommender systems: A multilayer framework for matching human resources. In *System Sciences, 2007. HICSS 2007. 40th Annual Hawaii International Conference on* (pp. 169-169). IEEE. doi:10.1109/HICSS.2007.223

Keller, K. L., & Staelin, R. (1987). Effects of Quality and Quantity of Information and Decision Effectiveness. *The Journal of Consumer Research*, *14*(2), 200–213. doi:10.1086/209106

Kennedy, J. L. (1971). The system approach: A preliminary exploratory study of the relation between team composition and financial performance in business games. *The Journal of Applied Psychology*, *55*(1), 46–49. doi:10.1037/h0030599

Khalil, O. E., & Seleim, A. (2012). Culture and knowledge transfer capacity: A cross-national study. In M. Jennex (Ed.), *Conceptual models and outcomes of advancing knowledge management: New technologies* (pp. 305–332). Hershey, PA: IGI Global. doi:10.4018/978-1-4666-0035-5.ch016

Khan, N., & Sikes, J. (2014). *IT under pressure: McKinsey Global Survey results*. McKinsey & Company.

Khatri, N., Budhwar, P., & Fern, C. (1999). *Employee turnover: bad attitude or poor management*. Singapore: Nanyang Technological University.

Kim, A. J., & Ko, E. (2012). Do social media marketing activities enhance customer equity? An empirical study of luxury fashion brand. *Journal of Business Research*, *65*(10), 1480–1486. doi:10.1016/j.jbusres.2011.10.014

Kim, E., Lee, J. A., Sung, Y., & Choi, S. M. (2016). Predicting selfie-posting behavior on social networking sites: An extension of theory of planned behavior. *Computers in Human Behavior*, *62*, 116–123. doi:10.1016/j.chb.2016.03.078

Kim, J., & Marschke, G. (2005). Labor mobility of scientists, technological diffusion, and the firm's patenting decision. *The Rand Journal of Economics*, *36*(2), 298–317.

Kim, S., & Ju, B. (2008). An analysis of faculty perceptions: Attitudes toward knowledge sharing and collaboration in an academic institution. *Library & Information Science Research*, *30*(4), 282–290. doi:10.1016/j.lisr.2008.04.003

Kim, S., & Park, H. (2013). Effects of various characteristics of social commerce (s-commerce) on consumers trust and trust performance. *International Journal of Information Management*, *33*(2), 318–332. doi:10.1016/j.ijinfomgt.2012.11.006

Kindred, J., & Petrescu, C. (2015). Expectations versus reality in a university–community partnership: A case study. *Voluntary International Journal of Voluntary Nonprofit Organizations*, *26*(3), 823–845. doi:10.1007/s11266-014-9471-0

King, W. R. (2009). Knowledge management and organization learning: Annals of knowledge system (4th ed.). Springer. doi:10.1007/978-1-4419-0011-1

King, W. R. (2009). Knowledge management and organizational learning. In W. R. King (Ed.), *Knowledge Management and Organizational Learning* (pp. 3-13). Annals of Information Systems.

King, R. A., Racherla, P., & Bush, V. D. (2014). What we know and dont know about online word-of-mouth: A review and synthesis of the literature. *Journal of Interactive Marketing*, *28*(3), 167–183. doi:10.1016/j.intmar.2014.02.001

King, W. R. (2008). Knowledge transfer. In M. Jennex (Ed.), *Knowledge management: Concepts, methodologies, tools, and applications* (pp. 123–129). Hershey, PA: IGI Global. doi:10.4018/978-1-59904-933-5.ch010

Kirlik, A. (1993). Modeling strategic behavior in human-automation interaction: Why an" aid" can (and should) go unused. *Human Factors: The Journal of the Human Factors and Ergonomics Society, 35*(2), 221–242. PMID:8349287

Klassen, R. M., & Chiu, M. M. (2010). Effects on teachers self-efficacy and job satisfaction: Teacher gender, years of experience, and job stress. *Journal of Educational Psychology, 102*(3), 741–756. doi:10.1037/a0019237

Kleina, A., Ahlfb, H., & Sharmac, V. (2015). Social activity and structural centrality in online social networks. *Telematics and Informatics, 32*(2), 321–332. doi:10.1016/j.tele.2014.09.008

Kloke, K., & Krücken, G. (2010). Grenzstellungsmanager zwischen Wissenschaft und Wirtschaft? Eine Studie zu Mitarbeiterinnen und Mitarbeitern in Einrichtungen des Technologietransfers und der wissenschaftlichen Weiterbildung. In Beiträge zur Hochschulforschung, 32. Jahrgang, 3, 32-52.

Ko, D. G., Kirsch, L. J., & King, W. R. (2005). Antecedents of knowledge transfer from consultants to clients in enterprise system implementations. *Management Information Systems Quarterly, 29*(1), 59–85.

Koh, H. C., & Goh, C. T. (1995). An analysis of the factors affecting the turnover intention of non-managerial clerical staff: A Singapore study. *International Journal of Human Resource Management, 6*(1), 103–125. doi:10.1080/09585199500000005

Kontaxis, G., Antoniades, D., Polakis, I., & Markatos, E. P. (2011). An Empirical Study on the Security of Cross-Domain Policies in Rich Internet Applications. In *Proceedings of the 4th European Workshop on System Security (EuroSec)*, (pp. 295-300). doi:10.1145/1972551.1972558

Kopetz, H. (2011). Internet of things. In Real-time systems. Springer US.

Korzaan, M., & Lawrence, C. (2015). Advancing student productivity: An introduction to evernote. *Proceedings of the EDSIG Conference Conference on Knowledge Systems and Computing Education.*

Kosakowski, J. (1998). *The Benefits of Information Technology.* ERIC Digest.

Koskinen, K. U., Pihlanto, P., & Vanharanta, H. (2003). Tacit knowledge acquisition and sharing in a project work context. *International Journal of Project Management, 21*(4), 281–290. doi:10.1016/S0263-7863(02)00030-3

Kramer, L. (2011). The Power of Celebrity Endorsement Enhanced By Social Media. *Business Insider Australia.* Retrieved from http://www.businessinsider.com.au/the-power-of-celebrity-endorsements-enhanced-by-social-media-2011-3?r=US&IR=T

Kreps, G. (1981). *Organizational folklore: The packaging of company history at RCA* Paper presented at the ICA/SCA Conference on interpretive approaches to organizational communication, Alta, UT.

Krucken, G., Meier, F., & Muller, A. (2007). Information, Cooperation, and the Blurring of Boundaries – Technology Transfer in German and American Discourses. *Higher Education*, *53*(6), 675–696. doi:10.1007/s10734-004-7650-4

Krueger, R. A. (1988). *Focus groups: A practical guide for applied research*. Newbury Park, CA: Sage Publications Inc.

Kuchar, J. K. (1996). Methodology for alerting-system performance evaluation. *Journal of Guidance, Control, and Dynamics*, *19*(2), 438–444. doi:10.2514/3.21637

Kwan, M. M., & Cheung, P. (2006). The knowledge transfer process: From field studies to technology development. *Journal of Database Management*, *17*(1), 16–32. doi:10.4018/jdm.2006010102

Kwon, S. W., & Adler, P. S. (2014). Social capital: Maturation of a field of research. *Academy of Management Review*, *39*(4), 412–422. doi:10.5465/amr.2014.0210

Kyriakidou, O., & Gore, J. (2005). Learning by example: Benchmarking organizational culture in hospitality, tourism and leisure SMEs. *Benchmarking: An International Journal*, *12*(3), 192–206. doi:10.1108/14635770510600320

Laframboise, K., Croteau, A., Beaudry, A., & Manovas, M. (2009). Interdepartmental knowledge transfer success during information technology projects. In M. Jennex (Ed.), *Knowledge management, organizational memory and transfer behavior: Global approaches and advancements* (pp. 189–210). Hershey, PA: IGI Global. doi:10.4018/978-1-60566-140-7.ch012

Laihonen, H., & Koivuaho, M. (2011). Knowledge flow audit: Indentifying, measuring and managing knowledge asset dynamics. In B. Vallejo-Alonso, A. Rodriguez-Castellanos, & G. Arregui-Ayastuy (Eds.), *Identifying, measuring, and valuing knowledge-based intangible assets: New perspectives* (pp. 22–42). Hershey, PA: IGI Global. doi:10.4018/978-1-60960-054-9.ch002

Laihonen, H., & Lönnqvist, A. (2011). How knowledge assets are transformed into value: The case of knowledge flows and service productivity. In G. Schiuma (Ed.), *Managing knowledge assets and business value creation in organizations: Measures and dynamics* (pp. 173–187). Hershey, PA: IGI Global. doi:10.4018/978-1-60960-071-6.ch011

Lam, A. (2000). Tacit Knowledge, Organizational Learning and Societal Institutions: An Integrated Framework. *Organization Studies*, *21*(3), 487–513. doi:10.1177/0170840600213001

Landauer, T. K. (1995). *The trouble with computers: Usefulness, usability, and productivity*. Cambridge, MA: MIT Press.

Lane, P. J., Salk, J. E., & Lyles, M. A. (2001). Absorptive capacity, learning, and performance in international joint ventures. *Strategic Management Journal*, *22*(12), 1139–1161. doi:10.1002/smj.206

Langner, S., Hennigs, N., & Wiedmann, K.-P. (2013). Social persuasion: Targeting social identities through social influencers. *Journal of Consumer Marketing*, *30*(1), 31–49. doi:10.1108/07363761311290821

Laroche, M., Habibi, M. R., & Richard, M. O. (2013). To be or not to be in social media: How brand loyalty is affected by social media? *International Journal of Information Management*, *33*(1), 76–82. doi:10.1016/j.ijinfomgt.2012.07.003

Larson, J., Christensen, C., Foster-Fishman, P. G., & Keys, C. B. (1994). Discussion of shared and unshared information in decision-making groups. *Journal of Personality and Social Psychology*, *67*(3), 446–461. doi:10.1037/0022-3514.67.3.446

Lauring, J., & Klitmøller, A. (2015). Corporate language-based communication avoidance in MNCs: A multi-sited ethnography approach. *Journal of World Business*, *50*(1), 46–55. doi:10.1016/j.jwb.2014.01.005

Lauring, J., & Selmer, J. (2010). Multicultural organizations: Common language and group cohesiveness. *International Journal of Cross Cultural Management*, *10*(3), 267–284. doi:10.1177/1470595810384587

Lawyer, G. (2014). *Understanding the spreading power of all nodes in a network: a continuous-time perspective.* arXiv preprint arXiv:1405.6707

Leckie, C., Nyadzayo, M. W., & Johnson, L. W. (2016). Antecedents of consumer brand engagement and brand loyalty. *Journal of Marketing Management*, *32*(5-6), 558–578. doi:10.1 080/0267257X.2015.1131735

Lee, C. K., & Al-Hawamdeh, S. (2002). Factors impacting knowledge sharing. *Journal of Information & Knowledge Management*, 49-56.

Lee, D. H., & Brusilovsky, P. (2007, June). Fighting information overflow with personalized comprehensive information access: A proactive job recommender. In *Autonomic and Autonomous Systems, 2007. ICAS07. Third International Conference on* (pp. 21-21). IEEE. doi:10.1109/CONIELECOMP.2007.76

Lee, A. (2000). *Computer reservation systems: an industry of its own. Centre for Asian Business Cases, School of business.* The University of Hong Kong.

Lee, H., Reid, E., & Kim, W. G. (2014). Understanding knowledge sharing in online travel communities: Antecedents and the moderating effects of interaction modes. *Journal of Hospitality & Tourism Research (Washington, D.C.)*, *38*(2), 222–242. doi:10.1177/1096348012451454

Lee, J., & Moray, N. (1992). Trust, control strategies and allocation of function in human-machine systems. *Ergonomics*, *35*(10), 1243–1270. doi:10.1080/00140139208967392 PMID:1516577

Lee, K., Caverlee, J., & Webb, S. (2010). Uncovering social spammers: social honeypots + machine learning. In *Proceedings of the 33rd international ACM SIGIR conference on Research and development in information retrieval* (pp. 435-442). doi:10.1145/1835449.1835522

Lee, M., Rodgers, S., & Kim, M. (2009). Effects of valence and extremity of eWOM on attitude toward the brand and website. *Journal of Current Issues and Research in Advertising*, *31*(2), 1–11. doi:10.1080/10641734.2009.10505262

Lee, T. W., Mitchell, T. R., Sablynski, C. J., Burton, J. P., & Holtom, B. C. (2004). The effects of job embeddedness on organizational citizenship, job performance, volitional absences, and voluntary turnover. *Academy of Management Journal*, *47*(5), 711–722. doi:10.2307/20159613

Lee, Z., Lee, J., & Sieber, T. (2002). ERP-based knowledge transfer. In D. White (Ed.), *Knowledge mapping and management* (pp. 79–87). Hershey, PA: IRM Press. doi:10.4018/978-1-931777-17-9.ch009

Lehner, F., & Maier, R. K. (2000). How can organizational memory theories contribute to organizational memory systems? *Information Systems Frontiers*, *2*(3/4), 277–298. doi:10.1023/A:1026516627735

Leonardi, P. M., Huysman, M., & Steinfield, C. (2013). Enterprise social media: Definition, history, and prospects for the study of social technologies in organizations. *Journal of Computer-Mediated Communication*, *19*(1), 1–19. doi:10.1111/jcc4.12029

Leung, D., Law, R., Van Hoof, H., & Buhalis, D. (2013). Social media in tourism and hospitality: A literature review. *Journal of Travel & Tourism Marketing*, *30*(1-2), 3–22. doi:10.1080/10548408.2013.750919

Leung, L. (2013). Generational differences in content generation in social media: The roles of the gratifications sought and of narcissism. *Computers in Human Behavior*, *29*(3), 997–1006. doi:10.1016/j.chb.2012.12.028

Levine, S., & White, P. E. (1961). Exchange as a conceptual framework for the study of interorganizational relationships. *Administrative Science Quarterly*, *5*(4), 583–601. doi:10.2307/2390622

Levy, M. (2009). WEB 2.0 implications on knowledge management. *Journal of Knowledge Management*, *13*(1), 120–134. doi:10.1108/13673270910931215

Levy, S. J. (2006). How New, How Dominant? In R. F. Lusch & S. L. Vargo (Eds.), *The Service-Dominant Logic of Marketing. Dialog, Debate, and Directions*. Armonk, NY: M.E. Sharpe.

Liang, D. W., Moreland, R., & Argote, L. (1995). Group versus individual training and group performance: The mediating role of transactive memory. *Personality and Social Psychology Bulletin*, *21*(4), 384–393. doi:10.1177/0146167295214009

Liang, T. P., & Lai, H. J. (2002). Effect of store design on consumer purchase: An empirical study of online bookstores. *Information & Management*, *39*(6), 431–444. doi:10.1016/S0378-7206(01)00129-X

Liang, T. P., & Turban, E. (2011). Introduction to the special issue, social commerce: A research framework for social commerce. *International Journal of Electronic Commerce*, *16*(2), 5–14. doi:10.2753/JEC1086-4415160201

Liberman, N., & Trope, Y. (1998). The role of feasibility and desirability considerations in near and distant future decisions: A test of temporal construal theory. *Journal of Personality and Social Psychology*, *75*(1), 5–18. doi:10.1037/0022-3514.75.1.5 PMID:11195890

Lichy, J., & Kachour, M. (2016). Understanding how students interact with technology for knowledge-sharing: The emergence of a new social divide in France. *International Journal of Technology and Human Interaction, 12*(1), 83–104. doi:10.4018/IJTHI.2016010106

Li, J., & Lee, R. P. (2015). Can knowledge transfer within MNCs hurt subsidiary performance? The role of subsidiary entrepreneurial culture and capabilities. *Journal of World Business, 50*(4), 663–673. doi:10.1016/j.jwb.2014.09.004

Lingel, G. (2016). *The Best Freelancing Sites of 2016*. Retrieved from http://www.lifehack.org/368286/the-best-freelancing-sites-2016

Lin, H. F. (2007). Knowledge sharing and firm innovation capability: An empirical study. *International Journal of Manpower, 28*(3/4), 315–332. doi:10.1108/01437720710755272

Lin, J., Hung, S., & Chen, C. (2009). Fostering the determinants of knowledge sharing in professional virtual communities. *Computers in Human Behavior, 25*(4), 929–939. doi:10.1016/j.chb.2009.03.008

Lin, K. Y., & Lu, H. P. (2011). Why people use social networking sites: An empirical study integrating network externalities and motivation theory. *Computers in Human Behavior, 27*(3), 1152–1161. doi:10.1016/j.chb.2010.12.009

Lippincott, J. (2010). "Benim bilgim": Dijital kütüphaneler, sosyal ağlar ve kullanıcı deneyimi. Bilgi Yönetiminde Teknolojik Yakınsama ve Sosyal Ağlar 2. Uluslararası Değişen Dünyada Bilgi Yönetimi Sempozyumu Bildiriler Kitabı, 22-24 Eylül 2010, Hacettepe Üniversitesi Bilgi ve Belge Yönetimi Bölümü: Ankara.

Litvin, S. W., Goldsmith, R. E., & Pan, B. (2008). Electronic word-of-mouth in hospitality and tourism management. *Tourism Management, 29*(3), 458–468. doi:10.1016/j.tourman.2007.05.011

Liu, K. L., Chang, C. C., & Hu, I. L. (2010). Exploring the Effects of Task Characteristics on Knowledge Sharing in Libraries. *Library Review, 59*(6), 455 468. doi:10.1108/00242531011053968

Liu, Q., & Eugene, A. (2011). *Modeling answerer behavior in collaborative question answering systems. In Advances in information retrieval* (pp. 67–79). Springer Berlin Heidelberg.

Liu, S. (2008). Knowledge sharing: Interactive processes between organizational knowledge-sharing initiative and individuals' sharing practice. In E. Bolisani (Ed.), *Building the knowledge society on the Internet: Sharing and exchanging knowledge in networked environments* (pp. 1–23). Hershey, PA: IGI Global. doi:10.4018/978-1-59904-816-1.ch001

Liviatan, I., Trope, Y., & Liberman, N. (2008). Interpersonal similarity as a social distance dimension: Implications for perception of others actions. *Journal of Experimental Social Psychology, 44*(5), 1256–1269. doi:10.1016/j.jesp.2008.04.007 PMID:19352440

Lops, P., De Gemmis, M., & Semeraro, G. (2011). Content-based recommender systems: State of the art and trends. In Recommender systems handbook (pp. 73-105). Springer US.

Louis, M. R. (1980). *A cultural perspective on organizations: The need for and consequences of viewing organizations as culture-bearing milieux*. Paper presented at the National Academy of Management Meetings, Detroit, MI.

Lu, J., Wu, D., Mao, M., Wang, W., & Zhang, G. (2015). Recommender system application developments: A survey. *Decision Support Systems, 74*, 12–32. doi:10.1016/j.dss.2015.03.008

Lyons, K. L. (2000). Using patterns to capture tacit knowledge and enhance knowledge transfer in virtual teams. In Y. Malhotra (Ed.), *Knowledge management and virtual organizations* (pp. 124–143). Hershey, PA: Idea Group Publishing. doi:10.4018/978-1-930708-65-5.ch007

Machikita, T., Tsuji, M., & Ueki, Y. (2016). Does Kaizen create backward knowledge transfer to Southeast Asian firms? *Journal of Business Research, 69*(5), 1556–1561. doi:10.1016/j.jbusres.2015.10.016

Machlup, F. (1983). *The study of information: Interdisciplinary messages*. Retrieved from http://philpapers.org/rec/MACTSO-9

Macnamara, J., & Zerfass, A. (2012). Social media communication in organizations: The challenges of balancing openness, strategy, and management. *International Journal of Strategic Communication, 6*(4), 287–308. doi:10.1080/1553118X.2012.711402

Maglitta, J. (1996). Smarten up! *Computerworld, 29*(23), 84–86.

Malhotra, Y. (2000). Knowledge management and new organization forms: A framework for business model innovation. *Information Resources Management Journal, 13*(1), 5–14. doi:10.4018/irmj.2000010101

Malhotra, Y. (2005). Integrating knowledge management technologies in organizational business processes: Getting real time enterprises to deliver real business performance. *Journal of Knowledge Management, 9*(1), 7–28. doi:10.1108/13673270510582938

Malinowski, J., Keim, T., Wendt, O., & Weitzel, T. (2006, January). Matching people and jobs: A bilateral recommendation approach. In *Proceedings of the 39th Annual Hawaii International Conference on System Sciences (HICSS'06)* (Vol. 6, pp. 137c-137c). IEEE. doi:10.1109/HICSS.2006.266

Malinowski, J., Weitzel, T., & Keim, T. (2008). Decision support for team staffing: An automated relational recommendation approach. *Decision Support Systems, 45*(3), 429–447. doi:10.1016/j.dss.2007.05.005

Mansell, A., Brough, P., & Cole, K. (2006). Stable Predictors of Job Satisfaction, Psychological Strain, and Employee Retention: An Evaluation of Organizational Change Within the New Zealand Customs Service. *International Journal of Stress Management, 13*(1), 84–107. doi:10.1037/1072-5245.13.1.84

Mariani, M. M., Di Felice, M., & Mura, M. (2016). Facebook as a destination marketing tool: Evidence from Italian regional Destination Management Organizations. *Tourism Management, 54*, 321–343. doi:10.1016/j.tourman.2015.12.008

Marino, M., Parrotta, P., & Pozzoli, D. (2016). Educational diversity and knowledge transfers via inter-firm labor mobility. *Journal of Economic Behavior & Organization, 123*, 168–183. doi:10.1016/j.jebo.2015.10.019

Marschan-Piekkari, R., Welch, D., & Welch, L. (1999). Adopting a common corporate language: IHRM implications. *International Journal of Human Resource Management, 10*(3), 377–390. doi:10.1080/095851999340387

Marshall, C., & Rossman, G. B. (2006). *Designing qualitative research* (4th ed.). Thousand Oaks, CA: Sage Publications Inc.

Mårtensson, M. (2000). A critical review of knowledge management as a management tool. *Journal of Knowledge Management, 4*(3), 204–216. doi:10.1108/13673270010350002

Martinez-Romo, J., & Araujo, L. (2013). Detecting malicious tweets in trending topics using a statistical analysis of language. *Expert System Application, 40*(8), 992–3000. doi:10.1016/j.eswa.2012.12.015

Masalonis, A. J., & Parasuraman, R. (1999). Trust as a construct for evaluation of automated aids: Past and future theory and research. *Proceedings of the Human Factors and Ergonomics Society Annual Meeting, 43*(3), 184-187. doi:10.1177/154193129904300312

Maslach, C., Schaufeli, W. B., & Leiter, M. P. (2001). Job burnout. *Annual Review of Psychology, 52*(1), 397–422. doi:10.1146/annurev.psych.52.1.397 PMID:11148311

Mayer, R. C., Davis, J. H., & Schoorman, F. D. (1995). An integrative model of organisational trust. *Academy of Management Review, 20*(3), 709–734.

McAfee, A. P. (2006). Enterprise 2.0: The dawn of emergent collaboration. *IEEE Engineering Management Review, 34*(3), 38–47. doi:10.1109/EMR.2006.261380

McBey, K., & Karakowsky, L. (2001). Examining sources of influence on employee turnover in the part time work context. *Career Development International, 6*(1), 39–48. doi:10.1108/13620430110381025

McCracken, G. (1989). Who is the Celebrity Endorser? Cultural Foundations of the Endorsement Process. *The Journal of Consumer Research, 16*(3), 310–321. doi:10.1086/209217

McCroskey, J. C., Fayer, J. M., & Richmond, V. P. (1985). Dont speak to me in English: Communication apprehension in Puerto Rico. *Communication Quarterly, 33*(3), 185–192. doi:10.1080/01463378509369597

McDermott, R. (1999). Why information technology inspired but cannot deliver knowledge management. *California Management Review, 41*(4), 103–117. doi:10.2307/41166012

McDermott, R., & ODell, C. (2001). Overcoming cultural barriers to sharing knowledge. *Journal of Knowledge Management, 5*(1), 76–85. doi:10.1108/13673270110384428

McGuire, W. J. (1969). The nature of attitudes and attitude change. The Handbook of Social Psychology, 3(2), 136-314.

McInnis, D.J. (2004). Where Have All the Papers Gone? Reflections on the Decline of Conceptual Articles. *ACR News*, 1-3.

McKnight, D. H., & Chervany, N. L. (2001). What trust means in e-commerce customer relationships: An interdisciplinary conceptual typology. *International Journal of Electronic Commerce*, 6(2), 35–59.

McKnight, D. H., Choudhury, V., & Kacmar, C. (2002). Developing and validating trust measures for e-commerce: An integrative typology. *Information Systems Research*, 13(3), 334–359. doi:10.1287/isre.13.3.334.81

McLaughlin, J. (2016). What is organizational culture? Definition & characteristics. *Business 107: Organizational Behavior*. Retrieved September 28, 2016, from http://study.com/academy/lesson/what-is-organizational-culture-definition-characteristics.html#transcriptHeader

McLaughlin, S. (2009). Improving supply chain performance through the implementation of process related knowledge transfer mechanisms. *International Journal of Knowledge Management*, 5(2), 64–86. doi:10.4018/jkm.2009040105

McLaughlin, S. (2013). Assessing the impact of knowledge transfer mechanisms on supply chain performance. In *Supply chain management: Concepts, methodologies, tools, and applications* (pp. 1477–1491). Hershey, PA: IGI Global. doi:10.4018/978-1-4666-2625-6.ch087

Mehta, A. (1994). How advertising response modeling (ARM) can increase ad effectiveness. *Journal of Advertising Research*, 34, 62–62.

Melville, N., Kraemer, K., & Gurbaxani, V. (2004). Review: Information technology and organizational performance: An integrative model of IT business value. *Management Information Systems Quarterly*, 28(2), 283–322.

Mentzas, G., Kafentzis, K., & Georgolios, P. (2007). Knowledge services on the Semantic Web. *Communications of the ACM*, 50(10), 53–58. doi:10.1145/1290958.1290962

Meyer, A. (1981). How ideologies supplant formal structures and shape responses to environments. *Journal of Management Studies*, 19(1), 45–61. doi:10.1111/j.1467-6486.1982.tb00059.x

Midyette, J. D., Youngkin, A., & Snow-Croft, S. (2014). Social media and communications: Developing a policy to guide the flow of information. *Medical Reference Services Quarterly*, 33(1), 39–50. doi:10.1080/02763869.2014.866482 PMID:24528263

Miller, P. (1998). *Mobilising the power of what you know*. London: Random House.

Millissa, F. Y. (2016). Service co-creation in social media: An extension of the theory of planned behavior. *Computers in Human Behavior*, 65, 260–266. doi:10.1016/j.chb.2016.08.031

Minbaeva, D. B. (2005). HRM practices and MNC knowledge transfer. *Personnel Review, 34*(1), 125–144. doi:10.1108/00483480510571914

Minbaeva, D. B. (2008). HRM practices and knowledge transfer in multinational companies. In K. O'Sullivan (Ed.), *Strategic knowledge management in multinational organizations* (pp. 1–27). Hershey, PA: IGI Global. doi:10.4018/978-1-59904-630-3.ch001

Mishra, & Yadav, B. (2013). Job Anxiety And Personality Adjustment Of Secondary School Teachers In Relation Of Gender And Types Of Teacher. *Educational Research International, 1*(1), 105-126.

Mishra, J., & Morrissey, M. A. (1990). Trust in employee/employer relationships: A survey of West Michigan managers. *Public Personnel Management, 19*(4), 443–463. doi:10.1177/009102609001900408

Mithas, S., Tafti, A., & Mitchell, W. (2013). How A Firm's Competitive Environment And Digital Strategic Posture Influence Digital Business Strategy. *Management Information Systems Quarterly, 37*(2), 511–536.

Mobasher, B. (2006). Web Usage Mining. In B. Liu (Ed.), *Web Data Mining: Exploring Hyperlinks, Contents and Usage Data*. Berlin: Springer.

Moen, J. (2005). Is mobility of technical personnel a source of R&D spillovers? *Journal of Labor Economics, 23*(1), 81–114. doi:10.1086/425434

Mohamad, S. F. (2008). Effects of communication on turnover intention: a case of hotel employees in Malaysia. *Graduate Theses and Dissertations*. 11164. Retrieved from http://lib.dr.iastate.edu/etd/11164

Mooney, R. (1999). Relational learning of pattern-match rules for information extraction. In *Proceedings of the Sixteenth National Conference on Artificial Intelligence*, (pp. 328-334).

Moreland, R. L., Argote, L., & Krishnan, R. (1997). Training people to work in groups. In Applications of Theory and Research on Groups to Social Issues. Plenum.

Morgan, E. (2016). Influencers cash in on social media's power. *ABC News*. Retrieved from http://www.abc.net.au/news/2016-03-24/influencers-cash-in-on-social-media-power/7274678

Moskaliuk, J., Bokhorst, F., & Cress, U. (2016). Learning from others' experiences: How patterns foster interpersonal transfer of knowledge-in-use. *Computers in Human Behavior, 55*, 69–75. doi:10.1016/j.chb.2015.08.051

Mou, Y., & Lin, C. A. (2015). Exploring podcast adoption intention via perceived social norms, interpersonal communication, and theory of planned behavior. *Journal of Broadcasting & Electronic Media, 59*(3), 475-493.

Mucan, B., & Özeltürkay, E. Y. (2014). Social Media Creates Competitive Advantages: How Turkish Banks Use This Power? A Content Analysis of Turkish Banks Through Their Webpages. *Procedia-Social and Behavioral Sciences, 2nd International Conference on Strategic Innovative Marketing, 148,* 137-145.

Munar, A., & Ooi, C. (2012). *What Social Media Tell Us About The Heritage Experience.* Retrieved from https://www.researchgate.net/profile/can_seng_ooi/publication/265060043_what_social_media_tell_us_about_the_heritage_experience_what_social_media_tell_us_about_the_heritage_experience/links/55faa40c08aeba1d9f369106.pdf

Munar, A. M., & Jacobsen, J. K. S. (2014). Motivations for sharing tourism experiences through social media. *Tourism Management, 43,* 46–54. doi:10.1016/j.tourman.2014.01.012

Munibalaji, T., & Balamurugan, C. (2012). Analysis of link algorithms for web mining. *International Journal of engineering and Innovative Technology, 1*(2).

Muschalla, B., Heldmann, M., & Fay, D. (2013). The significance of job-anxiety in a working population. *Occupational Medicine, 63*(6), 415–421. doi:10.1093/occmed/kqt072 PMID:23771887

Myers, J. G., Greyser, S. A., & Massy, W. F. (1979). The Effectiveness of Marketings R&D for Marketing Management: An Assessment. *Journal of Marketing, 43*(1), 17–29. doi:10.2307/1250754

Nahapiet, J., & Ghoshal, S. (1998). Social capital, intellectual capital, and the organizational advantage. *Academy of Management Review, 23,* 242–266.

Najafi-Tavani, Z., Zaefarian, G., Naudé, P., & Giroud, A. (2015). Reverse knowledge transfer and subsidiary power. *Industrial Marketing Management, 48,* 103–110. doi:10.1016/j.indmarman.2015.03.021

NaliniPriya, G., & Asswini, M. (2015). A survey on vulnerable attacks in online social networks. *Proceedings of 2015 International Conference on Innovation Information in Computing Technologies,* 1–6.

Naumann, E. (1993). Antecedents and consequences of satisfaction and commitment among expatriate managers. *Group & Organization Management, 18*(2), 153–187. doi:10.1177/1059601193182003

Neeley, T. B., Hinds, P. J., & Cramton, C. D. (2012). The (un)hidden turmoil of language in global collaboration. *Organizational Dynamics, 41*(3), 236–244. doi:10.1016/j.orgdyn.2012.03.008

Nelson, R. R., & Winter, S. G. (1982). *An Evolutionary Theory of Economic Change.* Cambridge, MA: Belknap Press.

Nelson, R. R., & Winter, S. G. (1982). The Schumpeterian tradeoff revisited. *The American Economic Review, 72*(1), 114–132.

Nemati-Anaraki, L., & Heidari, A. (2016). Knowledge sharing for improving effectiveness of university-industry collaborations. In *Business intelligence: Concepts, methodologies, tools, and applications* (pp. 955–972). Hershey, PA: IGI Global. doi:10.4018/978-1-4666-9562-7.ch049

Nezakati, H., Amidi, A., Jusoh, Y. Y., Moghadas, S., Aziz, Y. A., & Sohrabinezhadtalemi, R. (2015). Review of social media potential on knowledge sharing and collaboration in tourism industry. *Procedia: Social and Behavioral Sciences, 172*, 120–125. doi:10.1016/j.sbspro.2015.01.344

Ngoma, N. S., & Lind, M. (2015). Knowledge transfer and team performance in distributed organizations. *International Journal of Knowledge-Based Organizations, 5*(2), 58–80. doi:10.4018/ijkbo.2015040104

Nielsen, A. P. (2006). Understanding dynamic capabilities through knowledge management. *Journal of Knowledge Management, 10*(4), 59–71. doi:10.1108/13673270610679363

Nohria, N., & Ghoshal, S. (1997). *The differentiated network: Organizing multinational corporations for value creation.* San Francisco, CA: Jossey–Bass.

Nolen-Hoeksema, S., & Girgus, J. S. (1994). The emergence of gender differences in depression during adolescence. *Psychological Bulletin, 115*(3), 424–443. doi:10.1037/0033-2909.115.3.424 PMID:8016286

Nonaka, I., & Toyama, R. (2003). The knowledge-creating theory revisited: knowledge creation as a synthesizing process. *Knowledge Management Research & Practice, 1*(1), 2-10.

Nonaka, I. (1991). The knowledge-creating company. *Harvard Business Review, 69*, 96–104.

Nonaka, I. (1994). A Dynamic Theory of Organizational Knowledge Creation. *Organization Science, 5*(1), 14–37. doi:10.1287/orsc.5.1.14

Nonaka, I., & Konno, N. (1998). The concept of ba: Building a foundation for knowledge creation. *California Management Review, 40*(3), 40–54. doi:10.2307/41165942

Nonaka, I., & Takeuchi, H. (1995). *The Knowledge-Creating Company: How Japanese Companies Create the Dynamics of Innovation.* New York: Oxford University Press.

Nonaka, I., & Takeuchi, H. (1995). *The Knowledge-creating Company.* New York. Oxford University Press.

Nonaka, I., Takeuchi, H., & Umemoto, K. (1996). A theory of organizational knowledge creation. *International Journal of Technology Management, 11*(7–8), 833–845.

Nonaka, I., & Toyama, R. (2002). A firm as a dialectical being: Towards a dynamic theory of a firm. *Industrial and Corporate Change, 11*(5), 995–1009. doi:10.1093/icc/11.5.995

Nonaka, I., Toyama, R., & Konno, N. (2000). SECI, Ba and leadership: A unified model of dynamic knowledge creation. *Long Range Planning, 33*(1), 5–34. doi:10.1016/S0024-6301(99)00115-6

Nonaka, I., Toyama, R., & Nagata, A. (2000). A firm as a knowledge-creating entity: A new perspective on the theory of the firm. *Industrial and Corporate Change, 9*(1), 1–20. doi:10.1093/icc/9.1.1

Nonaka, I., von Krogh, G., & Voepel, S. (2006). Organizational knowledge creation theory: Evolutionary paths and future advances. *Organization Studies*, *27*(8), 1179–1208. doi:10.1177/0170840606066312

Noor, N. L. M., Hashim, M., Haron, H., & Aiffin, S. (2005). Community acceptance of knowledge sharing system in the travel and tourism websites: an application of an extension of TAM. *ECIS 2005 Proceedings*, 71.

Norberg, A., Dziuban, C. D., & Moskal, P. D. (2011). A time-based blended learning model. *On the Horizon*, *19*(3), 207–216. doi:10.1108/10748121111163913

Nylund, P. A., & Raelin, J. D. (2015). When feelings obscure reason: The impact of leaders' explicit and emotional knowledge transfer on shareholder reactions. *The Leadership Quarterly*, *26*(4), 532–542. doi:10.1016/j.leaqua.2015.06.003

O'Connor, P. (1999). *Electronic information distribution in tourism and hospitality*. CAB international.

O'Connor, P., & Frew, A. J. (2002). The future of hotel electronic distribution: Expert and industry perspectives. *The Cornell Hotel and Restaurant Administration Quarterly*, *43*(3), 33–45. doi:10.1016/S0010-8804(02)80016-7

O'Reilly, T. (2005). *What is Web 2.0? Design patterns and business models for the next generation of software*. Available: http://www.oreilly.com/pub/a/web2/archive/what-is-web-20.html

O'Reilly, T. (2007). What is Web 2.0: Design patterns and business models for the next generation of software. *Communications & Stratégies*, *1*(65), 17–37.

Oakley, R. L., & Salam, A. F. (2014). Examining the impact of computer-mediated social networks on individual consumerism environmental behaviors. *Computers in Human Behavior*, *35*, 516–526. doi:10.1016/j.chb.2014.02.033

Obar, J. A., & Wildman, S. (2015). Social media definition and the governance challenge: An introduction to the special issue. *Telecommunications Policy*, *39*(9), 745–750. doi:10.1016/j.telpol.2015.07.014

OCass, A., & Fenech, T. (2003). Web retailing adoption: Exploring the nature of internet users web retailing behavior. *Journal of Retailing and Consumer Services*, *10*(2), 81–94. doi:10.1016/S0969-6989(02)00004-8

Oestreicher-Singer, G., & Zalmanson, L. (2013). Content or Community? A Digital Business Strategy For Content Providers in the Social Age. *Management Information Systems Quarterly*, *37*(2), 591–616.

Ohanian, R. (1990). Construction and Validation of a Scale to Measure Celebrity Endorsers Perceived Expertise, Trustworthiness, and Attractiveness. *Journal of Advertising*, *19*(3), 39–52. doi:10.1080/00913367.1990.10673191

Okada, E. M. (2005). Justification Effects on Consumer Choice of Hedonic and Utilitarian Goods. *JMR, Journal of Marketing Research*, *42*(1), 43–53. doi:10.1509/jmkr.42.1.43.56889

Okhuysen, G. A., & Eisenhardt, K. M. (2002). Integrating Knowledge in Groups: How Formal Interventions Enable Flexibility. *Organization Science*, *13*(4), 370–386. doi:10.1287/orsc.13.4.370.2947

Olivera, F. (2000). Memory systems in organizations: An empirical investigation of mechanisms for knowledge collection, storage and access. *Journal of Management Studies*, *37*(6), 811–832. doi:10.1111/1467-6486.00205

Oracle. (2012). *Is social media transforming your business?* An Oracle White Paper. Retrieved from http://www.oracle.com/us/products/applications/social-trans-bus-wp-1560502.pdf

Orlikowski, W. J. (1996). Improving organizational transformation over time: A situated change perspective. *Information Systems Research*, *7*(1), 63–92. doi:10.1287/isre.7.1.63

Ott, J. S. (1989). *The organizational culture perspective*. Pacific Grove, CA: Brooks/Cole Publishing Company.

Oxforddictionaries.com. (2016). *Definition of knowledge in English*. Retrieved October 10, 2016, from http://www.oxforddictionaries.com/definition/english/knowledge

Oxley, J. E., & Sampson, R. C. (2004). The scope and governance of international R&D alliances. *Strategic Management Journal*, *25*(8/9), 723–749. doi:10.1002/smj.391

Pagani, M. (2013). Digital Business Strategy and Value Creation: Framing The Dynamic Cycle of Control Points. *Management Information Systems Quarterly*, *37*(2), 617–632.

Page, K. M., & Vella-Brodrick, D. A. (2009). The what, why and how of employee well-being: A new model. *Social Indicators Research*, *90*(3), 441–458. doi:10.1007/s11205-008-9270-3

Panahi, S., Watson, J., & Partridge, H. (2012). Social media and tacit knowledge sharing. Developing a conceptual model. *World Academy of Science, Engineering and Technology*, *64*, 1095-1102.

Panahi, S., Watson, J., & Partridge, H. (2012). Social media and tacit knowledge sharing : Developing a conceptual model. *World Academy of Science. Engineering and Technology*, *64*, 1095–1102.

Pan, B., MacLaurin, T., & Crotts, J. C. (2007). Travel blogs and their implications for destination marketing. *Journal of Travel Research*, *46*(1), 35–45. doi:10.1177/0047287507302378

Pang, B., & Lee, L. (2008). Opinion mining and sentiment analysis. *Foundations and Trends® in Information Retrieval*, *2*(1–2), 1-135.

Paparrizos, I., Cambazoglu, B. B., & Gionis, A. (2011, October). Machine learned job recommendation. In *Proceedings of the fifth ACM Conference on Recommender Systems* (pp. 325-328). ACM. doi:10.1145/2043932.2043994

Parasuraman, R., & Riley, V. (1997). Humans and automation: Use, misuse, disuse, abuse. *Human Factors: The Journal of the Human Factors and Ergonomics Society, 39*(2), 230–253. doi:10.1518/001872097778543886

Parasuraman, R., Sheridan, T. B., & Wickens, C. D. (2000). A model for types and levels of human interaction with automation. Systems, Man and Cybernetics, Part A: Systems and Humans. *IEEE Transactions on, 30*(3), 286–297.

Parise, S. (2009). Social media networks: What do they mean for knowledge management? *Journal of Knowledge Technology Case and Application Research, 11*(2), 1–11. doi:10.1080/1 5228053.2009.10856156

Park, H., Rodgers, S. & Stemmle, J. (2011). Health organizations' use of Facebook for health advertising and promotion. *Journal of Interactive Advertising, 12*(1), 62-77.

Park, D. H., & Kim, S. (2008). The effects of consumer knowledge on message processing of electronic word-of-mouth via online consumer reviews. *Electronic Commerce Research and Applications, 7*(4), 399–410. doi:10.1016/j.elerap.2007.12.001

Paroutis, A., & Al Saleh, A. (2009). Determinants of knowledge sharing using Web 2.0 technologies. *Journal of Knowledge Management, 13*(4), 52–63. doi:10.1108/13673270910971824

Parrotta, P., & Pozzoli, D. (2012). The effect of learning by hiring on productivity. *The Rand Journal of Economics, 43*(1), 167–185. doi:10.1111/j.1756-2171.2012.00161.x

Parsons, A. (2013). Using social media to reach consumers: A content analysis of official Facebook pages. *Academy of Marketing Studies Journal, 17*(2), 27.

Payne, G. T., Moore, C. B., Griffis, S. E., & Autry, C. W. (2011). Multilevel challenges and opportunities in social capital research. *Journal of Management, 37*(2), 491–520. doi:10.1177/0149206310372413

Pazzani, M. J., & Billsus, D. (2007). Content-based recommendation systems. In *The adaptive web* (pp. 325–341). Springer Berlin Heidelberg. doi:10.1007/978-3-540-72079-9_10

Peachey, T., Hall, D. J., & Cegielski, C. (2008). Knowledge management and the leading information systems journals: An analysis of trends and gaps in published research. In M. Jennex (Ed.), *Knowledge management: Concepts, methodologies, tools, and applications* (pp. 1450–1463). Hershey, PA: IGI Global. doi:10.4018/978-1-59904-933-5.ch119

Pekka-Economou, V., & Hadjidema, S. (2011). Innovative organizational forms that add value to both organizations and community: The case of knowledge management. *European Research Studies, 14*(2), 81–95.

Percy, W., & Kostere, K. (2006). *Qualitative research approaches in psychology.* Capella University.

Perrin, A. (2015). Social media usage: 2005 - 2015. *PewResearchCenter: Internet, Science & Tech.* Retrieved October 10, 2016, from http://www.pewinternet.org/2015/10/08/social-networking-usage-2005-2015/

Perrow, C. (1984). *Normal Accidents, Living with High-Risk Technology*. New York: Basic Books.

Peters, T. J., & Waterman, R. H. Jr. (1982). *In Search of Excellence: Lessons from America's Best-Run Companies*. New York: Harper & Row.

Pezzillo Iacono, M., Martinez, M., Mangia, G., & Galdiero, C. (2012). Knowledge creation and inter-organizational relationships: The development of innovation in the railway industry. *Journal of Knowledge Management, 16*(4), 604–616. doi:10.1108/13673271211246176

Pfeffer, J. (1981). Management as symbolic action: The creation and maintenance of organizational paradigms. In L. L. Cummings & B. M. Staw (Eds.), Research in Organizational Behavior (vol. 3, pp. 1-52). Greenwich, CT: JAI Press.

Pfeffer, J. (1993). Barriers to the Advance of Organizational Science: Paradigm Development as a Dependent Variable. *Academy of Management Review, 18*(4), 599–620.

Pfeiffer, H., & Tonkin, E. (2012). Personal and Professional knowledge management. *Bulletin of the American Society for Knowledge Science and Technology, 38*(2), 22–23.

Pinto, H., Cruz, A. R., & de Almeida, H. (2016). Academic entrepreneurship and knowledge transfer networks: Translation process and boundary organizations. In L. Carvalho (Ed.), *Handbook of research on entrepreneurial success and its impact on regional development* (pp. 315–344). Hershey, PA: IGI Global. doi:10.4018/978-1-4666-9567-2.ch015

Polanyi, M. (1966). The logic of tacit inference. *Philosophy (London, England), 41*(155), 1–18. doi:10.1017/S0031819100066110

Polányi, M. (1966). *The Tacit Dimension*. London: Routledge & Kegan Paul.

Policy, T. L. (2010). *Fifth Pakistan Labour policy*. Pakistan: Academic Press.

Poole, J. P. (2013). Knowledge transfers from multinational to domestic firms: Evidence from worker mobility. *The Review of Economics and Statistics, 95*(2), 393–406. doi:10.1162/REST_a_00258

Poon, A. (1993). *Tourism, Technology and Competive Strategies*. Wallingford, UK: CAB International.

Porter, C. E., & Donthu, N. (2006). Using the technology acceptance model to explain how attitudes determine Internet usage: The role of perceived access barriers and demographics. *Journal of Business Research, 59*(9), 999–1007. doi:10.1016/j.jbusres.2006.06.003

Porter, M. E. (1990). *The Competitive Advantage of Nations*. New York: Free Press. doi:10.1007/978-1-349-11336-1

Powell, A., Piccoli, G., & Ives, B. (2004). Virtual teams: A review of current literature and directions for future research. *ACM SIG MIS Database, 35*(1), 6–36. doi:10.1145/968464.968467

Priestley, J. L., & Samaddar, S. (2007). The role of ambiguity in the transfer of knowledge within organizational networks. In G. Putnik & M. Cruz-Cunha (Eds.), *Knowledge and technology management in virtual organizations: Issues, trends, opportunities and solutions* (pp. 211–219). Hershey, PA: Idea Group Publishing. doi:10.4018/978-1-59904-165-0.ch009

Priestly, J. L. (2006). Knowledge transfer within interorganizational networks. In E. Coakes & S. Clarke (Eds.), *Encyclopedia of communities of practice in information and knowledge management* (pp. 307–316). Hershey, PA: IGI Global. doi:10.4018/978-1-59140-556-6.ch052

Prieto, I. M., Revilla, E., & Rodríguez-Prado, B. (2009). Managing the knowledge paradox in product development. *Journal of Knowledge Management*, *13*(3), 157–170. doi:10.1108/13673270910962941

Punin, J., Krishnamoorthy, M., & Zaki, M. (2002). LOGML: Log markup language for web usage mining. In WEBKDD 2001—Mining Web Log Data Across All Customers Touch Points (pp. 88-112).

Qu, H., & Lee, H. (2011). Travelers social identification and membership behaviors in online travel community. *Tourism Management*, *32*(6), 1262–1270. doi:10.1016/j.tourman.2010.12.002

Rad, A. A., & Benyoucef, M. (2010). A Model for Understanding Social Commerce. *Conference on Information Systems Applied Research, 3*, 12-25.

Ramayah, T., Yeap, J. A. L., & Ignatius, J. (2013). An empirical inquiry on knowledge sharing among academicians in higher learning institutions. *Minerva: A Review of Science, Learning and Policy*, *51*(2), 131–154.

Rampton, J. (2016, Mar 16). *Top 10 Freelance Job Sites in 2016*. Retrieved from http://www.johnrampton.com/top-10-freelance-job-sites-in-2016/

Ranft, A. L., & Lord, M. D. (2002). Acquiring new technologies and capabilities: A grounded model of acquisition implementation. *Organization Science*, *13*(4), 420–441. doi:10.1287/orsc.13.4.420.2952

Rautio, A. (2012). Social Media ROI as part of Marketing Strategy Work. Observations of Digital Agency Viewpoints (pp. 15-40)

Razmerita, L., Kirchner, K., & Sudzina, F. (2009). Personal knowledge management: The role of web 2.0 tools for managing knowledge at individual and organisational levels. *Online Knowledge Review*, *33*(6), 1021–1039. doi:10.1108/14684520911010981

Rehman, M., Mahmood, K. B., Salleh, R., & Amin, A. (2011). Review of Factors Affecting Knowledge Sharing Behavior. *2010 International Conference on E-business, Management and Economics, 3*, 223-227.

Reinhard, M., & Schmalholz, H. (1996). Technologietransfer in Deutschland: Stand und Reformbedarf. Berlin: Academic Press.

Reychav, I., & Weisberg, J. (2009). Good for Workers, good for Companies: How Knowledge Sharing benefits Individual Employees. *Knowledge and Process Management, 16*(4), 186–197. doi:10.1002/kpm.335

Ricci, F., Rokach, L., & Shapira, B. (2011). *Introduction to recommender systems handbook.* Springer, US. doi:10.1007/978-0-387-85820-3_1

Richards, D. (2007). Collaborative knowledge engineering: Socialising expert systems. In *11th International Conference on Computer Supported Cooperative Work in Design* (pp. 635–640).

Richter, A., Stocker, A., Müller, S., & Avram, G. (2011). Knowledge management goals revisited - A cross-sectional analysis of social software adoption in corporate environments. In *22nd Australasian Conference on Information Systems* (pp. 1–10).

Rickards, T., Smaje, K., & Sohoni, V. (2015, September). Transformer in chief: The new chief digital officer. *McKinsey Digital,* 1-6.

Ridzuan, A. A., Sam, H. K., & Adanan, M. A. (2008). Knowledge management practices in higher learning institutions in Sarawak. *Asian Journal of University Education, 4*(1), 69–89.

Riege, A. (2005). Three dozen knowledge sharing barriers managers must consider. *Journal of Knowledge Management, 9*(3), 18–35. doi:10.1108/13673270510602746

Rifkin, J. (1995). *The End of Work: The Decline of the Global Labour Force and the Dawn of the Post-Market Era.* Putnam Publishing Group.

Rive, P. (2008). Knowledge transfer and marketing in second life. In P. Zemliansky & K. St.Amant (Eds.), *Handbook of research on virtual workplaces and the new nature of business practices* (pp. 424–438). Hershey, PA: IGI Global. doi:10.4018/978-1-59904-893-2.ch030

Rodriguez, M., Peterson, R. M., & Krishnan, V. (2012). Social medias influence on business-to-business sales performance. *Journal of Personal Selling & Sales Management, 32*(2), 365–378. doi:10.2753/PSS0885-3134320306

Roemer, L. K., Bigelow, S. M., & Borsato, E. P. (2009). Strategies to meet knowledge transfer needs. In A. Dwivedi (Ed.), *Handbook of research on information technology management and clinical data administration in healthcare* (pp. 564–581). Hershey, PA: IGI Global. doi:10.4018/978-1-60566-356-2.ch035

Romhardt, K. (1997). Processes of knowledge preservation: Away from a technology dominated approach. In Proceedings der 21, "Deutschen Jahrestagung für Künstliche Intelligenz", 9.

Rothberg, H. N., & Klingenberg, B. (2010). Learning before doing: A theoretical perspective and practical lessons from a failed cross-border knowledge transfer initiative. In D. Harorimana (Ed.), *Cultural implications of knowledge sharing, management and transfer: Identifying competitive advantage* (pp. 277–294). Hershey, PA: IGI Global. doi:10.4018/978-1-60566-790-4.ch013

Rudawska, A. (2015). System nagród jako mechanizm wspierający wewnątrzorganizacyjne dzielenie się wiedzą. *Studia i Prace Wydziału Nauk Ekonomicznych i Zarządzania, 34*(4), 289–301.

Rugman, A. M., & Verbeke, A. (2001). Subsidiary-specific advantages in multinational enterprises. *Strategic Management Journal*, *22*(3), 237–250. doi:10.1002/smj.153

Rugman, A. M., & Verbeke, A. (2004). A perspective on regional and global strategies of multinational enterprises. *Journal of International Business Studies*, *35*(1), 3–18. doi:10.1057/palgrave.jibs.8400073

Ruhanen, L., & Cooper, C. (2004). Applying a knowledge management framework to tourism research. *Tourism Recreation Research*, *29*(1), 83–87. doi:10.1080/02508281.2004.11081434

Rulke, D. L., & Galaskiewicz, J. (2000). Distribution of Knowledge, Group Network Structure, and Group Performance. *Management Science*, *46*(5), 612–625. doi:10.1287/mnsc.46.5.612.12052

Saari, L. M., & Judge, T. A. (2004). Employee attitudes and job satisfaction. *Human Resource Management*, *43*(4), 395–407. doi:10.1002/hrm.20032

Sakaki, T., Okazaki, M., & Matsuo, Y. (2013). Tweet analysis for real-time event detection and earthquake reporting system development. *IEEE Transactions on Knowledge and Data Engineering*, *25*(4), 919–931. doi:10.1109/TKDE.2012.29

Saks, A. (1995). Viewpoints: A symposium on the usefulness of literacy research. *Research in the Teaching of English*, 326–348.

Sambamurthy, V., Bharadwaj, A., & Grover, V. (2003). Shaping Agility through Digital Options: Reconceptualizing the Role of Information Technology in Contemporary Firms. *Management Information Systems Quarterly*, *27*(2).

Santoro, M. D., & Bierly, P. E. (2006). Facilitators of knowledge transfer in university-industry collaborations: A knowledge-based perspective. *IEEE Transactions on Engineering Management*, *53*(4), 495–507. doi:10.1109/TEM.2006.883707

Sarala, R. M., Junni, P., Cooper, C. L., & Tarba, S. Y. (2014). A sociocultural perspective on knowledge transfer in mergers and acquisitions. *Journal of Management*, *42*(5), 1230–1249. doi:10.1177/0149206314530167

Sarkar, M., & Banerjee, S. (2016). Exploring social network privacy measurement using fuzzy vector commitment. *Intelligent Decision Technologies*, *10*(3), 285–297. doi:10.3233/IDT-160256

Sarter, N. R., & Woods, D. D. (1993). *Cognitive engineering in aerospace application: Pilot interaction with cockpit automation*. Mofferr Field, CA: Nasa Ames Research Centre.

Sarwar, B., Karypis, G., Konstan, J., & Riedl, J. (2001, April). Item-based collaborative filtering recommendation algorithms. In *Proceedings of the 10th international conference on World Wide Web* (pp. 285-295). ACM.

Sashi, C. M. (2012). Customer engagement, buyer–seller relationships, and social media. *Management Decision*, *50*(2), 253–272. doi:10.1108/00251741211203551

Saul, H. (2016,). Instafamous: Meet the social media influencers redefining celebrity. *Independent.* Retrieved from http://www.independent.co.uk/news/people/instagram-model-natasha-oakley-iskra-lawrence-kayla-itsines-kendall-jenner-jordyn-woods-a6907551.html

Scardamalia, M. (2002). Collective cognitive responsibility for the advancement of knowledge. In B. Smith (Ed.), *Liberal education in a knowledge society* (pp. 67–98). Chicago, IL: Open Court.

Schall, M. S. (1981). *An exploration into a successful corporation's saga-vision and its rhetorical community.* Paper presented at the ICAl SCA Conference on Interpretive Approaches to Organizational Communication, Alta, UT.

Schein, E. H. (1985). *Organizational Culture and Leadership.* San Francisco, CA: Jossey-Bass.

Schermerhorn, J. R., Hunt, J. G., & Osborn, R. N. (1994). *Managing organizational behavior.* New York: Wiley.

Schermerhorn, J. R. Jr. (1977). Information sharing as an interorganizational activity. *Academy of Management Journal, 20*(1), 148–153. doi:10.2307/255469 PMID:10305920

Schlagwein, D., & Hu, M. (2016). How and why organisations use social media: Five use types and their relation to absorptive capacity. *Journal of Information Technology,* (May): 1–28.

Schmallegger, D., & Carson, D. (2008). Blogs in tourism: Changing approaches to information exchange. *Journal of Vacation Marketing, 14*(2), 99-110.

Schneider, D. A. (2006). Practical Considerations for Real-Time Business Intelligence. *BIRTE Workshop, Business Intelligence for the Real-Time Enterprises* (1-3). Seoul, Korea: Springer.

Schreyer, P. (2000). *The contribution of information and communication technology to output growth.* STI Working Paper.

Schutt, R. K. (2006). *Investigating the social world: The process and practice of research.* Thousand Oaks, CA: Sage.

Scott, B. G., & Weems, C. F. (2010). Patterns of actual and perceived control: Are control profiles differentially related to internalizing and externalizing problems in youth? *Anxiety, Stress, and Coping, 23*(5), 515–528. doi:10.1080/10615801003611479 PMID:20155530

Scott, N., Cooper, C., & Baggio, R. (2008). Destination networks: Four Australian cases. *Annals of Tourism Research, 35*(1), 169–188. doi:10.1016/j.annals.2007.07.004

Scott, W. R. (2014). *Institutions and Organizations: Ideas, Interests, and Identities.* Los Angeles, CA: Sage.

Search Engine Land. (2014). *About Local Consumer Review Survey 2014.* Retrieved from http://searchengineland.com/88-consumers-trust-online-reviews-much-personal-recommendations-195803

Seidler-de Alwis, R., & Hartmann, E. (2008). The use of tacit knowledge within innovative companies: Knowledge management in innovative enterprises. *Journal of Knowledge Management, 12*(1), 133–147. doi:10.1108/13673270810852449

Senge, P. M. (1998). The leader's new work. *Leading Organizations,* 439-457.

Serdar, D., Jacobs, M., Nayir, D. Z., Khilji, S., & Wang, X. (2013). The quasi-moderating role of organizational culture in the relationship between rewards and knowledge shared and gained. *Journal of Knowledge Management, 18*(1), 19–37.

Shabib, N., Gulla, J. A., & Krogstie, J. (2013). On the Intrinsic Challenges of Group Recommendation. In *RSWeb*. RecSys.

Shafaei, A., & Razak, N. A. (2016). International Postgraduate Students' Cross-Cultural Adaptation in Malaysia: Antecedents and Outcomes. *Research in Higher Education,* 1–29.

Shah, S. S., Aziz, J., Jaffari, A. R., Ejaz, M. W., Khattak, A., & Rehman, K. R. A. (2011). Mentoring and its effects on turnover intentions in perspective of Pakistan's telecom sector. *Information Management and Business Review, 3*(3), 133–138.

Shani, A., & Pizam, A. (2009). Work-related depression among hotel employees. *Cornell Hospitality Quarterly, 50*(4), 446–459. doi:10.1177/1938965509344294

Shaw, G., & Williams, A. (2009). Knowledge transfer and management in tourism organisations: An emerging research agenda. *Tourism Management, 30*(3), 325–335. doi:10.1016/j.tourman.2008.02.023

Sheldon, P. (1997). *Tourism Information Technologies.* Oxford, UK: CAB.

Shen, K. N., Yu, A. Y., & Khalifa, M. (2010). Knowledge contribution in virtual communities: Accounting for multiple dimensions of social presence through social identity. *Behaviour & Information Technology, 29*(4), 337–348. doi:10.1080/01449290903156622

Sherif, K., & Sherif, A. (2008). Think social capital before you think knowledge transfer. In M. Jennex (Ed.), *Current issues in knowledge management* (pp. 53–65). Hershey, PA: IGI Global. doi:10.4018/978-1-59904-916-8.ch005

Sher, P. J., & Lee, V. C. (2004). Information technology as a facilitator for enhancing dynamic capabilities through knowledge management. *Information & Management, 41*(8), 933–945. doi:10.1016/j.im.2003.06.004

Shimp, T., & Andrews, J. C. (2013). *Advertising promotion and other aspects of integrated marketing communications.* Cengage Learning.

Shoaib, M., Noor, A., Tirmizi, S. R., & Bashir, S. (2009). Determinants of employee retention in telecom sector of Pakistan. *Proceedings of the 2nd CBRC,* 14.

Siehl, C., & Martin, J. (1981). *Learning organizational culture.* Working paper, Graduate School of Business. Stanford University.

Sigala, M., & Chalkiti, K. (2012). Knowledge management and Web 2.0: preliminary findings from the Greek tourism industry. *Social Media in Travel, Tourism and Hospitality: Theory, Practice and Cases*, 261.

Sigalaa, M., & Chalkiti, K. (2015). Knowledge management, social media and employee creativity. *International Journal of Hospitality Management*, *45*, 44–58. doi:10.1016/j.ijhm.2014.11.003

Sigala, M., & Chalkiti, K. (2014). Investigating the exploitation of web 2.0 for knowledge management in the Greek tourism industry: An utilisation–importance analysis. *Computers in Human Behavior*, *30*, 800–812. doi:10.1016/j.chb.2013.05.032

Silberman, N. A. (2005). Beyond theme parks and digitized data: what can cultural heritage technologies contribute to the public understanding of the past? *Interdisciplinarity or The Best of Both Worlds: The Grand Challenge for Cultural Heritage Informatics in the 21st Century*. Available at: http://works.bepress.com/neil_silberman/39/

Silerman, D. (2006). *Interpreting qualitative data* (3rd ed.). Thousand Oaks, CA: Sage Publications.

Singh, A., Rose, C., Visweswariah, K., Chenthamarakshan, V., & Kambhatla, N. (2010, October). PROSPECT: a system for screening candidates for recruitment. In *Proceedings of the 19th ACM international conference on Information and knowledge management* (pp. 659-668). ACM. doi:10.1145/1871437.1871523

SINTEF. (2013). Big data, for better or worse: 90% of world's data generated over last two years. *Science Daily*. Retrieved January 13, 2015 from www.sciencedaily.com/releases/2013/05/130522085217.htm

Skitka, L. J., Mosier, K. L., & Burdick, M. (1999). Does automation bias decision-making? *International Journal of Human-Computer Studies*, *51*(5), 991–1006. doi:10.1006/ijhc.1999.0252

Skok, W., & Kalmanovitch, C. (2005). Evaluating the role and effectiveness of an intranet in facilitating knowledge management: A case study at Surrey County Council. *Information & Management*, *42*(5), 731–744. doi:10.1016/j.im.2004.04.008

Smartinsights.com. (2016). *Global social media research summary*. Retrieved October 11, 2016, from http://www.smartinsights.com/social-media-marketing/social-media-strategy/new-global-social-media-research/

Smith, C., & Jenner, P. (1998). Tourism and the Internet. *Travel & Tourism Analyst*, (1), 62-81.

Smith, E. A. (2001). The role of tacit and explicit knowledge in the workplace. *Journal of Knowledge Management*, *5*(4), 311–321. doi:10.1108/13673270110411733

Smith, T. (2009). The social media revolution. *International Journal of Market Research*, *51*(4), 559–561. doi:10.2501/S1470785309200773

Sobkowicz, P., Kaschesky, M., & Bouchard, G. (2012). Opinion mining in social media: Modeling, simulating, and forecasting. *Political Opinions in the Web, 29*(4), 470-479.

Social, M. S. (2015). *How Australian people and businesses are using social media.* Retrieved from: www.sensis.com.au/socialmediareport

Sohail, M. S., & Daud, S. (2009). Knowledge sharing in higher education institutions: Perspectives from Malaysia. *VINE: The Journal of Information and Knowledge Management Systems, 39*(2), 125-142.

Solli-Sæther, H., & Gottschalk, P. (2010). Knowledge transfer. In H. Solli-Sæther & P. Gottschalk (Eds.), *Managing IT outsourcing performance* (pp. 132–141). Hershey, PA: IGI Global. doi:10.4018/978-1-60566-796-6.ch007

Solmaz, B., Tekin, G., Herzem, Z., & Demir, M. (2013). İnternet ve social media kullanımı üzerine bir uygulama. *Selçuk İletişim, 7*(4), 24–32.

Solomon, M. R., Ashmore, R. D., & Longo, L. C. (1992). The Beauty Match-up Hypothesis: Congruence between Types of Beauty and Product Images in Advertising. *Journal of Advertising, 21*(4), 23–34. doi:10.1080/00913367.1992.10673383

Soto-Acosta, P., Perez-Gonzalez, D., & Popa, S. (2014). Determinants of Web 2.0 technologies for knowledge sharing in SMEs. *Service Business, 8*(3), 425–438. doi:10.1007/s11628-014-0247-9

Sowmya, K., & Panchanatham, N. (2014). Job Anxiety as an Outcome of Organizational Politics in Banking Sector-Chennai. *International Journal of Management & Innovation, 6*(2).

Sparr, J. L., & Sonnentag, S. (2008). Fairness perceptions of supervisor feedback, LMX, and employee well-being at work. *European Journal of Work and Organizational Psychology, 17*(2), 198–225. doi:10.1080/13594320701743590

Spector, P. E. (1997). *Job satisfaction: Application, assessment, causes, and consequences* (Vol. 3). Sage publications.

Srivastava, T., Desikan, P., & Kumar, V. (2005). Web Mining – Concepts, Applications and Research Directions. *Foundations and Advances in Data Mining*: Studies in Fuzziness and Soft Computing, *180*, 275–307. doi:10.1007/11362197_10

Stankosky, M., & Baldanza, C. (2001). *A systems approach to engineering a KM system.* Unpublished Manuscript.

Stankov, U., Lazic, L., & Dragicevic, V. (2010). The extent of use of basic Facebook user-generated content by the national tourism organizations in Europe. *European Journal of Tourism Research, 3*(2), 105.

Starbuck, W. H. (1992). Learning by knowledge-intensive firms. *Journal of Management Studies, 29*(6), 713–740. doi:10.1111/j.1467-6486.1992.tb00686.x

Stasser, G., & Stewart, D. (1992). Discovery of hidden profiles by decision-making groups: Solving a problem versus making a judgment. *Journal of Personality and Social Psychology, 63*(3), 426–434. doi:10.1037/0022-3514.63.3.426

Stasser, G., & Titus, W. (1987). Effects of information load and percentage of shared information on the dissemination of unshared information during group discussion. *Journal of Personality and Social Psychology, 53*(1), 81–93. doi:10.1037/0022-3514.53.1.81

Stasser, G., Titus, W., & Wittenbaum, G. M. (1995). Expert roles and information exchange during discussion: The importance of knowing who knows what. *Journal of Experimental Social Psychology, 31*(3), 244–265. doi:10.1006/jesp.1995.1012

Statista. (2016). *Leading social networks worldwide as of April 2016, ranked by number of active users (in millions)*. Retrieved from http://www.statista.com/statistics/272014/global-social-networks-ranked-by-number-of-users/

Stenius, M., Hankonen, N., Ravaia, N., & Haukkala, A. (2016). Why share expertise? A closer look at the quality of motivation to share or withhold knowledge. *Journal of Knowledge Management, 20*(2), 181–198. doi:10.1108/JKM-03-2015-0124

Sternthal, B., Dholakia, R., & Leavitt, C. (1978). The Persuasive Effect of Source Credibility: Tests of Cognitive Response. *The Journal of Consumer Research, 4*(4), 252–260. doi:10.1086/208704

Stevenson, M., & Greenwood, M. A. (2006). Learning Information Extraction Patterns Using WordNet. In *Proceeding of The Third International WordNet Conference* (pp. 95-102).

Storey, M. A., Treude, C., Deursen, A., & Cheng, L. T. (2010). The Impact of Social Media on Software Engineering Practices and Tools. *FoSER '10 Proceedings of the FSE/SDP workshop on Future of software engineering research, 359-364*. doi:10.1145/1882362.1882435

Stoyanov, A., & Zubanov, N. (2012). Productivity spillovers across firms through worker mobility. *American Economic Journal: Applied Economics, 4*(2), 168–198. doi:10.1257/app.4.2.168

Strategy, A. (2015). Banking on Digital-Three actions banks can take to generate more value from their digital investments. Academic Press.

Strauss, A., & Corbin, J. (1990). *Basics of qualitative research: Grounded theory procedures and techniques*. Newbury Park, CA: Sage Publications.

Stringhini, G., Kruegel, C., & Vigna, G. (2010). Detecting spammers on social networks. In *Proceedings of the 26th Annual Computer Security Applications Conference*, (pp. 1–9).

Suh, B., & Han, I. (2003). The impact of customer trust and perception of security control on the acceptance of electronic commerce. *International Journal of Electronic Commerce, 7*(3), 135–161.

Sultan, N. (2013). Knowledge management in the age of cloud computing and Web 2.0: Experiencing the power of disruptive innovations. *International Journal of Information Management, 33*(1), 160–165. doi:10.1016/j.ijinfomgt.2012.08.006

Summers, J. O. (2001). Guidelines for Conducting Research and Publishing in Marketing: From Conceptualization Though the Review Process. *Journal of the Academy of Marketing Science, 29*(4), 405–415. doi:10.1177/03079450094243

Surowiecki, J. (Ed.). (2005). *The Wisdom of the Crowds*. New York: Anchor Books.

Swan, J., Newell, S., Scarbrough, H., & Hislop, D. (1999). Knowledge management and innovation: Networks and networking. *Journal of Knowledge Management*, 3(4), 262–275. doi:10.1108/13673279910304014

Swets, J. A. (1998). Measuring the accuracy of diagnostic systems. *Science*, 240(4857), 1285–1293. doi:10.1126/science.3287615 PMID:3287615

Syed-Ihksan, S. O. S., & Rowland, R. (2004). Knowledge management in a public organization: A study on the relationship between organizational elements and the performance of knowledge transfer. *Journal of Knowledge Management*, 8(2), 95–111. doi:10.1108/13673270410529145

Szöllosi-Janse, M. (2004). Wissensgesellschaft in Deutschland: Überlegungen zur Neubestimmung der deutschen Zeitgeschichte uber Verwissenschaftlichungsprozesse. *Geschichte und Gesellschaft (Vandenhoeck & Ruprecht)*, 30, 277–313.

Tapscott, D., & Caston, A. (1993). Paradigm Shift: The New Promise of Information Technology. McGraw Hill, Inc.

Taylor, S., & Todd, P. A. (1995). Understanding information technology usage: A test of competing models. *Information Systems Research*, 6(2), 144–176. doi:10.1287/isre.6.2.144

Teas, K. R., & Palan, K. M. (1997). The Realms of Scientific Meaning Framework for Constructing Theoretically Meaningful Nominal Definitions of Marketing Concepts. *Journal of Marketing*, 61(4), 52–67. doi:10.2307/1251830

Tee, M. Y., & Karney, D. (2010). Sharing and cultivating tacit knowledge in an online learning environment. *International Journal of Computer-Supported Collaborative Learning*, 5(4), 385–413. doi:10.1007/s11412-010-9095-3

Teng, J. T. C., & Song, S. (2011). An exploratory examination of knowledge sharing behaviors: Solicited and voluntary. *Journal of Knowledge Management*, 15(1), 104–117. doi:10.1108/13673271111108729

Tenzer, H., Pudelko, M., & Harzing, A.-W. (2013). The impact of language barriers on trust formation in multinational teams. *Journal of International Business Studies*, 45(5), 508–535. doi:10.1057/jibs.2013.64

Tesser, A., & Paulhus, D. (1983). The definition of self: Private and public self-evaluation management strategies. *Journal of Personality and Social Psychology*, 44(4), 672–682. doi:10.1037/0022-3514.44.4.672

Tett, R. P., & Meyer, J. P. (1993). Job satisfaction, organizational commitment, turnover intention, and turnover: Path analyses based on meta analytic findings. *Personnel Psychology*, 46(2), 259–293. doi:10.1111/j.1744-6570.1993.tb00874.x

Tho, N. D., & Trang, N. T. M. (2015). Can knowledge be transferred from business schools to business organizations through in-service training students? SEM and fsQCA findings. *Journal of Business Research*, *68*(6), 1332–1340. doi:10.1016/j.jbusres.2014.12.003

Thornton, P. H. (2004). *Markets From Culture: Institutional Logics and Organizational Decisions in Higher Education Publishing*. Stanford, CA: Stanford University Press.

Thornton, P. H., & Ocasio, W. (1999). Institutional logics and the historical contingency of power in organizations: Executive succession in the higher education publishing industry, 19581990. *American Journal of Sociology*, *105*(3), 801–843. doi:10.1086/210361

Thornton, P. H., & Ocasio, W. (2008). Institutional logics. In R. Greenwood, C. Oliver, K. Sahlin, & R. Suddaby (Eds.), *The Sage Handbook of Organizational Institutionalism* (pp. 99–129). Los Angeles, CA: Sage. doi:10.4135/9781849200387.n4

Thornton, P. H., Ocasio, W., & Lounsbury, M. (2012). *The Institutional Logics Perspective: A New Approach to Culture, Structure, and Process*. Oxford, UK: Oxford University Press. doi:10.1093/acprof:oso/9780199601936.001.0001

Thorp, J. (2003). *The information paradox: realizing the business benefits of information technology*. McGraw-Hill Ryerson.

Tichy, N. M. (1982). Managing change strategically: The technical, political, and cultural keys. *Organizational Dynamics*, *11*(Autumn), 59–80. doi:10.1016/0090-2616(82)90005-5 PMID:10298937

Tobin, R. (2016). Social media: Platform use keeps rising. *Travel Weekly*. Retrieved from http://www.travelweekly.com/ConsumerSurvey2016/Social-media-platform-use-keeps-rising

Tojjari, F., Esmaeili, M. R., & Bavandpour, R. (2013). The effect of self-efficacy on job satisfaction of sport referees. *European Journal of Experimental Biology*, *3*(2), 219–225.

Tolbert, P. S., David, R. J., & Sine, W. D. (2011). Studying choice and change: The intersection of institutional theory and entrepreneurship research. *Organization Science*, *22*(5), 1332–1344. doi:10.1287/orsc.1100.0601

Tosi, H. L., Mero, N. P., & Rizzo, J. R. (2000). *Managing organizational behaviour* (4th ed.). Oxford, UK: Blackwell Blackwell Business.

Trant, J. (2009). Studying social tagging and folksonomy: A review and framework. *Journal of Digital Information*, *10*(1).

Treem, J. W., & Leonardi, P. M. (2012). Social media use in organizations: Exploring the affordances of visibility, editability, persistence, and association. *Communication Yearbook*, *36*, 143-189.

Trope, Y., Liberman, N., & Wakslak, C. (2007). Construal levels and psychological distance: Effects on representation, prediction, evaluation, and behavior. *Journal of Consumer Psychology: The Official Journal of the Society for Consumer Psychology*, *17*(2), 83.

Trope, Y., & Liberman, N. (2011). Construal level theory. In P. Van Lange, A. W. Kruglanski, & E. T. Higgins (Eds.), *Handbook of Theories of Social Psychology*. London: Sage Publications.

Troutman, C. S., Burke, K. G., & Beeler, J. D. (2011). The Effects Of Self-Efficacy, Assertiveness, Stress, And Gender On Intention To Turnover In Public Accounting. *Journal of Applied Business Research*, *16*(3). doi:10.19030/jabr.v16i3.2043

Trusov, M., Bucklin, R. E., & Pauwels, K. (2009). Effects of Word-of-Mouth versus Traditional Marketing: Findings from an Internet Social Networking Site. *Journal of Marketing*, *73*(5), 90–102. doi:10.1509/jmkg.73.5.90

Tsai, C., Shen, P., & Chiang, N. (2012). An investigation of the relationship between intellectual capital and knowledge transfer: An exploratory case study of Taiwanese bands. *International Journal of Art, Culture and Design Technologies*, *2*(2), 43–56. doi:10.4018/ijacdt.2012070104

Tsoukas, H., & Vladimirou, E. (2001). What is organizational knowledge? *Journal of Management Studies*, *38*(7), 973–993. doi:10.1111/1467-6486.00268

Tung, V. W. S., & Ritchie, J. B. (2011). Exploring the essence of memorable tourism experiences. *Annals of Tourism Research*, *38*(4), 1367–1386. doi:10.1016/j.annals.2011.03.009

Tutar, H. (2012). *Yönetim bilgi sistemi*. Ankara: Seçkin Yayıncılık.

Tziner, A., & Eden, D. (1985). Effects of crew composition on crew performance: Does the whole equal the sum of its parts? *The Journal of Applied Psychology*, *70*(1), 85–93. doi:10.1037/0021-9010.70.1.85

Uchihira, N. (2014). Knowledge transfer in product-based service design. In M. Kosaka & K. Shirahada (Eds.), *Progressive trends in knowledge and system-based science for service innovation* (pp. 258–272). Hershey, PA: IGI Global. doi:10.4018/978-1-4666-4663-6.ch014

Udo, G. J., Guimãrães, T., & Igbaria, M. (1997). An investigation of the antecedents of turnover intention for manufacturing plant managers. *International Journal of Operations & Production Management*, *17*(9), 912–930. doi:10.1108/01443579710171280

Ugolini, F., Massetti, L., Sanesi, G., & Pearlmutter, D. (2015). Knowledge transfer between stakeholders in the field of urban forestry and green infrastructure: Results of a European survey. *Land Use Policy*, *49*, 365–381. doi:10.1016/j.landusepol.2015.08.019

UNESCO. (2005). *Towards knowledge societies*. Paris: UNESCO.

Usman, S., H. & Oyefolahan, O. (2014). Determinants of Knowledge Sharing Using Web Technologies among Students in Higher Education. *Journal of Knowledge Management, Economics and Information Technology*, *4*(2).

Usoro, A. (2013). Social media for knowledge sharing in African development institutions: A viewpoint paper. *Computing and Information Systems*, *17*(1), 28–30.

Usunier, J. C. (1998). *International and cross-cultural management research.* SAGE Publications Ltd.

Van de Ven, A. H., & Koenig, R. Jr (1975). *Pair-Wise Inter-Agency Relationships: theory and preliminary findings.* Working Paper, Department of Administrative Sciences, Kent State University.

Van den Hooff, B., & de Ridder, J. A. (2004). Knowledge sharing in context: The influence of organizational commitment, communication climate and CMC use on knowledge sharing. *Journal of Knowledge Management, 8*(6), 117–130. doi:10.1108/13673270410567675

Van den Hooff, B., Elving, W. J. L., Meeuwsen, J. M., & Dumoulin, C. M. (2003). *Knowledge Sharing* in Knowledge Communities. In M. H. Huysman, V. Wulf, & E. Wenger (Eds.), *Communities and Technologies.* Deventer: Kluwer Academic Publishers. doi:10.1007/978-94-017-0115-0_7

Van Eijsden, G. A. (2000). *Banking in the Digital Economy* (Doctoral Dissertation). Technical University Eindhoven.

Vance, D. M. (1997). Information, knowledge and wisdom: the epistemic hierarchy and computer-based information system. In B. Perkins & I. Vessey (Eds.), *Proceedings of the Third Americas Conference on Information Systems.* Academic Press.

Veling, L., Murnane, S., Carcary, M., & Zlydareva, O. (2014). *The Digital Imperative.* IVI White Paper Series.

Ventola, C. L. (2014). Social media and health care professionals: Benefits, risks, and best practices. *Pharmacy and Therapeutics, 39*(5), 356–364. PMID:24883008

Verbeke, A. (2010). International acquisition success: Social community and dominant logic dimensions. *Journal of International Business Studies, 41*(1), 38–46. doi:10.1057/jibs.2009.70

Viejo, A., & Sánchez, D. (2015). Enforcing transparent access to private content in social networks by means of automatic sanitization. *Expert Systems with Applications, 42*(23), 9366–9378. doi:10.1016/j.eswa.2015.08.014

Vijaya, M. S., & Sudha, V. P. (2013). Research Directions in Social Network Mining with Empirical Study on Opinion Mining. *CSI Communications, 37*(9), 24–27.

Volady, L. (2013). *An Investigation of Factors Influencing Knowledge Sharing Among Undergraduate Teacher Education Students.* Retrieved September 9, 2013, from http://volady0002.wordpress.com/knowledge-sharingamong-undegraduate-students/

Von Krogh, G. (1999). *Developing a knowledge-based theory of the firm.* St. Gallen: University of St. Gallen.

Von Krogh, G. (2011). Knowledge Sharing in Organizations: The role of communities. In E.-S. Mark & L. Marjorie (Eds.), *Handbook of Organizational Learning and Knowledge Management* (pp. 403–432). Wiley & Sons.

von Krogh, G. (2012). How does social software change knowledge management? Toward a strategic research agenda. *The Journal of Strategic Information Systems*, *21*(2), 154–164. doi:10.1016/j.jsis.2012.04.003

Vuori, V. (2011). *Social Media Changing the Competitive Intelligence Process: Elicitation of Employees' Competitive Knowledge*. Academic Dissertation. Available: http://dspace.cc.tut.fi/dpub/bitstream/handle/123456789/20724/vuori.pdf

Vuori, V. (2011). *Social media changing the competitive intelligence process: Elicitation of employees' competitive knowledge*. Tampere University of Technology. Retrieved October 10, 2016, from http://dspace.cc.tut.fi/dpub/bitstream/handle/123456789/20724/vuori.pdf

Vuori, V., & Okkonen, J. (2012). Refining information and knowledge by social media applications: Adding value by insight. *VINE Information and Knowledge Management*, *42*(1), 117–128.

Wagner, C., & Bolloju, N. (2005). Supporting knowledge management in organizations with conversational technologies: Discussion forums, weblogs, and wikis. *Journal of Database Management*, *16*(2), 1–8.

Wahlroos, J. K. (2010). *Social Media as a Form of Organizational Knowledge Sharing. A Case Study on Employee Participation*. Unpublished thesis of the University of Helsinki. Retrieved from https://helda.helsinki.fi/bitstream/handle/10138/24624/Thesis.Johanna.Wahlroos.pdf?sequence=1

Walsh, J. P., & Ungson, G. R. (1991). Organizational Memory. *Academy of Management Review*, *16*(1), 57–91. doi:10.5465/AMR.1991.4278992

Wang, J., Smailes, E., Sareen, J., Schmitz, N., Fick, G., & Patten, S. (2012). Three job-related stress models and depression: A population-based study. *Social Psychiatry and Psychiatric Epidemiology*, *47*(2), 185–193. doi:10.1007/s00127-011-0340-5 PMID:21234534

Wangpipatwong, S. (2009). Factors Influencing Knowledge Sharing Among University Students. *Proceedings of the 17th International Conference on Computers in Education*, 800-807.

Wang, S., & Noe, R. A. (2010). Knowledge sharing: A review and directions for future research. *Human Resource Management Review*, *20*(2), 115–131. doi:10.1016/j.hrmr.2009.10.001

Wang, T., Keng-Jung Yeh, R., Chen, C., & Tsydypov, Z. (2016). What drives electronic word-of-mouth on social networking sites? Perspectives of social capital and self-determination. *Telematics and Informatics*, *33*(4), 1034–1047. doi:10.1016/j.tele.2016.03.005

Wang, Z., & Wang, N. (2012). Knowledge sharing, innovation and firm performance. *Expert Systems with Applications: An International Journal*, *39*(10), 8899–8908. doi:10.1016/j.eswa.2012.02.017

Wan, Z., Haggerty, N., & Wang, Y. (2015). Individual level knowledge transfer in virtual settings: A review and synthesis. *International Journal of Knowledge Management*, *11*(2), 29–61. doi:10.4018/IJKM.2015040103

Warr, P. (1990). The measurement of well being and other aspects of mental health. *Journal of Occupational Psychology*, *63*(3), 193–210. doi:10.1111/j.2044-8325.1990.tb00521.x

wearesocial.com. (2016). *Digital in 2016*. Retrieved October 10, 2016, from http://wearesocial.com/uk/special-reports/digital-in-2016

Wegner, D. M. (1986). Transactive memory: A contemporary analysis of the group mind. In G. Mullen & G. Goethals (Eds.), *Theories of Group Behavior*. New York: Springer-Verlag.

Weick, K. E. (1991). The nontraditional quality of organizational learning. *Organization Science*, *2*(1), 116–123. doi:10.1287/orsc.2.1.116

Weick, K. E. (1995). *Sensemaking in Organizations*. Thousand Oaks, CA: Sage.

Weigmann, K. (2015). Lessons learned in germany. *EMBO Reports*, *16*(2), 142–145. doi:10.15252/embr.201440011 PMID:25582450

Weikum, G., & Theobal, M. (2010). From information to knowledge: harvesting entities and relationships from web sources. In *Proceedings of the twenty-ninth ACM SIGMOD-SIGACT-SIGART symposium on Principles of database systems*, (pp.65-76). doi:10.1145/1807085.1807097

Weill, P., Subramani, M., & Broadbent, M. (2002). Building IT infrastructure for strategic agility. *MIT Sloan Management Review*, *44*(1), 57.

Weinberg, B. D., & Pehlivan, E. (2011). Social spending: Managing the social media mix. *Business Horizons*, *54*(2), 275–282. doi:10.1016/j.bushor.2011.01.008

Wells, K. B., & Sturm, R. (1995). Care for depression in a changing environment. *Health Affairs*, *14*(3), 78–89. doi:10.1377/hlthaff.14.3.78 PMID:7498906

Werthner H., & Klein S. (1999). *Information technology and tourism. A challenging relationship*. Springer Computer Science.

Werthner, H., & Klein, S. (1999). ICT and the changing landscape of global tourism distribution. *Electronic Markets*, *9*(4), 256–262. doi:10.1080/101967899358941

West, M. A., Garrod, S., & Carletta, J. (1997). Group decision-making and effectiveness: unexplored boundaries. In C. L. Cooper & S. E. Jackson (Eds.), *Creating tomorrow's organizations a handbook for future research in organizational behaviour*. New York: John Wiley & Sons.

Whelan, E., Parise, S., De Valk, J., & Aalbers, R. (2011). Creating employee networks that deliver open innovation. *MIT Sloan Management Review*, *53*(1), 37–44.

Wickens, C. D., Conejo, R., & Gempler, K. (1999). Unreliable automated attention cueing for air-ground targeting and traffic maneuvering. *Proceedings of the Human Factors and Ergonomics Society Annual Meeting*, *43*(1), 21-25. doi:10.1177/154193129904300105

Wiener, E. L. (1981). Complacency: Is the term useful for air safety. *Proceedings of the 26th Corporate Aviation Safety Seminar*.

Wiewiora, A., Trigunarsyah, B., & Murphy, G. (2012). Knowledge transfer in project-based organisations: The need for a unique approach. In *Organizational learning and knowledge: Concepts, methodologies, tools and applications* (pp. 262–274). Hershey, PA: IGI Global. doi:10.4018/978-1-60960-783-8.ch116

Wilkesmann, U. & Würmseer, G. (2007). *Wissensmanagement an Universitäten.* Discussion papers des Zentrums für Weiterbildung Universität Dortmund, 03.

Witherspoon, C. L., Bergner, J., Cockrell, C., & Stone, D. N. (2013). Antecedents of organizational knowledge sharing: A meta-analysis and critique. *Journal of Knowledge Management, 17*(2), 250–277. doi:10.1108/13673271311315204

Wong, C.-S., Wong, Y., Hui, C., & Law, K. S. (2001). The significant role of Chinese employees organizational commitment: Implications for managing employees in Chinese societies. *Journal of World Business, 36*(3), 326–340. doi:10.1016/S1090-9516(01)00058-X

Wu, C.-W. (2016). The performance impact of social media in the chain store industry. *Journal of Business Research, 69*(11), 5310–5316. doi:10.1016/j.jbusres.2016.04.130

Wu, J., Liu, N., & Xuan, Z. (2011). Simulation on knowledge transfer processes from the perspectives of individuals mentality and behavior. *International Journal of Knowledge and Systems Science, 2*(4), 1–13. doi:10.4018/jkss.2011100101

Wu, S. H., & Hsu, F. B. (2001). Towards a knowledge-based view of OEM relationship building: Sharing of industrial experiences in Taiwan. *International Journal of Technology Management, 22*(5), 503–524. doi:10.1504/IJTM.2001.002975

Xia, H., & Gupta, A. (2008). Common knowledge sharing model of 24-hour knowledge factory of grid computing based on case based reasoning. *International Journal of Knowledge Management, 4*(3), 1–18. doi:10.4018/jkm.2008070101

Xiang, Z., & Gretzel, U. (2010). Role of social media in online travel information search. *Tourism Management, 31*(2), 179–188. doi:10.1016/j.tourman.2009.02.016

Xiao, H., & Smith, S. L. J. (2010). Professional communication in an applied tourism research community. *Tourism Management, 31*(3), 402–411. doi:10.1016/j.tourman.2009.04.008

Xu, X., & Du-Babcock, B. (2012). Impact of English-language Proficiency on Chinese Expatriates' Adjustment to Overseas Assignments. *Global Advances in Business Communication, 1*(1), 4.

Yagolnitser, M. A. (2015). Diagnosis of Conditions for the Formation of Innovation Clusters in Russian Regions: Mathematical and Statistical Approach. *International Journal of Econometrics and Financial Management, 3*(1), 38–43.

Yamao, S., & Sekiguchi, T. (2015). Employee commitment to corporate globalization: The role of English language proficiency and human resource practices. *Journal of World Business, 50*(1), 168–179. doi:10.1016/j.jwb.2014.03.001

Yan, G., He, W., Shen, J., & Tang, C. (2014). A bilingual approach for conducting Chinese and English social media sentiment analysis. *Computer Networks, 75*, 491–503. doi:10.1016/j.comnet.2014.08.021

Yang, C., Harkreader, R. C., & Gu, G. (2010). *Recent Advances in Intrusion Detection. In* Lecture Notes in Computer Science: Vol. 6961. *Die free or live hard? empirical evaluation and new design for ghting evolving twitter spammers* (pp. 318–337). Berlin: Springer.

Yang, J. (2007). The impact of knowledge sharing on organizational learning and effectiveness. *Journal of Knowledge Management, 11*(2), 83–90. doi:10.1108/13673270710738933

Yang, J. T., & Wan, C. S. (2004). Advancing organizational effectiveness and knowledge management implementation. *Tourism Management, 25*(5), 593–601. doi:10.1016/j.tourman.2003.08.002

Yang, J.-T. (2004). Job-related knowledge sharing: Comparative case studies. *Journal of Knowledge Management, 8*(3), 118–126. doi:10.1108/13673270410541088

Yang, S., Lin, S., Carlson, J. R., & Ross, W. T. Jr. (2016). Brand engagement on social media: Will firms social media efforts influence search engine advertising effectiveness? *Journal of Marketing Management, 32*(5-6), 526–557. doi:10.1080/0267257X.2016.1143863

Yassin, F., Salim, J., & Sahari, N. (2013). The Influence of Organizational Factors on Knowledge Sharing Using ICT among Teachers. *Procedia Technology, 11*, 272–280. doi:10.1016/j.protcy.2013.12.191

Yesil, S., & Dereli, S. F. (2013). An empirical investigation of organisational justice, knowledge sharing and innovation capability. *SciVerse Science Direct, 75*, 199–208.

Yesina, J. L., Stepanenkova, N. M., & Agaphonova, E. E. (2015). Forms and Mechanisms of Integration of Science, Education and Business-Community in the Context of Innovative Changes in the Regional Economy. *Creative Economy, 9*(12), 1491–1508.

Yi, J. (2009). A Measure of Knowledge Sharing Behavior: Scale Development and Validation. *Knowledge Management Research & Practice, 7*(1), 65–81. doi:10.1057/kmrp.2008.36

Yoo, K. H., & Lee, W. (2015). Use of Facebook in the US heritage accommodations sector: An exploratory study. *Journal of Heritage Tourism, 10*(2), 191–201. doi:10.1080/1743873X.2014.985228

Yoon, S. J. (2012). A social network approach to the influences of shopping experiences on E-WOM. *Journal of Electronic Commerce Research, 13*(3), 213–223.

Yu, H., Liu, C., & Zhang, F. (2011). Reciprocal recommendation algorithm for the field of recruitment. *Journal of Information & Computational Science, 8*(16), 4061–4068.

Yu, T., Lu, L., & Liu, T. (2009). Exploring factors that influence knowledge sharing behavior via weblogs. *Computers in Human Behavior*. doi:10.1016/j.chb.2009.08.002

Zaglia, M. E. (2013). Brand communities embedded in social networks. *Journal of Business Research, 66*(2), 216–223. doi:10.1016/j.jbusres.2012.07.015 PMID:23564989

Zagorski, B. (2007). Major depressive episodes and work stress: Results from a national population survey. *American Journal of Public Health, 97*(11), 2088–2093. doi:10.2105/AJPH.2006.104406 PMID:17901431

Zahra, S. A., & George, G. (2002). Absorptive capacity: A review, reconceptualization, and extension. *Academy of Management Review, 27*(2), 185–203.

Zander, U., & Zander, L. (2010). Opening the grey box: Social communities, knowledge and culture in acquisitions. *Journal of International Business Studies, 41*(1), 27–37. doi:10.1057/jibs.2009.76

Zapata-Cantú, L., Ramírez, J., & Pineda, J. L. (2012). HRM adaptation to knowledge management initiatives: Three Mexican cases. In *Human resources management: Concepts, methodologies, tools, and applications* (pp. 170–190). Hershey, PA: IGI Global. doi:10.4018/978-1-4666-1601-1.ch012

Zapata-Cantú, L., Treviño, T., Morton, F., & Monterrubio, E. L. (2016). Digital technologies as media to transfer knowledge in IT firms. In A. Goel & P. Singhal (Eds.), *Product innovation through knowledge management and social media strategies* (pp. 204–217). Hershey, PA: IGI Global. doi:10.4018/978-1-4666-9607-5.ch009

Zeng, B., & Gerritsen, R. (2014). What do we know about social media in tourism? A review. *Tourism Management Perspectives, 10*, 27–36. doi:10.1016/j.tmp.2014.01.001

Zhang, J., & Baden-Fuller, C. (2010). The influence of technological knowledge base and organizational structure on technology collaboration. *Journal of Management Studies, 47*(4), 679–704. doi:10.1111/j.1467-6486.2009.00885.x

Zhang, M. J. (2007). An empirical assessment of the performance impacts of IS support for knowledge transfer. *International Journal of Knowledge Management, 3*(1), 66–85. doi:10.4018/jkm.2007010105

Zhang, T. T., Kandampully, J., & Bilgihan, A. (2015). Motivations for customer engagement in online co-innovation communities (OCCs): A conceptual framework. *Journal of Hospitality and Tourism Technology, 6*(3), 311–328. doi:10.1108/JHTT-10-2014-0062

Zhang, Z. Y. (2015). Security, trust and risk in multimedia social networks. *The Computer Journal, 58*(4), 515–517. doi:10.1093/comjnl/bxu151

Zhang, Z., & Gupta, B. B. (2016). Social media security and trustworthiness: Overview and new direction. *Future Generation Computer Systems.* doi:10.1016/j.future.2016.10.007

Zheng, R. Z., & Truong, T. N. (2017). A framework for promoting knowledge transfer in SNS game-based learning. In R. Zheng & M. Gardner (Eds.), *Handbook of research on serious games for educational applications* (pp. 66–91). Hershey, PA: IGI Global. doi:10.4018/978-1-5225-0513-6.ch004

Zimmermann, H. (2000). *Understanding the Digital Economy: Challenges for new Business Models.* SSRN Electronic Journal.

Zmuda, N. (2013). *Pepsi Beverage Guru Unveils His Plan to Win the World Over.* Retrieved from <http://adage.com/article/news/pepsi-beverage-guruunveils- plan-win-world/228641>

Zou, H., & Ghauri, P. N. (2008). Learning through international acquisitions: The process of knowledge acquisition in China. *Management International Review*, *48*(2), 207–226. doi:10.1007/s11575-008-0012-1

Zurada, J. M. (1992). *Introduction to artificial neural systems* (Vol. 8). St. Paul: West.

Index

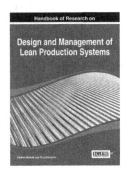
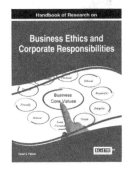

Stay Current on the Latest Emerging Research Developments

Become an IGI Global Reviewer for Authored Book Projects

Premier Reference Source
Emerging GIS Applications for Emergency and Disaster Management

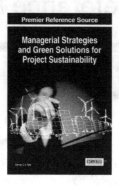
Premier Reference Source
Managerial Strategies and Green Solutions for Project Sustainability

Premier Reference Source
Comparative Approaches to Using R and Python for Statistical Data Analysis

Premier Reference Source
Solutions for High-Touch Communications in a High-Tech World

The overall success of an authored book project is dependent on quality and timely reviews.

In this competitive age of scholarly publishing, constructive and timely feedback significantly decreases the turnaround time of manuscripts from submission to acceptance, allowing the publication and discovery of progressive research at a much more expeditious rate. Several IGI Global authored book projects are currently seeking highly qualified experts in the field to fill vacancies on their respective editorial review boards:

Applications may be sent to:
development@igi-global.com

Applicants must have a doctorate (or an equivalent degree) as well as publishing and reviewing experience. Reviewers are asked to write reviews in a timely, collegial, and constructive manner. All reviewers will begin their role on an ad-hoc basis for a period of one year, and upon successful completion of this term can be considered for full editorial review board status, with the potential for a subsequent promotion to Associate Editor.

If you have a colleague that may be interested in this opportunity, we encourage you to share this information with them.

Information Resources Management Association

Become an IRMA Member

Members of the **Information Resources Management Association (IRMA)** understand the importance of community within their field of study. The Information Resources Management Association is an ideal venue through which professionals, students, and academicians can convene and share the latest industry innovations and scholarly research that is changing the field of information science and technology. Become a member today and enjoy the benefits of membership as well as the opportunity to collaborate and network with fellow experts in the field.

IRMA Membership Benefits:

- **One FREE Journal Subscription**
- **30% Off Additional Journal Subscriptions**
- **20% Off Book Purchases**
- Updates on the latest events and research on Information Resources Management through the IRMA-L listserv.
- Updates on new open access and downloadable content added to Research IRM.
- A copy of the Information Technology Management Newsletter twice a year.
- A certificate of membership.

IRMA Membership $195

Scan code or visit **irma-international.org** and begin by selecting your free journal subscription.

Membership is good for one full year.

Printed in the United States
By Bookmasters